Gal Kirn

The Partisan Counter-Archive

Media and Cultural Memory/ Medien und kulturelle Erinnerung

Edited by
Astrid Erll · Ansgar Nünning

Volume 27

Gal Kirn

The Partisan Counter-Archive

Retracing the Ruptures of Art and Memory in the Yugoslav People's Liberation Struggle

DE GRUYTER

ISBN 978-3-11-068139-0
e-ISBN (PDF) 978-3-11-068206-9
e-ISBN (EPUB) 978-3-11-068215-1
ISSN 1613-8961

Library of Congress Control Number: 2020939766

Bibliographic information published by the Deutsche Nationalbibliothek
The Deutsche Nationalbibliothek lists this publication in the Deutsche Nationalbibliografie; detailed bibliographic data are available on the Internet at http://dnb.dnb.de.

Cover image: Edi Šelhaus: Youth from Bobno polje that created
a star. 1945. Babno polje. Black and white negative, 6 x 9 cm.
Muzej novejše zgodovine Slovenije.
Typesetting: Integra Software Services Pvt. Ltd.
Printing and binding: CPI books GmbH, Leck

www.degruyter.com

Foreword

My turn to Partisan memory and monuments dates back to 2009, when the Museum of Modern Art in Ljubljana (Tanja Lazetić and Zdenka Badovinac) organised a series of events and an edited volume, in which my text – primarily dealing with "national reconciliation" in memory and revisionist politics in Slovenia – appeared. I had no idea that my first article on the sad fate of Partisan monuments and the emergence of revisionist monuments in the post-Yugoslav context would kindle so much interest and eventually result in this book. This research project has travelled with me across a few institutions and scholarships that deserve a special mention. First, as a fellow at the Institute of Cultural Inquiry, Berlin, I was able to conduct research on Partisan poetry and revolutionary temporality (as part of the project Multistability and Kippbild, 2010–2012). I need to thank the entire group of scholars there for their generous feedback and, most notably, Christoph Holzhey. Furthermore, I would like to thank the Humboldt Stiftung for granting me a postdoctoral fellowship (2014–2016), in which I conducted research on Partisan film documents from WWII. Some of these investigations were published in the book *Partisans in Yugoslavia*, which Miranda Jakiša co-edited with Nikica Gilić (2015). I have to thank Christine Gölz and Matteo Colombi for their invitation to the Leibniz Institute for the History and Culture of Eastern Europe (GWZO) and for their feedback on the topic of Yugoslav film and memory (chapter 3). Finally, I would like to thank TU Dresden and, in particular, the Institute for Slavic Studies and Prof. Christian Prunitsch, who hosted me as an Open Topic Fellow (2017–2020), where I received the opportunity to re-organise my research material in the form of a book.

Special thanks go to various individuals and institutions that have helped me or provided me with the archival material: first of all, to the Museum of Contemporary History (Ljubljana) for its generosity and the professional work of Jožica Šparovec, Katarina Jurjavčič and the director Kaja Širok. Also, I would like to thank the Slovenian Archive and Radovan Čukić from the Museum of Yugoslavia (Belgrade), the AVNOJ Museum in Jajce, the digital archive of www.znaci.net and the League of Croatian Antifascist Veterans (Zagreb) for their granting permission to reproduce visual material in this book. Furthermore, Robert Burghardt, Božidar Flajšman, Michael Allen, Marko Krojač and Goranka Matić deserve a special mention for the use of their photographs of Partisan monuments. My special thanks go to the owners of the rights for reproduction of the Partisan artists Tomaž Krpič, Andrej Gerlovič, Janin Klemenčič, Alenka Puhar, Luka Vidic, Matej and Manja Pavšič and Vedrana Madžar who not only granted me permission but were also keen to assist me with additional information on the Partisan artists and their artworks that I have been

https://doi.org/10.1515/9783110682069-202

able to reproduce here. Last but not least, I would like to thank Želimir Žilnik for inspiration and for sharing his personal trajectory on Jazak's antifascists. Thanks to these people, this book contains several unknown, or hardly known, artworks and photographs, which may hopefully trigger further investigations in a field of research that has remained mostly limited to the ex-Yugoslav region and fringes of academia.

There are many groups and individuals that have influenced, helped, improved and sharpened my thoughts and contributed to this book. First and foremost, my thanks and debt go to Miklavž Komelj, who published a long study on Partisan poetry in Slovene a decade ago, which affected me deeply. It comes as no surprise that some of Komelj's topics resonate strongly with the book that is in your hands, while I tried to expand these topics both to different art materials and also temporally and spatially away from the horizon of Slovenia to the whole of Yugoslavia. Miklavž Komelj commented intensively on parts of my chapters (especially 1 and 2) and added several thoughts on the interpretations of a few poems. To his selfless help I can only respond with my deepest gratitude, and I am sure he will recognise his influence in more than a few passages. Furthermore, I have had lively discussions with members of the collective ThK, Ana Vujanović and Marta Popivoda, whose theatrical re-enactment of Partisan women (memories) and their current film project on the testimony of the Partisan resistance remains of vital inspiration. Also, I need to acknowledge another member of the ThK group Bojan Djordjev for his help with the translation of Partisan poems. To Ivana Momčilović I am heavily indebted for her continual support in writing and struggling, but also for herself being actively involved in rethinking Yugoslavia and the Partisan experience. I would like to thank Jernej Habjan for giving me the incentive to co-edit the first international volume on recent theoretical work on Partisan art and politics (*Slavica Tergestina*). I must also mention Davor Konjikušić for exchanging his materials and thoughts on Partisan photography, and I would also like to warmly thank the collective KURS (Miloš Miletić and Mirjana Radovanović) for their invitation to present some of my research in Belgrade (2017). In a similar vein, Katerina Kolozova and Artan Sadiku's invitation to the summer school in Skopje 2015 resulted in a lecture that was discussed by participants and integrated into the introductory chapter. Finally, I would like to thank Paula Barreiro López to invite me into the collective research team on Partisan Resistance(s) that aims to expand the political and artistic scope of partisan struggles.

The central theoretical inspiration for a return to the Partisans and for a way of connecting theory and praxis I owe to the Collective WHW, Darko Suvin, Ozren Pupovac, Srečko Pulig and especially Rastko Močnik and Boris Buden whose way of thinking has seeped deeply into my own work. I am deeply grateful to Peter Stanković's work on Partisan film, to Aldo Milohnić and Goran Sergej

Pristaš, for their selfless help in highlighting a few important cues for interdisciplinary research on Partisan performance and theatre. Mirt Komel's comments on chapter 1, especially with respect to the notion of surplus memory and accumulation, as well as Elena Vogman's insightful comments on the methodology and interpretation of past resources were of vital importance. Moreover, my dear friend Alan Kučar deserves a special mention for our continual dialogue on this and other related matters. Finally, I want to warmly thank Ana Hofman for commenting on aspects of Partisan poetry and song (chapter 2); Ana Dević for making remarks on the introductory chapter; Dominique Hurth for helping me to reflect on Brussels' revisionist monument in chapter 4; Mateo Ivčević, Milan Radanović and Sanja Horvatinčić for their knowledge of history and of the monuments; and Ankica Čakardić for a few great suggestions on women's antifascist legacy. My special thanks also go out to Jodi Dean and the Circle for Critical Theory from Nisyros for a lively discussion on my paper on the Partisan figure today and to Vjeran Pavlaković for his work on revisionism in the post-Yugoslav context and the round table discussion on populism and memory organised by Chiara de Cesari and Ayhan Kaya. I especially benefited from Gönül Bozoglu's comments, which helped me improve parts of chapter 4. Last but not least, my book would not be the same without Nathaniel Boyd and Andrew Hodges, who have improved not only my English and style of writing, but were also generous enough to illuminate some evident contradictions in my reasoning. In addition, I would like to thank Lydia White and Stella Diedrich for their assistance and guidance with finalising the book project. The list of credits is becoming long and points to the fact that despite the solitary experience of theoretical writing, one is always already involved in a collective journey.

Finally, my warm thoughts and thanks also go to my family in Slovenia, especially to my parents and my brother back home, who helped me to retrieve some material and who have offered long-term support. Let me also warmly greet my close family in Berlin, my partner Niloufar Tajeri with whom we started our project named Archive to Sub-Urban Dissent, which in many ways enriched my considerations on the Partisan counter-archive. I would also like to thank my sons Shayan and Diyako, who gave me strength when I needed it most, especially towards the end of the writing process.

At the very end, I would like to return to the beginning. How did I become interested in the Partisan resistance in the first place? It all started in 1943, when my great-grandfather Franc Kirn entered a Partisan shock-brigade from the XIV. Division and was captured and interned in a Dresden concentration camp – in the city where I currently work! – while my grandfather, Franc's son, Vladislav Kirn, like a large majority of Partisans, entered the struggle at a very young age. He was 16 years old when he worked in the Trbovlje mine and joined the Partisans in 1943.

Later that year, he joined the second battalion of Prešeren's shock-brigade and participated as part of a tiny assault troop in the major victory of Partisans against local fascists at Turjak. He was shot and captured by Nazis later that year. After a series of tortures by local fascists while he was being treated in a local hospital, he was sent to Dachau concentration camp, where he survived for a year and a half. As he was more of the silent type and did not boast about his bravery, I heard most of the stories of Partisan courage through my grandmother, after he had already died. And just when I started writing this book, my grandmother Fani also died. This book therefore wishes to interrupt the silence of the dead and is thus also a dedication to my (great-) grandparents, to their deeds and testimonies, which sparked a series of thoughts and flashes of memory that have produced lasting effects and affects. This is something that goes beyond a mere familial tie; there were many Partisans across Europe and the world that stood up against colonial domination and fascist occupation that should not be forgotten. Thus, at the end I conclude by dedicating the book to the Partisan struggle itself, to its memory that should not be forgotten and to the deep and determined belief that it was not only worth it but necessary to resist fascism and fight for another world. This book addresses both this bygone past and our potential future. A short poem "Love in Storm," written by the Partisan poet Matej Bor whose poems were printed such Partisan printing house depicted on the Figure 1, encapsulates the unbreakable spirit of emancipatory desire and revolt:

> Tonight I saw your palm,
> how it got squeezed in the firm fist
> in the darkness of the Ljubljana streets.
> And you know of what I thought, poet-Partisan?
> If only my poem were like your palm,
> all soft and tender like the cherry blossom in spring
> and that it were as resistant as your fist,
> whenever you witness the fascist parade.[1]

1 All permissions for translations of the Matej Bor poems are courtesy of Matej and Manja Pavšič.

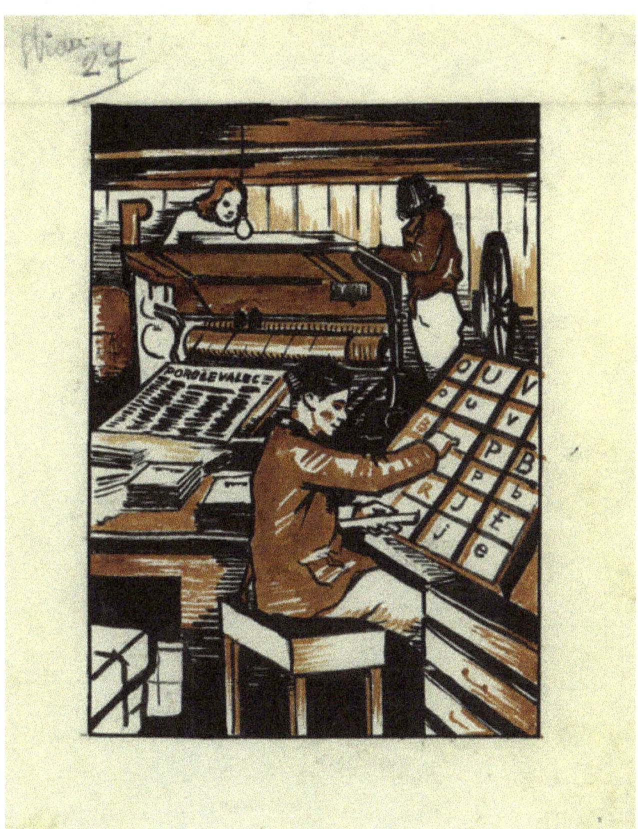

Figure 1: *Typesetters* by Ive Šubic. Courtesy of the Museum of Contemporary History, Ljubljana (hereinafter MNZS).

Contents

Introduction: The "Primitive Accumulation" of Revisionist Memory: A Plea for the Partisan Counter-Archive

> The idea of accumulating everything, of establishing a sort of general archive, the will to enclose in one place all times, all epochs, all forms, all tastes, the idea of constituting a place of all times that is itself outside of time and inaccessible to its ravages, the project of organising in this way a sort of perpetual and indefinite accumulation of time in an immobile place, this whole idea belongs to our modernity. Michel Foucault (1986, 26)

Let us return briefly to the year 1989, to images of the collective and enthusiastic destruction of Berlin Wall. This victorious image announces the surprisingly peaceful way in which "history ends" within the larger socialist East. Socialism ceases to exist. There is now only the triumph of the West with its capitalist modernisation, which seems to become completely global. Within two years' time, however, a historic anti-climax has taken place: in 1991, war ravages Europe once more, for the first time since WWII. The socialist and federal Yugoslavia disappears. In its place, the democratically elected governments of the new nation-states emerge, which desire a transition to liberal capitalism and form ethnically pure communities. To achieve this, they wage civil wars, while parts of the "international community" support different republics and the (il)legal arms trade flourishes. Post-socialist governments send their people to wars, dispossess them of social ownership and rob them of their own democratic past, a past that had actually brought down socialism. The new political powers and revisionist ideology take aim most notably at Yugoslavia; obfuscating the socialist and Partisan past becomes the most popular culture of memory and genre of daily politics and journalism. The destruction of monuments and books is soon accompanied by the politics of ethnic and legal cleansing. Our screens project images of a much more depressing future: the tanks of the Croatian Army shell the city of Mostar's bridge, which had stood in place for centuries as a symbol of multicultural and religious tolerance and as a remainder of the Ottoman legacy. We see the images of the underground tunnels in the besieged and shelled Sarajevo, a city that once prided itself on having had a strong Partisan and multicultural past during WWII and in the socialist Yugoslavia. The fascist dead have been resurrected in order to haunt the land of the living, and the once defeated, vicious past is thus now materialised in the painful images of those clinging to life in the concentration camps. This story symbolically ends in the site of the first genocide after WWII: Srebrenica, the new "realm of memory," where more than eight thousand male inhabitants (young and old men) were executed, a scene that was painfully tol-

https://doi.org/10.1515/9783110682069-001

erated by the spearheads of the "international community": NATO and the UN. Are, then, these images of genocide and the indifference of the international community images that commemorate the end of the century? And what are the images that we pack in our mental suitcases and computer hardware for the new millennium?

From the "end of history" to the memorial speculation of a nation

From a dominant historiographic, political and journalistic perspective in the West, the clear image that has cemented our views post-1989 is undoubtedly the fall of the Berlin Wall. Tearing down the walls and curtains heralded a democratic promise to the East and potential democratic renewal for the West.[2] But for those coming from Yugoslavia, this story did not end so well: 1989 materialised in 1991 in a very different way. If we, then, take history dialectically, we should speak of the fall of socialism in the historical sequence of 1989–1991. Instead of peaceful transition, we actually encounter the inauguration of new ethnic borders and wars, new walls and a clear asymmetry between the core and periphery. The new walled, even "waned-sovereign"-state system (Brown 2010) was not merely the wishful thinking of local nationalist politicians and war criminals from the ex-Yugoslavia, but was later baptised by the Dayton Peace Treaty. The latter confirmed the politics of ethnically cleansed areas, for which new nationalists were fighting for from the beginning.[3] Dayton echoed the central slogan of new nationalists: social life in a multi-ethnic and multi-religious society is not possible. Moreover, socialism and Yugoslavia were always already a fake and "artificial entity." Our only possibility is the political entity of one nation in one state within a capitalist horizon. The ethnically cleansed point of view is thus one of the main contributions to the memorial legacy of the post-Yugoslav context and has been inscribed in a more general wave of anti-totalitarian legacy.

Today we are speaking almost three decades after the violent dissolution of Yugoslavia and 15 years after the enthusiastic enlargement of the European Union, which fully integrated the East into the common market area. Despite a recent capitalist crisis that has exhausted neoliberal utopia and hopes of transition, the

2 Ironically, 30 years after the fall of the Berlin Wall, the EU has erected six times as many walls on its borders than the original length of the Berlin Wall. As Akkerman reports, building walls has become a part of the fast-growing defence industry (Akkerman 2019).

3 For a critical appraisal of the Dayton Process from a critical distance and within the longer-term perspective of market unification see Živković (2015).

neoliberal austerity politics and political divisions continue, while the rise of the extreme right has forced any critical thinker to reconsider the premature claim of Fukuyama's "end of history" (1992). Fukuyama himself (2018) admitted that his statement was premature and that some forms of socialism would be welcomed today. The deep political, economic and increasingly environmental crises are forcing us into a sort of apocalyptic judgement, which made Žižek claim that we have now definitely entered the "end times" (2011). Rather than giving in to apocalyptic fears, what is unfolding in front of us is the increasing destabilisation of the once stable horizon of a European future with its utopian core of (neoliberal) capitalist mantra and anti-totalitarian memory. This is further visible in the waning political legitimacy of the centre parties with their ideologies, which are seeing their major competitor coming from the extreme right, while they continue to do everything – austerity and taking a tough anti–immigrant stance – to make the extreme right stronger.[4] The long persistent trope that condemned both "extremisms" as equally bad is strengthened by the anti-totalitarian mantra that equates fascism with communism, which is obscuring the fact that the communist and Partisan forces combatted and contributed in a major way to the victory over fascism in WWII. In times when autocratic and far-right governments exist in the West/Europe and strong parties of the extreme right have become a new European norm, the condemnation of fascism and the commemoration of the antifascist legacy has now been long gone from the memory agenda. Instead of indulging in the mere musealisation of WWII or evoking moral prescriptions of "never again," should we not seriously tackle and engage with antifascist, antiracist and yes, also anti-austerity struggles past and present? In a period when the rise of Islamophobia, xenophobia against all minorities and refugees, patriarchal sentiments against women, and even a return to the white-washing of the colonial and fascist past are spoken of in official political discourses, the return to a Partisan past seems theoretically and politically urgent. The recent tragic events of post-Yugoslavia and its cleansing of the antifascist and communist past through wars resonates with a wider constellation within contemporary Europe. The ex-Yugoslav "politics of memory" has been dominated by right-wing nationalist revisionism that has navigated from the open rehabilitation of fascist collaborationism during WWII to the mobilisation of 1000-year-old dreams of mythical kingdoms.

---

4 Tariq Ali has made a convincing argument that demonstrated in what ways the neoliberal policies of the centre parties (dominant political forces) enabled the rise of the extreme right-wing (Ali 2015). Thus, one should not underestimate the threats of the "extreme centre" that within the mainstream media portrays left and right extremism as the same problem/danger to liberal democracy.

The passing of three decades since the break-up of Yugoslavia has given us enough distance to critically survey the abandonment of its antifascist and Partisan past and to retrace certain emancipatory fragments in order to awaken the Partisan legacy from its symbolic death. To paraphrase Boris Buden (2009), if the future today seems more closed than ever before, with the paradigm of utopia buried, then the past – history – has become more undecided and uncertain than ever.[5] The withering away of the grand narrative of communism and Marxism has been replaced by a plurality of small narratives and personal testimonies within the macro-trajectory of neoliberalism and historical revisionism (anti-totalitarianism) that evokes clear (post)colonial imprints. The post-socialist shake-up has had strong consequences for the central pillars of post-war Europe, which were based on antifascism, an ideology of peace and a social contract that implied a welfare state and the protection of human rights. The grand narrative and these material conditions have withered away along with socialism.

This short diagnosis of 'memorial' destiny may lead to some grim and disheartening conclusions. However, in 1929, Antonio Gramsci, who found himself in a fascist prison, brilliantly wrote, in his prison letter of 19 December 1929, a slogan of emancipation that remains just as pertinent today: "it is necessary to direct one's attention violently towards the present as it is, if one wishes to transform it. Pessimism of the intelligence, optimism of the will." (Gramsci 1999, 395). If *pessimism of the intelligence* means practicing a strong critique of the existing state of affairs, then *optimism of the will* insists on the necessity of participating in social change despite all odds against it. This brings me to the central point of departure for this book, which starts with a critical evaluation of the dominant nationalist archive, its revisionist discourses and practices that target the Partisan past and antifascist legacy of WWII (*pessimism of the intellect*), while also attempting to point to one possible way of retracing and retrieving experience and artworks that relate to the event of Partisan Yugoslavia (*optimism of the will*). The central mission of this book will thus address two deeper questions: what can we learn from the Partisan past for our current situation? Moreover, how, if at all, are we able to mobilise past emancipatory resources (Williams 1989), especially from the field of art, to strengthen a utopian dream of a different future?[6]

This book presents a selection of some known – at least for the public in former Yugoslavia – and some forgotten Partisan materials and artworks scattered

5 As Frederic Jameson claims, the time of utopia has also been completely substituted by the genre of dystopia in popular culture, which can be seen as a long-term reaction to the first realisation of utopia in the October Revolution and socialism (2005).

6 Susan Buck-Morss's return to the Soviet avant-garde is unquestionably one such theoretical work to which my methodology subscribes and has been inspired by (Buck-Morss 2002).

across the post-Yugoslav space. Before I dissect these selected art and cultural works, I need to critically depart from the current situation, presenting why it has become so difficult to speak about the Yugoslav Partisan legacy. It has been argued that the Yugoslav, socialist and Partisan project and movement have reached their practical and symbolic end. While it presents itself as a set of dominant retrospective lenses, revisionism implies a *re-visioning* of the community's past, present and future. This has occurred during all major social transitions in the former East countries. However, the specificity of the legacy of Partisan and socialist Yugoslavia is that Yugoslavia was able to liberate itself on its own from the fascist occupation and it did not belong to either the NATO/West or the Stalin/Informbiro/Warsaw pact, but rather contributed to the creation of the "non-aligned alternative" (Kirn 2019b; Prashad 2007). This marked the Yugoslav trajectory of political and economic autonomy that developed a solid model of self-management and an economy of solidarity within and outside of the federation (Samary 1988; Woodward 1995a, 1995b; Suvin 2014). These experiences were thoroughly revised and demonised in the late 1980s and the 1990s, in turn reflected in a set of neoconservative memorial practices and nationalist realms of memory.[7] The memorial constellation could be referred to as "nationalist revisionism" and entailed a thorough rewriting and re-imagining of Yugoslav history. Historical revisionists paint the entire history through the lens of the idea of nation, a view that treated the people of the Balkans as subjects incapable of 'normal' democratic governance (Buden 2003; 2009). This reasoning among other things points to a strong degree of "(self-)orientalisation" (Said 1978) under general neo-imperialist policies within the region.[8] Furthermore, ethnic methodologism/ethnocentrism (Woodward 2003) also permeated within different academic disciplines that approached the topic of transition.

The dominant ideology of ethnocentrism in capitalist transition was opposed by two critical approaches, which differently evaluated the dissolution of Yugoslavia. To simplify, the first approach focused on the critique of nationalism and marginalisation (with one great contribution made by Wachtel 1998, relating in particular to the cultural apparatus) but did not speak of the capitalist transition, whereas the second, a (neo-) Marxist approach focused mostly on the capitalist transition, understanding nationalism and revisionist ideology as a secondary

---

7 A detailed analysis of these memorial strategies is dealt with in chapter 4.

8 An array of important theoretical articles have been written on the epistemological, but also factual, critique of nationalist revisionism. For details see Arsenijević and Jovanović (2007); Centrih (2008); Kosi and Centrih (2007); Kuljić (2010); Luthar (2014, 2017); Močnik (1995, 2008); Petrović (2013b). Also, in terms of postcolonial analysis and the critique of (neo-)imperialist policies throughout the Balkans, see Boatca (2019) and Rexhepi (2018).

phenomenon. One major challenge within critical discourse was the question of how to bring these two critiques into a solid historical narrative that would point to the strategic nexus between the (nation-)state and capital. One possible path to connecting them is to see revisionism as a state ideology that is materialised in the "ideological state apparatuses" (Althusser 2008): the political apparatus, school, Church, media and, most notably, cultural institutions such as (new) national museums – e.g. Budapest's House of Terror Museum – and memorial parks, along with the renaming of streets and new nationalist rituals and commemorations. Another path is to link such nationalism directly to the capitalist transition as articulated by Nikola Dedić:

> Nationalism is not a phenomenon that is separate from the "logic of transition." On the contrary, nationalism made room for the establishment of neoliberalism, and genocide is a radical consequence of the privatisation that began in the 1990s. Afterwards, with the empowerment of "democratic" transitional governments and privatisation laws (which most of the former Yugoslav states adopted in the late 1990s and early 2000s), genocide was finally legalised. Genocide, ethnic cleansing and *nationalism*, therefore, *served* as the basis for the *accumulation of surplus value*, and paved the way for the integration of the former Yugoslav societies into the system of global capitalism. (2006, 184, *my emphasis*)

Even if Dedić concludes with the instrumental relation between nationalism and the "accumulation of surplus value," this rich passage directs us to another concept that is relevant for a concise understanding of the transition from socialism to capitalism, namely to Karl Marx's "primitive accumulation of capital." For most of Volume 1 of *Capital* ([1867]1990), Marx was preoccupied with logically understanding capital and (surplus) value, while only the very few final chapters (part 8) focused on the historical formation of capital. Marx's historical analysis speaks of an encounter between capital and labour that has a very different rationality to the bourgeois myth of Robinson Crusoe. Rather than the individual creativity of Robinson, or Smith's "invisible hand" of the market, a set of real historical preconditions had to take place.[9] Marx rereads the bourgeois narrative of mythical origins as a biblical story of "original sin" that divides society into diligent and deserving capitalists (the figure of Robinson) and those who are lazy, poor, racialised, surplus subjects and as such can only, if necessitated by capital,

9 Althusser observed that even something that looks like an eternal form of governance, state, or the only seemingly functional economic system like capitalism, actually came into being in a series of encounters that were not predestined. It was not necessary that the elements and encounter between labour and capital took hold even if they did in the end (Althusser 2006). This does not minimise the existence of a certain necessity to capitalist logic, to commodity fetishism, capital's subjectivity, the extraction of surplus value, appropriation of rent, etc.

contribute their labour power. Historically speaking, this is *fake news*. What Marx's analysis brings into the discussion, by contrast, is how the origins of capitalism were linked to non-economic constraints, namely, to the social process comprised of legal policies, state violence and colonialism (cf. Labica 2001). The "primitive accumulation of capital" was conducted internally to guarantee the necessary labour power for manufacturers by expropriating the communal lands of peasants, therein both punishing and pushing vagabonds and beggars into factories (production), while colonialism, apart from the brutalities meted out on the enslaved and slaughtered populations, entailed the external expansion of capitalist markets. This concept is useful not only for the historical evaluation of the 'origins' of the capitalist mode of production that has to do with some long-gone 'primitive' models of capitalism; rather, Marx enables us to detect the repetitive 'primitive' patterns of the accumulation of capital that carry very violent policies within each cycle of systemic crisis for anything presenting itself as an obstacle to capital.

This concept can also be, with further specifications, used to understand the post-socialist transition.[10] Evidently, the whole range of extra-economic policies and pressures, from market reform and denationalisation laws to austerity politics and foreign credits, were needed to execute the transition, but I would like to add another twist. What one finds in many critical approaches to the post-socialist transition is a separation between theorists of ideological critique (the critique of historical revisionism and liberalism as dominant ideology)[11] and those that practice a critique of political economy (neoliberal capitalism). If ideological critique tends to overwrite analysis with its critique of nationalism (and wars) and focuses on the analysis of *state* agency, then a critique of political economy observes nationalism as a secondary phenomenon and something that was practically absent in times of socialism, while focusing on *capital*'s agency. Instead of going for a mutually exclusive alternative, the concept of the "primitive accumulation of capital" evaluates both poles of the transition process at the same time and enable us to fully understand the temporality and structural

---

10 Mirt Komel read the Yugoslav ethnic wars in the 1990s through the topic of primitive accumulation (2008), while a good collection of texts with a focus on the post-Yugoslav context and a few other Eastern European countries can also be found in the volume edited by Gajić and Popović (2011). The Mayday School of Workers-Punks University in Ljubljana was organised around this topic and also published a small booklet, see www.delavske-studije.si/primitive-accumulation-in-the-post-socialist-transition-and-the-eu-accession-period/.

11 For a good analysis of ideological transition see Buden (2009); for a critique of post-fascism, see Močnik (1995) and Kuzmanić (1999), especially in regard to xenophobia in Slovenia towards migrants and people from the former Yugoslav republics.

causality of the early transition process. If post-socialism is a transitory social formation dominated by capitalist elements, one should acknowledge that, during the wars, it was state and ideology (the politico-ideological entity) that guided historical processes and determined the reality, and with this, the economic transition as well. Furthermore, due to the state of exception, the process of economic transition to capitalism was more easily conducted. War can be seen as the ultimate 'spending' (waste and ruination) of the resources, infrastructure, wealth and people accumulated and born in socialism. War and the transition to capitalism entailed huge amounts of violence needed to dismantle socialist forms of management and belief, a general form of stable employment (a private market in labour power), a selling out of the accumulated and socialised means of (re)production and infrastructure (privatisation).[12] This process resulted in the killing of around 140,000 people, the marginalisation of entire social groups and minorities, class stratification, increasing pauperisation and large waves of migration. The post-socialist transition was structured as a "modernisation" campaign and conducted in compliance with foreign investment agencies and European Union prerogatives (Živković 2015). However, one should not forget that the post-socialist transition was effectively organised from within and as a consequence of the internal fractures of self-managed development (Kirn 2019b).

The economic struggle was accompanied by a consistent and long-term counter-revolutionary transformation of the historical narrative and ideological apparatuses that targeted not only the memory of socialist times, but also, in particular, the events surrounding WWII. Even within the post-Yugoslav context, the national drama presented itself as a 'double occupation,' at first by fascism/Nazism (Germans, Italians) then by Stalinism/Titoism (Soviets, Yugoslavs), which was only resolved by the final heroic victor: the nation. The latter was a constantly tragic figure that was most of the time subjugated to the cruel play of external forces, while from the 1990s onwards, it was able to live freely in independence. Evidently, the historical memory of WWII had to be thoroughly revised, since it needed to exculpate many events and groups within each nation that had practiced open historical collaboration with fascism. The social forces that carried out this ideological assault were grounded in anti-communism and a more general wave of the re-traditionalisation of societies through nationalism, patriarchy and the Church. As early as in 1987, when analysing the tendencies

12 For a good historical overview of the transition process in Yugoslavia see Močnik (2008). See also the edited volume completed by Veselinović (2011). As Woodward (1995b) pointed out, employment in socialist Yugoslavia was neither full nor stable, however, the conditions of those employed were much more secure and distribution of value more just and discussed among workers compared with nowadays in the postsocialist context.

of civil society and opposition to the socialist one-party system, Tomaž Mastnak spoke of a possible "totalitarianism from below" (Mastnak 1987), which pushed for the nationalisation and traditionalisation of (civil) society. The 1990s did not bring a solid balance between the new state and civil society, but instead saw the merger of civic actors with new and old political parties in the new state (Kirn 2017a; cf. Pupovac 2008). Neoliberal globalisation should, apart from the strictly free market, promote fluid national identities. But this did not take place; rather, a major conservative backlash that has been defined along the line of the "invention of tradition" (Hobsbawm and Ranger 1983), which in post-socialist context clearly fixed the nation to its supposed pre-modern authenticity and forged an inseparable bond of nation with religion:

> 'Invented tradition' is taken to mean a set of practices, normally governed by overtly or tacitly accepted rules and of a ritual or symbolic nature, which seek to inculcate certain values and norms of behaviour by repetition, which automatically implies continuity with the past. In fact, where possible, they normally attempt to establish continuity with a suitable historic past. (1983, 1)

Within the post-socialist context, the very visible body of the nation was now presented as the eternal ether of a distant – for each nation specific – past. The sequence of the late 1980s and 1990s worked on the "structure of feeling" (Williams 1961) of memorial-historical continuity and largely succeeded in re-interpreting recent and distant history as a whole in light of the methodological unity of nation. Nationalist modernisation took place despite being an already theoretically outdated and sublated epistemological project, which was deconstructed and criticised by various critical feminists, post-colonialists and Marxist theorists from the 1970s onwards.[13]

The process of the "invention of tradition" is thus not understood only through the capacity to adapt and substitute the 'real' tradition as suggested by Hobsbawm, but can be brought into strong correlation with Marx's concept of the "primitive accumulation of capital." I suggest understanding this connection through the name the "primitive accumulation of memory/state." It is evidenced through a thorough reinvention of memory and tradition – further

13 In a collective effort by Étienne Balibar and Immanuel Wallerstein (1991), they launched a critical approach that accounted for the relative autonomy of instances (economy, ideology, politics) and political categories that relate to race, gender and class. Similar criticisms as those directed towards the methodological privileging of nation were directed against the proponents of neoliberal modernisation who put progress back on the agenda without any critical reservations and despite its obsoleteness as a theoretical concept (see the introduction to the edited volume of Burchardt and Kirn, 2017a).

explaining the creation of a nexus between the nation-state (former republics of Yugoslavia) and capital. One of the paradoxes of the transitional process is that if the memory-related accumulation of state intensified feelings of national pride and ethnic hatred, then at the same time the primitive accumulation of capital in the new states has expropriated people of their social ownership: in short denationalisation robbed them of the material base (for their national pride). In the conventional Marxian frame it is the economic instance that determines other instances (e.g. politics, ideology, culture), while in the civil war of the 1990s, the interplay between instances manifested in the "primitive accumulation of the state." In other words, instances of politics practiced a large degree of autonomy and became a precondition for neoliberal economic transition. The very violence of the new states did not have to be concealed (Žižek 2008a), but became the dominant language and practice of post-Yugoslavia.

The accumulation of memory by the state was deployed by means of thoroughly *symbolic* violence with respect to the past and was tied to the physical destruction of Partisan monuments and the erasure of books and ideas that evoked non-aligned, modernist, Partisan and socialist times. Furthermore, this intensified through the ethnic and legal cleansing of people that did not comply with the ideas and newly imagined borders of the great new nation-states. In this new narrative, the Partisan legacy was seen as the most disturbing element that unsettles memories of the past and visions of the future. How, then, do newly constituted national communities, which aspire to become a part of the transnational world and Europe, move 'forward'? In order to reconcile nations from within, *Yugoslavia* needed to be dumped in the dustbin of the twentieth century, which came to be seen as a century of totalitarian violence and catastrophes. Thinking about the twentieth century in terms of moralisation and the body count in terms of politics brings us to a situation of intellectual blockage, whereby any emancipatory politics is already from the beginning deemed to be a possible path to the gulag/camp (Badiou 2005), while the revolutionary legacy in the "ages of extremes," which also had positive material consequences, is forgotten (Hobsbawm 1994). More concretely, "Yugoslav totalitarianism" (Dyker and Vejvoda 1994) was seen both as "responsible for repressing ethnic issues" as well as propagating the conspiracy that "post-Yugoslav nationalism" was merely a "continuation of Yugoslav socialism by other means, conducted essentially by the same agencies and actors." (Jovanović 2012, 151) This retrospective entity of totalitarian Yugoslavia not only fulfils the fantasies both of liberal and nationalist critics alike, but also pushes us to forget the major lesson that Partisan and socialist Yugoslavia brought into historical and political reality. Yugoslavia was a name and an entity built on transnationalism and federalism, constituted through a revolution that started as multinational antifascist solidarity. Before it became one of Tito's and the new Yugoslavia's official ideological slogans, the latter major maxim of "brotherhood and unity," was an attempt at and practice of struggling against fascism and living together in a Partisan collective. One is tempted to say that it was precisely because of the uniqueness of the Partisan event and the relative autonomy and economic prosperity of socialist Yugoslavia that the recent regressive recourse to post-Yugoslav revisionism, to wars and iconoclasm in relation to the recent past, has been so dramatic. Subotić pointed out that the anti-communist ideology went so far as to integrate Holocaust memory and symbols into commemorating the crimes of the communist past even if the latter had nothing to do with the Holocaust (Subotić 2019).

Post-Yugoslav revisionism, in its discursive and commemorative forms, is not exceptional if we compare it with the revisionist process in the (East) European context. We should remember that the first major memorial regression took place in the heart of (old) Europe. The academic 'encounter' between German revisionist historian Ernst Nolte and the *nouveaux philosophes* that dominated French debates is exemplary in this regard and had a strong influence on understanding recent European history. If the demise of socialism has been correctly analysed through the rise of neoliberalism and an attack on the welfare state,[14] then a neoconservative assault on the emancipatory narratives of the past (Buden 2009) – revolutionary, communist, socialist or anticolonial – should not be overlooked. Dominico Losurdo (2015) traced the ways in which right-wing revisionists, from Furet to Nolte, have demonised the whole legacy of the (non-)European revolutionary and Enlightenment past to the revolutions of the twentieth century. This shift was openly demonstrated on the highest political level in 1985, when the German Prime Minister Helmut Kohl organised a visit and mourning session at Bitburg cemetery with the US president Ronald Reagan. In the wake of the commemoration of Normandy, they decided to commemorate 2,000 German soldiers at a cemetery in Bitburg, which was also the final resting place for 50 SS soldiers. This ideological attack, which gave the trope of totalitarianism a new symbolic power (Traverso 2017a, 2017b),[15] did not end with its own theoretical defeat in the *Historikerstreit* of the late 1980s. What actually happened was that revisionist historiography was translated into one of the most potent narratives of the new nation-states in the former East and recent musealisations of the socialist/European past. This trope materialised in a range of cultural and

14 A few critical analyses of neoliberalism were undertaken by Harvey (2005); Klein (2008); Monbiot (2017); Streeck (2016), and others.

15 The point of departure for the totalitarian trope dates back to 1939 and the Molotov-Ribbentrop Pact that brought cooperation between Germany and the Soviet Union. I will discuss this symbolic date for the anti-totalitarian paradigm in detail in the last part of chapter 4.

academic institutions, especially in the former East: museums, research centres and magazines, but also monument parks, documentary films and commissions all attempted to evidence the history of totalitarian – this time communist and Partisan – violence.[16] In the concrete post-Yugoslav transition, right-wing historical revisionism translated into ethnic wars and the cleansing of the revolutionary and antifascist past. The new agents of the post-Yugoslav transition collectively, even if separated by their ethnic communities, embarked on a clear course of historical regression: moving from the federalism, multi-ethnicity and transnationality of Yugoslavia to the ethnically exclusive concept underpinning the new states (Kirn 2015a). They moved from a more just redistribution of surplus value and the legal empowerment of workers to more brutal forms of extraction and hierarchical social organisation that imposed stark class divisions, pauperisation and a peripheral positioning within the European capitalist economy.

The memorial accumulation of the new state and its proponents – *new historians* – negated the established tenets (Anderson 2010; Deutsch 1996; Hobsbawm 1992) that modern nations did not exist before the 'spring of the nation' in the nineteenth century. Moreover, primitive memorial accumulation dug deep into the past to retrieve its symbolic capital. The new historians helped to provide research material for national myths, legends and stories. Instead of speculating about the future – as capital, new historians were speculating on history! The revolutionary surplus of the Partisan revolution was substituted by a national mythos – reconciliations, tragedies, victories and defeats relating to distant past events. In more concrete terms, this memorial speculation operated on a diverse range of phantasmatic events: Serbian nationalist ideology, for example, was launched on the 600-year commemoration of the Battle of Kosovo field and defeat to Ottomans that became a source of potent trauma (1389); the imaginary of great Croatia appropriated the Middle Age Kingdom of Croatia (925–1102), whose territory occupied most of what is currently Bosnia and Herzegovina and Croatia. Furthermore, the imaginary of the new country of Bosnia and Herzegovina, while split from the start, arguably operates on the tradition of the Middle Age Kingdom

16 From museums of totalitarian art (Amsterdam, Sophia) and the *Museum of Totalitarianism* (Kiev) to the *House of Terror* (Budapest) and museums of recent national histories, all have made a convergent point about the historical confluence of or continuity between the two totalitarianism(s) in the former Eastern Bloc (Radonić 2009, Ghodsee 2014). For a detailed and critical analysis of the musealisation of the East in the case of the *House of Terror Museum* in Budapest, see Buden (2009) who correctly claims that people in the East soon had to forget that they were the ones who conducted democratic changes at the end of the 1980s; deprived of the political past they had to recognise their lack of a democratic culture and performed a kind of self-orientalising gesture. For a broader view on the long-term political criminalisation of communism through EU institutions and political discourse, see Neumayer (2018).

and Ottoman empire. Slovenian nationalist ideology plunged even further back to the early medieval Carinthian Kingdom of the eighth century and called for the realisation of the millennial dream of the first independent state. Such speculative forces redrew continuity into national temporality and most recently reached their climax in Northern Macedonia. The deepest memorial imagination has been drawn from Alexander the Great. It does not matter whether Alexander the Great was born in the Greek part of Macedonia or that he did not speak any Macedonian, what matters is the sheer intensification of the 'archive fever' across the sister republics that finally succeeded in returning to the very ancient 'origin' of the archive.

The process of archival origin, as Derrida (1995) showed well, has the etymological root of *arche*, meaning both the beginning and a political authority – *archons* are leaders and also those who guard and interpret the archive. This has to do with spatial and interpretive sovereign authority, which draws a full methodological circle between the nation and its (historical) destiny. This thesis will be elaborated in chapter 1 and I will explain in what way the method and the Partisan counter-archive differ from nation-state archives. This difference relates both to the nature of authority (central state authority vs. the Partisan deterritorialising liberation movement), its space (a capital city and established institutions vs. the mobile and popular councils of people's liberation) and also to the modality of alternative memorial production and dissemination. Rather than departing from the completeness and already known nature of the subject of the nation, safeguarded by the new state, the Partisan counter-archive takes as its starting point the process of openness and the subject of 'revolutionary people,' which in real terms referred most notably to peasants and women who were previously completely excluded from historical narratives.[17] The Partisan counter-archive tackles what I called the Partisan and counter-archival "surplus," which avoided being easily integrated into either socialist Yugoslavia or the capitalist states of today. New nation-states presently speculate over mythical pasts, while they only adjust to capital that speculates with their future. This is another reason to use the prefix *counter-*[18] since the new national archive overwrote Yugoslav, and more generally socialist/revolutionary, history with a sole protagonist (the

17 The Yugoslav example is not unique. There exist diverse experiences across East Europe in specific time periods. One fascinating example and account of the anti-fascist and pro-communist history of Bulgaria's WWII experience has been written by Ghodsee (2015).

18 There have been a few solid attempts to rethink and apply the prefix 'counter-' to the past. I was inspired most notably by Mirzoeff's (2011) book, whose critique of dominant visuality highlights its link in sustaining existing authority and power relations. Mirzoeff is interested in decolonial genealogy and dismantling racial hierarchies and visualisations, while this project

ethnic nation) and sold people's future. Something resembling a counter-archival insurgent practice is thus engaged not only in a rereading of the past, but also in nurturing the counter-archival surplus and giving people back the symbolic power to imagine the future once again.

Musing on the absurdities of the memorial accumulation and speculation over the memory of the new nation-state can easily become an ironic but also arrogant exercise that displays the 'spirit' of the ruling classes in the new nation-states. However, rather than bitterly dwelling on this distraction of distant origins, one ought to detect a more tragic reversal played by the resurrected ghosts of the history of the twentieth century. All the new nationalist ideologies had particular stakes in the WWII period and, as Walter Benjamin has already warned us, "*even the dead* will not be safe from the enemy if he wins. And this enemy has not ceased to be victorious" (1968, 255). Benjamin spoke of the ruling class and threat of fascism in the 1930s, which realised itself in the horrors of WWII, while the post-Yugoslav ethnic wars of the 1990s showed how easy it can be to discard the moral norm of 'never again' and even decades of strong work on the memory culture of antifascism. It is noteworthy that many countries and their right-wing political elites in the post-Yugoslav context rehabilitated those defeated in WWII and baptised them as true patriots of respective nations. These defeated ghosts were the local fascist collaborators: Chetniks, Ustashas, Home Guards and others. The slogans of these true "patriots" and ideas of great nations were openly displayed on the pedestal of the new wars. In concrete memory politics, it was these true 'patriots' and forgotten heroes that were recognised as the real victims of the totalitarian and Partisan past. Some were later publicly or privately commemorated with memorial inscriptions and monuments, a process that shall be described in chapter 4.

The dominant archive of Partisan Yugoslavia: Anti-totalitarianism, reconciliation and nostalgia

So far, I have mostly focused on the narrative and imaginary of right-wing historical revisionism and its *negative* function, designed to forget the history of revolutionary struggles. Importantly, this narrative has also imagined new 'sites of memory' (victims of totalitarian crimes, the rehabilitation of fascist collaborators) that has produced a new set of practices and rituals that have strengthened the

perhaps wishes to extend this from the visual film culture to oral, poetic examples and monuments. I will return to the question of the prefix 'counter-' in chapter 1.

ideological cohesion of the new nation-states. The post-Yugoslav discursive space is further marked by two other ideological orientations.

First, there is nationalist reconciliation that wants to reconcile irreconcilable trajectories. In this narrative, it does not matter whether the victims of totalitarian terror were Partisans or local collaborators; in the final instance, what matters is that they were all human beings. War is absurd. This apologetic stance of an atemporal and false universality is supplemented by national(istic) reconciliation, which fixes the dialogue on World War II by concluding: "The victims in wars were all human beings and we need to take into account that they all belong to one nation." This narrative decontextualises what the sides in the struggle were and why national liberation was fought for in the first place, while also successfully bringing a false universality to the specific nationalist cause: the idea of reconciliation is inextricably linked to nationalism. The new nation-state takes a moralistic stance and claims the ultimate decency of producing humane monuments and memories of past wars that will aid in neutralising both past-and-present antagonisms. Moral norms of human civility and the prescription of yet another "never again" aim to do away with the brutality and causes of past events. For this narrative and the emerging monuments of reconciliation, Young's (1992) criticism is still very valid. Instead of working through memory and raising critical awareness of the past, reconciliation relegates the work to the monument that does the memory work for us. This makes us not interactive and conscious agents of our history, but rather "inter-passive" spectators (Pfaller 2019) who are supposed to only look into the reconciled present with a feeling of predetermined national belonging. Despite the differences between the narratives of fascist collaboration and nationalistic reconciliation – narratives translated into political terms as extreme right-wing and liberal poles – they share the general anti-totalitarian ideology.[19]

Another narrative also present in the post-Yugoslav context is called Yugonostalgia and as the name suggests this narrative idealises everything connected to

---

19 The ideological trope of anti-totalitarianism has a long history. It began in the late 1930s in the US context where communism was first clearly equated with fascism. This equation was shared by the international community, by leftist non-communist, social democrat and liberal intellectuals and politicians, and was also spread by means of exhibitions and journals that rallied around the banner of freedom. Recently, the first comprehensive and critical exhibition that showed how modernist art was integrated into US foreign policy and cultural domination through freedom and anti-totalitarianism was organized by HKW in late 2017 with the name *Parapolitics: Cultural Freedom and the Cold War.* The latter was curated by Anselm Franke, Antonia Majača, Paz Guevara and Nida Ghouse, see also their publication *Parapolitics* (2020).

Partisan times and the socialist Yugoslavia.[20] The constant reference to the great leadership of Tito and the invention of a paradise that never existed contribute to a more general attitude of escapism and the commodification of memory. Despite its troublesome dwelling on the past, on the atemporality of Yugoslavia and its embracing of the 'good' dictator, this narrative does not subscribe to the nationalist memory so pervasive in the region.

Despite political differences, I argue that anti-totalitarian memory and Yugonostalgia both reduce the complexity of the Yugoslav past, while national reconciliation aims to forget the past by blurring political differences and orienting itself toward the future of the nation-state and its enlightened subjects. In terms of their historical contextualisation and clear teleology, these three narratives belong to what I call the dominant "archive of Yugoslavia." These narratives present a shared discursive formation with a set of rules about what can be visible and said about the Yugoslav past and, moreover, what should remain silent and invisible. What does their 'teleological,' predestined view of history consist of? These three narratives all ascribe a certain origin, goal, and subject to the historical process: there is a well-defined 'origin' (the nation, the moral norms of the civilised nation, the making of Yugo-stalgia), 'goal' (the nation, humanity and the maturity of the new nation-state, Yugoslavia), and 'subject' (the nation, citizens of the nation/the poet, Tito).[21] If the first and second narrative deal with the legitimisation of the present by demonising or forgetting the Partisan past (and glorifying the nationalist past/present), the Yugonostalgic account remains stranded in the Partisan past and, in particular, in the 'glorious' Yugoslav past. Yet, while these accounts differ in their political conclusions, they share the same teleological structure that affirms necessity in history, inasmuch as the predestined origin, goal and subject work as the fixed and sacred core of an ideological, political and memorialising project.

Until recently, it seemed that the narrative and goal of reconciliation was winning the ideological battle of the past. There was a wave of politicians that at least discursively appealed to people from all the former Yugoslav republics by

---

20 A key work that covered nostalgic practices mostly related to Tito was written by Mitja Velikonja (2009). Tanja Petrović made a strong case for where to find some emancipatory material even within the nostalgic practices (2013), especially as a critique of nationalism in the region and in providing a point of cohesion between youth, their history and their present.

21 A philosophical critique of teleological thinking along the ideological chain origin-subject-goal in Marxist theory and a certain form of Hegelianism has been elaborated by Louis Althusser (1976).

apologising for war crimes.[22] Films were made that poked fun at the extreme right and openly embraced reconciliation,[23] while a few monuments were erected to promote reconciliation.[24] However, with the intensification of the economic crisis and a general move towards extreme right-wing populism across Europe in the wake of the refugee crisis, the narrative of the open rehabilitation of fascism is yet again on the rise across the whole of post-Yugoslavia. This direct rehabilitation of local fascism takes different forms: from the popularisation of fascist songs and the celebration of Hague war criminals as heroes – be they released, condemned or deceased – to the erection of monuments to war criminals from recent wars and fascist collaborators from WWII, and the organisation of paramilitary groups that intend to defend the homeland in front of migrants/refugees. This might be the grim landscape of post-Yugoslav culture and the politics of memory, but it is our point of departure. Can critical theory contribute to and call for an expansion of this horizon by mobilising Partisan material that has been forgotten, demonised or emptied through nostalgic ritualisation?

A plea for a Partisan counter-archive: Partisans of the world, retrieve past fragments of and for an emancipatory future!

The dominant revisionism succeeded to a large degree in neutralising and demonising the Partisan past, while precisely such a preoccupation with this period of history – even if negative – points to its symbolic strength. There is something symptomatic at work with either negative or utterly nostalgic

---

22 For a brief moment after the first round of the European enlargement process, there seemed to be a series of state visits and warm handshakes between leading politicians from the region, with Serbia's political representatives publicly recognising war crimes in Srebrenica, etc. See the political events and attempts at reconciliation in the bibliography (online resources).

23 Dragojević's *Parada* (2011) has become one of the most popular and also internationally renowned films (awarded the Berlinale), which takes a journey through the gay pride in Serbia, which, due to a strange mix of circumstances, is defended by a very unexpected coalition of war criminals from the 1990s coming from different camps, such as Ustashas, Chetniks and Muslim extremists. Instead of a clear political message, we receive a depoliticised and highly dubious moralising relativisation that attracts via humorous coexistence and the complicity of extremes. Golubović's *Krugovi* (2013) departs from a heavily inflected Christian perspective that draws a continuity between maintaining the burdens from the past and the impossibility of integration into any community until we have some sort of reconciliation between perpetrators and victims.

24 The symptomatic case is the *Monument to the Victims of All Wars* in the centre of Ljubljana, which became the most important site for state commemoration and diplomat visits. This monument is discussed in chapter 4.

returns to the Partisan past. I argue that this is where we can trace certain excess – what I call the *Partisan surplus* – that persists despite dramatic changes in historical circumstances that undo all the major pillars fought for in the Partisan struggle. The call for the Partisan counter-archive is not to be understood merely as a critique of the dominant archive of Yugoslavia in the three forms presented above, be it ‘nationalised’ (anti-totalitarianism), moralised (reconciliation) or privatised/culturalised (nostalgia). This book will attempt to excavate moments and (art)works from the past that form emancipatory fragments and that can potentially transfer them into the present. The Partisan counter-archive is a ‘construction site,’ where semi-forgotten artworks and political acts enter into a more palpable – and, I hope, lasting relationship in and beyond post-Yugoslav context.

This book is a first attempt at a synthesis returning to the triangulation of Partisan art, politics and memory that moves from Partisan to socialist and finally post-socialist times. There are certain regional discussions in former Yugoslavia that are becoming more vocal ever since the first serious public break with the discourse of nationalist revisionism and nostalgia occurred. This break happened in 2004, when the first exhibition *On Partisan Print* curated by Lilijana Stepančić was launched. This event, and a remarkable catalogue, first of all triggered a small but fascinating theoretical discussion on the alternative margins between Miklavž Komelj and Rastko Močnik (for an English translation and edition see Habjan and Kirn, 2016), while its echoes put the topic of the Partisan struggle and Partisan art on the theoretical, cultural and even political agenda across the former Yugoslavia. Furthermore, the specific monumental Partisan legacy found international fame thanks to Jan Kampenaers’ photo-book *Spomenik*, published in 2010. While its aesthetic quality, which vividly captures Partisan monuments, cannot be questioned, its neutralising starting point leads to a problematic operation of return: Kampenaers decided in favour of the title *Spomenik*. Spomenik in Serbian-Croatian and Slovenian means *monument*, which leaves a readership from the ex-Yugoslavia (and beyond) perplexed, since it obfuscates the fact that all these monuments are actually called monuments to the revolution or the Partisan monument, or monuments to the People’s Liberation Struggle. Furthermore, a rather short and inaccurate foreword by Neutelings deserves an additional critical note. The aestheticisation of the monuments is coupled with a thorough decontextualisation.[25] Neutelings first argues that these people (he is probably

25 For a good criticism see Heatherley (2016). There were also, within the post-Yugoslav context, analyses similar (and prior) to Kampenaers’ intervention, where the aestheticisation of the major artistic-monumental works of socialist Yugoslavia were presented. One symptomatic case is the

referring to Yugoslavs ... ?) were indifferent to these monuments. Not only does this statement lack any academic support, he even claims that this indifference can be understood because:

> different ethnic groups fought one another from different points on the ideological spectrum [...] for this reason, the war monuments could assume neither a heroic nor a patriotic guise [...] they had to be neutral enough to be acceptable to both victims and perpetrators [...] The Spomeniks were places of forgetting, while they should have been places of remembering. They formed a cheerful backdrop for the bright future awaiting the socialistic model society, the official policy line of which was to smooth over all of the former conflicts. (Neutelings 2010, 17)

This passage firstly transforms the figure of the Partisan into an ethnic category (the next two chapters will present a detailed refutation of such a claim), which stands in fundamental opposition to the multinational belonging of the Partisan struggle. His further argument also misreads the abstract gesture of late socialist modernism itself, which had no reason to please or reconcile the populations through these monuments. This argument would be valid when taking into account the array of new revisionist monuments erected since the demise of socialism (see chapter 4). Rather than any function of reconciliation, major Partisan monuments were erected at a time when nationalism saw its first post-war resurgence in the late 1960s and early 1970s. The case studies of Partisan monuments that I describe in chapter 3 point out that a typical totalitarian formula in the Yugoslav context does not work: Partisan monuments were not simply prescribed and financed from above in order to 'forget' the civil wars. Rather, an array of agents and social groups were engaged in the process of commemoration, in thinking and working through the question of how to remember the struggle, its protagonists and the revolution itself.[26] If we agree that the abstract form of monuments leaves room for ambivalence and imagination, their proper name, *monuments to revolution*, together with the accompanying museums and school excursions leave a very explicit antifascist and pedagogic message. Obviously, the major changes of the post-1991 transition resulted in a withering away of the historical context and political institutions that defended or transferred the Partisan legacy, which is why Neutelings and many aestheticising returns to this period currently have difficulties in grappling with the Partisan legacy.

documentary *Damnatio Memoriae*, which importantly presents the destroyed destiny of Partisan monuments in Croatia (Žižić 2001).

26 Heike Karge (2010) wrote a key book on the topic of Yugoslav Partisan monuments, where she shows that the process of negotiation and financing was not at all simple and guided from above, but a process consisting of major disagreements and distributed financing.

Despite the transformed circumstances, the radical quality of the monuments of revolution has not disappeared and should be taken as a serious object of study and work. One of this book's claims is that they succeeded in extracting and radicalising a politico-aesthetic gesture that demands serious meditation on the triangulation between Partisan politics and art that stemmed from the Partisan rupture. These monuments posed major questions that have also become a guiding thread of the Partisan counter-archive: how can a rupture be commemorated in aesthetic form? What kinds of form/medium/artistic means were the most inventive and disruptive in the Yugoslav context? These questions shall be answered in chapters 2 and 3, in which I present many case studies that form the heterogeneous body of the counter-archive. The Partisan counter-archive's records are structured around a few key criteria that I will present in the first chapter, while the aim of the book is to present the theoretical and artistic force of those works that attempted to formalise the Partisan surplus, i.e. the remainder and reminder of the Yugoslav revolution and Partisan struggle. Monuments to revolution were one such conceptual, aesthetic and political undertaking, which during the 1960s and 1970s in socialist Yugoslavia attempted to formalise such a surplus (see Figure 2).

Furthermore, the documents of the Partisan counter-archive are historically and spatially scattered throughout the former republics of Yugoslavia that have undergone different degrees of amnesia and revisionist zeal from the 1990s until today. The scattered and forgotten fragments of the Partisan past – besides taking into account the absence of institutional support – make critical research difficult. However, since the exhibition on Partisan print in 2004, there has been an array of works and groups that have begun dealing with the Partisan past in a productive way. Schematically, I would categorise the recent works into the following groups: firstly, authors, such as Miklavž Komelj, that focus on the period of WWII only (1941–1945); secondly, authors who are interested in socialist art in Yugoslavia that represented Partisan struggle and often used a Partisan narrative as a mythology of the new state (Partisan films and monument analysis); thirdly, groups and works that, in the light of the destruction of the Partisan legacy (since the 1990s), have attempted to preserve the monuments[27]; and finally those that have retrieved the antifascist message and breathed new meaning by means of political, theoretical and artistic appropriation.[28] There also exists a small

27 There are actions commemorating Partisan events organised by different Partisan veteran organisations, as well as younger initiatives from Mostar's AKC Abrašević, to young antifascist organisations in Croatia that focus on educational and youth work and the upkeep of Partisan monuments, which have often ended in confrontations with local authorities and extremists.

28 There are various artists and artist groups/collectives that have continually dealt with this topic: from WHW, Blok and Kurs to artists such as David Maljković, Andrej Grubić and Sanja

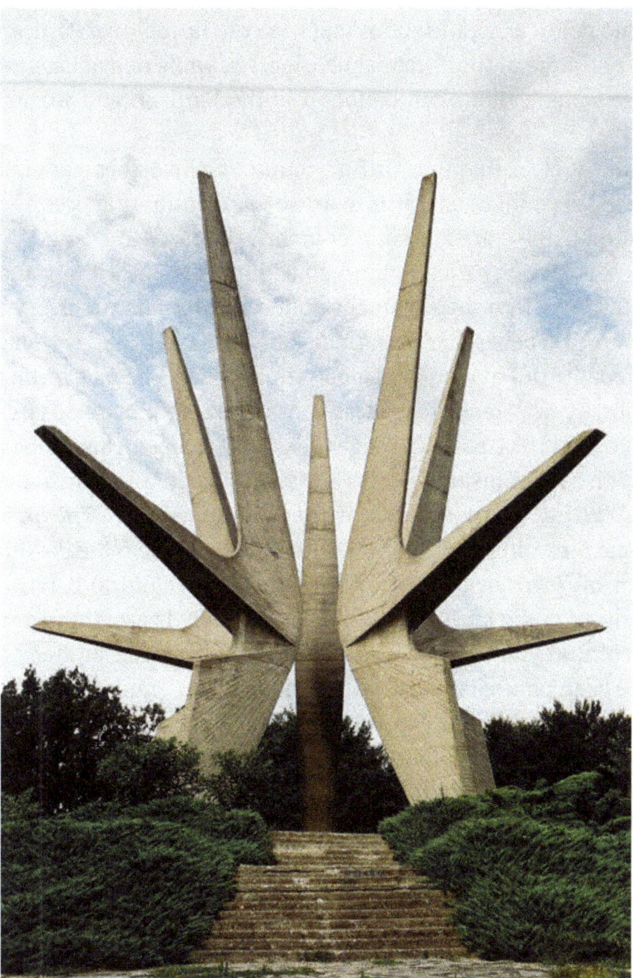

Figure 2: Monument to the Fallen Soldiers of the Kosmaj Detachment – Kosmaj Memorial Complex, produced by Vojin Stojić and Gradimir Medaković (1970). Courtesy of Robert Burghardt.

Iveković, who from as early as the 1990s uncovered the legacy of antifascism, and those artists who attempted to reconstruct, recuperate and artistically document the struggle. Bojan Djordjev also completed a staging of various Partisan poems that is documented online (2014: https://bojandjordjev.wordpress.com/2014/10/29/nije-to-crvena-to-je-krv/). The work of Nemanja Cvijanović "Comrades Follow Me Hurrah!" deals with Partisan artwork from WWII (a chessboard made in the camp), while adding a contemporary twist to and comment on the current situation. Also, the work of Goran Sergej Pristaš and Mila Pavićević combines the Partisan choreography, network of cultural and political organisations that work on the topics of Partisan remembrance and the critique of (post-)fascist revisionism, while one of its most surprising and vital reactualisations can be found in the Partisan and women choirs (e.g. Kombinatke).

Chapter 1 will make it clear that the Partisan counter-archive does not offer a panoramic/positivistic account of all-Partisan artworks, cultural practices and theoretical works. Rather, the Partisan counter-archive is based on a certain notion of excess/surplus that revolves around something that could not and cannot be made to easily fit into the dominant political order and archive, be it socialist Yugoslavia or the post-socialist nation-state. Partisan excess/surplus has to do with the modality of Partisan struggle itself, here conceived as revolutionary process that firstly 'awakened' the masses, while in the process masses themselves became a constitutive and major agent of social change. This chapter provides the reader with a short historical overview and conceptualisation of the Partisan struggle in WWII as a "rupture with strong consequences." The antifascist struggle became a revolutionary event that led to a complete break with the pre-war Kingdom of Yugoslavia, which had tremendous cultural-political consequences. The advent of the masses on the stage of history is exemplified in the mobile amateur cultural groups as well as in thousands of poems written by anonymous poets, Partisan photography, theatre performances, graphic designs, illustrations and even exhibitions. Revolutionary struggle became a site of encounter for radical artworks and politics that has not stopped yielding consequences either since WWII or since 1991. The 'essence' of Partisan surplus, then, cannot be reduced to either its artistic or to its political nature, but rather brings forth and reconfigures both fields, of aesthetics and politics, in a new fashion.[29]

This is the central hypothesis from which the counter-archive has grown, while the records of the counter-archive follow a few criteria: firstly, the records resist easy incorporation into official commemorations in the public sphere (through the state), since they have articulated a surplus that prevents easy systematisation into one field; secondly, I am interested in how different Partisan

---

archive of film and photography of liberation of Zagreb as a fascinating way of re-enacting and reconstructing liberating Partisan art and life (2015). There are a few films that work on Partisan memory from a left-wing but also personal perspective: Marta Popivoda's film *Landscapes of Resistance* (forthcoming), and a documentary film from Jakob Weindner *To, česar burja ni odnesla* (2014) to name a few.

29 In this respect it is indebted to a certain formulation from Rancière's politics of aesthetics and the aesthetics of politics based on the notion of an "aesthetic break" (2008). The latter will emerge, will be made visible-sayable-audible only by a radical dissonance with the established "distribution of the sensible," that is, the way we see, listen and speak about matters.

records have gone beyond former canons and expectations; thirdly, I have chosen records that have been particularly successful in providing alternative protocols and forms to commemorate the Partisan rupture. The fact that these records lie scattered around post-Yugoslavia speaks both to the specific nature of the Partisan struggle and the counter-archive: they are both *de-territorialised* and as such 'incapable' of easy state centralisation. The Partisan counter-archive does not claim authenticity or neutrality: the very modality of Partisan surplus propels it beyond present and past state ideologies. The Partisan counter-archive holds this surplus dimension open and does not foreclose it – it is neither reducible to the politics of the (former or current) state, nor to the aesthetic ideology of authenticity and experience. The case studies will point out how we can move beyond the mere ritualisation and performance of the ideological banner of socialist Yugoslavia and thus avoid a nostalgic temptation that easily boils down to what Benjamin called "leftist melancholia" (Benjamin 1999, 423–27).[30] The case studies will also ask if and how a Partisan rupture was sustained in socialism and whether it can be sustained in the current age of national-neoliberalism. The conceptualisation of the counter-archive has been inspired by figures such as Walter Benjamin and Susan Buck-Morss, but also Jacques Rancière as well as a group of authors from the post-Yugoslav context.

Each of the following chapters analyses specific examples from poetry, films, monuments, photography and other intermedial forms, which among other aspects show how the dominance of one medium over another (from poetry to sculpture and films). Consequently, I will show how the Partisan rupture was "remediated" in different historical periods, answering questions as to how, in what way and why it was (de)mobilised through the Partisan art and memory. The subsequent three chapters are organised around two main axes: the historical and the axis guided by the medium/art that conveys/continues the Partisan rupture.

Chapter 2 will depart from the Partisan archive during the time of intense Partisan struggle (1941–1945). Due to the context of occupation and war, a shortage of cultural infrastructure and material carries a deep mark on this period. Yet despite this material scarcity and the practical impossibility of engaging in cultural activity in times of war – *inter arma musae silent* – an array of fascinating artworks was produced during this period. I will translate and analyse a few examples of Partisan poetry that first expressed the strong need to commemorate the rupture and succeeded in articulating a form of revolutionary temporality:

30 For a fascinating discussion on the troubles and political inefficacy with "leftist melancholia" see Brown (1999) and Dean (2018), while Traverso (2017b) takes a more affirmative approach.

the "not-yet-existing" or, in French, the *futur antérieur* (cf. Badiou 2005). The second part of this chapter will be dedicated to the analysis of the very first Partisan films and how Partisans made films "by other means" (Levi 2012), using hidden cameras in occupied cities or recording songs in Partisan cartoons, and the footage of the Partisan struggle.

Chapter 3 takes place in the midst of the cultural explosion and renaissance of interest in political emancipation found in the mature self-management of the 1960s–70s. The media-art analysis here will deal with the proliferation of Partisan films and monuments. Can we confirm or reject the thesis held by some cultural theorists that cultural works and practices of the Partisan event existed only to mythologise the new Yugoslav state? The backdrop of this discussion is perhaps the waning ideological legitimacy of the socialist project, the market reform that was introduced in 1965 when unemployment and protests pointed toward a serious crisis for the first time. It seems that this fuelled the ideological need to over-invest in the Partisan past – thus memory and representation became one of the most intense points of ideological and cultural confrontation. The first example will analyse a few critical films that subverted the dominant representation of Partisan struggle. The second example will deal with the late modernist movement of sculptors, architects and designers who produced 'monuments to revolution' and thus answered the question of how to formalise and commemorate revolution.

Chapter 4 will present the dissolution of Yugoslavia through the revisionist cultural politics that organised the iconoclastic destruction of Partisan monuments, undoing the Partisan legacy and constructing a revisionist memorial landscape. The post-socialist context will be shown to be a veritable example of what I have called the "primitive accumulation of memory," which has been affected by different strategies. This was done, on the one hand, through complete silencing, destruction and obliteration and, on the other hand, through nationalist reconciliation and open fascist rehabilitation. Thus, the terrain has become full of rich examples of "disputed memory" (Sindbæk Andersen and Törnquist-Plewa, 2016). These strategies shall be evaluated in terms of both the discursive and monumental practices/protocols that have contributed to the withering away of the Partisan legacy in the period since 1991 and this section will end with a short analysis of the newest anti-totalitarian pan-European monument that is being erected in Brussels.

Finally, despite this counter-archive being so strongly based on the no-longer-existing political space of Yugoslavia, it does not seek to stay within the confines of its exceptional experience. Rather, the counter-archive is waiting to be further explored as an insurgent methodology and expanded to other political and cultural Partisan counter-agencies and insurgencies that have occurred in counter-history. There are many such experiences that have remained obscured or limited to the confines of academic/artistic settings and treated as curiosities of a long-gone, failed past. The Partisan counter-archive could travel to the radicalisation of the French revolution in Haiti and the first Partisan black republic, to the communards of the Paris Commune and the Taipei Revolts, but also to the Partisan struggle after the October Revolution and the Moroccan guerrilla units led by Abd el-Krim el-Khattabi, and once again to the international brigades and antifascists in the Spanish Civil War and the Partisans of WWII. The Partisan moment after WWII continued in the anticolonial struggles that stretch across different continents and urban guerrillas to militant feminist, antiracist and environmental movements – each of which have been fighting important struggles that have had strong artistic and political effects. The work of critical (counter-) archival studies consists in systematising and articulating counter-archival traces and effects. How such counter histories and memories of an emancipated past will be remediated, retold, and resocialised in the present in the form of a new emancipatory politics is not only a theoretical task, but also entails a political practice that remains to be awakened in our present and for our future.

Chapter 1
The Three Impossibilities of the Partisan Counter-Archive: Politics, Art and the 'Anti-memory' of Rupture

> Guerrilla warfare is a people's warfare; an attempt to carry out this type of war without the population's support is a prelude to inevitable disaster.
>
> Che Guevara, 1963 (*Guerrilla Warfare – A Method*)

> I don't care a spit
> for tons of bronze;
> I don't care a spit
> for slimy marble.
> We're men of kind,
> we'll come to terms with our fame;
> let our
> common monument be
> socialism
> built
> in battle.
> Vladimir Mayakovsky, 1930 (*At the top of my voice*)

This chapter consists of three parts: in the first part I will assess the political dimensions of the People's Liberation Struggle (1941–1945), namely, how this struggle succeeded in subtracting from the old political powers (the Yugoslav government-in-exile, London) and in winging against the fascist collaborationists and the fascist occupation, therein triggering social revolution; in the second part of the chapter I will analyse the emergence and significance of Partisan art that created a symbolic imaginary for the struggle itself; and in the last part of the chapter I will ask how and why the Partisan struggle – as early as during the war – expressed a need and a strong desire to commemorate the contemporaneous rupture.

Various revolutionary consequences stemmed from the People's Liberation Struggle, ranging from the materialisation of federalism, international solidarity and socialist struggle to women's emancipation and cultural revolution.[31] The

31 Pupovac (2008). In my book on socialist Yugoslavia (Kirn 2019b), I elaborated a political analysis of "Partisan rupture with strong consequences" and also the genesis of resistance in the pre-war Yugoslavia, as well as political, social and economic changes that unfolded after World War II.

https://doi.org/10.1515/9783110682069-002

most important for this book will be the analysis of Partisan revolution from the perspective of a specific encounter between politics and art, which was accompanied, during the struggle itself, by the powerful commemorative expression/imagination of that very Partisan revolution. This potent encounter, the richness of artists' form and their complex temporality, form the basis of the Partisan counter-archive. The project travels through the fields of politics, art and memory and departs from questions such as: how was it possible to perform revolutionary acts in the harshest circumstances and despite all the odds? How did the Partisan counter-archive reorient and construct a new future? And how did that gesture and practice herald and symbolically facilitate the new world? I will also attempt to answer the question of what the Partisan counter-archive embodies and what incited it initially to begin a process of decolonised and liberated commemoration: was it the figure of the Partisan, the struggle itself, Partisan Yugoslavia and "unity and brotherhood," or was it rather the modality of the de/re/territorialisation of liberated territories? The modality of "becoming Partisan" will be central to the conception of the counter-archive and this is why the next sections will present several major characteristics of pre-war Yugoslavia and the beginnings of the Partisan struggle.

1.1 The *ancien régime* of Yugoslavia prior to WWII: The "prison-house of nations" and economic exploitation

The interwar Yugoslavia emerged after World War I as a Kingdom of Serbs, Croats and Slovenes. The heterogeneous territories with diverse people and nations came together in the aftermath of the dissolution of the Austro-Hungarian monarchy and under the tutelage of the Serbian aristocracy, which formed a part of the "small entente" during the war. From the very beginning the kingdom was split by major political and economic antagonisms. These were present in the very first constitution of 1921 that subscribed to a centralist and unitarist conception of Yugoslavia, which won out over the 'autonomist' and clerical version supported mostly by the Croatian Peasant Party and the Slovenian Clerical Party.[32] After the

32 The extreme nationalist divisions exacerbated the severe socio-economic situation, where the bourgeois parties and monarchists tightened around a unitarist conception, which was countered by the autonomist current. The Croatian Party of Peasants and to some extent also the Slovenian Clerical Party were against the monarchist dynasty of Karađorđević and against unitarism. For the development of autonomist ideas see Banac (1984, 226–48). It is also noteworthy that after the first general elections in the kingdom in 1920, the Communist Party became the third largest party. Due to the revolutionary unrest in post-war Europe the ruling class banned

imposition of royal dictatorship in 1929, the kingdom received a new name: *The Kingdom of Yugoslavia*, whereby all political life was limited to superficial struggles between the two biggest officially permitted parties.[33] The new kingdom not only existed at "the periphery of the capitalist world system," but according to a recent study by Lev Centrih, the state found itself at the "periphery of the European semi-periphery that was dominated by fascist regimes" (Centrih 2011, 112). In the mid-1930s, the ruling class in Yugoslavia increasingly relied on the Italian and German economy and drew its political ideas from their theories of fascist corporativism. To define the old Yugoslavia from the mid-late 1930s as a semi-fascist dictatorship is not at all a controversial claim, if one takes into account the brutal exploitation of the people and domination of small nations/nationalities and repression of all political opponents (Magaš 1993, 23–27). Any political activity was banned and many activists or members of leftist groups and organisations were exiled, imprisoned or executed. From at least 1935, the Kingdom of Yugoslavia instituted a set of prison-camps for political opponents, most notably for communists and fervent nationalists.[34] Since the level of economic exploitation was particularly severe, the period before WWII was marked by numerous strikes and illegal protests. The latter were met with police brutality, capital punishment and the forced migration of protest organisers.

In these circumstances, support for socialist and communist forces began to rise even if the Communist Party remained weak, fragmented and until 1937 operated in exile. This was also the year when the party leadership took a few major decisions: to support the republican side in the Spanish Civil War by all means, to gradually prepare a united popular front against fascism and to revise its former policy of Yugoslav centralisation.[35] Yugoslav Communists started adopting federalist ideas, which were confirmed in a series of new autonomous parties: for example, the Communist Party of Slovenia and Communist Party of Croatia were formed (Magaš 1993, 27–28) Tito's rise to power within CPY came precisely in this time. But as the Kingdom of Yugoslavia intensified the repression during the time

---

the party in the constitution of 1921. Mayors that were legally elected to municipal office – as in the case of the mayor of Belgrade – were prevented from entering office, later imprisoned, and politically neutralised.

33 See also Centrih's excellent summary of factional struggles (2011, 112–133).

34 For more details on Yugoslav concentration camps in the 1930s see *Opća enciklopedija JLZ* (1978, V, 500–504).

35 The historian Ivo Banac rightly analyses the ambivalent position linking, on the one hand, the vision of *narodno jedinstvo* (national unity) and Marxist internationalism (1984, 328–339), on the other. In the beginning of the 1920s, "communist leaders were overconfident of their ability to ride the continental red wave" (Banac 1984, 330) and that is why they did not capitalise on the national question.

of the Spanish Civil War and immediately before WWII, most of the CPY leadership were imprisoned. On the eve of war in early 1941, the CPY membership counted only 7,000 members. However, this relatively small grouping had a strong and long-term illegal organisational network in the Kingdom of Yugoslavia, and was joined by some 200 fighters-survivors from the Spanish Civil War and concentration camps (Pavlaković 2016), who all held a strong belief in social transformation.

These pre-war conditions opened a path for Yugoslav Communists to become a central political force that began organising the antifascist struggle throughout Yugoslavia soon after the fascist occupation.[36] Communist parties were central agents in liberation fronts that united all antifascist organisations, but as I will show below the communist organisations themselves went through a major transformation: both opening up and democratising from below. By the end of the war, the Communist Party of Yugoslavia counted more than 140,000 members most of whom came from the rural countryside and who were deeply engaged in the Partisan struggle.

1.2 World War II: Fascist occupation and the Partisan uprising

The invasion of Yugoslavia began on 6 April 1941 and was completed by 17 April 1941, when the Yugoslav Royal Army declared an unconditional surrender with very little resistance and even voluntary disarmament by its forces. The Kingdom of Yugoslavia, a semi-fascist dictatorship, was substituted by a thoroughly fascist one imposed by foreign rule. Yugoslavia was divided into different zones of occupation – Italian, Hungarian, Bulgarian and German occupation zones and protectorates. The central part with Croatia and most of present-day Bosnia and Herzegovina was handed over to the political administration of *Ustashas* who formed a fascist puppet state called the *Independent State of Croatia* (1941–1945). Under these circumstances, a part of the old political elite openly collaborated with the fascist regime, while a part of the political elite, along with the royal family, migrated to London. The latter remained the internationally recognised Yugoslav government-in-exile, while in practical terms the royal Yugoslav government-in-exile gradually lost popular support and had little ideological legitimacy in occupied Yugoslavia. From the very start of the war, the civilian population was exposed to brutal terror due to racial laws and decrees: forced labour and migration, torture and extermination became normal under the new occupation

---

36 There were more than 1,500 Yugoslav volunteers, mostly communists, who joined the International Brigades. See also Pavlaković (2004).

regimes and their racist policies. The network of concentration camps, including on Yugoslav territory, were horrific sites of mass killings, where hundreds of thousands of Roma, homosexuals, political opponents, antifascists, communist youth, women, Partisans, Jews and other nationalities and minorities were killed.[37] This situation of extreme terror in the occupied zones led a massive number of people to participate in the Partisan antifascist struggle, which offered not only a place of refuge/survival, but imagined and finally promised and realised an imaginary of a different world.

To be sure, at the very beginning of the war, it was not crystal clear who was fighting against the occupation regime and for what. There were different self-proclaimed "patriotic" groups, who were not Partisan and who formed their own military units and militias in order to guard the homeland. Firstly, there were nationalistic Serbian units called Chetniks, led by Draža Mihailović, who became the recognised representative of the royal power of the Yugoslav government-in-exile. At the very start of the war, Chetniks retained a degree of autonomy and fought on some occasions against the Nazi occupiers. They also received, up until mid-1943, great amounts of material assistance from the British forces, while as early as from the autumn 1941 they began to openly attack antifascist Partisan forces and collaborate with Nazi forces. This is well documented in transcriptions/archives and in their direct military engagement on the terrain.[38] Apart from their policies of ethnic cleansing in Bosnia and Herzegovina, they fought together with the Nazis and Croatian Ustasha in major offensives against Partisan forces in 1943.[39] All across Yugoslavia fascist local collaborators started organising against the Partisans. In Slovenia, the local anti-communist militia mobilised clerical-fascist youth and part of the peasantry to join the White Guard,[40] who

37 To name just a few concentration camps: Rab was the largest concentration camp on an island in Europe (see Jezernik 1999) or Gonars (Pirjevec 2008). Both were under the authority of fascist Italy, while the infamous camp Jasenovac was run by the Croatian Ustasha, where around 100,000 people were killed (Dedijer 1992; Israeli 2013).

38 See the recent historical studies of Radanović (2012, 2014); Yugoslav Partisans also confiscated the Chetniks' archives that document all the cooperation-agreements between the Chetniks and Nazis. This was used in the trial after the war against Mihailović (Latas 1999). This historical fact is nowadays overshadowed by the revisionist theories and populist politics (Radanović 2015), which first of all forget that collaboration was a crime. Chetniks have become increasingly depicted as the only proper patriots.

39 Mihailović's Chetniks mostly attacked Partisans (Petranović 1988, 241–243) and were militarily defeated in Bosnia after the so-called Battle of Neretva, that is, in the fourth fascist offensive against the Partisans.

40 The official name carries an openly anti-communist orientation and its legacy from the October Revolution.

collaborated with Italian fascists. After the capitulation of Italy in 1943 and the heavy defeats that the Partisans inflicted, local collaborationists regrouped and were renamed the Home Guard.[41] The latter came directly under Nazi command and swore oaths to Hitler on various occasions. In Kosovo and Macedonia, SS-Albanian units, Skander-beg, operated, whereas the bourgeois nationalist Albanian units of *Balli Kombëtar* remained in a more ambivalent position. However, in the end they collaborated with Nazis and Chetniks in order for Kosovo to remain without Partisan resistance.[42] In Bosnia a Muslim *Handžar* SS division was integrated into military actions of the Nazi army.

Local fascist collaborationists consisted of extreme nationalists who were ostracised in the pre-war Kingdom of Yugoslavia, while much of their leadership came from the old ruling class. With forced conscription in many rural areas, a lot of young peasants also entered the collaborationist forces. The intensity of civil war can be partially explained by the pre-war political antagonisms and ethnic hatred that resulted from the national question's suppression. Civil war meant that people fought against people from the same regions, villages and sometimes even families, which testified to the intense ethical and political challenges (over belonging). Fascist terror led to a significant number of civilian deaths and military casualties in Yugoslavia. All in all, more than 10% of the entire population was lost during the war.[43] If we add to this the imprisonment, torturing and raping of the local population – we can get a picture of the extreme proportions of devastation. Above all, the local fascist collaborators were ethnically exclusive in terms of their membership and operated on one central principle: *ethnic hatred*. However, from the very start of the war, alleged patriotism was already morally problematic: on the one hand, this was displayed in the murder of their 'own'

---

41 There is film footage of the anti-communist gatherings of local collaborationists. One good and accessible example was a major gathering of local fascists in Ljubljana in 1944, which was filmed by an infiltrated Partisan activist Rudi Omota (http: //www.youtube.com/watch? v=3p-NoQqPBg0). This material was also used in court after the war in order to convict the collaborationists. I will come to the question of whether this kind of material should be considered a part of the Partisan counter-archive in the next chapter, but the short answer is no.

42 See Magaš (1993, 32–34).

43 See Tomashevich (2001, 733). In the European context apart from the Jewish population and Roma people, people from the Soviet Union, Poland and Yugoslavia suffered the largest death toll, amassing losses of more than 10% of their whole population. These numbers can be compared with the casualties of the European and Japanese colonial regimes from Portuguese East Timor and the British Empire "handling" of the Bengali famine to French Indochina and the Dutch East Indies. See Keegan (1989) for different numbers, while the general table of casualties is presented here: https://en.wikipedia.org/wiki/World_War_II_casualties.

people who did not obey them, or who were 'racially' different, while, on the other, they were in service to their real masters – the fascist occupiers.

One should not forget that if it is true that the Partisan resistance in Yugoslavia was the biggest in occupied Europe and by the autumn of 1944 already counted around 650,000 Partisans, the fascist-collaborationist forces were among the strongest in Europe as well: in the autumn of 1944 they amounted to more than 250,000 people.[44] Admittedly, a portion of the local population was forcefully mobilised, however, that does not overshadow the historical fact that in many parts of Yugoslavia, fierce battles raged between Partisans and local collaborationists. In this respect Hannah Arendt was not only right when she spoke of the "banality of evil" (1977), of all those who facilitated deportations of Jews to concentration camps and in so doing were accomplices who greased the gears of the fascist state – this was also true of all those military and political units that actively supported the fascist regime – without which it would not have been able to sustain itself for so long. These were years of a strong international solidarity among fascists across Europe and the world.

In contrast to moral pragmatism and the principle of ethnic hatred, the Partisan liberation struggle represented the only political force that was open to all nations and nationalities, to men and women. The Partisans were thus the only 'Yugoslav' and gender-mixed armed group that operated in the whole of Yugoslavia. Moreover, the Yugoslav Partisans operated and cooperated beyond the 'ethnic' borders aiding in the formation of other Partisan detachments.[45] Late in 1943, detachments of the Italian Army that had resisted serving the Nazis switched sides and became involved in the *Garibaldi* Partisan Division – more than 5,000 Italian soldiers became Partisans and fought the Nazi occupation.[46]

Partisan struggle becomes a site and movement that operates around the central Partisan criterion of belonging to an main Partisan criterion consists of belonging to an international antifascist struggle and practicing antifascist solidarity, which goes both against the Schmittian view of 'ethnic'/telluric belonging on the one hand, and against the mainstream journalistic definition

44 Cf. Radanović (2014).

45 Yugoslav Partisans co-organised Partisan actions in Bulgaria, Albania, Austria and Italy. The attempt to constitute a Partisan body for the coordination of the antifascists in the Balkans was stopped by the British Allies. After WWII it was Yugoslavia who helped Greek Partisans in the civil war up until the international isolation of Yugoslavia in 1948 (Karamanić 2009). Tempo-Vukmanović in charge of Balkan coordination discussed these issues in detail in his memoirs (1982), see also Petranović (1991).

46 Lando Manucci's text on Garibaldi's division can be consulted online: http: //www.montenegrina.net/pages/pages1/istorija/cg_u_2_svj_ratu/divizija_garibaldi_u_crnoj_gori_lando_manuci.html.

of the Partisans as someone connected to a political party, on the other. The Merriam Webster Dictionary defines a partisan as "a firm adherent to a party, faction, cause or person, especially one exhibiting blind, prejudiced and unreasoning allegiance." The second part of the sentence works as an ideological supplement that assigns a very concrete feature to Partisans: the absence of any regulative idea or faculty of reasoning – a partisan exhibits blind and unreasoning allegiance. This sombre representation delegitimises the figure of the (Yugoslav) Partisan from the outset and brings it into the horizon of fanaticism, eternally resigning the Partisans to a realm of irrational politics. Not only does revolt and resistance against fascist occupation in harsh circumstances demand political courage, it also departs from an abstract and very rational maxim: *we have the right/reason to revolt*, to paraphrase Badiou (2005). Each Partisan took an oath, which slightly differed across regions, while Tito himself drafted one of the earliest versions on 26 September 1941:

> We, the people's Partisans of Yugoslavia, have taken up arms to wage a relentless struggle against the bloodthirsty enemies who have enslaved our country and are exterminating our peoples. In the name of liberty and justice for our people, we swear that we shall be disciplined, persevering and fearless, that we shall spare neither blood nor life in fighting the fascist invaders and all traitors to the people until they are completely annihilated.
>
> (Tito [1941] 1966, 31)

The subject concerned is "we, the people's Partisans of Yugoslavia," which already points to the collective dimension of Partisans – not starting with I (and stating your name as in the Army of the Kingdom of Yugoslavia), but starting with a collective enunciated position, which comes from the people and is directed at all Yugoslavia. The specific Partisan oath used in Slovenia was even more political, explicitly stating allegiances in war, as well as stating that as a

> Partisan of liberation and the People's Army of the Slovenian Nation, I fight on the side of the Workers-Peasant-Red Army and other people that struggle for freedom [...] for brotherhood and peace among nations and people, for the better future of working people [...] the Partisan shall fight against fascist masters and barbarians; and [finally I swear] that I will not leave Partisan detachments – until the complete victory over the fascist occupiers and complete liberation of the Slovenian nation [...] For freedom in struggle.
>
> (From Lešnik and Tomc 1995, 84)

This oath not only highlights the Red Army as the major side for which the Partisans in Slovenia fight, it also already mentions "working people" as an emerging political subject (Pupovac 2008) that foresees a very different political imaginary, a specific synthesis between the working class, peasants and people. It ends on a more poetic call that freedom is only possible in and through struggle.

As a contrast, let me quote an oath made by local collaborationists in Slovenia, the *Home Guard*, who under SS Command performed a collective oath on the birthday of Adolf Hitler on 20 April 1944:

> I swear to the almighty God that I will be loyal, courageous and submissive to my superiors, and that in joint struggle with the German Armed Forces under the command of the leader of Great Germany, the SS detachments and police, I will fight against bandits and against communism, and also against its allies, and fulfil my duties conscientiously for the Slovenian homeland and as a part of free Europe. For this fight I am ready to sacrifice my life. May God help me. (from *Slovenec*, 21 April 1944)

This oath's point of departure is a clear conservative ideology, subjugated to God, superiors, the order of Great Germany and clearly attached to the ethnic principle of cleansed nations. However, the oath also discloses – in its purest form – the moral and political ambivalence and hypocrisy between Nazi Germany and its fake news of "free Europe" on the one hand, within which the Slovenian homeland is designated, while years of war saw how people from Slovenia had been forcefully exiled, tortured, executed and sent to concentration camps, while resistance movements were interpreted as groups of bandits and as such were summarily executed.

In juxtaposition to the false patriotism of local collaborationists, the term Partisan stands as the name for a collective struggle that made an immense sacrifice for liberation. The Partisan figure is thus not some male and militaristic figure, but rather a figure of a collective-in-resistance. This collective embodied the Partisan principle that was directed against the principle of the ethnic hatred of WWII. In other words, the Partisan principle was based on multinational antifascist solidarity, which declared the equality and unity of all nations and working people. The Partisan movement opened up a new horizon for Yugoslavia that was based on universal politics:

> The Yugoslav Partisan movement incited the first mass people's uprising in occupied Europe, and the large-scale revolutionary movements of the twentieth century. (the Yugoslav Revolution was the biggest revolutionary uprising after the Spanish Civil War)[47]

It is factually and politically incorrect to reduce the People's Liberation Struggle (*Narodno-osvobodilni boj*, hereinafter PLS) to its national component, even if the notions of people and nation were often intermingled. Part of the confusion stems from the very naming of the resistance, which merges "the nation" [*narod*]

47 Komelj (2008, 24).

and "the people" [*ljudstvo*] into a single term: the nation.[48] Furthermore, if we reduced the PLS to mere national liberation, then Partisans would be there to liberate specific nations and aim to build a nation-state. The PLS put into practice a heterogeneous political subjectivity of the people and all nations on Yugoslav territory. To be more precise, the most inventive part of the Partisan struggle was its dialectical convergence in a revolutionary process of the working classes, nations, progressive youth and women. Thus, there was not a single aspect of the struggle that held more or less importance than another: neither national (a mere struggle against the occupation, a struggle for equality among nations and nationalities) nor a simply social revolutionary struggle (the autonomy of liberated territories with consequences for later socialist transformation) – it was one and all of these.

There is a valid reason why the Partisan movement did not call or name their activities and formation merely a Partisan army organisation. Rather, from the beginning onwards, it was a *struggle* that entered centre stage, reflected in the names of the Partisan units: at times called after poets and figures from the local resistance tradition, at other times from the region where they were formed, yet also carrying the 'proletarian' signifier. All these different denominations highlight the varied construction of a community-in-struggle, while also allowing for the political construction of an enemy that cannot be simply substantiated in an ethnic sense. The opponents were then not some substantive ethnic group, such as 'Italians' or 'Germans,' but those that belonged to the political camp of fascism, local fascist collaborators included.

The struggle for people's liberation therefore travels dialectically between social and national liberation, as proposed by Ozren Pupovac who speaks of the

---

48 The Slovenian language distinguishes between people [*ljudstvo*] and nation [*narod*], even though in political and theoretical texts these two concepts are used interchangeably and we should interpret them with regard to the specific context (Komelj 2008). In the Serbo-Croatian-Bosnian language the difference between nation and people is sometimes blurred, as the word is the same: *narod*. For more information on the historical development of the concepts of nation, nationality and ethnicity in the Yugoslav context see Banac (1984, 23–27). Banac's study also argues that nationalism is a modern concept and situates the development of national awareness in the late nineteenth century. Nevertheless, occasionally his thesis transforms into emphasising nationalist ideology as an eternal and ahistorical formation. Karl Deutsch offers a more precise definition of nationalities as groups of people on the path towards their political, economic and cultural autonomy (Deutsch, 1996). During World War II a variety of terms were used in the Partisan struggle, with the exception of the French version of the nation or the unitarian Yugoslav nation, which has had an exceedingly negative connotation since the Kingdom of Yugoslavia.

emergence of a "revolutionary people."[49] Pupovac argues that the PLS practiced a political principle, which did not only relate to

> a single people or a single nation, but rather to all the nations and peoples within the repressive monarchic regime as well as to all the people beset by domination, whether on the basis of class, gender, nationality or religion.[50]

The Yugoslav struggle for people's liberation represents one of the few examples of antifascist politics that developed a positive programme. The Partisan struggle affirmed a framework in which the former symbolic meanings and the old Yugoslavia gradually lost their ideological significance. When Jacques Rancière speaks of the existence of real rupture ("politics" that interrupts the order of "police"), he argues that it needs to entail a process of "de-identification." In the precise context of the Partisan struggle, "de-identification" is an appropriate term as we can see it posited against the (local) fascist ethnic hatred and racial hierarchy, while also against the old stereotypes of national character. To illustrate this point, it suffices to refer to one minor case: the Liberation Front – the Partisan political power in Slovenia – that on 1 November adopted and published a declaration. Point 4 of the programme called upon the people not to change the allegedly servile tendency of national character, but to transform more deeply the human nature that functioned as a natural fact:

> With the liberation action and activation of the Slovenian masses, the Liberation Front will transform the Slovenian national character [...] In fighting for their national and human rights, they are creating a new model of active Sloveneness.[51]

This speaks of the profound political ambition of the Partisan project that wanted to construct a new world and a new (wo-)man, and which cannot be addressed other than through the encounter of class and nation(s). Furthermore, the very *modus operandi* of guerrilla activities and thinking can be perhaps best thought through the concept of deterritorialisation. But as Deleuze and Guattari propose,

49 There are diverse alternative conceptions of "the people"; cf. Jacques Rancière (2002) and Laclau (2005). I expand on this notion elsewhere Kirn (2015a), while one of the most comprehensive radical political edited volumes was written by Badiou, Butler and Didi-Huberman (2016).

50 Pupovac (2008, 16).

51 Nine fundamental points of the Liberation Front were adopted, the first seven of these at the 4th session of the Supreme Plenum of the Liberation Front on 1 November 1941. The analysis of the Assembly of all National Liberation Struggle Committee deputies in Kočevje between 1 and 3 October 1943 also attests to the duality of the social revolution (Kristan 1973, 600–609). This duality had been at work from the very beginning, but in 1943 it incorporated the masses and attained a wider Yugoslav dimension.

the first theorem of this concept is that "one never deterritorialises alone" (2003, 174), rather, if the movement – i.e. body of resistance – and analytical work are strong, it always *reteritorialises*.[52] The Partisan principle of deterritorialisation should be seen both as being critical of the presupposed linkage between population, territory and state (Carl Schmitt's conception of the Partisan is overdetermined by a *Blut und Boden* ideology, which Schmitt terms "telluric"[53]) with its dominant mode of politics (the nation-state or its radicalisation in a fascist regime), but also as something that does not float up in the air and which would always be short in duration, even without any (counter-)institutional form. Rather, the Partisan imaginary and the principles of solidarity in a new world materialised in the liberated territories that came into existence from the autumn of 1941 onwards. The deterritorialisation, the movement from one zone to another, and the multiplication of pockets of resistance resulted in decolonisation and *reterritorialisation* in the newly liberated zones.[54] The map of liberated territories became increasingly visible and tainted the purity of fascist rule throughout Yugoslavia, but also extended to more general European and global horizons. The map below depicts the contours of fascist occupied Europe in May 1943 and the pockets of liberated zones (see Figure 3).

1.3 The Antifascist Council for the People's Liberation of Yugoslavia: The creation of the Partisan (anti-)state Yugoslavia in November 1943

With the Partisan armed struggle, the wheels of the Yugoslav revolution never stopped turning; they were in "constant flux." This is what Svetozar Tempo, a Partisan charged with coordinating Balkan Partisan activities, took as the principle lesson from and legacy of the PLS (1982). The constant movement of Partisan detachments was linked to their guerrilla tactics in light of fascist military offensives, but also to their own planning and coordination. Despite the absence of efficient communicative devices among the Partisan units scattered across

52 See also the section (2007, 291–297). Primož Krašovec analysed the principle of deterritorialisation in the Partisan struggle (2007).

53 I wrote a more detailed critique of Schmitt's allegedly formalistic account (2004) of the Partisans elsewhere (Kirn 2019b). See also Alberto Toscano (2008) for an emphasis on the telluric in Schmitt's multipolar world, which instantiates a "clashes of civilisation" discourse.

54 The main post-war socialist ideologue of self-management Edvard Kardelj wrote, in 1943, the treatise on the liberated zones and councils. This treatise and the political practice of liberated zones resonated with the originary form of Partisan self-management.

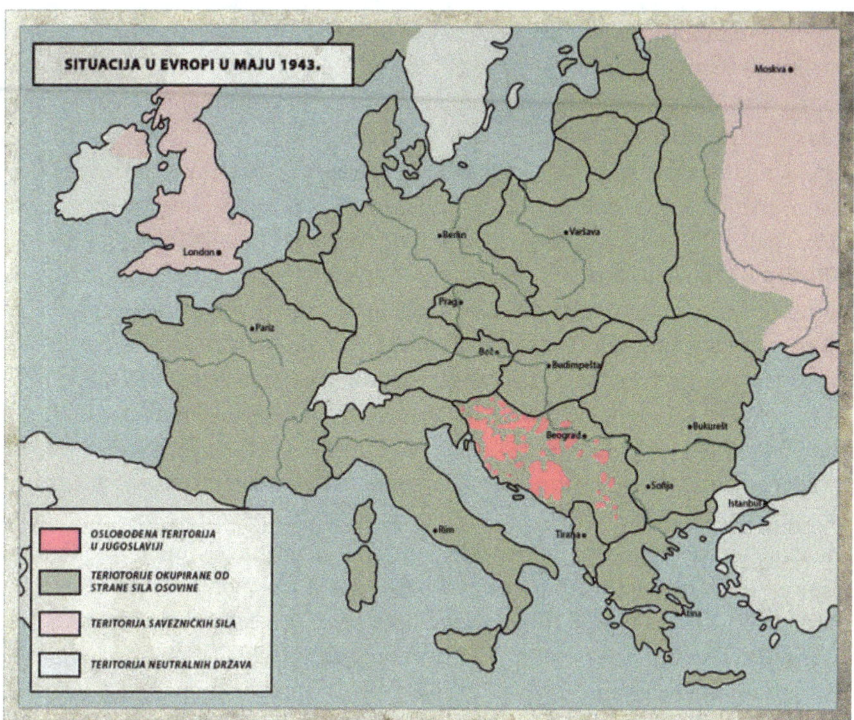

Figure 3: Map of Europe in May 1943, from the textbook *Hronologija NOB 1941–1945*: Green denotes Axis-occupied territory, pink denotes Allied territories, and violet denotes the liberated territories of the Partisans in Yugoslavia.
Source: https://commons.wikimedia.org/wiki/File:Jugoslavija_i_Evropa_maj_1943.jpg.

the Yugoslav territory, the Partisan central command attempted to coordinate military and political activities, draft major political decisions and also hold communication abroad with antifascist allies. In October 1942, Bihać became a historic space where the Antifascist Council for the National Liberation of Yugoslavia (hereinafter AVNOJ) was formed and assembled all the Committees of the Deputies of the National Liberation. The AVNOJ and the Supreme Headquarters became the central hub that partly steered the regional and national resistance nodes – the movement. In reality, AVNOJ could not oversee political and military actions at the local level due to slow-moving communication, while the specificity of the regional occupation, offensives and relation of forces were also issues. The Regional and Field Committees of the National Liberation Struggle thus remained largely autonomous and had to demonstrate a profound political and military inventiveness in order to successfully organise the supply chain of food, living and military necessities, while also to politically and culturally organise the local population in the liberated territories. The task was to begin the construction of the broadest possible forms of people's power, the People's Liberation Councils.

As was the case throughout the world, 1943 proved to be a major turning point for the Partisan liberation struggle in Yugoslavia. The PLS was close to defeat but famously survived two major offensives in central Bosnia. Early in 1943 the Fourth Offensive *Fall Weiss* was unleashed around the Neretva River, with more than 150,000 units of Axis forces, Ustashas and Chetniks, accompanied by 200 airplanes, heavy artillery and tanks. They were tasked with the annihilation of the Partisan General Command, its main forces and the Partisan hospital. The latter counted some 3,000 wounded, while General Command had some 17,000 Partisans ready for combat. This meant that the Partisans were outnumbered 10 to 1. Besieged on many occasions as well as being aerially bombarded, almost 10,000 Partisans – including 700 women fighters – lost their lives. However, via a surprise outmanoeuvre, crossing the bridge over Neretva, destroying it, while crossing back at night with wounded, they turned imminent defeat into one of the more epic victories in the struggle, which also caught Chetnik formations by surprise and defeated their forces in Bosnia. Just a few months later, after hundreds of kilometres on the run carrying both wounded and typhoid-ridden Partisans, the fifth offensive around the river Sutjeska began, codenamed *Schwarz*. Once again the Partisans survived the offensive, even though they suffered large losses.[55] After breaking through the fascist siege, Partisan detachments moved into eastern Bosnia and liberated substantial territories. This is where the major political rupture would take place.

The second meeting of AVNOJ took place in the liberated territories around Livno, in Jajce, between 21 and 29 November 1943. Encouraged by the capitulation of Italy, and the serious defeats of the Axis on the Eastern Front and North Africa, the Yugoslav deputies of the National Liberation Struggle seized the historical opportunity. The assembly brought together Partisan delegates from the whole of Yugoslavia, who decided on the future of the new political entity. The deputies – men as well as women[56] – adopted the AVNOJ Declaration, which was the most significant political document: a real breakthrough in WWII. The declaration was a kind of Partisan constitution that proclaimed the independence of

---

55 These events were later worked through in major commemoration projects and re-mediated in all possible forms: from monuments and museums to poems and films. I shall come back to this topic in detail in chapter 3.

56 Even if this was not formally written down, women through their participation in the struggle gained a right to vote, which during the war meant they voted and could be voted into the political organs of the liberation struggle. Officially, women received the right to vote immediately after the war in socialist Yugoslavia.

the antifascist resistance and the future political system of Yugoslavia. It openly negated the rights and constitution of the old Yugoslavia and the government-in-exile. This decision was a revolutionary act, a cutting off, in his absence, of the king as the sovereign of the former Kingdom of Yugoslavia. The king was 'beheaded' peacefully from afar, while later, also with the UK's insistence, given a democratic chance: the king's return and the regime of the new Yugoslavia would be decided by the people at a post-war people's referendum.[57] Other vital points in the Partisan constitution were no less revolutionary[58]: a federal and new Yugoslavia was established and immediately granted the equality of all nations and nationalities as well as their "right to self-determination"[59]; members were elected for the National Committee of the AVNOJ, which was declared the revolutionary government, assisted, in terms of organisation, by the AVNOJ and its National, Regional and Local Committees of the National Liberation Struggle; and, last but not least, Tito became a marshal and the supreme leader of the Partisan movement (see Figure 4).

The AVNOJ deputies were not engaged in a mere utopian daydream but relied on the immense popular support and transformative experience of Partisan resistance. The new Partisan Yugoslavia was fought for and imagined, in short it was being created. This is even more forceful when we take into account that the Allies did not see the Partisan movement as the real representative of the Yugoslav people. Moreover, it is well documented how British forces – in particular – calculated their choices between the Chetniks and the Partisans, meditating on possibly opening a front in the Balkans. In the light of discussions over spheres of influence (Yugoslavia stood in the middle between the British and Soviet

57 Nešović and Pagon (1973).

58 The Declaration of the AVNOJ opens with the following sentence: "On the basis of every nation's right to self-determination, including the right to secession or unification with other nations, and in accordance with the true disposition of all the Yugoslav nations, expressed during the three-year joint National Liberation Struggle that forged an indivisible brotherhood of all nations of Yugoslavia, the Anti-Fascist Council for the National Liberation of Yugoslavia hereby issues the following Decree" (Nešović and Pagon 1973, 238).

59 With one important exception, the question of Albanians in Kosovo was a pressing issue already during the war. The Albanian anti-fascist activists and Partisans were leaning towards the idea of merging with Albania, while the Communist Party of Yugoslavia tried to postpone this issue until after the war. Kosovo was also the only area where armed resistance took place after the Partisans had already liberated it: in February 1945. The Kosovo question also remained at the core of the dispute between the Communist Party of Yugoslavia and the Communist Party of Albania (Magaš 1993, 33–34; Ramet 2006, 155–156). Regardless of the political and revolutionary nature of the Yugoslav project, which was open to all nationalities, we cannot ignore the symbolic/cultural restriction of the very name *Yugoslavia*, which refers to the place and adherence of all South Slavs (Karamanić 2006).

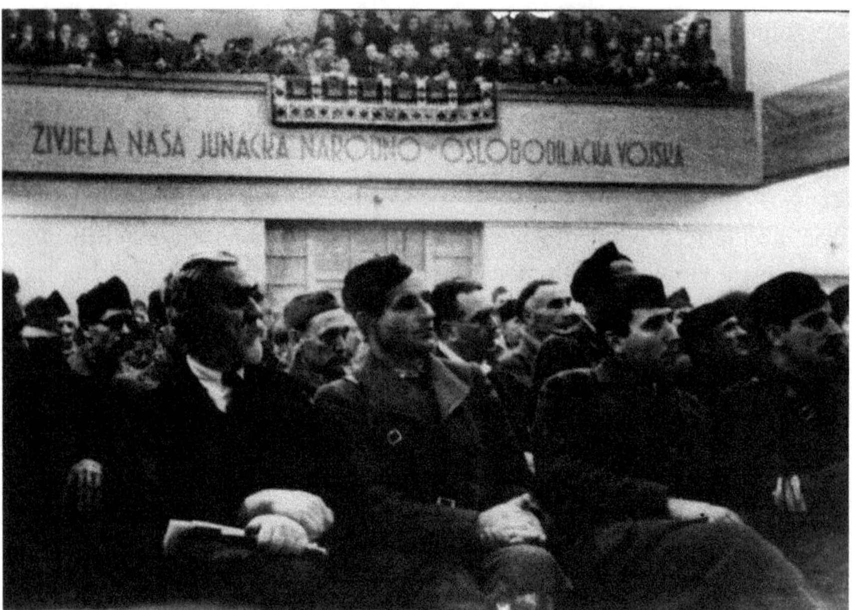

Figure 4: The second meeting of AVNOJ, the historic proclamation of the revolutionary government of Yugoslavia, 27 November 1943, Courtesy of the AVNOJ Museum, BiH.

sphere[60]), the Partisan decision of self-authorisation bordered on madness, paraphrasing what Hegel meant by "jump[ing] into emptiness." Partisan Yugoslavia did not organise any effort for international recognition, and had no central state apparatus, or even a capital city[61]; it rather organised wartime resistance in

60 Donny Gluckstein follows Mandel's thesis on the two wars within one war: the first was obviously waged against fascism, while the second was waged against imperialism. Gluckstein (2012) explains how this played out in various resistance movements across Europe, where the Balkans, which is split into two major spheres of influence, implemented three very different outcomes: the countries that came under Soviet influence (Bulgaria), those under British/US (Greece) and the Yugoslav and Albanian case that remained relatively autonomous due to diverse political factors.

61 One could argue that the concept of a centre was foreign to the Partisan movement, however, one could speak of many centres – informal capitals of the "Partisan state." Some Partisans used this paradoxical notion of the "Partisan state" while in the Republic of Užice (Kostja 1981), Bihać (see also the edited volume of works that were published for the duration of republic, Kapetanović et al. 1964) and Jajce (the second meeting of AVNOJ 1943, see Petranović 1977). After the capitulation of fascist Italy, the Dalmatian island of Vis remained a free and autonomous zone, which – after the Nazi attempt to liquidate Tito and the General Command in the airdrop on Drvar – harboured all the central political and military organs of the Partisan Movement. With

extremely precarious material conditions. The bold declaration of the new revolutionary power signalled to people in Yugoslavia that they join the resistance *en masse* and acknowledge the constitutive powers, while it also signalled – even pressured – the Allies to come to a decision on the question of Yugoslavia. A few days later, the Allies met at a conference in Tehran and confirmed the Partisan struggle as the only Allied and antifascist force on the territory of Yugoslavia.[62] This was not yet an act of recognition for the future Yugoslavia, but a confirmation of the political autonomy of the Yugoslav Partisans.[63] *De facto* recognition came once the Yugoslav Partisans – with the help of the Soviet Allies – liberated Belgrade in October 1944 with a low number of casualties in the Partisan and Soviet camps. What is also noteworthy is the political fact that the liberation of the capital city was completed by the Yugoslav Partisan forces that were fighting on the front in cooperation with the Soviet Red Army. The Partisan takeover of Belgrade as the capital city of Yugoslavia was of symbolic value in showing to the Allies the capacity of the Partisans to be able to liberate autonomously. It was also something that would stand as a strong reminder of a Yugoslav autonomous future. The Yugoslav Partisans were recognised de facto internationally as autonomous political agents. Soviet Command did not only ask for permission to enter Yugoslav liberated zones, they also planned the attack and movements under joint command. By the end of war, there were more than 800,000 Partisans organised in four Yugoslav armies, which made it the largest resistance movement and army in Europe.[64] This was not without consequences for both the split with Stalin in 1948 and for their contribution to the creation of a third independent non-aligned global movement beyond the block divisions in the 1950s.[65] As I

---

the full support of the local population and a British flotilla, Vis remained a strategic centre up until the liberation of Belgrade in late October 1944. The centre of the Slovenian Partisan resistance remained the region of Bela Krajina, which was mostly liberated during the war.

62 A year later the king of Yugoslavia and a part of the government-in-exile publicly supported the Partisan struggle, calling upon the population to join the National Liberation Struggle. The Allies, especially Churchill, strived to ensure that the Partisan leadership formed as broad a government as possible, which would include a part of the government-in-exile and pave the way for the general transition to the new Yugoslavia. On 8 March 1945 Tito and Šubašić signed an agreement that appeased the British and formally brought together all of the political forces. This was a compromise with a calculation that the British forces would refrain from interfering with Yugoslavia's internal matters after the war.

63 This angered Stalin, who demanded that Tito call off the temporary revolutionary government (see Ramet 2006, 157–159), which the Supreme Headquarters refused to do.

64 See Thomashevich (2001). For a detailed overview of data relating to the Partisan struggle in WWII see: http: //www.vojska.net/eng/world-war-2/yugoslavia/.

65 I name this the Partisan rupture by other means. The split with Stalin was supposed to break Tito and the Party's authority and divide people, however, what followed was a launch of an

have argued elsewhere (Kirn 2019b), one can see the autonomous road to socialism and non-alignment as a continuation of Partisan politics by other means. Partisan rupture yielded strong consequences that echoed beyond the borders of Yugoslavia, and deep into the post-war period, joining other revolutionary events of the twentieth century. However, this political event would not have been possible without the strong cultural practice, imagination and artistic activity that is so vital for the Partisan counter-archive.

1.4 Partisan cultural revolution

The Partisan rupture created new organs of the people's power, which entailed strong changes in cultural practices, as both cultural production and dissemination were revolutionised and democratised.[66] As Ivana Momčilović rightly pointed out, there was an influential pre-war legacy and ties that existed between various Yugoslav art movements and political groups,[67] especially between surrealism, realist artists and the Communist Party. These activities can be distilled around a series of important discussions that have been labelled the "controversy on the left" in the 1930s, which repeated and further explored some arguments on the international left between the avant-garde, modernism and socialist realism.[68] How is one able to break with the bourgeois autonomy of art? What kind of cultural production and dissemination should one conceive and implement? Who is the audience of the tendencies in the new art? What is the importance of the form and content of leftist artwork? The controversy pitted different positions that opted to radicalise both form and content.[69] Socialist realist and avant-gardist positions remained strong before, during and after WWII, and continued to be

independent path of socialism that was first promoted as workers' self-management in 1950 and later co-created the non-aligned movement that went beyond Cold-War bipolarity. For details see Kirn (2019b).

66 This section is in a large way indebted to the work and conversations with Miklavž Komelj (2008), I also need to thank Ivana Momčilović for some insights into Yugoslav Surrealism.

67 Especially the groups Zemlja and Život completed major experiments in bringing art production and exhibition to the rural countryside and remained involved politically in times of open repression and censorship. On Život group see Knežević (2017), for the Zemlja group see Hanaček and Vuković (2017), while for the most recent take on the relationship between surrealism and the Partisans see Komelj (2017, 55–65).

68 For a good overview see also Hanaček (2019).

69 In this respect Walter Benjamin's thesis on "tendential art" sublates the dichotomy of content and form and resonates with the main thrust of engaged art at that time.

discussed up until the official rejection of socialist realism in the famous Third Congress of Yugoslav Writers in 1952 with Miroslav Krleža's speech.[70]

More significant than the pre-war discussion was the historical fact that a large majority of intellectuals, cultural workers and artists joined the Partisan uprising as early as in 1941 and continued to do so later. For the communist leadership, it was vital to win over intellectuals and cultural workers to the struggle since this would have a major influence on the ideological struggle and on the organisation of educational and cultural activities. There were numerous established artists and cultural workers who entered into the struggle, perhaps one of the most famous being the legendary surrealist Koča Popović, who became a commandeer of the First Proletarian Brigade,[71] or Mitra Mitrović, an early communist-feminist and literary scholar who became one of the leaders of the Antifascist Women's Organisation, a minister for education and a member of AVNOJ.

Numerous artists and cultural workers who came over to the Partisan resistance did not only organise cultural activities and work on their artistic practice, but also fought with arms and were active in political organisations. Partisan artists thus became Partisan-poet-fighters, who on a conceptual level followed the avant-garde maxim, whereby art form also becomes a form of life. It soon became clear that Partisan art contributed to the struggle in a major way, which is why we should see it as a constitutive part of the liberation struggle. Also, in terms of political organisation, artists and cultural workers became organised. The Slovenian case demonstrates this aspect from the very beginning when the Liberation Front was formed, that is, only a few days after the capitulation of the Kingdom of Yugoslavia, on 26 April 1941. The front was formed by four partners: the Communist Party, Christian Socialists, Sokol associations and finally a group called the *cultural workers*. The Partisan leadership was soon convinced they had to win cultural workers and artists for the cause of liberation. This is how we should read the direct call to poets (and artists in general) to join the Partisans that was written by the great Slovenian poet Oton Župančič. The poem "Pojte za menoj" ("Sing after me" later called "Do you know your debt, poet?") was not signed and was first published in *Slovenski poročevalec* on 6 September 1941, and later in *Delo* in December 1941. Furthermore, the Liberation Front issued a decree on "cultural silence," which called that any collaboration – even

70 See Krleža (1952), for some historical details of the struggle on the artistic left in Yugoslavia, see also Lasić (1960) and the more recent overview in Visković (2011) and Močnik (2018).

71 The list of Partisan-artists would be too long; let us just briefly say that they came over in a predominant way to the Partisan camp, while a tiny elitist layer of privileged artists remained within the fascist collaborationist, or royalist side. This is also reflected in the poor quality of collaborationist art/culture.

cultural – should be forbidden from December 1941 onwards.[72] The call to boycott the fascist apparatus was accompanied by a call to construct Partisan culture and create the cultural means to liberate people and nations.

The struggle over the hearts of people was practiced in Serbia in a similar vein, where on 14 August 1941 the *Association of Serbian Antifascist Artists* published the "Call to the Serbian People" that called for the remaining cultural workers and artists to join the Partisans:

> We are expelled from our homes, libraries, newspapers and galleries and we have joined the struggle, coming together with you into the forests, doubly armed, with both pen and gun, with paintbrush and bomb. (quoted in Miletić and Radovanović 2016, 80)[73]

The vital importance of Partisan culture and art was first fully confirmed and practiced in the first liberated zone named the Republic of Užice, proclaimed on 24 September 1941 and lasting for more than two months. The first Partisan republic (a territory as big as present-day Slovenia) had a strong material base, since it operated the first running (real) Tesla hydro-facility, which provided electricity for the factory production of ammunition, textiles and a printing house. There was a substantial number of intellectuals and cultural workers involved in the organisational and cultural matters there, especially in developing Partisan print. It was here that one of the first issues of *Borba* (early November 1941), the newspaper of the Communist Party, published its first large cultural edition and a special collection of international antifascist songs. Miletić and Radovanović (2016, 2017) explain that also the first Partisan "Artist Unit" was created in order to organise printing, cultural and political events (see Figure 5). They also produced artworks in the "Partisan Atelier," prepared theatre performances that were collectively dramatised/directed, trained with choirs, collected together the antifascist Partisan songs and other activities. One of the surviving members of the Artist Unit, Milutin Čolić, recounts the following:

> At the start we were only twenty soldiers – artists, and this was very unusual and possibly a unique experience: for example, one evening the group would go to defend the hills around Užice in order to quell the attack by the Chetniks, while the next evening we would put

72 For details see Klemenčič and Žagar (2004, 180).

73 Petranović (1977) explains that already very early in the war the enemy counter-propaganda activity had started working. When the Nazis found out that the Partisans had a radio station, they began emitting their own fake news reports with the intent of deceiving the listeners of the radio station and speaking of the capitulation of Partisans etc. In response to this fake radio station the call of the *Association of Antifascist Artists* was sent out and as Petranović remarks, there were but a few individuals behind this *Association*. The struggle over the meaning and legitimacy of the struggle was treated with utmost concern by the communist and Partisan leadership.

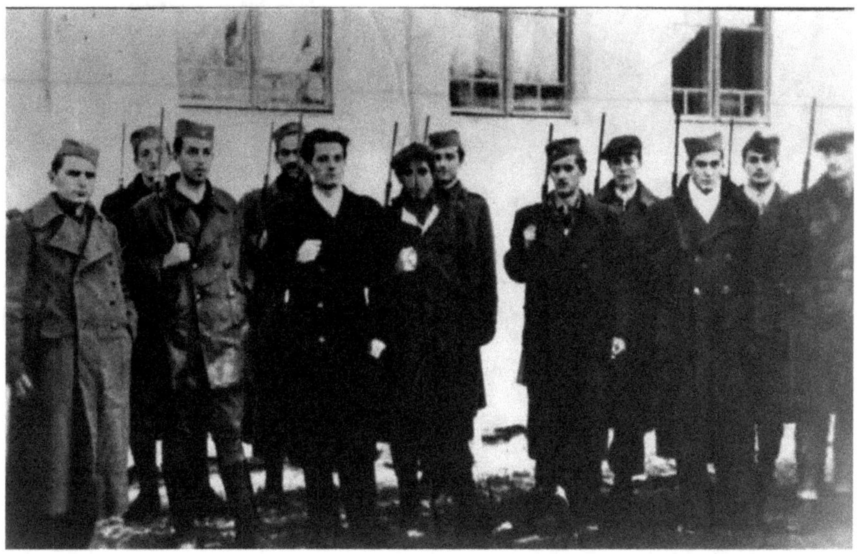

Figure 5: A Partisan "artist unit" in Užice, October 1941. Courtesy of the Archive of Užice.

> our guns down beside the scene, and go up on the stage where we would recite the words of Čapek, Mušić or Goethe; there was this evening where we had a rehearsal of Goethe's Egmont, which was disrupted by the first offensive of the German Army. (Čolić 1981, 313)

Ambitious tasks and material results speak not only of a cultural policy of the liberation struggle that cannot be reduced to a dictate of the Communist Party and its leadership, but of a great role that was gained and attributed to Partisan art. It is not coincidental that the very first Partisan unit was called the "Artist Unit" and not a "Cultural Unit," nor was simply part of the propaganda section of the Communist Party (which also existed). This small detail, which insists on a differentiation between art and culture, is not an academic or local curiosity, but can give us some clues to understanding the major transformation that Partisan artistic practices brought about. The emergence of Partisan art meant that they first needed to reinvent not only the conditions of artistic production (cf. Komelj 2008) and of dissemination, but also new artistic forms. Needless to say, Partisan artists were not apolitical, nor were they speaking from the space of an imaginary Partisan art community. They were openly political and many of them took part in the military struggle itself (see Figure 6).

Within the Partisan political institutions, fierce discussions were continually held on the role of Partisan art. What should the content and form of the cultural events for peasants and Partisan groups be? Was not the war against fascism and the guerrilla struggle aimed at realising national liberation? And if national

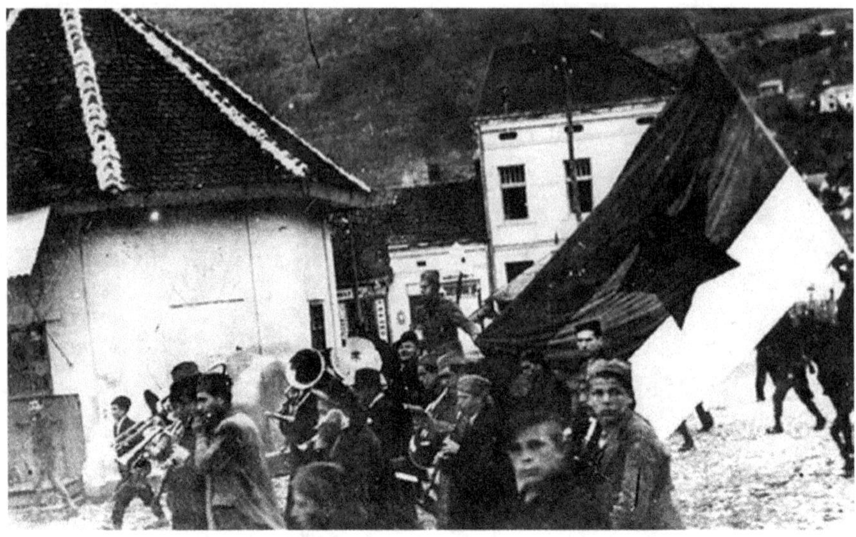

Figure 6: A Partisan cultural event in Užice, November 1941. Courtesy of Predrag Kovačević and the webpage https://uzicanstveno.rs/.

liberation is the highest goal, would Partisan art not be better off when assuming a purely propagandistic function? Evidently, the propagandistic argumentation, to boost and elevate the morale of the troops and motivate the local population to enter the struggle, was present all throughout the war. However, the leadership of the Communist Party and of the National Liberation Councils recognised the importance of the "avant-gardist" tendency. The latter was frequently adopted within the Agitprop Commission and was often repeated on various occasions. A strong representative of the "avant-gardist" position within the Agitprop Commission (she was also a member of Antifascist Women's Organisation) was Mitra Mitrović, who on 10 January 1943 published an article entitled "A Few Questions on the Cultural-Educational Work" in the main Communist Party newspaper *Borba*. Mitrović rejected the pragmatic view that Partisan art should only show what allegedly "people are able to understand" and adapt its quality and form to the masses:

> What people 'are able to understand' is usually conceived in a very one-sided way and at the expense of the cultural empowerment of the very people [...] Also in our own experience in this relatively short period of time when we were able to make culture available to the people without obstacles, this proved to us that people instinctively take up and are moved only by those works that have artistic quality [...] now that we are creating the foundation of a new people's culture, we need to move the people to create and engage in cultural matters and this is why we need to be very aware of the seriousness of this work. (quoted in Miletić and Radovanović, 2016, 113)

This seriousness of how to organise cultural work, its infrastructure, while at the same time not falling behind in terms of art quality and form, was affirmed on various occasions and in the works of the PLS. The deep engagement testified to a strong awareness that something new was emerging; that a new political and cultural life was being built and would not be waited for to appear following some indefinite interval after the end of the war. This is further confirmed by the lively activities even within the occupied cities where all work had to be completed underground and in a very conspiratorial way. The trust present among many members was quintessential since the fascist secret police were constantly on the backs of those organising the illegal network. The latter, for example in Ljubljana,[74] spread out from an illegal radio station (*Kričač*) and printing presses (*Podmornica*),[75] to poster-graphic-design workshops (see Figure 7), gathering spaces for reading and food-clothing production and supply, as well as to caring for the children of Partisans and the internees/imprisoned.[76]

Illegal networks in big cities were of major importance in the early phases of the war, but from at least mid-1942 onwards, the cultural infrastructure and majority of Partisan activists from urban cities moved to the countryside. This had to do with the expansion of liberated territories and the building of a political and cultural infrastructure – printing houses, cultural homes, Partisan academies – in the countryside (Centrih 2011). The countryside with a largely illiterate population was long associated (and still is) with a metaphor of backwardness and conservative values organised through the (local) Church. As such, the peasantry was continually viewed as a conservative force, including by many of those on the communist left. But during the PLS, the peasantry and the countryside in general became an increasingly politicised space, transformed along with the major social base of the Partisan struggle. It was here that the vast majority of Partisan battles and people's organising of political and cultural life took place.[77] Thus, as Miklavž Komelj (2008, 58–59) rightly argues, until the end of the war the Yugoslav countryside was more progressive than the urban centres (see Figure 8).

---

74 After the war, a "national hero" status was given to the following cities: Drvar, Prilep, Cetinje, Belgrade, Zagreb, Ljubljana, Novi Sad and Priština.

75 For an overview of illegal networks see the edited volume by Repe and Pirjevec (2008).

76 The monograph *Ilegalčki* describes the activities involved in the organised care for the children of Partisan parents, who were provided with temporary shelter and food while their parents fought (see Štrajnar and Velagić, 2004).

77 As in the subsequent anti-colonial and guerrilla struggles, the peasant population formed the heart and central social base of the revolutionary process.

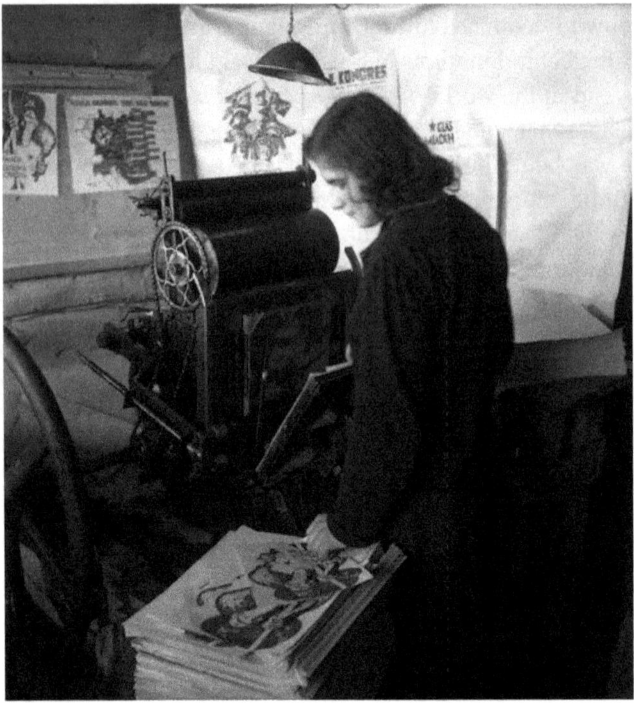

Figure 7: Partisan woman in the printing house Donas, 1944, Davča, unknown author. Courtesy of MNZS.

Additionally, this new cultural policy and infrastructure went hand-in-hand with the immense engagement and sacrifice of women. Partisan liberation entailed women's liberation in Yugoslav society, which was, over the whole of the war-stricken Europe of that time, and before the war, deeply permeated by conservative-patriarchal values. Women who joined the Partisans – Partisan women[78] – soon became organised on all fronts: culturally, politically and militarily. They saw Partisan struggle as a path to collective emancipation and formed their own organisation: The *Antifascist Women's Organisation* (AFŽ). It is noteworthy that by the end of the war, the AFŽ counted two million members, became autonomous and was formally recognised by the General Command and AVNOJ as a major partner in the struggle. The official estimates are that around 110,000 Partisan women fought with arms and 25,000 died in combat,

78 See the volume *Partizanke* (Milinović and Petakov 2010), which is comprised of interviews with different Partisan women that were engaged in the PLS.

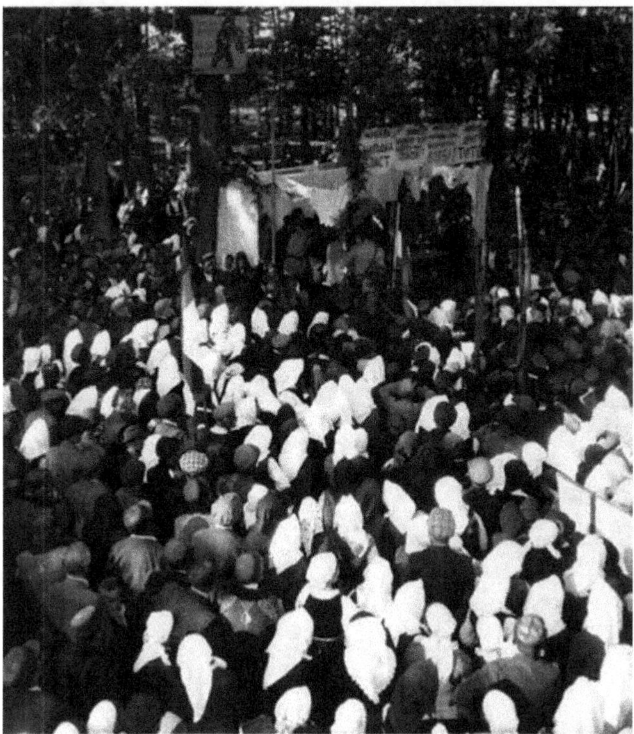

Figure 8: A cultural event as a meeting point for the local population, Partisans, and cultural workers. Courtesy of the AVNOJ Museum, BiH.

a figure too often forgotten when thinking about the revolution and resistance struggle in Yugoslavia.[79] The figure of the woman-Partisan has been revived today and continued in its own way by the Rojava YPJ women organisation. It is around this female "limit-experience" (Foucault 1977) that one can abstract a figure of 'maximalist' ethics: the woman-Partisan was involved in military work and fighting, nursing and caring for the wounded; she was engaged in political-cultural work, education and cultural organisation; and finally, again, in taking care of children and the elderly. If we take into account the cultural infrastructure's organisation, the AFŽ and Communist Youth (SKOJ) were the most important organs for the organisation of the youth, illiterate, women in the villages and also for the dissemination of ideas via reading and writing

79 On the recent exhibition, partially also accessible online, one can get a glimpse of activities that women organisations carried out: http://izlozba.sabh.hr/.

groups and poem recitals. They also held their own meetings and published their own newspapers (see Figure 9).[80]

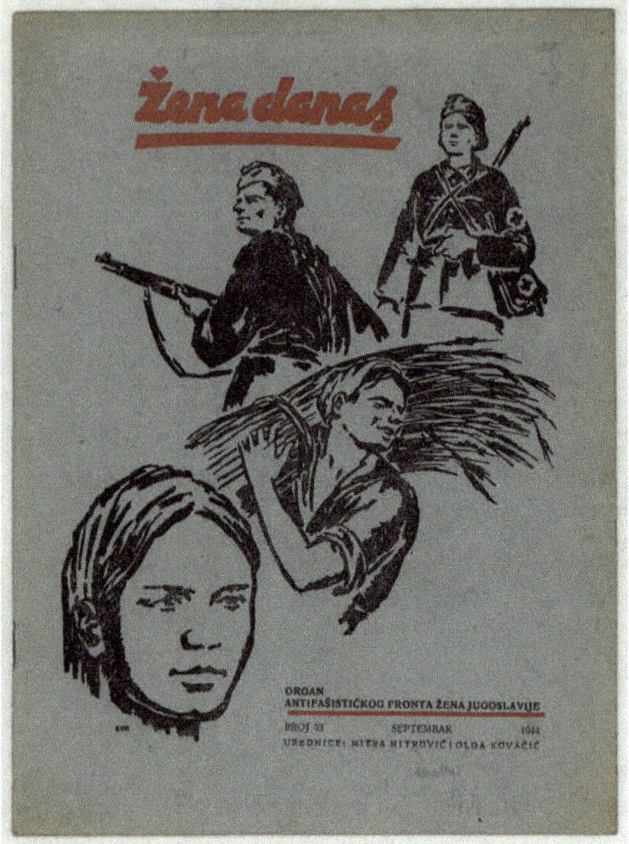

Figure 9: The AFŽ newspaper *Žena Danas*, 1944, no. 33, edited by Mitra Mitrović and Olga Kovačić. Courtesy of the National and University Library (Zagreb).

The Partisan cultural production existed in all resistance movements across Europe that developed their own cultural apparatus and propaganda sections. However, I would argue that the sheer numbers of artworks and variations of artistic practices in the Yugoslav case are immense. As concerns poetry

80 For more information see the Barbara Jančar-Webster's detailed study (1990) and more recently an edited volume by Dugandžić and Okić (2016). I also wish to thank Barbara Blasin for her assistance in finding some AFŽ newspaper issues.

alone, around 40,000 poetic works were written during the four years of war (Dedijer 1980, 929), with Slovenia counting some 12,000 poems and songs! A large majority of these poems and songs were not written by established poets, but by unknown and anonymous Partisans. Anonymous poetry had to do with both the emancipatory character of the new artistic practice and also ran contrary to the preconception of a poet as an individual genius/lighthouse of the nation on the one hand, and as a form of protection to not let oneself be exposed by name (which could endanger one's own life and the lives of relatives and friends). This cultural phenomenon of the immense production of anonymous poems and songs – singing was a vital bind of Partisan community – can be seen as a part of the movement of the masses entering an artistic-cultural stage of production (socialisation against exceptional individualisation). The modern canon linked to the entity of the proper name of the individual author, the way in which the signifier and biography inscribe themselves in poetic work, was proclaimed dead in the Partisan woods – before Roland Barthes' "death of the author." The practice of giving oneself one or even more Partisan names was pervasive and already a part of the pre-war revolutionary tradition. In the more general context of fascist occupation, there was a strong conviction that until the end of fascist domination all culture in the occupied territory should be anonymous and engaged in the Partisan cause, while the fascist-collaborationist cultural apparatus should be boycotted. The anonymity assigned to the collectivity of masses, their emancipation and cultural expression became a concept and an essential part of Partisan practice.[81]

PLS and Partisan artistic activity practically realised what for pre-war and post-war Yugoslavia was seen as a crazy, irrational, and impossible task: peasants becoming Partisans-poets. This runs close to the Rancièrian inspired method/project that rethought the expectation that workers/proletarians should drink or sleep late at night. What Rancière rather traces is a counter-history of workers' self-emancipation and education, where long nights were used to read and write poems (Rancière 1981). Evidently, we can speak of a major difference in that the Partisans found themselves at war, where a blurring between life and death, day and night, and a suspension of the 'normal' division of labour takes place. However, even if the war took the workers and peasants out of their daily work routine, it was the resistance and the openness of the struggle that made it possible that any Partisan could also become a poet. One example of the earliest and

81 In 1942, Louis Adamič, a Slovenian migrant to the USA who supported the Yugoslav Partisans, argued that anonymity posed an existential problem, although it is necessary for survival. He argued that "in such circumstances only the most solid civilised people can retain their integrity and avoid not being split into personality and un-responsibility" (quoted in Komelj 2008, 75–76).

most popular poems performed loudly in the Partisan units was Miodrag Tatović's "I am a Partisan, and proud of it." Miodrag was a worker from Ljig who started writing poems when the war broke out. World War II was full of darkness, but also productive darkness in which those who were supposed to remain as (semi-) illiterate workers, peasants, and women read out, wrote down and sang the Partisan poems and songs out loud. The cultural field in war became a democratised space contrary to a revisionist reading that conceives the cultural revolution as directed from above, or practiced by a small fraction of the communist elite. The Partisans' cultural activity burst out of expectations of what and how art can be produced in wartime with such scarce material, while these cultural outbursts could also not be completely controlled by the Communist Party. Furthermore, the Communist Party itself was transformed through the process. This proliferation of cultural forms and practices proceeded organically within the process of the liberation struggle itself, where revolutionary art and politics met each other. Miklavž Komelj points this major shift out well:

> It was not necessary that masses who spoke up for the first time formulated revolutionary slogans; they were included in the revolutionary process simply by the very gesture of speaking up. The liberation struggle also brought the freedom of expression, that is, to people whom this right was denied before; but they fought for it and started exerting it.[82]

This was not a merely symbolic entering of the masses, who remained passive and confirmed the directives of the leader Tito. Rather, what emerged was a veritable cultural renaissance exemplified in the mobile amateur and professional cultural groups, the creation of thousands of poems and songs written by anonymous poets, photography, graphic designs, paintings, statues, theatre performances, dances, exhibitions and even Partisan films. The masses were becoming "emancipated spectators" (Rancière 2011) and at points also active producers and participants in cultural-artistic works. The line between artistic production (of elite avant-gardists) and reception (the illiterate masses) was undermined, blurred and posited anew. The division of labour was blurred and bourgeois expectations were shattered. Partisan art was outside of the normal junctures of the market and the (fascist) state; instead it pushed to invent its own and new conditions.

Under the harsh circumstances, Yugoslav Partisan art succeeded in creating precarious but rich space and art formats, where images, gestures and words became weapons that were posited against the weapons of mass destruction. Put

82 Komelj (2008, 104–105).

poetically, the words and images of the Partisans and masses became weapons of mass creation. The creation of an imaginary of resistance, of new people, of a new Yugoslavia. Of a new world. Utopia materialised? Partisan art succeeded not only in reinventing the material conditions of art production, but it also contributed to the redefinition of art itself by inventing new intermedial forms as we will see in the next chapter. I already mentioned that during the fascist occupation the former cultural institutions were emptied out and substituted by the representatives of fascists and an allegedly racially superior culture/civilisation. The struggles of Partisan art and cultural workers thus unfolded along two lines: firstly, they fought against fascist-collaborationist propaganda, and, secondly, they also subverted the pre-war "bourgeois" canon along with its state-sanctified autonomy (the Kingdom of Yugoslavia).

Partisan art could only rely on its own immense cultural activity, which during the struggle invented a new form of engaged artistic autonomy. This thesis runs against two mainstream conceptions of (Partisan) art: either Partisan art is treated as a propaganda form (directed by the communist elite), or it is appropriated in a kind of academic modernism that retrospectively reads it as guaranteed by the state, which at that time did not exist. The Partisan conception of artistic autonomy is, however, radically different from the bourgeois idea of autonomy, which is always presupposed by either market forces, or by a central institution – the state – that grants and guarantees the autonomy and material conditions for art and its institutions. There is nothing purely artistic about artistic autonomy as Adorno noted long ago, and the whole set of aesthetic criteria, which legitimise what is, and what is not art (a canon), what and why something can be or not be exhibited on the altar of national culture, or for the art market, are all questions that have never been neutral or purely aesthetic. Partisan "aesthetic" practice formed a rupture both with existing cultural institutions and their canon, while it also invented new artistic intermedial forms. In this respect Partisan art shared a few features with the avant-gardists of the earlier twentieth century who radically protested against the established canons, formats and institutions.

Unquestionably, the claim that Partisan art was openly political art is uncontroversial, for as Komelj correctly argues, it "inseparably linked its own freedom with the people's liberation" (Komelj 2008, 31). However, Partisan art did not exist only as an ornament to victory over the enemy, mobilising for war and boosting the morale of Partisan troops. Furthermore, the sheer number and – in some cases – the aesthetic rupture/quality of artworks, and the massive efforts and discussion over the role of Partisan art bespeaks a specific engaged autonomy. Partisan art cannot be merely juxtaposed on the same level as fascist art, which subjugated art to war (technology). Marinetti's attempt aimed to overcome

Cicero's old formula of *inter arma musae silent* and took war as a realisation of the end of the arts. Marinetti called for another Emperor of the Holy Roman Empire that Benjamin paraphrased as "Fiat ars, pereat mundus," which means "Let art flourish and the world pass away" (Benjamin 2008, 55). For fascist art and Marinetti, humankind's experience of "its own annihilation" becomes "a supreme aesthetic pleasure" (Benjamin 2008, 42), and a whole art project and mission ending in war. The fascination with acceleration and the technology of war is not connected only with the historical emergence of industrialisation, but also with intimate links between the new fascist forces and the way art is instrumentalised in the fascist subjugation of art to war. To this prescription, Benjamin would famously respond with the communist prescription of the "politicisation of aesthetics" (Benjamin 2008, 42). This is more than his earlier conception of "tendential art" since Partisan art on the one hand needs to respond and overcome the glorification of war and the fascist desire of humankind's annihilation, while on the other hand it needs to go beyond (capitalist, or Soviet) state propaganda to mobilise the masses during the war. Partisan art thus presents itself as an alternative that struggled for a new role of art that was able to resist what Adorno posited as "the course of the world, which permanently puts a pistol to men's heads." (Adorno 2007, 180)

Finally, it is only through this new role of Partisan art that we can understand that Partisan struggle in Yugoslavia (and in many other Partisan moments of the twentieth century) was so enormously culturally productive. Only then can we understand why Partisans wrote thousands of poems, and wrote and composed songs that would be sung by the masses during and long after the war. Only then can we understand why the General Command of the Partisan resistance in Slovenia supported the printing of thousands of copies of avant-garde Partisan poetry by Karel Destovnik Kajuh and Matej Bor. It can be perplexing to understand why Partisans spent so much diligence and time designing, editing and printing a few thousand copies of collections of poems by anonymous and famous poets. However, rather than a mere curiosity, the collective volumes of anonymous Partisan poems and the body of other artworks function as a placeholder for a space of "compossibility" (Badiou 1992, 2005), of a radical encounter between Partisan art and politics. Furthermore, this body of artwork testifies to an intense awareness and seriousness when dealing with symbolic creation and the imaginary of liberation struggle, and with reflecting on the tense relationship between past, present and future. To conclude, Partisan art was neither simple propaganda nor a mere ornament to the struggle, but a vehicle and a force that imagined and radically strengthened the military and political fight for liberation. The PLS, then, cannot be thought without Partisan art, and also not, as I will show, without the desire to commemorate this immense rupture.

1.5 A theoretical note on the Partisan counter-archive

In the light of the Partisan/resistance generation's farewell across Europe, one can find an array of attempts to document and present various voices – mostly in the form of interviews – of resistant fighters. One such example is the European-wide project that resulted in an online *Archive of Resistance*. This is a laborious video archival project that conducted precious interviews with the last Partisan generation from all around Europe. In my own Slovenian context another fascinating attempt has been undertaken by students from the Academy of Film, Theatre and Radio, who made an impressive and online bilingual archive of Partisan theatre, documents, objects (e.g. puppets from a puppet theatre, props, photos), and interviews with the Partisans who worked in the liberated territory. I find these attempts relevant, while I would also like to stress that they operate in already established documentary registers: the collection of personal testimonies (individual axis) and the documentation of objects produced in the Partisan struggle (musealisation; monuments).

The Partisan counter-archive shall rather focus on something that cannot be as easily musealised or reduced to micro-narratives and testimonies. As mentioned above, there was a tremendous eruption of cultural works among the masses, which opened up an emancipatory horizon that made visible the political space of the liberated territory and the position of the Partisan movement as engaged in conflictual and contradictory relationships: those between the past and future; between the novelty and redefinition of the past tradition of the oppressed; between the emancipation of the nation, people and the new Yugoslavia. These challenging oppositions and questions foresee the complexity of what I argue emerged as the early forms of the Partisan counter-archive. How do we work through this counter-archival legacy? And why do I add "counter-" in the first place? The introductory chapter highlighted both the mainstream readings of the Partisan past (revisionist/demonising and nostalgic), to which my enterprise is openly opposed, joining the counter-hegemonic forces that reclaim the Partisan legacy. This section and the next chapter will highlight that the prefix "counter-" stands firstly for the Partisan activity itself, and testifies to the fact that liberated territories were not 'sovereign' and centralised mini-states holding their (national) archives, but were rather undergoing a "deterritorialising" of established power and empowering popular institutionalising organs that could be called counter-institutions. In addition, from an aesthetico-historical perspective, the prefix "counter-" is a convincing signifier. My work was inspired by the work of Mirzoeff (2011), whose account of counter-history evidenced a direct implication of dominant visualisation in sustaining established authority and power relations. Mirzoeff is mostly interested in decolonial genealogy and in dismantling racial hierarchies and visualisations, while my project wants to thematically extend the visual film culture to poetic examples and monuments. I will return to this prefix in the following paragraphs.

The Partisan counter-archive aims to retrace a desire inscribed in an array of Partisan artworks and asks: How come was there such a desire to commemorate the Partisan rupture in that dark time? Also, how come was there such a strong awareness and aesthetic work invested in this challenging initial problem, of commemorating Partisan revolution? Every revolutionary upheaval – and the Partisan movement was undoubtedly such an upheaval – disturbs the coordinates of the possible, practicing and pointing to a specific "surplus" in the situation. This gesture to transform the world has to do with a certain impossibility and excess that overcome the series of dominant prescriptions of the status quo: it goes against and beyond the maxim "there is no alternative to the existing (occupation)"; it goes beyond ethnic identity in ethnic/fascist wars. Such Partisan courage and comradeship built through the struggle enabled the impossibility to be dealt with and might be one of the central reasons why an array of Partisan artists and artworks started to take root and show that something new, something revolutionary, was taking place. And then the question emerges of how to commemorate rupture, this surplus? Does not this surplus – by the definition given by Freud (1964) – get immediately excluded from memory, as it is something too traumatic to be dealt on the subjective level, connected with such tremendous violence?[83] Moreover, and once deploying the retroactive logic of fantasy, does not the fact that the work of memory took place through (Partisan) art already point to this impossible commemoration that needed this necessary detour, a subtle displacement in the light of daily horrors and death? Was Partisan art and then my attempt at making the counter-archive one of the ways of recording and retaining human dignity, or one of the ways of thinking through the traumatic/Real? If Partisan art already needed to create new conditions for artistic activity in the midst of harsh circumstances and past ideology, then the Partisan counter-archive has to also rethink the conditions of expected protocols to commemorate the past and foresee a different future.

The next chapter offers a concise analysis of a series of artworks that point to a certain repetitive form that was vested with a deep memorial concern. Partisans wrote powerful poems and literary testimonies, created and invented (moving) images that already warned themselves and us who come after not to forget the

83 Especially important are his works and his concept of *Nachträglichkeit* (lit. afterwardness – a retroactive logic) which describe the functioning of trauma/fantasy. For details on this question see Laplanche and Pontalis (2004).

time, experience and event of rupture. At first glance, one can see this desire to commemorate the rupture as a reflection of the immediate fear and the general precarious constellation: the instability of the future and personal insecurity in times of brutal war. If one paraphrases Marx, it seems indeed that *all that is solid melted into air,* and in WWII *human existence melted into air with bombs and gas.* Everyone knew or saw not just one but many people, relatives or friends who died in the course of war, be it as civilians, hostages to be executed or Partisans, those in concentration camps and prisons, but also those who died as fascist collaborators. Death seemed closer and more stable than life and the future. There was a major shake-up of daily conditions with the omnipresence of death, which even radicalised fears and WWI-related traumas, now moving from the fronts to the homes where no one was spared. This radicalised existential anxiety and radical doubt in humanity can provide a partial answer of why there was a need to commemorate resistance in the view of probable death. Was Partisan struggle seen and commemorated as the only path to how human dignity and existence might survive?

Apart from the immediate existential concern and fear of not being forgotten (be it an individual or collective cause), another important path is remembering the utmost dedication and determination that led to the victory of the Partisans. Joining the Partisans seemed to many – interviewed later[84] – as the only ethical and political choice. This choice was accompanied by a strong will and enthusiasm for freedom and liberation, organising community-in-resistance and creating the cultural means together to imagine and realise a new world. There was something in this existential engagement in the Partisans – being also a part of the Partisan struggle and consequent rupture – that moved beyond the physical borders of life and death, beyond the linear temporality of the past, present and future. The Partisan determination in another world contributed to an intense awareness of the rupture.[85] This awareness and self-reflection triggered the need and desire to expand and commemorate the struggle itself. The questions that

84 Recently, two films from the ex-Yugoslav context have focused on this clear political determination and maximal ethics – dedication to the Partisan cause, with women Partisans as protagonists: Marta Popivoda's forthcoming film on a fearless Partisan who not only survived Auschwitz but also co-organised a revolt in that concentration camp. The second captivating film was made by Želimir Žilnik on the first woman antifascist organiser Dragica in Istria, a dedicated fighter in WWII, a translator for the BBC, and the person that was sent to deliver the strategic *no* to Stalin in 1948. A tragic irony of party purges in the early 1950s meant that she had to spend a few years of her life in the re-education camp *Goli otok* where Yugoslav 'Stalinists' were sent for a few years and after returning to 'normal' life, continued to be monitored.

85 In many of the diaries of poets and leaders (e.g. Kocbek, Popović) one finds a strong thematisation and expression of the awareness of the rupture.

guide this early Partisan counter-archive are then: what are the proper forms, directions and temporalities of the counter-archive? Does it imitate, or even reflect further the modality of Partisan politics and art – this transforming and deterritorialising movement? Or, does the counter-archive attempt to find a space for the preservation of the Partisan surplus? Is the future only open if the rupture succeeds and is continued? By which means?

The aim of the Partisan counter-archive is therefore not to uncover some objective or ultimate truth in some lost document as Foucault has already taught, for any return to an allegedly original scene as something pure reinstates a primary identity. Such, origins have more to do with projections, with a romanticisation of heroic times (even if the Partisan times were heroic), which could easily bring us into the danger of falling into a nostalgic account. The counter-archive does not pretend to cover a vast canonical archive that makes a property claim, and honours the elders, because of their seniority alongside honour obligations to the family kinship. The Partisan counter-archive is interested in the dimension of the Partisan rupture's universality and how selected artworks carried the effects of the Partisan rupture far beyond the immediacy of WWII. The counter-archive retrieves the emancipatory traces of rupture that were "re-mediated" (Erll and Rigney 2009) and translated into a set of discourses and artworks that shaped and contributed to collective memory in socialist Yugoslavia. As I will show in chapter 4 this emancipatory Partisan memory was dismantled in the post-Yugoslav context. In this respect, once again, Foucault's lesson is clear: one needs to "cultivate the details and accidents that accompany every beginning; it will be scrupulously attentive to their pretty malice." (Foucault 1977, 139) "Details" and "accidents" were an integral part of the Partisan movement. How else can one explain the avant-gardist desire and practice in the Partisan struggle that set itself against the pre-war and predominant socialist realist propagandistic definition of art? It was precisely between the realist and avant-gardist stances that partisan art forcefully emerged. How else can we explain the complex trajectory of the Partisan memory of the very rupture, which was already critical of its future (ab)use? Launching a new counter-archival perspective is only possible by "putting into question the very historical subject which one tries to attain" (Agamben 2009, 217).

The counter-archive is thus set against the more objectivist historiographical use of the archive that takes it as a neutral depository or as the most secure source of the past. Jacques Derrida explained well that the word archive comes from the Greek word *arche*, which has a double meaning.[86] The first and more obvious meaning is linked to a beginning, while the second meaning is more important

86 For the entire elaboration see Derrida's text (2005).

for my research: Derrida links *arche* to *commandment* (commanding, guiding). *Arche* implies *archons*, that is, the political leadership that "stores" the beginning. As such there is nothing authentic or innocent at the very beginning, but rather the inscription of asymmetrical power relations. This beginning necessary unfolds in the commanding operations, which Derrida links to a specific space – the central archive, which becomes located in the heart of a polis, the capital of the empire, or simply in the nation-state. This is also the place where the interpretation of the archive and documents takes place, which can result in legal or other ideological forms. The archive thus becomes the central ideological resource that legitimises the continuation of the beginning, which is often described through epic defeats and victories, presently including the romantic times of the 'glorious' nations. Obviously, with the complexity of the rationalising process and capitalist (post-)modernisation, *archons* are no longer the same group of people, but have become 'diversified' – expert-interpreters, cultural managers, memory urban planners and the future data analyst, who all become instrumental to the constant "accumulation of memory." The expert class is deeply embedded in post-socialist governmentality, which in times of historical revisionism offers at best a nationalistic reconciliation (of fascists and Partisans), and at worst openly rehabilitates variants of fascism.

Conversely, Derrida's deep insights into the modality of the archive are a valid guide to elaborate on the notion of the counter-archive. What stands at the beginning of the counter-archive can thus not simply be a 'national (dis-)unity' that aims to reconcile and heal the wounds of the presupposed nation. National (dis-)unity might operate around primal traumatic events, such as (civil) war, terror, occupation, colonialism. Rather than the task of reconciliation, the Partisan counter-archive strives to commemorate the revolutionary core and surplus that wants to be forgotten, neutralised or demonised in the dominant revisionist ideology/archive. The Partisan counter-archive defines the beginning in terms of the following terms: surplus, asymmetry and struggle. I opt for the term surplus whose quality is that it cannot be easily appropriated in any (neither in a socialist, nor in a post-socialist) institutionalised state. This does not mean that all that exists is the transitional, ephemeral truth of unrealised (Partisan) subjectivities and their revolutions. Rather, their unity takes place in the real struggles of the oppressed, and not in some retrospective memorial ritualisation that aim for ethnic-national reconciliation. The counter-archive affirms and guards the multiplicity of the struggle and is opposed to archives based on racially or ethnically presupposed categories. The struggle against national unity might be one of the slogans of the counter-archive.

In philosophy this was often cited as the fight against the One and its presupposed eternal categories. I have already mentioned the figure of Walter Benjamin who worked prophetically around an alternative notion of memory/history, while also the seminal work *A Thousand Plateaus* of Deleuze and Guattari succeeded in articulating the struggle against the One in the field of memory. Or, rather what they coin as "anti-memory" (Deleuze and Guattari 2003, 294) is opposed to "long-term memory," which finds its base in bureaucratic accounting and the tracing and segmenting of points on presupposed 'units' (race, family, nation etc.). Long-term memory links these units within a linear temporality that moves from past to present, retaining an eternal substance. Long-term memory, or what I call the current nationalist(ic) archives sustain a dominant "representation of the old present" (Deleuze and Guattari 2003, 295), while, on the contrary, "anti-memory" is traversed by the process of "becoming" and building further on an emancipatory legacy. This is where the Partisan counter-archive enters into the discussion, locating the lines that go in between the mainstream nodal points and focus on the ruptures with long-term memory. There is something peculiar about the very temporality of anti-memory, since it "can act at a distance, come or return a long time after, but always under conditions of discontinuity, rupture and multiplicity" (Deleuze and Guattari 2003, 16). This definition strongly resonates with the return to and modality of the Partisan counter-archive.

Interestingly, Deleuze and Guattari revisit this topic once again at a later stage when they speak of a "monument to revolution." In *What is Philosophy* they very much sound like early Constructivists who take art to be a privileged space and practice of memory (cf. Schreel 2014). Art is a "composition of sensations" that are directed at nothing outside of themselves and embrace what they term "anti-memory." This thought is paradoxically elaborated in the highly dialectical concept of a "monument to revolution." This "monument" encapsulates the core desire of the Partisan counter-archive that

> does not commemorate or celebrate something that happened but confides to the ear of the future the persistent sensations that embody the event: the constantly renewed suffering of men and women, their recreated protestations, their constantly resumed struggle. Will this all be in vain because suffering is eternal and revolutions do not survive their victory? But the success of a revolution resides only in itself, precisely in the vibrations, clinches, and openings it gave to men and women at the moment of its making and that composes in itself a monument that is always in the process of becoming, like those tumuli to which each new traveller adds a stone. The victory of a revolution is immanent and consists in the new bonds it installs between people, even if these bonds last no longer than the revolution's fused material and quickly give way to division and betrayal.
>
> (Deleuze and Guattari 1994, 176–177)[87]

87 Deleuze and Guattari's "monument to revolution" silently refers to the core legacy of Tatlin's *Monument to III.International.* Tatlin's model attempted to commemorate the revolution in

The counter-archive is thus oriented to the future rather than the past, while the central lesson of revolution is that it will reside precisely through "the vibrations, clinches, and openings," where art will play a major role. The counter-archive operates on a temporality and spatiality that are discontinuous and that instead of past heroism speaks and engages with future-oriented echoes and visions. Despite these traces perhaps being rare moments, gestures, images, words and figures, they can contribute to the imaginary of Partisan resistance beyond borders and time.[88]

In the Yugoslav context, Partisan rupture had strong effects that carried over radical excess. The major challenge of this book is to select and interpret various re-mediations, refractions and translations of Partisan rupture in various art/media forms. It is noteworthy that the Partisan counter-archive did not have a capital city with a centralised state and a party system. Rather, it was the counter-archive that was on the constant move and that already during the very liberation

---

movement and designed future-oriented, interventionist and socialised monuments that redefined the former sovereigntist-national-imperial monuments. For Tatlin to start imagining revolutionary monumental policy, of which he was in charge, he needed to rethink what the monument to revolution might be. But if Tatlin's attempt was a cutting-edge and alternative within the more general monumental propaganda of the emerging Soviet Union, did we not more often deal with the "monument to revolution" from the perspective of defeat? The killings of workers during strike or protest, the executions of antifascist fighters and/or Partisans? Has our time not also rendered a monument to revolution obsolete and practically impossible?

88 As mentioned above, the Partisan counter-archive is not – even within the post-Yugoslav context – a pioneering activity, and generally it can be aligned with some excellent examples of online and other archives that worked on the radical critique of the dominant canons while attempting to "decolonise" (Mirzoeff 2011; Basu and De Jong 2016; De Jong 2016) and "deprivatise" (Buck-Morss 2012, MacKay 2018) the material, resources and vision/reception itself. There are many attempts and counter-archives that share such trajectories and can be accessed online: http: //www.coloursofresistance.org/ (mostly on black liberation), http: //monumenttotransformation.org/atlas-of-transformation/index.html (a collective work mostly inspired by art works); http: //www.internationaleonline.org/research/decolonising_practices/ (especially on decolonising art-theoretical practices), https: //www.pagesmagazine.net/en/articles/archive-of-suburban-dissent-1-introduction (especially on riots), https: //interferencearchive.org/, and also Didi-Huberman's attempt to retrieve diverse instances of uprising(s) that share certain universal features: http: //soulevements.jeudepaume.org/cartographie/. The prominence of untying dominant archives and supplementing existing canons and museums has become prominent at least from 2012. In the international arena it was Documenta 13 that presented a large array of works and connections between the counter-archive(s): publishing collections of revolutionary poems, re-enacting lost monuments to rethinking ways of making traumatic events visible and audible in a new way. There is however an important question: If and how far can such international arenas and publications on the alternative, counter-archives undo the deeper structural injustices?

itself launched a commemorative trajectory of the oppressed from the perspective of the oppressed. In this respect, the Partisan counter-archive challenges the politics of mourning (Butler 2014),[89] which runs close to leftist melancholy. Rather, the counter-archive takes a stance that the history of emancipation can and should also take lessons from the victories of the oppressed that succeeded in bringing about a veritable social transformation. The Partisan counter-archive remembers Partisan rupture, and also imagines new connections, echoes and visions of/to the future, in which the oppressed did and could (again) cease to be the oppressed. This includes the memory of destruction and the cessation of oppression.

This leads me to the *central* feature of the counter-archive that defines what Diana Taylor names "curated selection" (2003, 19). My selection of artworks is based on what I call a *surplus*[90] of selected artwork that is associated with Marx's concept of "surplus value" and Lacan's concept of "surplus enjoyment" that have been antagonising and foundational concepts of Marxism and psychoanalysis. As Samo Tomšič (2015) showed well, these two concepts have played a prominent role within French structuralism and even for later discussions in the poststructuralist tradition. From an epistemological perspective developed by Louis Althusser (1991), both the ground-breaking discoveries of Marx and Freud do not lie in producing a complete positivist empirical study of the human mind vis-à-vis the unconscious and statistical measurement of wealth and the degree of capitalist exploitation. Rather, both Marx and Freud made a decisive theoretical rupture within existing ideologies: for Marx, it was bourgeois political economy and the blind spot of "surplus value," while for Freud, it was the field of psychology and the conscious subject. Despite these scientific contributions to the humanities, both Marxism and psychoanalysis remain peculiar sciences, since their objects of study and their major concepts – class struggle and sexual indifference – are traversed by antagonism/conflict (Althusser 1991). In other words, there is no easy reconciliation of the class split of society or of the split subject after analysis. Within the perspective of these conceptual ruptures, the

---

89 The edited volume of Eng and Kazanjian (2013) introduces a much-needed political twist in memory studies that are often dominated by the figure and narrative of victimhood. As if there is nothing – one can certainly rely on the history of emancipatory struggles. The most fascinating recent turn to affirm the idea of return is by Enzo Traverso (2017a), who states that traumas and defeats of our grandparents can also lead us and even mobilise us to political action and reflection. Also, another French philosopher named Laurelle seems to rehabilitate the victim as a figure through which one can rethink history (2015). This book evidently takes another trajectory.
90 For details on the conceptual tackling of the surplus in Marx and Freud, see Samo Tomšič's chapter on loss and surplus (2015, 64–79).

notion of "surplus value" and, by homology, "surplus enjoyment" in psychoanalysis, we can trace this excess that permeates and structures the objective and subjective reality: capitalist exploitation and sexual difference. This dimension to surplus structurally falls out of the neat equation of costs and investments and presents itself as a blind spot of dominant political economy.

I would like to devise such a conceptual device within the context of the Partisan counter-archive. If the political economy of a national archive is neatly measured, canonised and structured according to the greatest aesthetic achievements of national culture within established institutions, financed and organised by a centralised authority, then the introduction of the term – by analogy – *counter-archival surplus* disrupts the neat balance of national-aesthetic substance and offers a counter-institutional and insurgent modality. The lesson of the counter-archive is to stand always for the oppressed and excluded, their struggles from below and the need to be remembered, which is very much in line with the standpoint of Marx. Furthermore, in line with Freud and psychoanalysis, the work of the counter-archive will make no claim or promise of any easy memory reconciliation after the traumas of wars and revolutions. Rather, it will take seriously the lesson of splits, holes and the selectiveness of any such project.

Furthermore, to grasp the modality of the counter-archive, I will need to reply to the question of what happens after the Partisan rupture occurs in the realm of the (counter-)memory, and in what way the rupture is continued by other means? Since, as is argued above, the counter-archive is not organised around a sacred 'origin' that irreversibly changed the world, I am interested in a series of material inscriptions of rupture that have, in their own way, continued the Partisan legacy in the socialist and post-socialist context. The counter-archival surplus will be located at diverse sites of struggle, as temporal, spatial and aesthetic interruptions that target (then) existing forms of domination and exploitation, but also of visuality, as Rancière says in relation to the regime of the *sayable-visible*. Another vital feature of a surplus is that it cannot be easily co-opted by dominant institutions, and is opposed to any quasi-democratic gesture to include a small layer of oppression(s) in the established historical canon in order to absolve colonial guilt or for merely representative ornamental purposes, while leaving the established structures and domination untouched. In other words, the counter-archival surplus does not want to practice a quasi-democratic inclusion of difference, but to perform and make visible radical dissent with the established order/archive. This project departs from a structuralist epistemological perspective, yet in its concrete analysis of artistic material it is inspired by a line of contemporaries of structuralism, most notably of Deleuze/Guattari on a "monument to revolution" (2005), Jacques Rancière's "archive of proletarians"

(1981) and Didi-Huberman's meticulous archival research that explored visions, words, and gestures of resistance (2016).[91]

Returning to case studies in the specific Yugoslav situation, a few peculiar and ambivalent trajectories of the counter-archive exist: chapter 2 takes as a starting point the cases that produced strong commemorative/artistic practices that pointed to an awareness of the rupture with the situation of the liberation struggle in World War II; in chapter 3 I trace how the Partisan rupture was maintained in memory and remembered in a productive and critical way against the dominant mythologisation in socialist Yugoslavia; and lastly, in chapter 4 I trace the destructive and demonising commemorative practices in the post-Yugoslav context that target the explicitly Partisan revolutionary core: surplus and rupture. This book shall then navigate the thin line between different "impossibilities" that remember or forget Partisan Yugoslavia long after it has been symbolically and physically relegated to the dustbin of history. The Partisan counter-archive highlights the ways in which the selected case studies from different historical periods made use of the counter-archival surplus. Since I am speaking of three very different historical periods with very different kinds of artistic material, my task implies significant unpacking and a close reading. Furthermore, the political and aesthetic surplus has been triggering destructive answers from its inception: from the fascist regime that wanted to destroy and burn the sounds and images of resistance, to recuperation of the legacy, the waning legitimacy of the socialist project from the 1970s and finally up to the period of the 1990s, which rehabilitated the nationalistic archive(s) and partially destroyed or forgot the Partisan legacy. The most recent narratives contribute to the covering up or vilifying of the surplus of Partisan rupture. This politicisation of the archive is what Laura Jane Smith and Gary Campbell speak of as immanent to the field of heritage:

> If we accept that heritage is political, that it is a political resource used in conflicts over the understanding of the past and its relevance for the present, then understanding how the interplay of emotions, imagination and the process of remembering and commemoration are informed by people's culturally and socially diverse affective responses must become a growing area of focus for the field. (2015, 18)

For Susan Buck-Morss, not only diagnosis but a specific prescription in our return to a utopian and/or emancipatory past is needed; one that demands a critical training of the eye for the emancipatory "mode of reception" (2012) and, one could

---

91 Didi-Huberman takes an array of already well known and highly aesthetic examples from the history of uprisings, while his archive does signal a need to move beyond the national context and re-narrate micro and macro transformative events through a set of universal gestures.

add, a critical training of the ear that can listen for the sounds of the oppressed. Buck-Morss calls to decolonise, denationalise, and deprivatise the legacy of the oppressed:

> History is layered. But the layers are not stacked neatly. The disrupting force of the present puts pressure on the past, scattering pieces of it forward into unanticipated locations. No one owns these pieces. To think so is to allow categories of private property to intrude into a commonly shared terrain wherein the laws of exclusionary inheritance do not apply [...].
> (in Jacir and Buck-Morss 2012, 83)

The Partisan counter-archive does not want to forget the lessons of defeat – even if the emancipatory movements have already long excelled in "leftist melancholia" (Benjamin 1999) – but it primarily wants to learn and mobilise emancipatory resources and victories of the oppressed with the potential of spilling over. The counter-archive will then perform a double task: on the one hand it commemorates the past-and-present voices and sounds of oppression, occupation, exploitation, while at the same time, it nurtures and organises those voices, gestures and images into the emancipated future. The construction of the Partisan counter-archive demands a critical method of reading the past and the existing state of affairs, and setting the emancipatory past in motion as a venue that can open up gaps in the dominant discourse and archive by dispersing the fragments of emancipation in our present. Returning Susan Buck-Morss to her major inspiration for "method," this book also registers the debt to Walter Benjamin and his way of thinking through the precarious legacy, oblivion and resurrection of the dead.

The task of the emerging counter-archive is not to offer an all-encompassing and exhaustive list of engaged Partisan artworks – a much thicker volume would be needed for this – but it agrees with Borghes' thesis that any classification is "arbitrary and conjectural" and thus limited. Moreover, as Cristina Baldacci claims, any classification that tends to organise the archive is

> lacking, uncertain, inclined to a perfection and thoroughness that can never be obtained. It's also a demonstration of the need for control, a make-believe representation that implies continuity [...] which is influenced by the choices and conceptual canons of its creator.
> (Baldacci 2013, 31)

The Partisan counter-archive challenges the method of classification with the central term of a surplus that brings dissent into the hegemonic apparatus of thought-memory-politics-economy. Abstracting from the general theoretical contours and the historico-political contextualisation of the Partisan rupture, I arrive at three distinct features of the Partisan counter-archive. These criteria were used for the selection of case studies in the next two chapters: firstly, the chosen artworks emphasise the 'unfinished' nature of the Partisan rupture that combined a 'negative' struggle (antifascism) and an affirmative programme (social revolution); secondly, they express the paradoxical and contradictory relationship between memory and revolution that is reflected in the form and content and even in specific innovation in Partisan production and dissemination (tendential art in Benjamin's sense); and thirdly, one can – and this is admittedly not in the hands of the analyst – point to the emancipatory potential of the resources for their current and future mobilisation. The alternative memorial strategies that are deployed speak about the Partisan past, but they also speak, first and foremost, to the future and the (im)possible task of constructing a new, classless and decolonised society. The selected material reflects thus both the author's limits and choices, and consciously positions the records and interpretations of the records against the mainstream 'reconciliation' discourse, where Partisans and fascists unite in the name of the nation and victimhood. Consequently, the figure of the Partisan will be consciously untied from any signifier of ethnic identity and the exoticisation of the country that exists only in its negative 'Balkanisation'. In this way, the figure of the Partisan does not imply a member of a party, but stands as a name that takes sides for trans-nationalist solidarity and social justice yesterday, today and tomorrow.

There is an apparent and productive paradox inscribed in the core of this book: how is it possible to rethink, formalise and articulate a counter-archival surplus, if this surplus – the paradoxical memory of the Partisan rupture – avoids being appropriated? Does this paradoxical memory on the rupture, even if one names it the counter-archive, not already neutralise the revolutionary modality? However, if one forecloses the work of memory and a critical reading of any emancipatory potentiality that counters the past-and-present status quo, a defeatist position is ascribed to oneself. Moreover, this can mean theoretically regressing to a more simplistic binary ideological constellation that sees rupture as something active and singular, yet memory as something passive and relegated to bygone history. This ideological binary sees rupture as a short single event in history, while memory as something static and only reflecting dominant ideology. In that case, the conceptions of rupture and memory remain very impoverished and at a standstill within the linear temporality of capitalist modernisation. If this chapter explained that (Partisan) rupture should be envisioned as a revolutionary process that encompasses all social fields, and has strong consequences, echoes and visions, then the work of counter-archival memory becomes one of its main consequences, which triggers new ruptures in the future to come.

Chapter 2
Early Partisan Photography, Film and Poetry (1941–1945): An Oath to Past and Future Struggles

> To articulate what is past does not mean to recognise 'how it really was.' It means to take control of a memory, as it flashes in a moment of danger. For historical materialism it is a question of holding fast to a picture of the past, just as if it had unexpectedly thrust itself, in a moment of danger, on the historical subject.
>
> Walter Benjamin, *On the Concept of History* (1940)

> Here every stone was a gun hole
> and every person a shield of freedom.
> The memory of these days should live
> permanently as the stone of these coasts defended by lives.
>
> The Partisan and poet Jure Frančević-Pločar (1943)[92]

2.1 Introduction: Armed struggle, armed memory

What are the most commanding images that infected the collective memory of the Partisan armed struggle? How did the armed struggles arm memory? Was it through films, documentaries – mental images and memes alike – or rather through poems, songs and stories that we formed our general imaginary of the armed struggle? In retrospect, images continually provided individual icons of struggle, such as Che

92 "Ovdje je svaki kamen bio puškarnica
i svaki čovjek štit slobode
Uspomena na te dane neka živi
trajno kao kamen
ovih životima obranjenih obala." (Online*: Slike Partizana*)
A "gun hole" here refers to a place to rest a gun. This poetic verse was written by Jure Franičević – Pločar who, in as early as 1943 had published the first Partisan collection of poems in Croatia with the title *Po rovovima*. Pločar wrote this verse in the winter of 1943–44 when the whole island of Vis was liberated, and when it worked and breathed together as one. For a few months the whole Yugoslav political and Partisan infrastructure was relocated to the island, awaiting the Nazi invasion. This poetic inscription is consecrated in this informal capital of the Partisan movement and the way in which the whole island, even nature, the island's stones and coasts, joined the antifascist cause. Life on the island, one could say, brings a strong sense of continuity, secluded – maybe frozen – while at the same time in constant flux – the coming and going of ships and the sea might have triggered this ever-green trope of a utopian island. Yet this utopia was realised in Vis. This quote remained part of two memorial inscriptions on Partisan monuments after the war, which 'disappeared' in the 1990s.

https://doi.org/10.1515/9783110682069-003

Guevara, Ho Chi Minh, Mao Tse Tung, Josip Broz Tito, Thomas Sankara, Dolores Ibárruri (La Pasionaria), Leila Khaled or Angela Davis. But does not the focus on individual leaders only reproduce a specific visual history and 'great personalities' as content? There are at least two other grassroot vernacular images that became emblematic for the alternative representation of armed struggle: one of an anonymous peasant guerrilla/Partisan and another of an anonymous woman-fighter. They both take up arms and fight an uphill battle against various forms of domination, including against the large and well-equipped armies of a central government, occupying forces and colonial armies.

Zooming out from an individualised representation to a more long-term historical view, one can trace the origins of the word "guerrilla" as connected to a specific type of military fighting in early nineteenth century Spain, after the invasion of Napoleon's army. It was against this major army that a series of successful counter-attacks by much smaller forces were waged and could not be subdued. They were, however, fighting for another empire and not for some sort of universal emancipation.[93] One can even go back, as Eric Hobsbawm (1969) suggests, to the rise of modernity and the intensification of peasant revolts that represented some of the first popular armed struggles, whose participants would often be referred to as 'bandits.' The latter – just like most peasant revolts – wanted to preserve the commons and not really overturn and transform the existing order. Hobsbawm (1969) suggested that fractions of the ruling class even embraced a certain amount of cyclical rioting and uprisings that would overthrow other competing and corrupt fractions, while not really endangering the core system of domination and exploitation. The public imaginary should thus be careful not to idealise those figures that actually desire a more just restoration of the Bastille, Winter Palace or Iron Throne. In this respect, the lineage of Yugoslav Partisans fits much better into the history of radicalised and emancipatory grassroot armed struggles, from the Haiti uprising or the Taiping revolt, which were both anticolonial and social-egalitarian, to the Paris Commune. The form of the armed struggle on the emancipatory horizon of global revolution became paradigmatic during the twentieth century when Lenin declared it key to revolutionary transformation: the armed struggle of people, workers, peasants became a part of revolutionary war. The latter, despite its militant and militaristic departure, was

93 The political inspiration for the guerrilla struggle and the 'figure of the Partisan' was not limited to the left imaginary; in a short study named *Theory of Partisan*, the fascist legal theorist Carl Schmitt (2004) located Partisan subjectivity as a key in undermining the bipolar order of nation-states. In juxtaposition to the revolutionary imaginary of Partisan struggle, Schmitt's conception overdetermined Partisan allegiance with a 'telluric' dimension. He rendered the Partisan a 'nationalist' and *counter*-revolutionary figure who most cares for *Blut und Boden* and dissolution into the cultural (racialised) spaces of multipolar spheres (Kirn 2019b; Toscano 2008).

defined as "the war to end all wars," and was to be seen and fought as the 'last war' that would also bring peace and an egalitarian society. This meant that the armed struggle was waged against extreme conditions of social injustice and repression, be it in the form of military occupation, colonialism or despotic domination. In this respect, it was the image of the October Revolution and its aftermath – where the Red Army had to fight both the White army and foreign military armies – that influenced the imaginary of the Partisan armed struggle before and during WWII, and anticolonial and anti–imperialist struggles in the so-called Third World after WWII.[94] These struggles also had ramifications on the West, ramifications that moved to its (sub) urban centres in the 1960s: from the urban riots of the dispossessed[95] to May 68 and the subsequent developments of left terrorist factions.[96]

This chapter will not cover the political, military, economic and legal aspects of the Yugoslav Partisan struggle, which has already been covered by various historical-political-economic studies in socialist and post-socialist times. Rather, I will focus on the cultural empowerment and symbolical armament of Partisan liberation.[97] The previous chapter pointed out the explosive encounter between Partisan art and politics, which cannot be relegated to the language of propaganda. This chapter will assess the hypothesis that: *Partisan (armed) struggle needed to arm Partisans and more generally people who supported the struggle*

---

94 The Third World, contrary to recent past and present views is not that which is lagging in modernisation be it the capitalist First World, or the socialist Second World. As Vijay Prashad showed well (2007), the Third World developed its own modernity based on non-alignment movements, anti-colonial and its own internal developments and became a political project based on a dream of universal emancipation.

95 One of the most poignant analyses on the general context of urban riots was undertaken by Mike Davis (1990/2006): racial segregation, police violence, de-industrialisation and rising poverty in the US inner cities presents a necessary entry point. See also Clover (2015) on the intensification of riots after 1960.

96 It is noteworthy that within theoretical-political discussions of the RAF, the concept of the urban-armed guerrilla was of utmost importance not only in some broad sense of international struggle and solidarity but as a means of radicalised political action viewed as the only way to trigger revolution. The extreme means of reaching this goal gave the secret service and repressive apparatus an upper hand that could neutralise any critique, which had very negative consequences for the left-progressive scene in Germany and Italy.

97 Evidently, there has been an array of substantial studies that looked at the work of Yugoslav Partisan theatre groups (e.g. Milohnić 2015), Partisan poetry (e.g. Komelj 2008), graphic design activities (e.g. Bassin, Lakovič and Visočnik, 1966; cf. Pavlinec 2004), Partisan painting (e.g. Bassin and Kori, 1971) and generally the more propagandist activities of the Partisan struggle (e.g. Repe 2004). With the notable exception of Komelj (2008), most of these works claim that Partisan *graphic work* presents a major artistic innovation (Stepančić 2004) and that Partisan art can be reduced to its agitational orientation.

in a political and most notably in an artistic way. The Partisan counter-archive selected those forms of artwork that helped to create a symbolic imaginary that cut radically into the present, and articulated a strong self-reflexivity and tense temporality between a memory of Partisan rupture and a future alternative world. I will try to answer the following questions: Who or what are the major protagonists of Partisan art(works)? What were the major media-art forms, the Partisan mode of production, dissemination and reception that the Partisans used and invented anew? And in what way did they relate to the Partisan rupture and the memory of it? Concrete case studies will present Partisan poems, songs, films and a few examples of posters and graphic designs, photographs and new intermedial forms, thus presenting an integral part of the early counter-archive.

2.2 The Partisan hunger for freedom

> Our poem and our freedom
>
> While they have already taken our freedom,
> they were not able to take away our song
> and if they shall dominate us even more,
> we shall need to sing more [...][98]

In retrospect, one can easily assess the difference in quality between the various Partisan art-media. However, Partisan art practices are all marked by a central capacity, that is, an indestructible will to create new forms of expression within conditions least favourable to art and even to life as such. Partisan poems, films and intermedial forms produce diverse monumental and micro-memorial effects that have expressed a desire to move beyond the physical and military necessities of the armed struggle. Partisan art moves beyond a physical hunger for food and the need for weapons in a time of war. The wartime testimonies of antifascists and Partisans all speak of periods of long-term hunger and exhaustion, while at the same time, of a hunger for life and a different world. In this respect, the richness

98 Če so nam že vzeli svobodo,
Nam pesmi ne morejo vzet,
Če več zatirali nas bodo,
Več bomo morali pet ... ! (in Paternu et al, 1998, 235). This poem was written under the pseudonym "mladi Primorec" in 1928 by a thirteen-year-old activist named Pinko Tomažič. He was active in the antifascist resistance in the fascist occupied part of Slovenia (then Italy). His name was taken up by the major and still existing Partisan choir "Tržaški partizanski zbor Pinka Tomažiča." Pinko Tomažič was executed on 15 December 1941 by Italian fascist forces.

of Partisan artworks and discussions redefined – even transvalued – the meaning and physical need of hunger.[99]

The politicisation of hunger has been present across a long history of riots, revolutions and wars and most famously assembled around the internationalist slogan of *bread, peace* and *freedom*. The slogan stretched from the 1912 strikes in the US to the famous Bolshevik decrees on land and peace in late October 1917 (Lenin [1917] 1975). Deleuze and Guattari take Lenin and his slogan seriously and define it as constituting "an incorporeal transformation that extracted from the masses a proletarian class as an assemblage of enunciation *before* the conditions were present for the proletariat to exist as a body" (2003, 83). This speaks of revolutionary temporality and of the political subjectivisation that materialised under Lenin's slogan uttered across the entire international workers' movement, and which had major effects on the twentieth century (Prashad 2019).

The trope of hunger for freedom is present in many Partisan poems and songs in the Yugoslav context. The People's Liberation Struggle (PLS) is a struggle for freedom and liberation, with the main goal clearly posited in its name. Let me start with one poem that immediately became a popular song often sung in the evenings, on marches and at cultural events.[100] It had a strong mobilising power among the resistance fighters and people, and was composed in 1941 by Matej Bor, while the musical score (Janez Kuhar) was added in 1944. The song bore the title *Jutri gremo v napad* (*We Go to Attack Tomorrow*), whose last verse has remained a perennial in resistance culture and refers back to the above slogan:

> Wanderer wind, give us your hand
> Lazy moon, follow us faster!
> We march and march
> Gun on shoulder
> Into attack for freedom, for bread.

The Partisans march and fight against occupation and are oriented toward a future horizon that will give them freedom and bread. No bread without freedom, no freedom without bread.[101] This trope repeats itself across much of the resistance

---

99 I would like to thank the inspiring lecture-performance of Zena Edwards, which advocates for the complexity of hunger often discarded as a mere physical human need, cf. online: https: // youtu.be/3wdNMbsuGkA (2018).

100 I would like to thank Ana Hofman for bringing to my attention this transition between poem and song, since the singing itself (a sonic activity) had a vital affective power in mobilising and creating a community-in-resistance (Hofman 2016).

101 "Veter potepuh, podaj nam roko!
Mesec lenuh, hitreje za nami!
Mi gremo, gremo

poetry and literature. What I am interested in, however, are the poetic examples that subtract freedom from the sphere of hunger, human needs and survival. Rather, there is a selection of poems that take freedom extremely seriously and point out its deadly dimension, and perhaps even inaugurate it as the ultimate agent, or form of agency of the Partisan struggle. Kajuh's famous poem "We Enter Freedom through Death" speaks of a bleeding new art created in times of war:

> Canvasses bleeding have we substantiated
> Over the land,
> with our broken fingers pinning them
> across the mountains,
> the mountains and the roads,
> across all the ravines.
>
> our skins we have made into
> painting canvasses,
> we, modern-day Raphaels [...]
> On these canvasses of ours
> We have thrown landscapes
> of death and dying,
> we carve them with impressions
> of struggle and rebellion.
>
> Look at our canvasses,
> these are works of art,
>
> in them revolutionary thought
> greatness begets,
> blood flowing from them
> ravaging like mines.
>
> These are our canvasses,
> spread over the land,
> to carve our path
> to freedom through death.
> And when, all scolded and tired,
> we finish our canvasses
> in the pavilion of the New Times
> exhibit them we shall;
> and no one will regret the blood
> we spilled for the paint.[102]

s puško na rami
v napad za svobodo, za kruh." From Matej Bor's poem *Tam nekje v gozdovih*, 1944, accessible here: http // kombinatke.si/2010/02/11/jutri-gremo-v-napad/, permission for translation by Matej and Manja Pavšič.

102 Translation by Gal Kirn and Darko Suvin. Most of the mentioned poems are accessible online on *Slike Partizana* (https: //slikepartizana.wordpress.com/2016/11/25/preko-smrti-stopamo-v-svobodo-karel-destovnik-kajuh/).

Poetry becomes one large painting *to* and *of* the struggle; one could even trace certain theological moments that cross the dead skins of Partisans that now become canvasses, while their flesh and blood is used for paint. Moving beyond the Christian ritual of eating bread and drinking wine, all the powers – the whole (even dead) body, soul and thought need to be completely dedicated to the Partisan painting and path to "freedom through death." Moreover, this trace radicalises the Christian universalist gesture of resurrection by placing it into the avant-garde legacy with its central desire to transgress the border between life and death (cf. Komelj 2008). The author of this poem does not locate the gates of the "New Times" on the other side, in the Heavenly Kingdom, where the dead might arrive, but in a Partisan pavilion where Partisan artists will exhibit their artworks with their own blood and sacrifice of their dead comrades. The new pavilion will not be an artist's oasis, or something commemorating the past, but will display the liberation's coming.

The painstaking path to freedom is radicalised in what is one of the most striking passages of Yugoslav Partisan poetry written by Ivan Goran Kovačić (1913–1943). Kovačić was a Partisan poet from Croatia, who experienced the most dramatic fighting and sieges of a Partisan units in Sutjeska. Briefly before his death he wrote a poem called "Our Freedom" and dedicated it to the commander of the Fourth Montenegrin Proletarian Brigade, Petar Komnenić. This is not a poem that sets the goal of simply reaching freedom, rather, this poem brings freedom the status of a brutal terror-stricken "object of desire." To be touched by freedom means to fall in and/or for the struggle, to face and dance with death. (see Figure 10). In the words of Kovačić:

> Freedom devours flesh and swallows blood,
> Freedom shatters legs and breaks arms,
> Graveyards and torment are her gifts.
> Freedom is terrible, cold and stiff.
>
> Her army is skeletons, corpses;
> Her door is the awful jaws of death,
> Her clothes are torn up,
> And her flags black with blood and smoke.
> Freedom roars as bombs and grenades do...[103]

The figure of freedom in Kovačić's poem is not perceived as the light at the end of tunnel, rather, it becomes the underlying colour of the tunnel itself. Freedom is thrown onto the battlefield of principles and gains an autonomous and dark character that "devours flesh" and "swallows blood." Freedom summons a

103 Excerpts from the original, which is rhymed ABBA, have been taken from Djordjev (2014).

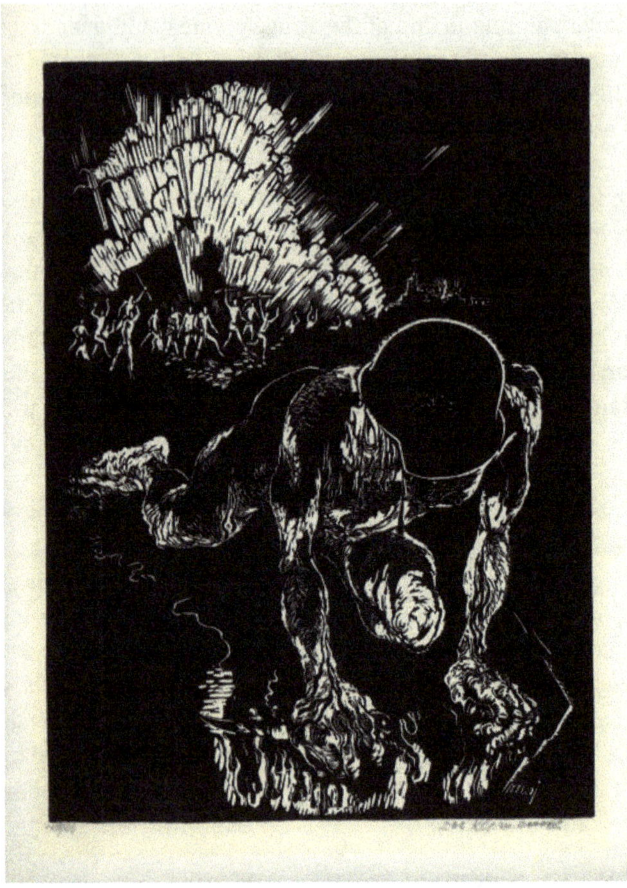

Figure 10: *Wounded beast flees,* linocut by Dore Klemenčič-Maj. From the graphic portfolio: *In the Name of Christ's Wounds*, 1944. Courtesy of MNZS.

zombie army that consists of skeletons and corpses. Does Kovačić make freedom a lethal figure very much like the war itself, which is marked by the figure of *fortuna* who is impossible to fight for or against? However, this seemingly supernatural and eternal force of freedom in the end coincides with the strength of the Partisan resistance. As Kovačić's concluding verse expresses:

> Freedom, now you tread along the Death Gorge,
> And your nag is bleeding and falls.
> Give us your bony hand, and then
> You'll be transfigured by our blood [...]

> You don't sing songs but you don't lament:
> You thunder, scream, curse, and roar,
> Like our bomb, machine gun and rifle.
>
> Crawl, Freedom, you shouldn't fly,
> Let rags cover your bones,
> But at some point, over our dead pile
> You'll wreak revenge with Life on Death.[104]

Kovačić's poem is a strange 'transfiguration' of freedom, which initially – and almost blindly – leads an army of skeletons and the dead. It is the drops of Partisan blood that begin the transformation. This means that freedom no longer has wings (it cannot fly away, or dominate over everyone indiscriminately), but has to crawl among the Partisans, helping them in the end to avenge the Partisan dead with life. The Partisan struggle against fascism is bloody and there is no way to exit from the battle into some pure moral universe where one would remain 'free' from death or judgement. Even if not on the battlefield, or from a safe historical distance, the Partisan struggle demands to be listened to as a battle cry against fascist barbarity and for social transformation. Again, and here more explicitly, the poem subverts the Christian trope of the transfiguration of Christ that is associated with rituals of wine (blood). The poem moves against any external direction whereby the subject is supposed to follow freedom (Jesus, who has been touched by the hand of God). In contrast, freedom here is thought of from the interiority of struggle, and is touched internally by the blood of Partisans. The struggle itself is the proper Partisan messiah, or rather those who come forward and 'interpellate' the freedom to the Partisan cause. The poem makes it clear that the fight for freedom is never granted, nor is it meditated upon up in the air: it is rather fought for. This poem does put Partisans on an equal footing with fascists and their bloodthirsty animality, yet it cannot be simply read as a literal hunger for bread, freedom and life. Here, freedom has a hunger all of its own: it is a hunger for itself, a hunger for *Our Freedom* that goes beyond the borders of life and death.

The extreme circumstances of suffering and hope, the fear of annihilation[105] and the capacity to build political autonomy in the liberated territories triggered a profound poetic sensitivity that expressed Partisan everyday life, but also the

104 Taken with permission from Bojan Djordjev's brochure (2014), translated by Žarko Cvejić and slightly edited by myself.

105 This intense feeling of hope and despair, the determination for bread and freedom, can be seen in the personal tragic fate of the Croatian poet, who after surviving one of the bloodiest battles at Sutjeska – comes back to a village near Foča to help his Serbian friend Dr. Salimović – where they are captured and shot by Chetniks.

expectation of a new life. In the very first Partisan collection of poems *Pesmi*, published in January 1942, Matej Bor published a striking poem that describes the transition towards this new world. Bor was involved in cultural activities as part of the Partisan resistance from early on and his poems were read by many young people and cultural workers who decided to enter the Partisan struggle. He concludes his poem "V Novi Svet" ("Into the New World") in the following way:

> Under the sky, from winds, from loudspeakers
> There scream and scream marches,
> The seas embrace the bloody continent
> The seas, sticky from blood and gasoline
> Lick and lick the continent [...]
> Drums, leaflets, periodicals and loudspeakers,
> Lying, trickery, horror, stinking.
> Europe and its gods and cannons
> Hastens/drowns into the abyss!
>
> Over the oceans of blood and gasoline,
> There sails, sails toward us – the new world.
> From blood, smoke, fire, gas
> The proletariat jumps out!
> From every heart
> Should burst out – not the rose:
> A bayonet!
> Repress love in yourself –
> If you don't love the new world![106]

---

106 Izpod neba, iz vetrov, iz megafonov
pa rjovejo, rjovejo marši,
morja oblivajo krvavi kontinent,
morja, mastna od krvi in bencina,TS
ližejo, ližejo, kontinent ...
Bobni, letaki, časniki, megafoni,
Laž, zvijača, strahota, smrad.
Evropa s svojimi bogovi in kanoni
drvi v prepad!

Po oceanih krvi in becina
Pa plove, plove k nam – novi svet.
Iz krvi, ognja, dima, plina,
Plane proletariat!
Iz sleherenga srca
poženi – ne roža:
Bajonet!
V sebi zatri ljubezen –
kdor ne ljubiš novi svet! (1946, 39–40). Published by Partisan print in early 1942.

The strained expectation of a "new world" is set in an apocalyptic tone and – one should also add – in the quite realistic imagery of World War II Europe, of "blood, fire, smoke and gas." In this continent, its old morals and canons have been drowning "in the abyss." Even if Matej Bor did not know of Walter Benjamin's meditation on *Angelus Novus* (2003), the lines evoke a coming of the Partisan angel sailing towards us through oceans of capitalist progress, symbolised by the "blood and gasoline" that embraces our shores. This angel will not simply turn its face to see the fear of the forgotten (long) dead of fascism and capitalist 'progress.' In contrast, the author of the poem demands the repression and oblivion of the former concept of humanist love for the other, to reconcile with such predicaments that in a time of war speaks of the banality of evil, collaboration and self-preservation. In this war, one needs to take sides, one needs to be a Partisan as the generic definition of the term goes: *the one who takes a side*. This decision does not fall prey to warmongering and bloodthirstiness, the gasoline of the old world, but is hungry for and in love with the "new world." The verse rejects the utopia posited in the distant future and calls out for present struggle. The new world in spite of barbarity is already in front of us, where "from the blood, smoke, fire, gas the proletariat jumps out." The Partisan proletariat is born out of this fascist war, while instead of the rose, it will carry the bayonet and the banner of "love to the new world." This expectation and hunger for the "new world" that Matej Bor so intensively expresses has to do with the deep desire to transform the existing world as well as a desire to transform previous artistic and political forms. If these were some of the most emblematic poems that represented, narrated, inaugurated Freedom, what, then, were the most emblematic images and gestures that accompanied Freedom in the Partisan imaginary?

2.3 The most emblematic Partisan images and gestures of resistance

The foremost icons of the Yugoslav People's Liberation Struggle (PLS) that were accepted internationally and by the general population in Yugoslavia were undoubtedly Tito and a red star on a Partisan hat. However, I am interested in those images and gestures that subverted the canon of the future state, and also at the same time deeply moved Partisans – those who were not yet part of the struggle and those coming after them. This section is indebted to the theoretical remarks that Didi-Huberman made in his long-term research on resistance and uprisings. His central assertion claims that gestures are "bodily forms" and as such should be seen as an essential part of "forces that make us rise up" (2016, 301). The dramaturgy of gestures is connected to the "exclamation of words," which carry both conflict in relation to the existing order and an "indestructible desire" for emancipation.[107] Didi-Huberman's fundamental pattern of resistance universalises specific acts of human emancipation, when he speaks of performative moments that become larger than the individual. Here I would like to focus on two subjective figures that have survived as photographs: Stjepan Filipović and Lepa Radić, who both gained the most important order of "national hero" after the war.

Stjepan Filipović's gesture of resistance became immortal immediately after his execution in Valjevo. This survival has to do with the 'fortunate' circumstances and impeccable timing of a young female photographer, Slobodanka Vasić. The act of taking a photo of the Partisan fighter and distributing it – without official permission – was severely punished. This is why I argue that even if Slobodanka was not a Partisan at the time, the very act of taking the photo can be recognised as a Partisan act (see Figure 11).

Stjepan Filipović was a member of the illegal Communist Party before the war, a worker and a Partisan who had organised resistance since the very start of war. Filipović was captured in early 1942 and for more than a month he was heavily tortured. For this reason, his first execution had to be postponed because he could not even stand on his feet. The SS report notes stated that Filipović was an "impossible case" and could not be broken. This is why the final date of his execution[108] was chosen with a public viewing in mind, aimed at instilling fear in the local population. This intention failed during the very course of the execution.

The photo captures a physically unarmed Partisan who awaits execution. As the SS and eyewitness reports testify, Stjepan Filipović walked along the streets and yelled "Down with Hitler," "Down with fascist gangs, communism shall prevail." Being hit by a gun and pushed around, he never ceased to continue making his proclamations and gestures of resistance. His boldness confused the executioners somewhat, who then received a new order – to execute Filipović 15 minutes before the officially scheduled time of execution. Filipović saved "the best" till last. Moments before his physical death, he refused to be hanged by a local Serbian collaborationist and demanded that the real occupiers dirty their hands. Just prior to the hanging, he extended his hands, made fists, and threw them wide in the air exclaiming the central slogan of Partisan liberation: "Smrt fašizmu, sloboda narodu" – "Death to Fascism, Freedom to the People." One can only imagine what rousing effect and resonance such loud and forceful words had just prior to the deafening silence that followed the hanging corpse a moment

---

107 For a detailed elaboration, including case studies, see Didi-Huberman (2016, 94–289).

108 See Radanović (2012) and also the interview with Radanović (2015), who made a detailed historical study. The SS archive received an inscription by the SS lieutenant Ludwig Teichmann, who said of Filipović that he was an: "impossible case."

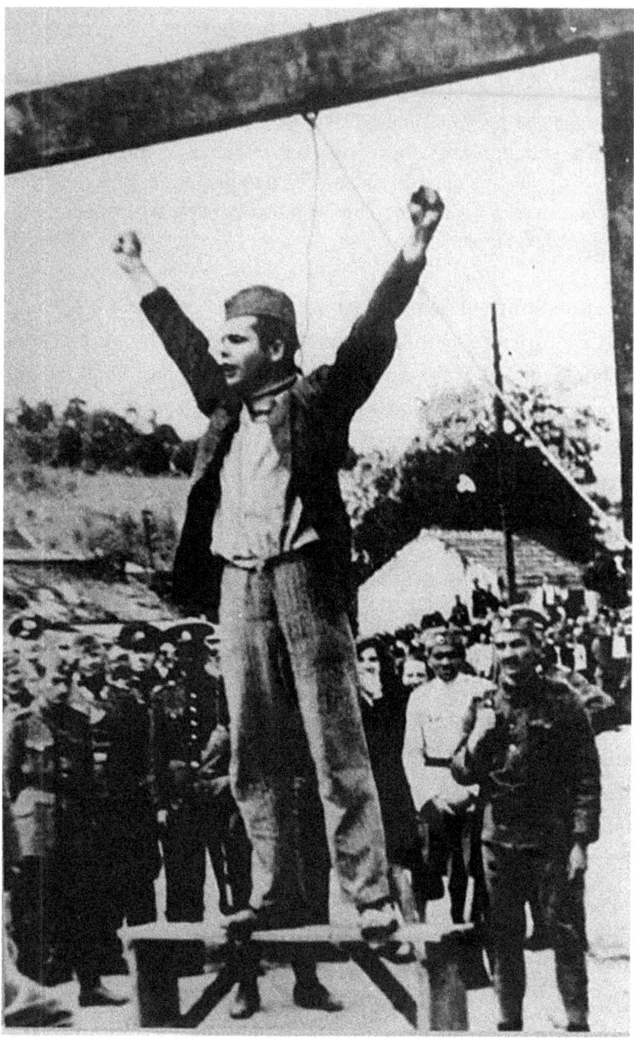

Figure 11: Stjepan Filipović before his execution in Valjevo, 1942, by Slobodanka Vasić. Source (public domain).

later. Crowds started to mutter, whisper his name, repeat the echoes and wonder about the courage of a Partisan.

His dead body hung for three more days only to then be taken to an unknown location to be buried. The story might trigger a biblical analogy with the resurrection of Lazarus or Christ, which also took place three days after their deaths, but, as WWII was a time of technical reproducibility, Stjepan Filipović was resurrected just hours after his real execution. Resurrected by a photo! Might we not say that the words Roland Barthes used to define a "punctum" are of particular relevance in this case as well?

> [...] the *punctum* is: *he is going to die.* I read at the same time: *This will be* and *this has been;* I observe with horror an anterior future of which death is the stake. By giving me the absolute past of the pose (aorist), the photograph tells me death in the future. What *pricks* me is the discovery of this equivalence ... I shudder, like Winnicott's psychotic patient, *over a catastrophe which has already occurred.* (1980, 96)

The event of execution and imminent death is tragic, however, it would have been even more tragic had this figure and event completely disappeared and remained forgotten. We need to thank the act of the photographer Slobodanka Vasić, which ensured we can still see this tragic but brave gesture today. After the execution, she returned to a small local shop, the photography studio *Foto Kosare*, where she had the negatives developed. Once the rumour of the photo spread, a commotion started and the local inhabitants bought the photos. Since the Nazi Command was stationed across the street, German soldiers saw that something was going on and so they searched the studio and seized all the photos soon after the shop had closed, confiscating the negatives and any photos they could get hold of. However, it remains unclear whether some photos remained in the hands of local people, or whether a local doctor who was part of the resistance slipped one photo away from the Nazi officer.[109] In any case, this photo of the Partisan resistance complemented the oral accounts and became part of the soon legendary legacy of Filipović's execution.[110]

The Nazis regarded the execution as a failure and they temporarily suspended public executions. This was a clear sign of symbolic victory and bravery that Filipović had won through his resilience. His gesture made him more alive than ever before and attained that immortality of freedom so well evoked by the poems of Karel Destovnik Kajuh and Ivan Goran Kovačić. To attain freedom through death means abolishing the natural laws and borders between the living and the dead. His gesture is directed against the fascist cult of death; it is a firm stance that resists occupation. In the post-war period, Filipović's image was broadly disseminated: the photo went on exhibition on various occasions in Yugoslavia and in international contexts, including being displayed in the hall of the UN in the early

---

109 See online: https: //libcom.org/history/stjepan-filipovic-everlasting-symbol-anti-facism.

110 Masumi Kameda wrote an article comparing Soviet and Yugoslav martyrdom, where he concludes that the Yugoslav Partisans attempted to "document the historical moment through the medium of photography and to reuse such photo-images in agitation and memorisation" (2013: http: //zaprokul.org.rs/pretraga/138_14. pdf).

1950s. It was also re-mediated in the form of articles, books, films, badges, postal notes and monuments in the socialist context.

Another emblematic image of Partisan gesture displays Lepa Svetozara Radić, a seventeen-year-old Partisan fighter who was in charge of the wounded in the Fourth Offensive against Partisan forces in central Bosnia. She was with a group of wounded and fought until the last bullets flew, besieged by the *Prince Eugen SS* division.[111] Heavily tortured, she nevertheless rejected giving up the names of the Partisan leadership. As the SS division report recounts, Lepa Radić "cannot be broken" and thus falls into the category of being yet another "impossible case." The first preserved photo shows her last walk to the place of her execution in Bosanska Krupa. She was convicted to death by hanging, a practice that was often used against women Partisans (see Figure 12).

The execution was public, but as the major offensive was still ongoing there were far less people present at her execution (survivors) than in the case of Filipović. According to eyewitnesses, she exclaimed, "Long live the Communist Party, and Partisans! Fight, people, for your freedom ... " Furthermore, Dušanka Kovačević recounts in her book the last moments of Lepa Radić: when Nazi captors tied the noose around her neck, she was offered a way out by revealing her comrades' identities. She responded, "I am not a traitor of my people. Those whom you are asking about will reveal themselves when they have succeeded in wiping out all you evildoers, to the last man ... "[112] The last sentence was interrupted, and a deep stillness and silence followed, while her eyes remained frozen and fixed at some point below, waiting and facing death. The photo shows a strong, calm resilience. This resilience, which was stronger than life, a surplus, reflected the deep resistance that permeated through the Partisan struggle. If Stjepan Filipović extended his arms in front of crowds of thousands, she had nothing but enemy soldiers and a few local villagers in front, with her hands tied at the back.

---

111 The majority of the Prinz Eugen Division consisted of *Volksdeutscher*: more than 55% of them were Germans that came from Banat and Serbia. For details on the work and crimes of this Division see Kovačević (1977, 45).

112 Her words were to a certain extent realised as the large majority of this SS division died in fights fleeing from Yugoslavia; some of the leaders were imprisoned and sentenced to death by hanging in the new Yugoslavia, while a few leaders of this SS division succeeded in escaping and remained in West Germany, where they became founders of the SS-lobby organization, HAIG. Most notably, the SS-Waffen Prinz Eugen general Otto Kumm 1943–1944 (1910–2004), held responsible for mass murders, was never extradited to Yugoslavia for a trial and escaped from an American-held prison in Dachau in 1947 to later live and lobby for pensions of the former SS staff and officers in West Germany (see https://en.wikipedia.org/wiki/HIAG).

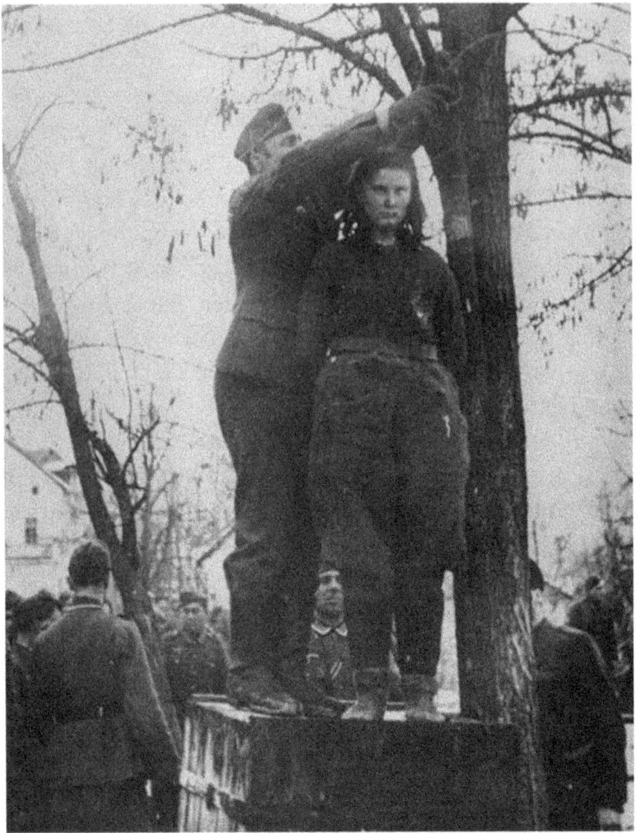

Figure 12: Moments before the execution of Lepa Radić. Public domain.

Just moments later, the photo displays her corpse hanging in the air, her head slightly tilted (see Figure 13). At the same time one cannot overlook the horrific *punctum*, for we see the gaze of a grinning soldier looking straight into the camera, while other soldiers look around, or walk down the street as if hangings are the most normal thing.[113] The gaze of the SS soldier shows how widespread the abuse and executions of the local population were, and gave fascist perpe-

113 The killings of hostages and the civilian population were a normal widespread practice in which not only the SS division but also the normal Wehrmacht army participated. Since the Yugoslav Partisans were not formally and internationally recognised as a government or army by 1944 (check chapter 1), the Nazi reprisals could be even more brutal, deeming them 'bandits' and explicitly targeting communists, Jews, and Roma, as well as any democratic or nationally aware individuals. As reprisals for one killed German soldier, whole villages were gathered and executed.

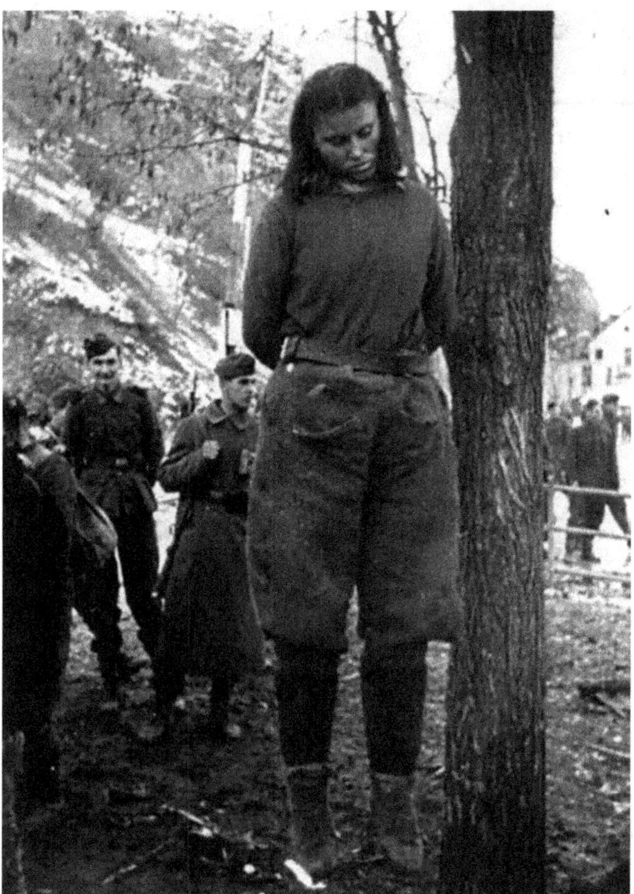

Figure 13: Lepa Radić, moments after her execution. Public domain.

trators and spectators a certain *jouissance* – a sadistic enjoyment in torturing, ending resistance and cleansing the 'unhealthy' part of their new social order. Despite having been taken by the SS soldiers, photos were found in a suitcase full of negatives in Zagreb after a Nazi soldier had been shot just before the city's liberation. It was not until 1968 that a nephew of Lepa recognised her photo in the then Mostar's Museum of the Revolution.[114]

The images point to specific differences between Stjepan and Lepa, or should we say differences between male and female Partisan heroism? There seems to be a clear juxtaposition between the outward performing gesture of Stjepan and

114 See Lukić (1968, online).

the inward resilience of Lepa, which might have persisted in the memories of witnesses long after. While these visual differences are evident, their ultimate gesture is a complete dedication to the liberation, and giving one's own life for this cause is of core importance. Evidently this is not the only criterion that makes these photos suitable for inclusion in a Partisan counter-archive – another important detail is that these photos were not taken by Partisans. The photo of Filipović was taken by a local female photographer who was not a member of the Partisan struggle, while the photos of Lepa Radić were even taken by an SS soldier! What counts for the Partisan counter-archive is not, then, a certain purist criterion of authentic Partisan production, nor does it follow a presupposed aesthetic criterion whereby works of art are only produced by renowned artists following specifically recognised artistic procedures. I do not want to claim that one should overlook the departing intentions of the photographers: either of a sadist or of a particular Nazi soldier's obsession to document, or the perhaps lucrative possibility of selling the photo of Filipović. On the contrary, my materialist analysis traces the consequences of the counter-archival material. These photos succeeded in capturing the most emblematic Partisan gestures and early symbols of Partisan resistance.

There is another emblematic photo that became famous during World War II. This photo displays the major symbol of Partisan struggle: the five-pointed star. It was on a cold winter's day in Babno Polje in 1944, when Edi Šelhaus asked the Partisan teacher Nada to organise a small staging of young schoolboys and girls posing for the Partisan icon – the star (see Figure 14). As Šelhaus (1982, 46–50) recounts, German planes often patrolled the area and thus staying outside displaying clear political messages would not endanger only lives but also expose the site as a space of local resistance. This photo was printed in the various Allied newspapers a few weeks later. It seems that this crazy idea to perform and capture the resilience of youth learning, while also forming a star in the middle of the field transgressed calculations of fear. By means of the human bodies under the direction of a teacher and a photographer, we receive one of the first performances of the symbol of the liberation struggle. This performance bore hope and unity to the divisions of a country ridden by civil war.[115]

115 These symbols would receive major cultural elaboration through the *étatisation* process in socialist Yugoslavia from the late 1940s onwards. This is especially true of the most famous holiday called *Štafeta mladosti*, which became a platform for the cultural experimentation of staging bodies and words, strengthening unity while also paradoxically strengthening ethnic identities. For a long-term visual analysis of this phenomenon, see the film of Popivoda (2013).

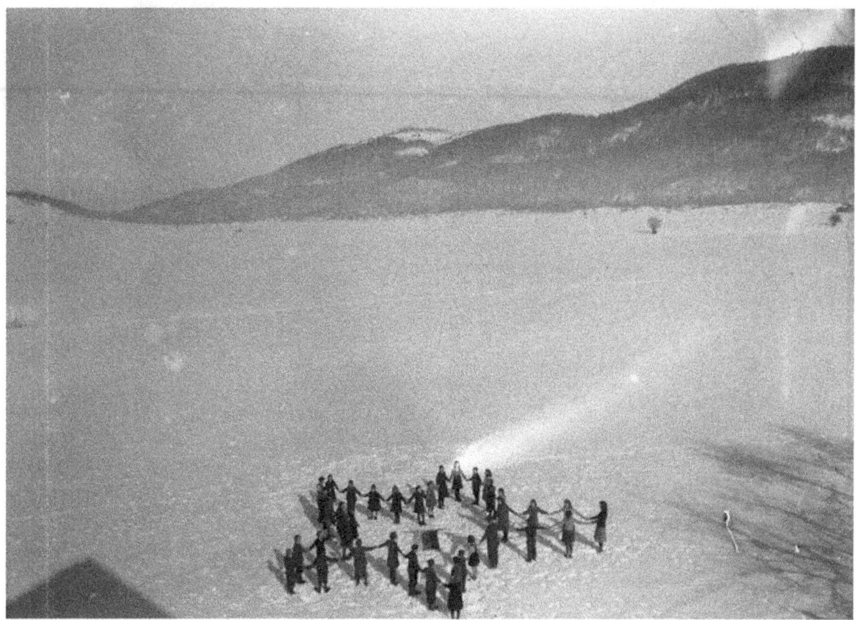

Figure 14: The Babno polje youth forming a star. Photo by Edi Šelhaus, winter 1944/45. Courtesy of MNZS.

They repeated the exercise and on another day formed the letters of Tito with their bodies, which in certain way announced future inscriptions of Tito as statesman (Figure 15). These Partisan gestures and symbols succeeded in staging a living monument to the community-in-resistance.

Finally, these diverse images bring us to a collective dimension of representation and pose a serious question: how do we, and how did Partisans conceive of the collective figure/image of Partisan struggle? Did they succeed in untying it from the individual hero or heroine, from Marshal Tito or even from the long-established symbol of the star? How can the imagery of Partisan struggle also be untied from the imagery of masculine virility and militarism that ornament the retrospective romanticist gaze of heroic times? Which form of collectivity would best portray the Partisan hunger for freedom? While researching a personal archive of the Partisan painter Dore Klemenčič, I saw a great array of sketches, posters and drawings that portray different Partisan women and men, resting or in action. But there was one image – a poster – that sticks out of the whole collection entitled *Partizanski skeči* (Partisan Sketches, see Figure 16). Dore Klemenčič painted this poster in mid-1943 – he was educated as a painter and during the war assigned to make illustrations and posters for Partisan newspapers and propa-

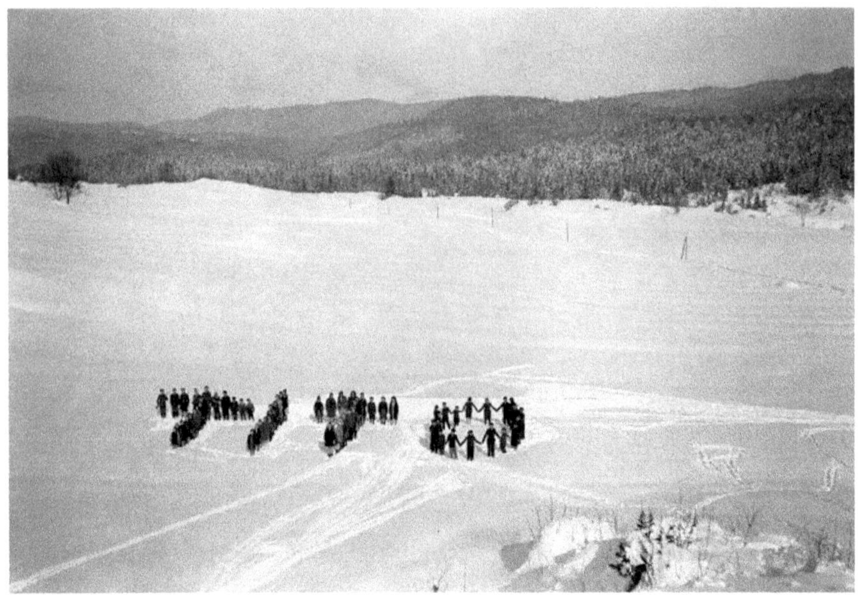

Figure 15: The Partisan teacher Nada Vreček with her pupils in the snow, creating the name of beloved comrade Tito. Photo by Edi Šelhaus, 1944. Courtesy of the Museum of Contemporary History, Ljubljana.

ganda leaflets especially in the region of Primorska.[116] I argue that the drawing of the poster below (Fig. 16) most poignantly symbolises the manifold character of Partisan hunger, the collective character of the Partisan struggle.

The poster is not a sketch of an individual Partisan figure, nor a caricature that Klemenčič practiced drawing throughout his time in the Partisans. Rather, this drawing stands out from his opus since the work displaces the individual Partisan into an abstract realm of various Partisan activities. Klemenčič's poster succeeds in sketching, thinking and commemorating the entire modality of the struggle. The poster is a solid example of suitable material for the counter-archive, since it complicates the more generally expected and accepted canon of the Partisan figure: one of a male or female fighter adorned with guns, smiling and at times carrying the star on the hat. This poster represents the fully armed and empowered Partisan struggle that redefines the notion of a weapon in war: from the obvious rifle to a guitar, a theatre mask and a book assembled under

116 For a detailed diary and memoirs see Klemenčič (1972). He had to travel in the fairly early stages of the war from Bosnia and Herzegovina to Slovenia and had some quite dramatic experiences in crossing competing enemy territories.

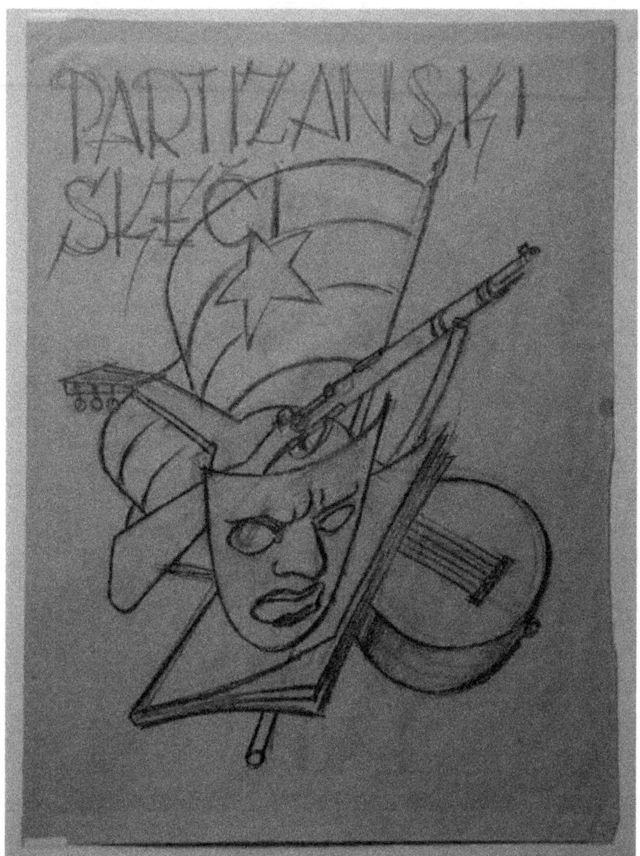

Figure 16: *Partisan Sketches*, a drawing for poster (1943) made by Dore Klemenčič-Maj. Courtesy of Janin Klemenčič and his personal archive.

the new flag of the new Yugoslavia, which carries a star. The poster expresses the equivalence of the different arms used in struggle and puts on display a deeper solidarity between political, cultural and military work that aims for liberation and arms for universal emancipation. This lucid transfiguration therefore displaces the individual Partisan figure as the holder and bearer of plural Partisan activities, while the main protagonist becomes the struggle itself.

This poster rethinks and formalises an abstract image of the Partisan collective, a welcoming image that subverts the dominant imagery of the male Partisan fighter. Apart from the collective protagonist of struggle, another rupture was to be found in the representation of a woman: she became a woman-fighter, which entailed a specific maximalist ethics of the struggle. There is an array of depictions of Yugoslav female Partisans within the print archive, from covers and photos, to illustrations

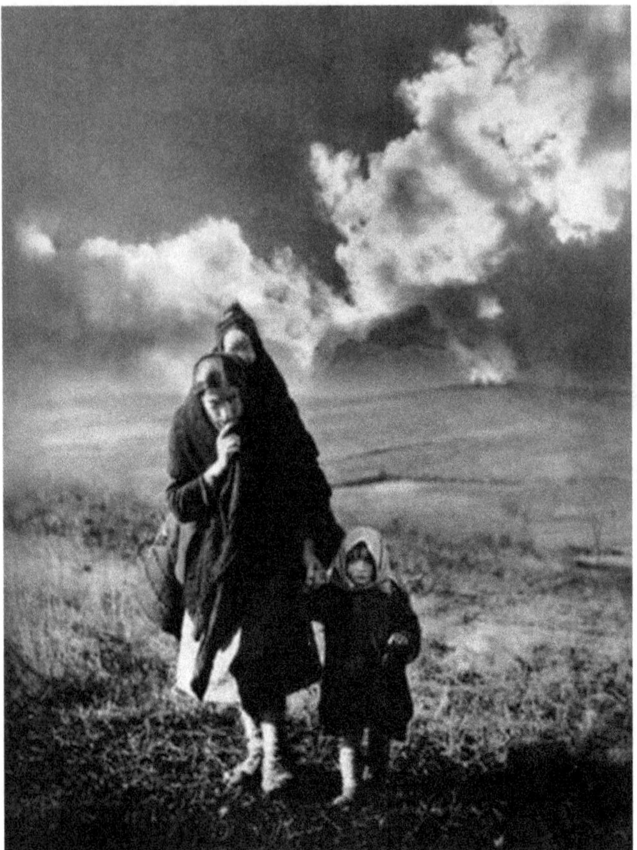

Figure 17: *Mati Knježepoljka*. Žorž Skrigin, 1943, Permission by Vedrana Madžar.

that display diverse representations of women (Vitorelli 2015). Probably the first iconic visual representations of a woman-partisan-peasant were based on the magnificent photo of a fleeing mother *Mati Knježepoljka* (see Figure 17) and another famous photo *Kozarčanka* (Figure 18) all taken in 1943 by Žorž Skrigin.

However, one can find also images of women fighters with guns, Partisan doctors, political commissars, cultural workers, peasant women who supported the Partisans and those who took care of the social reproduction of the struggle.[117] The many different roles taken on by women fighters were a vital part of the Partisan struggle and already early on in the war, women across Yugoslavia formed

117 A very helpful edited volume with texts, images and current interpretations of the AFŽ, the *Women's Antifascist Front* (Okić and Dugandžić, 2016), and also an online archive: http: //afzarhiv.org/.

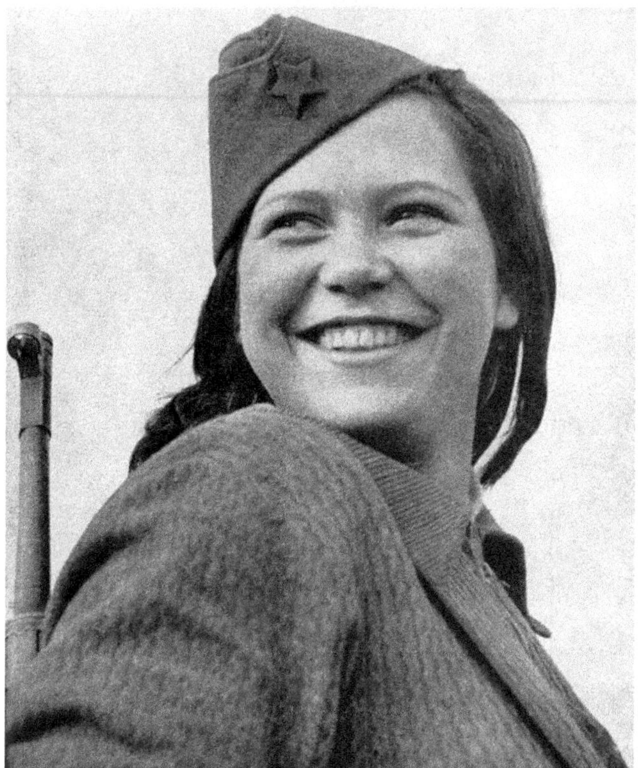

Figure 18: *Kozarčanka* (Kozara Partisan woman), Žorž Skrigin. Permission by Vedrana Madžar.

an autonomous political organisation – the Women's Antifascist Front (AFŽ), founded in 1942.[118] The figure of the Partisan woman that the AFŽ promoted was undoubtedly ahead of its time and one could argue more revolutionary than its male counterpart. Since the majority of women-peasants-workers came from very traditionalist and patriarchal contexts, they were then seen as carrying out all the activities that men carried out during the war – and more. One of the most famous images of a Partisan woman was designed by Hubert Kruljač (in cooperation with Franjo Mraz) in 1943 (see Figure 19).

This is not just any image from any poster, but the front cover of the very first issue of the female Partisan newspaper *Žena u borbi* (Woman in Struggle), which was printed by the Women's Antifascist Front of Croatia in June 1943. The

118 The founding event happened in Bosanski Petrovac on the liberated territory on 6 December 1942.

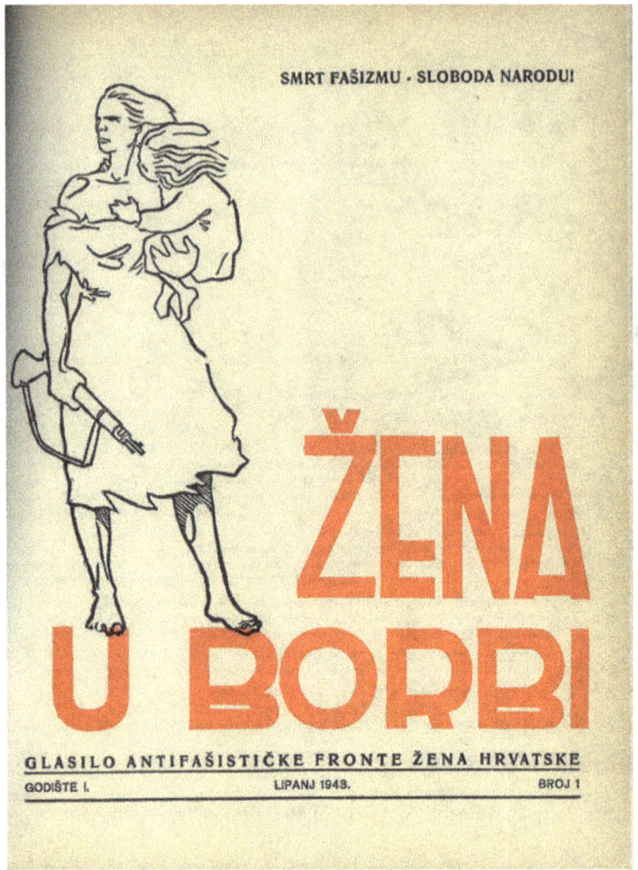

Figure 19: *Žena u borbi*, journal of the Women's Antifascist Organisation of Croatia, no. 1, 1943. Courtesy of the National and University Library (Zagreb).

newspaper was published regularly in the liberated territories and had a normal print run of 2,000 copies. Not only did women organize the printing of newspapers (see Figure 20), a majority of the contributions were written by the now educated farmer-women-partisans (see *Naša štampa u borbi za slobodu i socijalizam*, 1948), while the newspaper was first edited by two women, Marija Krajačić and Olga Kovačić, who had been active in previous women-run publications during and before the war.

The figure of the woman-fighter breaks with the traditionalist representation of women, which suggested they should stay at home and take care of the family, while men go to war. The Women's Antifascist Front promoted an image of a woman who performs all important tasks at the same time: fighting with a gun

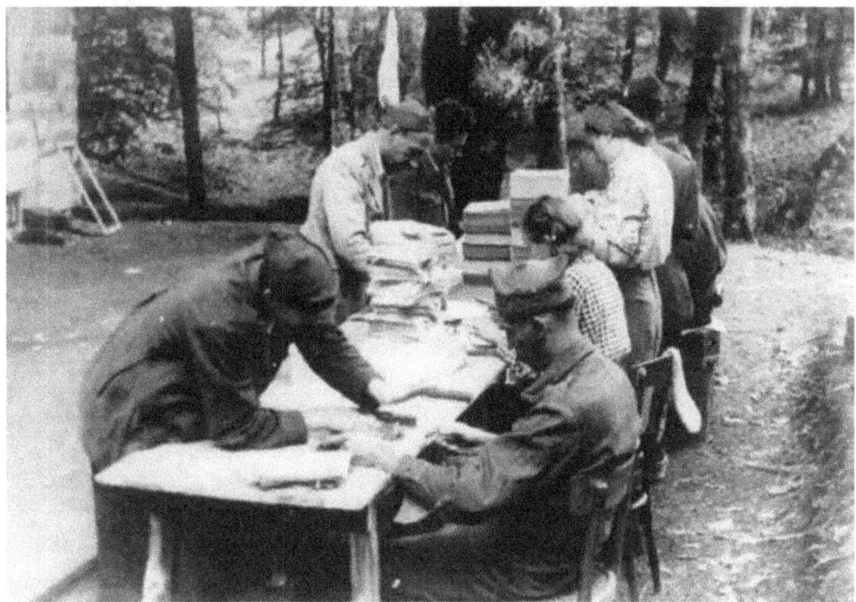

Figure 20: Partisan printing house in Papuk, Slavonia, 1943. Courtesy of znaci.net.

and taking care of the family, holding a child in her arms, writing political reports and poems, educating others and caring for the wounded.[119] Even if emblematised in one single woman-fighter – a concrete image – it repeats the gesture of the universality of the Partisan struggle evoked by Dore Klemenčič in his *Partisan Sketches*. This image was retained and re-appropriated later in history and political books on and also by women in socialist Yugoslavia. However, despite some significant improvements for women during socialism, it should be said that the communist leadership feared the real power of women and the tightly organised AFŽ. The latter gradually lost political power after the war and was dissolved in 1953.[120]

The Partisan counter-archive assembles varied poetic and visual representations that flout the conventions of tradition, here concretely, with the expectations and images of woman-fighters and collective struggle from World War II. The

119 There is a popular song "Young Partisan woman" that encapsulates the dedication and importance of women in the resistance (https: //www.youtube.com/watch? v=MQICfRlIs1s).

120 The awareness of the heroism of Partisan women was well described and recognised by their male counterparts on various occasions during the war in political, but also poetic and more literary material. Vladimir Dedijer's diaries, a member of Tito's closest entrourage, wrote concise diaries that have a special chapter dedicated to female Partisan heroism (1980, 698–709).

display of once marginal figures comes to the fore and highlights the dimension of collective transfiguration. The chosen poetic examples (e.g. Kajuh, Kovačić) brought forward the protagonist Freedom and the redefinition of the border between life and death, while the selected posters pointed to the collective figure of the Partisan struggle itself that moves beyond the concrete individual hero. I would record the poster of Dore Klemenčič as the central point of entry to the counter-archive: not only does it not depict an individual Partisan, it also redefines weapons that empowered and armed Partisans for the emancipatory struggle. A particular Partisan might be a member of this or that ethnic group, male or female, but what counts is their belonging to a universality that traverses all the particularities within the Partisan struggle. This is what made the Partisans different from other military collaborationist groups operating in the same areas.

The poster's slogan is a plea to win the struggle for "hearts and minds." Despite the heavy winter of the war and the brutality of the circumstances, the Partisans need to carry on living, to be even more 'hungry' for a different world rather than clinging to mere survival. Our imagination can give this poster limbs and faces; it can individualise the struggle present in all those young women and men who educated peasants in between the big battles and all those who stayed for months in Partisan hospitals taking care of the wounded, Allies and even enemy soldiers, as well as all those who stayed underground – metres under the ground – for hours on end in order to transmit radio signals, or print illegal newspapers and artwork; it can picture all those amateur theatre members who then formed Partisan theatre groups that turned the used parachutes of the Allies into decent costumes for their performances; it can see all those masses of anonymous poets, former peasants, who kept writing under the moon and by the campfire on small pieces of paper; it can grasp the military capacity of Partisan officers to outsmart a much more skilled and larger army; it can picture those peasant women who harboured and fed Partisans risking their lives for the cause. The list could go on for a while. The poster then evokes the collective figure of Partisan struggle that arms both themselves and others in the struggle *against* the occupation and *for* a different world. Partisan struggle thus expanded and transformed the notion of hunger and weapons. Arming in a Partisan way means acquiring the tools not to simply rise up in arms and stand against the enemy and occupier, but to arm the people in their quest for freedom. Partisan words and images became weapons that armed people for social change.[121] The question now remains of whether and how they armed their and our memory.

121 It was only after the liberation of Belgrade and the international recognition of Tito's Partisans that the Partisan movement became officially addressed as an army.

2.4 The poetic counter-archive: Geological research and an anthem to the future

The historian Branko Petranović completed a long-term detailed study of the Partisan liberation struggle and dedicated a large section of his book to Partisan print. His research concluded that more than "3,500 Partisan newspapers" were published during the war, as well as "151 collections of poetry, 111 books and brochures/booklets of art prose-literature and 102 collections of reports" (Petranović 1988, 371). More specifically, on Serbian territory, the diverse Partisan women's press organised by the Women's Antifascist Front in 1944 printed *Naša Žena* (Our Woman, AFŽ Serbia, Belgrade) with a print run of 30,000 copies, *Zora* (Dawn) with 50,000 copies, while in the region of "Vojvodina the three main women's newspapers regularly printed more than 100,000 copies" (Stojaković 2007, 15). Due to relatively high levels of illiteracy, many reading groups were organised where collective readings and discussions took place. In addition, one of the most diversified Partisan presses during the war, the *Propagandistic Section of the Executive Committee of the Liberation Front* published a booklet in 1944 entitled: "Partisan Printing Houses in Slovenia" (1944, see Figure 20).[122] The latter states that within a time span of only eight months, from December 1943 to July 1944, the regular publication of

> 169 different periodicals, among them two dailies and six weeklies [occurred]. Each month 340 Partisan newspapers were published and every month one article or a poem was contributed by more than 4000 Partisan officers and fighters that cooperated in the printing activities. (Krajnc 1944, 31)

This is an exceptional level of production, not only in relative but also in absolute terms when one compares it to the print production of other resistance movements across Europe. Once we turn to poetic production in Yugoslavia, a member of Tito's closest entourage, Vladimir Dedijer, assembled various political and cultural documents during the struggle. Dedijer also conducted extensive research in diverse archives over the decades after the war and asserted that more than 40,000 Partisan poems and songs were written during World War II (Dedijer 1980, 929), while some 12,000 poems and songs were gathered in Slovenia alone (Paternu 1987). Neither Partisan Yugoslavia nor socialist Yugoslavia had a central depository of Partisan artworks (and poems) and thus they remained scattered in the different museums to the People's Liberation Struggle as well as in the archives of the republics and the federation, yet also in various museums and

122 For an overview, see Repe (2004).

galleries of modern and contemporary art, and in personal archives. We can find poems and songs within old Partisan newspapers, brochures, children's books, as well as in designated publications for poetry and song. The most extensive project gathering the majority of Partisan poems in Slovenia was collected and edited in four volumes published by Paternu in collaboration with Irena Novak-Popov, Marija Stanonik and numerous lecturers and students from the Slavic Department of the University of Ljubljana. Most of these poems and songs are from Slovenia.[123] Other important publications are much smaller in scope, having gathered Partisan poems in Serbia, Croatia and other parts of Yugoslavia.[124] A large majority of these poems and songs remain untranslated into any non-South Slavic language. Another detail of key importance is that Partisan song, as part of the oral tradition – local and international – were not new Partisan songs, but actually old in terms of lyrics and/or melodies, where either new text or a new melody had been added (usually from Russian or other international revolutionary songs).[125]

Even if most of the Partisan poems remain scattered, certain poems that were transformed into songs appear to have a much stronger and lasting popularity and are now being sung by various alternative choirs (e.g. Kombinatke),[126] and rock or punk bands whose popularity has spread by means of social media, such as YouTube and Facebook. Only in recent years have new studies[127] been completed. These studies basically agree that Partisan poems represented an important symbolic imaginary and developed in a variety of forms: from the travesties of the old popular songs and a mixture of international revolutionary, folk and national-awakening poetry and songs to a vast array of new poems. I would add that the Partisan poems as a body of work was not only exceptional in terms of its enormous production, but also in terms of its diverse modes of dissemination: from more "traditional" poetry collections that were neatly designed[128] and song publications to collective declamations and adaptations in songs that were accom-

---

123 The four-volume anthology is entitled *Slovensko pesništvo upora 1941–1945* (Slovenian Poetry of Resistance 1941–1945). There have been a few documentary films that have addressed the topic of poetry and poets (e.g. *War Poetry* by Milan Ljubič, 1965).

124 Čubelić (1983), Rodić (1983), and Nedeljković (2017).

125 For details, see Hofman (2016). She refers to a songbook entitled "Zbornik partizanskih narodnih napjeva" (Hercigonja, 1962), where one can find numerous "variants" of one song.

126 They are a very active women's choir that also has a fully operational internet site: http://kombinatke.si/.

127 Komelj (2008), Hofman (2016), and Reč (2010).

128 The very first collection of poems was printed in Slovenia. The General Command of the Liberation Front ordered the printing of an edition by the avant-gardist and Partisan poet Matej Bor. The edition was entitled *Previharimo Viharje* (Overstorming the Storms) and printed in an illegal printing workshop in Brdo, in January 1942. There were almost 10,000 copies of this collection,

panied by more-or-less improvised music scores and instruments. "Partisan song was everywhere," remembers Šime Kronja, one of the citizens of Ruda, who witnessed the inauguration of the First Proletarian Brigade: "Partisan soldiers came to our town by singing" (in Bojić et al. 1966, 19) and this song enlisted new fighters and "echoed long after they had left our town." Poems and especially Partisan songs were everywhere, even in the most difficult times of battle and during the long exhausting marches in the snow. Reading poems out loud also occurred at cultural events, both formal and informal, as well as reading in silence, or aloud around the fire: Partisan poems and song became a red thread running through the struggle; it also became a vital oral legacy of the struggle after the war.[129]

This omnipresence and the collective nature of the production and dissemination of poems and songs speaks of a specific modality of Partisan poetry that can be named the "Partisan avant-garde." This is different to the specifically young cultural urban milieu before the war, which mostly reached an urban, elite audience. At the same time, some Partisan poets continued to experiment with very subtle poetic procedures,[130] while on the other hand the conditions of armed resistance pushed them into using more metric schemes and cooperating with music composers – realising the transition between poem and song. Močnik (2018) rightly suggested that the most circulated forms of visual Partisan culture "were distributed as leaflets and posters," while "poems were meant to be sung." Thus we can also speak of Partisan songs as the dominant oral expression of liberation.[131] Furthermore, for both Partisan poems and even less so for Partisan songs, they never existed for a specific elitist audience. Instead, the Partisan poems and songs came to full life at partisan performances (see Figure 21). They existed in and for the People's Liberation Struggle; they reflected an encounter between masses of anonymous and renowned poets, between all those who created poems for the first time and those who explored further poetic forms in

and it gained a further two editions during the war. It was immensely popular and many other Partisan artists refer to it as a sort of special inspiration.

129 This dimension to oral and sonic culture and legacy (in contradistinction to poem and written culture) was researched in detail by Ana Hofman (2016).

130 One of the most famous Slovenian Partisan poets, Karel Destovnik-Kajuh, experimented with the "inverted sonnet" (see Javoršek, 1981), while Peter Levec published a poem in six elegant elegiac distichs and resolved a century-long debate about the transfer of classic quantitative metric schemes into Slovene accentual-syllabic metrics ("The Burnt Village"). I would like to thank Rastko Močnik for bringing this case to my attention.

131 Matej Bor is a good example of this transition: after having joined the Partisan armed struggle, when he still used free verse and the "Mayakovskian" style 1941 he turned to more canonical verse and meter over a couple of months (1942), and then in less than a year to "popular" forms, where he cooperated in musical compositions (songs).

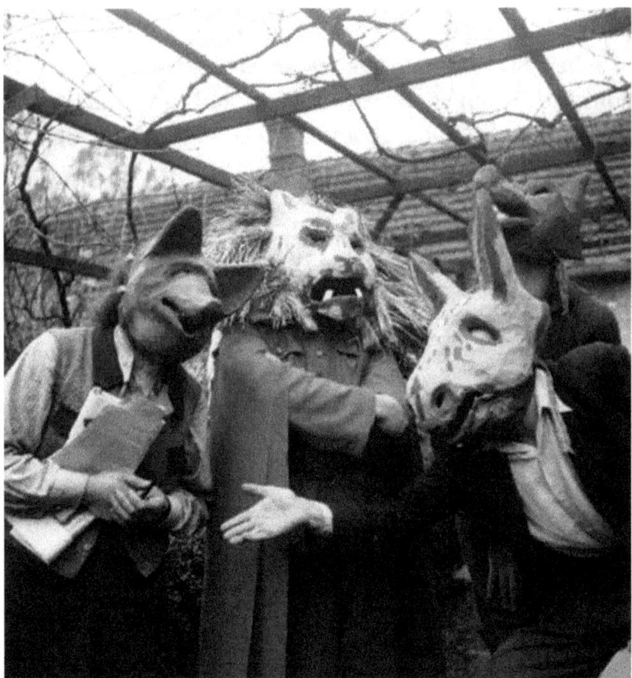

Figure 21: Partisan performance, Slavonia, 1944. Courtesy of the Association of Antifascists of Croatia.

the light of struggle and demanded that its vocation plunge deeper. This entailed an encounter between the pre-war avant-garde (constructivist, surrealist) poetry and folklore-popular songs. Written and oral culture, poem and song, contributed in a major way to the Partisan uprising: one could even argue that they became poetic and sonic performatives of the struggle. This does not mean the Partisan poems and songs had no predecessor. As we saw, they used international melodies and lyrics, but also a long oral tradition of resistance.

Furthermore, it comes as no surprise that the very first printed versions of Partisan poems and songs during WWII included a mix of popular, folk, internationalist revolutionary and local new Partisan poems and songs. The collection was called *Antifašističke pesme* (Antifascist Poems, or more adequately, Antifascist Songs) and was printed on 7 November 1941 on the first liberated territory in fascist occupied Europe. The first collection of antifascist songs was edited collectively, while one of its main editors was Dušan Nedeljković, a pre-war communist writer. Nedeljković wrote a foreword to the second edition 30 years later, where he described in detail what the central criterion of the editorial board for song selection had been. Nedeljković recounts how the editorial board conducted small surveys among Partisans and activists, asking them which songs were the most popular and why (Nedeljković 2017, 60–64).[132] The editorial board made a decision to publish old and new songs of resistance, which would put the newest song *Srpska partizanka* (Serbian Partisan Woman) on the same page with the Workers' and Soviet *International*. Due to the absence of original Soviet songs, the latter were transcribed from memory and improvised by those who spoke Russian. Additionally, the publication consisted of folk songs that related directly to past liberation struggles in the Balkans; *Ženska himna* (*Women's Anthem*); Bulgarian antifascist songs; and also a few poems written by workers, such as Miodrag Tatović from Ljig who wrote a poem that was sung to the melody of the more famous Soviet song "We shall defend this country/land." Last but not least, the fighter from Užice Velimir Joksimović wrote the song "The Commune of Užice Rose Up," which was based on an epic song (cf. Hercigonja 1962).

It is also important to note that it was completely normal practice in the early Partisan brigades to form choirs, which were made of up to 40 members. Petranović sums up well the starting zeal of such cultural innovators:

> A very unique phenomenon unfolded when poets-peasants, popular folk artisans without artist renown, began to write poems in decasyllable art forms and reflected on and celebrated the People's Liberation Struggle, while, on the other hand, those who were literate, writers, journalists in the liberated territory, were fully immersed in propagating the struggle. (1988, II, 375)

The writing, reading and singing of poems and songs was not the exclusive property of pre-war intellectuals and artists but rather sprang up organically from the Partisan movement (see Figure 22). This popular, mass and "lay" dimension of Partisan words and poems cannot be reduced neither to certain ethnic folk imaginary nor to internationalist frame. This was also due to a very practical reason, since most people from the peasant population already knew the old songs and melodies and so they simply inserted new lyrics that sonically "armed" the fighters (cf. Hercigonja 1972).

Partisan songbooks and poetry collections included translations of different foreign revolutionary songs. The collection *Pesmi* (Poems, 1943), published by the *Okrožna Tehnika* of the Communist Party of Slovenia, deserves special mention (see Figure 23). This collection consisted of 46 pages and 37 images that accompany 36 antifascist and revolutionary songs printed in six original languages: Slovenian, Serbo-Croatian, Russian, Bulgarian, Italian and Spanish. 1500 copies were printed and this was one of the more popular editions printed during the war. This points

132 In the first chapter of Ana Hofman's book (2016) there are a few sections that present some of the Partisan poems and songs that Nedeljković gathered and edited.

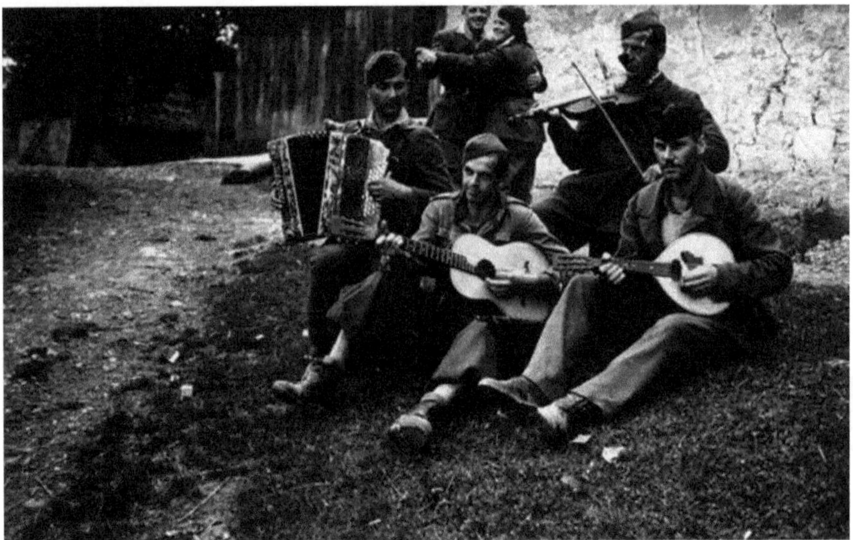

Figure 22: Partisan music group, unknown author, Croatia. Courtesy of Savez hrvatskih antifašista.

to the internationalist feature of Partisan song production that – despite regional specificities – shared a few denominators: a Partisan mass audience, dissemination and production; the mixing of avant-garde and folk elements; the dimension of anonymity. All these features contribute to the Partisan counter-archive.

2.4.1 Poems of revolutionary temporality

Deleuze and Guattari's "monument to revolution" entails an open and tense relationship between revolution and its poetic echoes for future struggles (2003, 176–177). But what if such a tense relationship and monument to revolution already begin within the revolution itself? As a matter of fact, within Partisan resistance literature and poetry, one can trace a widespread preoccupation with the notion of (precarious) time and memory: I would argue that there is a whole section of poetic production that could be called the poetic memory genre.[133] Predominantly these poems are written in the first person singular, with which the author addresses his or her beloved and/or fallen friends: comrades, wives, children, brothers and sisters, fathers and especially mothers. Many of these poems

133 Most of these poems can be found in Paternu et al. (1995, 1998).

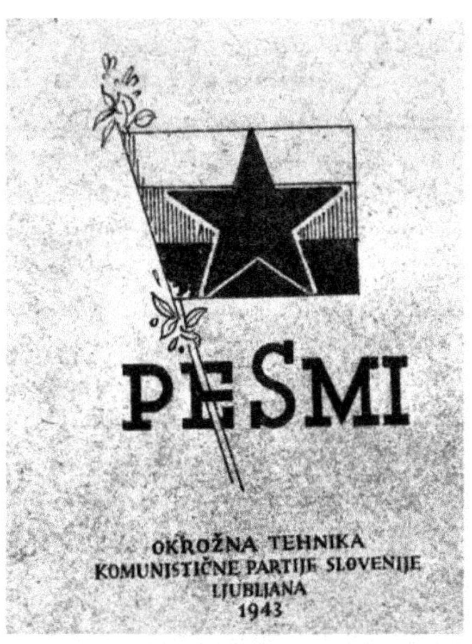

PESMI

OKROŽNA TEHNIKA
KOMUNISTIČNE PARTIJE SLOVENIJE
LJUBLJANA
1943

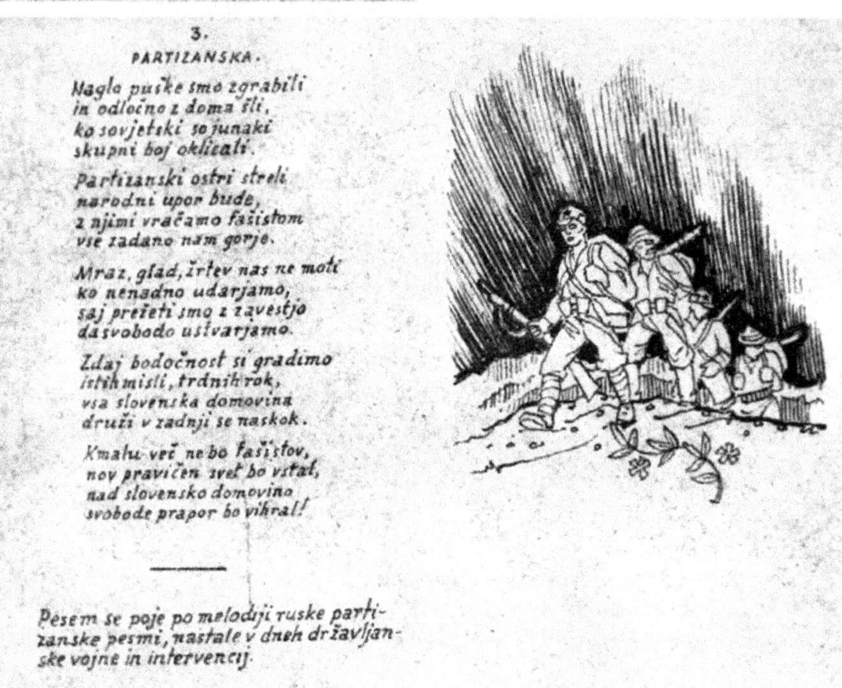

3.
PARTIZANSKA.

Naglo puške smo zgrabili
in odločno z doma šli,
ko sovjetski so junaki
skupni boj oklicali.

Partizanski ostri streli
narodni upor bude,
z njimi vračamo fašistom
vse zadano nam gorje.

Mraz, glad, žrtev nas ne moti
ko nenadno udarjamo,
saj prežeti smo z zavestjo
da svobodo ustvarjamo.

Zdaj bodočnost si gradimo
istih misli, trdnih rok,
vsa slovenska domovina
druži v zadnji se naskok.

Kmalu več ne bo fašistov,
nov pravičen svet bo vstal,
nad slovensko domovino
svobode prapor bo vihral!

Pesem se poje po melodiji ruske partizanske pesmi, nastale v dneh državljanske vojne in intervencij.

Figure 23: Miniature collection of Partisan poems named *Pesmi* from 1943. Designed and illustrated by Vlasto Kopač "Partisan song" that has addendum that the song should be sung according to the melody of Russian partisan song that was created in the days of their civil war and interventions. Courtesy of MNZS.

evoke or follow a classical dramatic structure: there is war and the necessity of individual sacrifice, and a premonition or the imminence of a Partisan's death. Such death is, however, not in vain, since mourning over death is necessarily linked to the horizon of freedom. There are numerous poems that can be read as testaments and goodbye letters, typically referring to the time of winter and waiting for the ever-delayed spring.[134] Furthermore, some of these poems are oriented towards the past, where the dwelling space of a "warm home" and a beloved family are the object of yearning. One can trace another recurring tension between the desire for an encounter (be it familial, sexual or more existential – with freedom and peace) and an awareness of its necessary delay due to war and an indeterminate future. There are also some poems written by or to the "unknown" Partisan who is buried in an "unknown grave."[135] Such poems form a dominant Partisan archive that commemorates the past from the perspective of present suffering, and calls for victims and/or fighters not to be forgotten. In such poetry, relatives and the beloved especially play the essential role of addressee. This is also a frequent form of poetry found among those interned or imprisoned (cf. Paternu et al. 1995, vol. III–IV). The structure of time here works on the level of content: the future stands for the (realised) promise of freedom, the end of war and peace, whereas the past is seen as a romanticised and idealised time of peace. Present suffering is exchanged for future freedom and also displaces romantic affections.

Juxtaposed to this more mainstream Partisan memory genre, the next sections focus on two types of Partisan poems: firstly, poems that subtly articulate the relations between past, present and future and practice revolutionary temporality; and secondly, an array of Partisan poems that were entitled "anthems," which declared multiplicity in unity and the rapturous character of Partisan poetry. These poems do not grasp time on the level of content (past – peace, present – war, future – promise of freedom/peace), but rather practice a strong awareness of the revolutionary temporality of that time. Time is out of joint and, set apart from the intensifying structure of the emotions of despair, sorrow,

134 Just to name a few examples of such a tendency: Viktor's poem "Memories from Youth Years" (in Paternu 1998, I, 155), Slavec's poem "For Freedom" (Paternu 1998, I, 183), Fani Okič's "Freedom" (Paternu 1998, I, 350), Bogo Flander's "Partisan's Spring" (Paternu 1995, 209) and many others.

135 Boris Beretič's "To the Fallen Partisan" (Paternu 1998, 370) and "To the dead Partisan" by Nada Cilenšek (Paternu 1998, 492), Kosta Racin's "Balade to an Unknown Soldier" (1943, accessible online: https://slikepartizana.wordpress.com/2017/04/20/balada-o-nepoznatom-vojniku-kosta-racin/). This dimension also strengthens the thesis on Partisan anonymity as one of the central aspects of the expanding mass cultural activity.

courage and enthusiasm, it formally breaks with the linear continuum and redefines the role of (Partisan) poetry itself. The Partisan counter-archival poems explicitly refer both to the collective dimension of the struggle and elaborate a refined revolutionary temporality between past, present and future.

2.4.2 Geology encounters Poetry: Comradeship is bigger than war?

Someday in a million years' time is a poem written by a Partisan named Iztok, who was a fighter in Prešeren's brigade. This poem appeared in the first issue of the Partisan newsletter *Triglavski Odmevi* (1943). The main addressee is humanity and, more notably, those that care to research the long distant past – *geologists* – and uncover the fossils of the Partisan struggle. What will s/he see and how will this Partisan past be understood and reconstructed under so many layers of barbarity?

> *Someday in a million years' time ....*
>
> One day, in millions of years, maybe geologists will write of how people lived these days.
>
> Their lips will curve into a bitter smile: *Oh, yes, at that time, a human being was only an animal, which is why his acts should not be taken as sins.*
>
> But if they could only know how our hearts were beating warmly all that time, that comradeship was more to us than we to ourselves, maybe then they would think differently about us, and then also understand our great pains.[136]

This poem posits at its core the contradictory relationship between the (distant) future (the geologist's present) and the complexity of the struggle of that time (the Partisan poet's past). The poet starts a dialogue with the future and asks the geologist if s/he will be able to understand this intensity, the Partisan rupture, without being blinded by the barbarism of war? Will there be some fragment in the fossil of the bleached bones that will testify to the dignity of the liberation struggle of that time? Also, why should one entrust this task to geology, rather than, for example, history or the emancipatory struggle of the future – will a geologist not also be embedded in the dominant ideology of his/her time?

The relationship between poetry and geology is not as arbitrary as a reader might think at first glance. There is a whole underground current within the history of science and poetry into which Iztok's poem is inscribed. We can trace their encounter at least from the early nineteenth century, when geology received scientific recognition and became popularised and exhibited to a more general

---

136 My translation. The original is taken from Paternu (1998, 209).

public. It was in 1831 that Honoré de Balzac came up with a fascinating reversal between geology and poetry, when speaking of Cuiver:

> Have you ever plunged into the immensity of space and time by reading the geological treatises of Cuvier? Borne away on the wings of his genius, have you hovered over the illimitable abyss of the past as if a magician's hand were holding you aloft? As one penetrates from seam to seam, from stratum to stratum and discovers, under the quarries of Montmartre or in the schists of the Urals, those animals whose fossilized remains belong to antediluvian civilizations, the mind is startled to catch a vista of the milliards of years and the millions of peoples which the feeble memory of man and an indestructible divine tradition have forgotten and whose ashes heaped on the surface of our globe, form the two feet of earth which furnish us with bread and flowers. Is not Cuvier the greatest poet of our century? Certainly Lord Byron has expressed in words some aspects of spiritual turmoil; but our immortal natural historian has reconstructed worlds from bleached bones [...] He treats figures like a poet [...] He searches a lump of gypsum, finds an impression in it, says to you, 'Behold!' All at once marble takes an animal shape, the dead come to life, the history of the world is laid open before you. (Balzac 1897, 21–22)

There is a certain doubling of geologists with a poet and Creator/God that not only reflects the careful study of the long-gone history of people, animals and the planet itself, but rather speaks of an almost magical ability to resurrect the dead and penetrate deep under the earth's surface. Probably the most lasting encounter between geology and poetry came with Goethe, whose erudite work did not use poetic expression as merely an aestheticisation of his geological and biological work, but as a necessary trajectory in understanding and reconstructing nature. The most fascinating 'synthesis' of this conviction comes through in his famous poem "Metamorphosis of Plants" (1798), which he writes at a time when he had already theorised a 'morphological' approach that assessed how forms cannot be discovered or analysed in a static way, but as constantly changing.[137] Metamorphosis is thus a key to the science of changing forms and came to the centre of his poetic and scientific research very much in line with Marx's own method of understanding society as structured by the class struggle. Furthermore, for Marx to understand capital in a positivist way, that is, as a static form of (the) accumulated wealth (of nations) was an erroneous epistemological departure. Such an epistemological standpoint should be juxtaposed to defining capital as something that is always transforming and

137 Morphology has to "manifest and show itself [...] The inorganic, the vegetable, the animal, the human, all manifests itself, appears as what it is, to our outer and inner sense. Form is something mobile, that comes into being and passes away. The science of form is the science of transformation" (1987, 349). For a detailed elaboration on morphological method in Goethe and connections to Marx, I must thank Elena Vogman (2018).

moving beyond obstacles. Capital can be regulated by a set of laws, but its revolutionising nature cannot be tamed by neither state nor morality: capital moves beyond a morality of good and evil. This is well epitomised in Marx's famous phrase on the transformation of forms under capitalist (re)production: "All that is solid melts into air." There is a certain homology at work here: Goethe's coupling of geology, biology and poetry tackled the transformation of plants and was directed at a deeper and truer understanding of nature, while both Marx in his own way of analysing and politicising class antagonism, and also the Partisan Iztok linked together geology and poetry in order to understand the transformation of society. If Partisan poetry can best embody and abstract the present rupture and even bring forth the future, then the task of us (Partisan) geologists, from the future is to reconstruct and sustain the rupture.

Another close reference to the relations between geology and poetry can be traced back to Mayakovsky, the major avant-gardist poet of the Soviet Union, and Srečko Kosovel, the major avant-gardist poet of Slovenia, who both wrote extensively in the 1920s. I want to argue that both authors lie in close mental and theoretical proximity to Iztok's geology of the Partisan future. Mayakovski and Kosovel both speak of a peculiar position from the future, a view from the future on their existence and times of rupture that will come from the standpoint of geology. Mayakovsky explicitly refers to the geologist as someone who in the midst of ruins and the (Brooklyn) Bridge will "succeed in recreating our contemporary world," thus pointing out the force of human imagination (cf. Vaingurt 2013). In one of his last poems before his death, Mayakovsky returns to the image of the bridge (Roman aqueduct) and equates geological excavation and poetic activity in their painstaking labour against tradition and oppression.[138] Instead

138 My verse
by labour
will break the mountain chain of years,
and will present itself
ponderous,
crude,
tangible,
as an aqueduct,
by slaves of Rome
constructed,
enters into our days.
When in mounds of books,
where verse lies buried,
you discover by chance the iron filings of lines,
touch them

of building bronze monuments, the only "common monument" to revolution for Mayakovsky is "socialism built in battle." The human imagination and battles that realise ideas are the only possible monuments to revolution itself and to the October Revolution. Srečko Kosovel – a close reader of Mayakovsky – nevertheless writes from the core of Europe permeated by counter-revolutionary tendencies (cf Komelj 2008). In one of his famous poems from 1925 entitled "Tragedy on the Ocean," Kosovel criticised the downfall of contemporary Europe and humankind in an apocalyptic tone of destruction, where the drowned have not drowned well enough to be really dead (Vrečko 2011; Komelj 2019; Komelj in Kosovel 2019). His criticism of the petit bourgeois mentality and individualism of European society makes the ocean the large cemetery of humankind, which will simply overgrow Europe. "In twenty thousand years" the geologist will enter the stage and he will step over the mountain, where "these islands shall be erected from the ground." The geologist will make an effort to "recognise the ocean in vain":

> The geologist will thus teach: These are parallel layers,
> here there was no struggle,
> here the ocean has covered silently,
> valleys, fields and mountains.[139]

If there is 'no struggle' and no political subject, then the work of the ocean (nature) is smooth and covers the past, which silently means that all the losses and victims will be forgotten. This speaks of the horrific feature of the "ocean without waves," which shrouds us in complete silence and darkness. What will then remain of humankind is an abyss, since the underwater world will keep covering the geological elements of "valleys, fields and mountains."

Iztok's poem in its own witty and even less optimistic way continues Kosovel's lines. Let us remember that the poem's central proposition is that even if a struggle takes place, such as that between Partisans and fascists, there is no guarantee that the ocean will not simply envelop it. There is no guarantee that the geologist will be able to read the whole intensive experience of the struggle out of the fossilised bones. Iztok fears future misunderstanding and even the abuse of Partisan memory. This poem succeeds in bringing polyphony and dissent to

---

with respect,
as you would
some antique
yet awesome weapon.
Accessible online: https://www.marxists.org/subject/art/literature/mayakovsky/1930/at-top-my-voice.htm.

139 Accessible online: https: //sl.wikisource.org/wiki/Tragedija_na_oceanu.

the process of deciphering and reconstructing the lesson of rupture. Iztok was definitely correct regarding the abuse of Partisan memory, but this occurred in much less than a million years: just two decades later the Partisan struggle was the subject of mythological spectacular films in socialist Yugoslavia, while from the 1980s onwards, "new geologists" excavated the previously victorious Partisan dead and turned them into totalitarian monsters guilty of major crimes.

This poem demonstrates a specific underground "aleatory encounter" (Althusser 2006) between geology and poetry and can tell us something about the changing protagonists of this encounter. There are at least three protagonists with their lines of interpretations that emerge within the geologico-poetic encounter: geologist-as-historian; geologist-as-poet-God; geologist-as-counter-archivist.

Firstly, a geologist can be defined as someone coming from the future, a representative of objective knowledge that follows specific scientific protocols and who can determine and reconstruct with a high degree of precision what this past was about. The geologist here would then become a historian or archaeologist with a critical distance from the matter.

Secondly, a geologist becomes a poet, who can either complement the past with the future, the poetic with objective discourse, or in a radicalised manner, a geologist can even substitute a poet by commanding strength in facts and speculations. This figure is very much in line with Balzac's quote that geologists can resurrect the dead and reconstruct not only the peculiar trait or form, but the whole history. As such, a geologist-poet comes close to the figure of a Creator, an objective time-machine. In the avant-gardist dictum, geology here sublates both science and art, since it commands the old (dead) and the new (living).

And thirdly, one can also make a case for the figure of a geologist-counter-archivist that reactivates the emancipatory fragments without any formal guarantee that people might read the rupture "correctly." This path is forked and traversed by two central aspects to my interest: there is an already well-known figure of "impossible" testimony, or of the extremely painful witnessing of horrific events, such as genocide and the Shoah (Levi 1988); while the next figure reactivates the impossibility of the Partisan struggle to defeat fascism against all odds. The most tragic defeat of the oppressed: alongside the most insane and improbable victory of the oppressed at the same time. In both aspects, the reactivation of memory is a serious activity that one has to undertake with the utmost political, theoretical and artistic creativity, care and responsibility. To take this geological-commemorative activity on a purely hermeneutical-textual level, the truth and lessons of the horrific past and victories of the oppressed can easily be endangered, reversed and forgotten. In our age, antisemitism (and Islamophobia) has been reaching new heights through the relativisation of the Shoah (Holocaust) and through launching attacks on minorities. The quest for multiple interpretations and understandings can even lead to a denial of the horrific past. The counter-archivist figure is thus not embedded in a quest for interpretation, but testifies, reflects and acts on certain horrific and victorious fragments so as to never repeat genocide (the defeat of the oppressed) or to continue repeating and expanding the rupture (the victory of the oppressed). This constitutes a geology of yesterday and tomorrow.

To return to Iztok's poem, how concretely does it read the radical novelty of the Partisan struggle? Does it really speak of a rupture that was irreversible, or does it point to certain deeper antagonisms? The poem finds the Partisan struggle located between two extremes: on the one hand, it evokes the brutal transformation of man into "only an animal," that is, into someone that kills as a moral regression from humanity to animality[140]; on the other hand, it also evokes the transformative dimension of a person and even "human nature," which is highlighted by the emergence of the politico-ethical principle of "comradeship." The latter was not only bigger than the Partisan as an individual, but also something in light of which the barbarity of war fades away. Comradeship and the Partisan's dedication to a universal cause will not be some royal path trodden by flowers but a path that brings "great pains." In her recent work, Jodi Dean has incisively tackled the complex entity of "comrade" and I believe that it is between what Dean defines as the third and fourth characteristics – "courage" and "enthusiasm" – that Iztok's testimony should be read from:

> Enthusiasm, energy is expected of comrades because it is that extra, that surplus benefit of collectivity, which enables them to do more, even to win. What distinguishes comrades from politically minded and hardworking individuals is the energy that accrues to collective work. Because they combine forces, they generate more than each could by working alone. Enthusiasm is the surplus that collective discipline generates. (Dean 2019, 88–89)

Comradeship (see Figure 24) as something that emerges from the community-in-struggle, from the very resistance, from resisting bodies and minds, articulates and embodies the specific surplus around which the counter-archive and Iztok's poem continues to revolve. This is why Iztok cannot speak of the moral geology of a future that would entail "working through" (*aufarbeiten*); what matters is to be able to "work upon" the struggle (*verarbeiten*) and upon the past and future relationality of Partisan comradeship.[141] Iztok's geologist carries the inherent

140 This view presupposes a certain superiority of human over animal that would ignore the horizon and scope of human activity and effects that it has on the planet, animals and fellow humans. For a fascinating journey from animality to humanity and back to the freedom of an animal, see Timofeeva (2018).

141 For a detailed critique of dominant ways of memorialising, see Adorno (2005, 89–103).

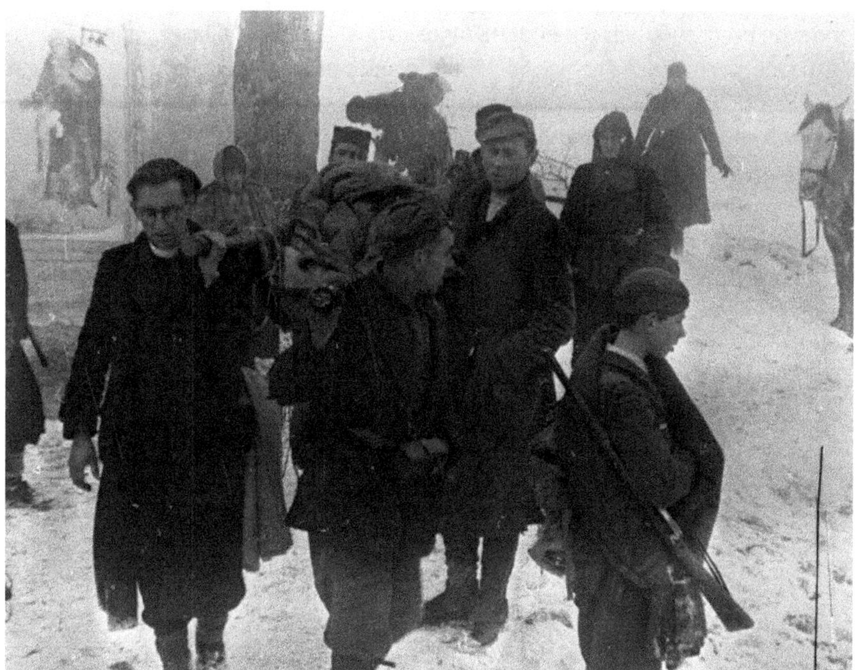

Figure 24: Transport of the wounded on Paški Kozjak after the breakthrough. The first on the left is a religious clergyman of the division Jože Lampret. Photographed by Jože Petek, 22 February 1944. Courtesy of MNZS.

tension of the Partisan, which thus cannot be resolved by moral categories of individual choice or the mere pragmatism of survival, but should be addressed in the light of the Partisan task: the liberation of the occupied country and the transformation of society. If one ought to measure the events in terms of a dominant humanist-Christian morality, the Partisan struggle and war would be defined as a series of "sins." This would bring a reconciliatory conclusion, namely that all sides committed crimes and sins, and are thus guilty, being perpetrators and victims.[142] One would then conclude that all the victims are the same and thus need to be commemorated in stone and images, or in poem and text. The reference to Christian morality is not without coincidence and can be traced throughout the Partisan cultural struggle. It is noteworthy that among Partisans there were different political groups and individuals affiliated to Christian socialism, or Islam

142 In the Slovenian context it was Spomenka Hribar in 1986 who called for national reconciliation and the embrace of Slovenian history through the signifiers of guilt and sin. I return to the analysis of reconciliation-revisionist arguments in chapter 4.

and who practiced their religion. In Yugoslavia at that time, a large majority of the Partisans came from a peasant background and were religious. Some detachments had their (lower) clergy and priests actively fighting against the fascist occupation. At the same time, those that professed their religion in the Partisans found themselves not so much in an antagonistic relationship to the Communist Party as the main organiser of antifascist resistance, but to different forms of institutionalised religion – churches and their dominant clergy. The latter in some places openly collaborated with the fascist occupying force, while on the other hand they wanted to keep a neutral position. This does not mean that a significant number of priests revolted against this – immoral position – and entered the Partisans (Kocbek 1949, 1982; see also Krnić 2018). Those who entered the Partisan struggle were aware that the struggle was more important than the positions taken by the dominant Church, with its retrograde external moralistic point that every side was committing sin equally. Furthermore, Iztok's poems also warn of a technological-forensic path that would complement morality with the counting of bones. Geology then works on the level of pure empirical facts, which results in counting bodies, enumerating battles, and making an objective judgement on war: every war is the same.

In juxtaposition to moral relativisation, Iztok's poem speaks of a "comradeship" that made the individual strive beyond selfish self-interest and a survival strategy (see emblematic photo of partisan comradeship from church, fig. 25). Is the counter-archivist and a future reader therefore invited to participate in a self-reflective and utopian practice that (re)constructs comradeship and imagines and fights for the possibility of a new world? This "thought-image" might already trigger the transition so well encapsulated by Hal Foster, when he speaks of the strategic transformation of "'excavation sites' into 'construction sites,'" which "suggests a shift away from a melancholic culture that views the historical as little more than the traumatic." (2004, 22). The geologist of the counter-archive stages a site for reconstruction and revives utopia for today and for a realised emancipatory politics of yesterday, while at the same time s/he cannot cover up the initial antagonisms that lead to brutal wars, or even less so, the antagonisms that relativise and rehabilitate fascism. Geology drowned in moral neutrality leads to the weakening of Partisan memory and of general memory regarding World War II.

2.4.3 A poem of the "last" struggle

The Partisan poet Karel Destovnik Kajuh (1922–1944) already became popular during the war and *immortal* after he fell in battle. His major collection *Pesmi* (Poems) was printed in 1943 by the cultural detachment of the Partisan Fourteenth Division. In 1943, he wrote one of his most striking poems, which relates

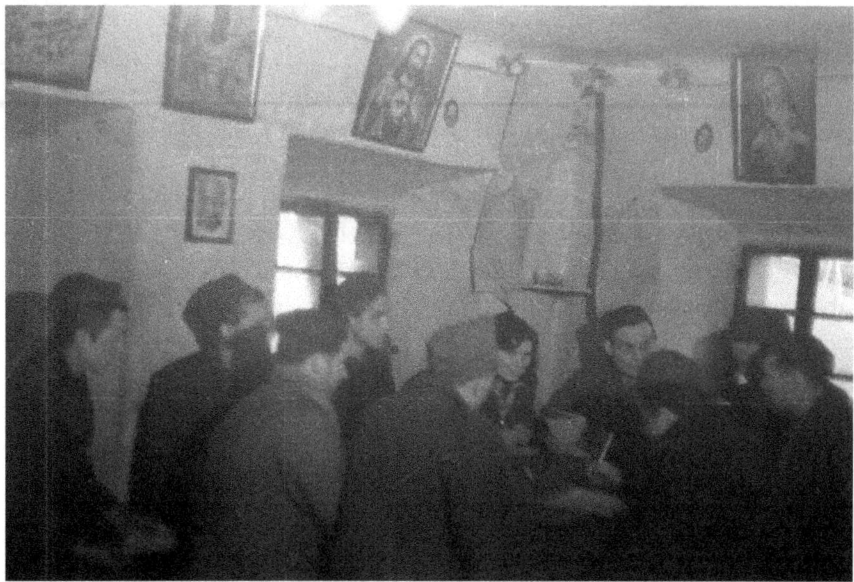

Figure 25: The political school of the XIV. Division during the German offensive, by Miloš Brelih, autumn 1943, Village at Hinje. Courtesy of MNZS.

to the complex temporality of struggle and poetry. In an expression of love, Kajuh named it "Fighter to a girl," but it was soon referred to as "Poem of the Struggle."

> Borec dekletu (Fighter to a Girl)
>
> Very different, differently one needs to sing,
> Than these accursed poets sing.
>
> Listen, girl, comrade, through whom I started to love people,
> Can you feel how my heart bleeds?
> Take, girl, with your hands my too hot blood!
> Do, please, scoop it up, you'll feel how it boils...
> This blood will sing a different poem,
> A poem sincere, and you'll be most glad of it.
>
> This poem will be a poem
> Of sincerity and work,
> Of life and death,
> Of fear and heroism
> A poem of love
> And a poem of hatred
>
> In this poem there will be a passionate desire,
> How to grab this damn life by its neck.
> This poem will be the poem of millions,

This poem will be the struggle,
Because it grew from my blood,
Because it grew out of dead bones.

From the ultimate struggle when people were killed.[143]

Kajuh's poem departs from the most intense feelings of love for a female-comrade and also love for his existential engagement in the Partisan cause. Such intense feelings of love and political determination are not pure – if they were, they would postulate a figure of the 'beautiful soul' of a fighter. Rather, the fighter's courage is combined with fear and hatred towards fascism. Kajuh's poem expresses a need to sing very "differently from how these accursed poets are singing." Devilish poems and songs are juxtaposed with the poem of emancipatory struggle. The latter shall make possible a path, it will demonstrate how to "grab this damned life by its neck," an allusion to Majakovski's poem "At the top of the voice," in

143 Special thanks to Darko Suvin who helped me with the translation of this poem into English. The original is rhymed, for details see below:
Čisto drugače, drugače je treba zapeti
Kakor pojo nam ti vražji poeti.

Čuj dekle, tovariš, ki v tebi sem vzljubil ljudi,
Kaj čutiš, kako mi srce krvavi?
Zajemi si, dekle, z dlanmi te moje prevroče krvi!
Daj, prosim, zajemi, saj čutiš, kako mi kipi ...
Ta kri ti bo pesem drugačno zapela,
Pesem iskreno, saj take boš najbolj vesela.

Ta pesem bo pesem
Poštenja in dela,
Življenja in smrti,
Strahu in junaštva
Pesem ljubezni
in pesem sovraštva.

V tej pesmi bo strastno hotenje,
zagrabit za vrat to prekleto življenje.

Ta pesem bo pesem milijonov,
ta pesem bo boj,
zato ker je vzrasla iz moje krvi,
zato ker je vzrasla iz mrtvih kosti,
iz mrtvih kosti
v boju poslednjem ubitih ljudi. (in Paternu 1995, 334).

which the poet is ready to step with his heel on the throat of the poem.[144] The last two verses sharpen the self-reflective function of the poem, which grows out of the struggle and out of blood. The temporality is evidently future-oriented ("this poem will be the poem of millions") and will become the struggle of millions that will "grow out of my blood" – thus relating this future to the present-day activity of the poet and the Partisans. At the very end there is a twist to the future past dimension: this poem shall grow from "dead bones" and all the dead still to come before the struggle and war is over. The People's Liberation Struggle is interpellated – or rather interpellates resistance, revolt and revolution on a global scale.

This dark representation of the dead enters into a tense relationship with both the poem and future struggle, and even more so with a departing verse of love and affection for the girl. On second thought, the poem's author started loving the people around him and the world again, when he fell in love with the comrade girl. It is thus both love for the girl and love for liberation that position this poem ambivalently. If anything, then the not-yet-existing political dimensions and the poem's not-yet-fulfilled love dimension relates to this ambivalence. As Komelj argues, the not-yet-existing is not about "the absence of concrete realisations, but the effect of all concrete realisations in a temporal tension that established the perspective of the 'ultimate' struggle as present" (Komelj 2008, 192). Kajuh is, despite the barbaric circumstances (see Figure 26) and necessity of blood, still able to express the anti-war attitude of this new, coming world. The Partisan does not follow the maxim of all imperialist wars fought only in the name of 'peace,' only for wars to eternally continue, in a battle for control and domination over land, resources, capital and people. The gesture of Kajuh in this poem is the opposite: it signals the future perspective of the last struggle; it is in the name of an 'ultimate war' for the cessation of all fascist and imperialist wars that this struggle is fought. It does not base itself on the logic of a presupposed racialised and national enemy, as evoked by the fascist logic of war. This anti-war Partisan logic operates on the basis of a Hegelian double negation, the "negation of negation," in the first sense negating the frame of imperialist war, but also in presupposing its own negation, through the perspective of the 'last' struggle.[145]

144 Komelj (2008, 435) and Cesar (1993) mention the major influence Mayakovsky had on Kajuh, the latter even dedicating one poem to Marx's photo and Mayakovsky's verse beneath the photo. I must thank the long conversations I had with Komelj on the strong relationship of Partisan poets in Yugoslavia with their Soviet avant-garde counterparts (from personal correspondence, 2018).
145 In this sense, Partisan struggle is staged on the proletariat horizon; that is, the proletariat not as an objective working class, but a peculiar class as "non-class," which will abolish class

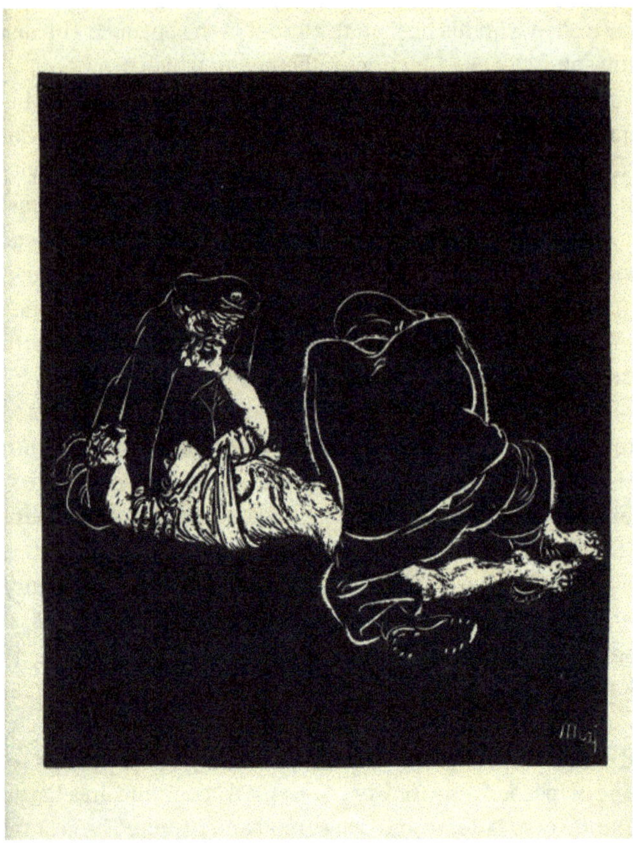

Figure 26: *Rapists*, linocut by Dore Klemenčič-Maj. From the graphic portfolio *In the Name of Christ's wounds,* 1944. Courtesy of MNZS.

2.4.4 One anthem splits into many: Agitators, women, struggle

On hearing the word anthem, one immediately associates it with a peculiar melody and words, i.e. with the symbolic representation of one's own nation-state. As is the case with any anthem, from its more liturgical origins to periods of national awakening, it is seen as an important performative part of the process of imagining and then "imagined community" (Anderson 2010), creating and recreating it through rituals and various media. Kelen (2014) conducted extensive

society, and with it, oppression and also itself as a class. For a detailed view of this Lukacsian interpretation of Marx see Balibar (2007).

research on the role and ways in which a particular poem – anthem – performs an ideological effect that weaves together and builds community. In short, singing in the same space, or in distant spaces, means the coming together of very different members in community. This performs and enacts the community itself.[146] Moving to the more specific context of war, anthems have been designed to fuel and increase patriotic feelings, from the marches of armies using drum tactics as they storm enemy troops to the phenomenon of anthems that relate to specific parts of the army. Think of the American military, for example, which gained a US Air Force hymn, US Navy hymn, US Marine hymn as well as the general US Army anthem.[147] What the military context of war provides is a well-orchestrated army of corps with direct calls for limbs, organs and a body, with a properly adapted musical accompaniment. Anthems represent the military's *body music politic*, which expresses the specific division of labour and the importance of each part of the general army, of which all parts are finally consolidated. The metaphor of the conductor and orchestra resonates with the political body being led (i.e. conducted) by the supreme sovereign who all parts, soldiers and citizens should obey.

At first glance, just as with the emergence of nation-states, one could also argue that national and popular liberation struggles during the twentieth century developed their own military poems and anthems. Yet I will claim that there were two major differences that should be ascribed to the (different) constitution of community-in-resistance as well as to its poetic creation of anthem. What struck me in the Partisan poetic material was the multiplication of anthems. "Anthems" proliferated, from an anthem for the specific unit, battalion or brigade (e.g. the "Anthem of the Venetian Brigade"), to the conventional "Artillery Anthem." There were also different anthems played to the revolutionary government AVNOJ during its inauguration (e.g. "Hej Slaveni"[148] and poems dedicated to Tito). There were also a series of generic Partisan anthems (e.g. Pintarič's "Partisan Anthem" and Kajuh's "Our Poem"), an anthem to historical personality and revolt (e.g. "Padaj silo i nepravdo")[149]; but also the

146 For details on the Partisan singing community and its reactivation today see Hofman (2016).

147 For the lyrics see: http://militarysalute.proboards.com/thread/728/service-songs-hymns.

148 This became an unofficial anthem of Yugoslavia, but was inserted in the constitution in 1988 on the brink of Yugoslavia's dissolution.

149 Matija Gubec (a major peasant hero of a revolt in 1575 for Croatians and Slovenians alike) or Matij Ivanić (the hero of the island of Hvar who, beginning in 1511, led a major revolt for several years against the entire Venetian Republic) were taken up and used as the titles for Partisan brigades, but also transformed into anthems for those very same brigades. Probably the most famous of all were the poems that refer to Matij Ivanić, such as *Padaj silo i nepravdo* (*Fall Authority, and Injustice*), which was re-appropriated in the twentieth century song *Slobodarka* (lit. *Freedom Giver*). See https: //hr.wikipedia.org/wiki/Slobodarka.

"Anthem of Women," "Anthem to Agitational Theatre," and the highly popular working class and Soviet Union's "International." In the more specific republican context, there was the example of the Slovenian anthem "Zdravljica" (by France Prešeren, the nation's greatest poet), the already forgotten "Slovenian anthem" by Anton Lavrin from 1944 and many others.

The proliferation of anthems speaks of the liberatory character of the plurality of Partisan voices that were equally contributing to the creation of a new Partisan republic. These anthems pointed to the horizon of the new Yugoslavia, which was based on multiple anthems but that did not follow a single 'interpellation' of individuals as 'citizen-subjects' into one 'nation-state' under the rule of one person (Tito). It is here – on the constitutional level – that we find the fundamental difference from the sovereigntist model: the Partisan anthem implies unity through a multiplicity of subjects, groups and positions. "Brotherhood and unity," formalised as a major slogan for the new Yugoslavia, cannot be understood without taking into account the fact that there was not one general anthem that would rule them all. There was neither a Yugoslav nation, nor a Yugoslav language. Any survey in 1941, 1943 or 1945 among the Partisans or Partisan leadership on the question of the Partisan, national and/or Yugoslav anthem would quickly show that there was no consensus on such an issue. Rather, strength was to be found in the multiplicity of anthems contributing to (the anthem to) the People's Liberation Struggle. Such anthems rather than the unity of 'nation' enunciate the position of the oppressed and the occupied who mobilise both past struggles and figures and who already speak from the future of a 'new world.' Finally, it is noteworthy that not all of these anthems were new: some of them were appropriated from the previous popular legacy of local resistance poems, while others made caricatures/parodies of or expanded (through parasitising the melody and musical score) on international revolutionary poems and songs. I will translate and briefly analyse three anthems, because they were able to expand on, think and commemorate the rupture on the emancipatory horizon. These three anthems are *Women's Anthem* (1941); *Anthem to Agitational Theatre* (1942) and *Partisan Anthem/Why Poems* (1943).[150]

"Women's Anthem" has quite a fascinating historical trajectory, even if the date of its inception is difficult to pin down. In Yugoslavia, women communists adopted the song in 1937 (Apih et al., 1976), but it was taken from the Soviet context, from Eimlers's film *Counterplan* (1932), for which Soshtakovich wrote a musical score in order to commemorate 15 years of the October Revolution. The original's lyrics are very different, whereas "Women's Anthem" clearly focuses

150 All these poems are in the edited volume by Paternu et al. (1995, 1998).

on women's emancipation. Before WWII only a tiny minority within the feminist communist struggle knew the poem, but this would change in November 1941. It was in the first liberated republic of Užice that the anthem received its earliest massive reception, since it was printed in the first Partisan songbook, *Antifascist Songs*.

> The bitter and dark past is disappearing behind us
> putting a century old dream behind us,
> we women are all black from slavery
> but we approach the day freely now.
>
> And also a woman, who has suffered the most
> up until now
> has joined in the struggle now and is raising
> her fist for more beautiful days.
>
> We call all women to the struggle,
> so let our voice be heard in the city and in the village
> we build a brighter future
> so let us sing a song at the top of our voice
>
> And also a woman, who suffered the most
> up until now
> has joined in the struggle now and is raising
> her fist for more beautiful days.[151]

---

151 My translation. See also: http: //kombinatke.si/Pesmipdf/zenska_himna.pdf
Za nami je temna preteklost,
za nami stoletni je san,
me žene iz sužnosti črne,
v svobodni zdaj stopamo dan.

In žena, ki molčala
je doslej vse dni,
zdaj v borbi dvignila je
pest za lepše dni.

V borbo vas kličemo žene,
naj čuje nas mesto in vas,
gradimo si lepšo bodočnost,
zapojmo si pesem na glas.

In žena, ki molčala
je doslej vse dni,
zdaj v borbi dvignila je
pest za lepše dni.

This poem soon became a popular song and spearheaded the political agency of the Women's Antifascist Organisation. Many women saw the liberation struggle as a historical opportunity and a major step forward from the traditionalist role that women had had in the Kingdom of Yugoslavia and all over the world. Partisan women received the political right to vote, and to be voted for, and for the first time in history they were able to fight with arms. This anthem clearly resonated with the collective path to the new free world that liberated all working women and especially those that "suffered the most for us" in terms of intersectional modes of exploitation and domination. Patriarchal ideology was particularly strong in rural areas, which went through a thorough social transformation during WWII. Partisan women and the AFŽ had a decisive role, becoming fighters and educators and leading the path towards emancipation (see Figure 27).[152]

The second anthem I would like to analyse is called "Anthem to Agitprop Theatre." This poem was written by Janez Kardelj[153] and carries a strong politico-aesthetical clarity aimed at answering the key questions of Partisan art: what is to be done for Partisan art (and not only for agit-theatre), and how is it to be done? The anthem crystallised as a result of a one-year process of cultural activities in the liberated zone around Kočevje (in southern Slovenia). Kardelj led a group of six other Partisans and cultural workers who organised cultural meetings, recited poems with a guitar and told agit-stories in the villages of Stari Log, Grintovec and others.[154] Additionally, this cultural group was preparing to perform some of the first Partisan theatre plays, for which the renowned poet Matej Bor contributed his first Partisan play *Heavy Hour*. The group, however, never staged these plays since in May 1942[155] it was interrupted by a fascist offensive. All the members of the cultural group – except for the poet Ivan Rob – died in the *Roška ofenziva* and it was only a year later that the *Agitprop Theatre* was formed, producing and performing their theatre plays. In addition, the *Theatre of People's*

This is a Slovenian version of the Women's Anthem that was translated by Vida Levstik, a theatre actress and an activist of the Women's Antifascist Front, who adapted the song and also conducted a women's choir. It was published in April 1944 in the collection *Pesmi za mladenke* (3).

152 In recent years in Slovenia, the women's self-managed choir Kombinatke adapted this song and also called for all "conscious men" to join the struggle for women and universal emancipation.

153 He was a brother of the more famous, major ideologue of the Communist Party of Yugoslavia, Edvard Kardelj, a left hand of Tito, who later wrote extensively on the theory and practice of self-management.

154 See Kraševec-Igor (1985, 32).

155 For details, see the online interview and documents: http: //www.Partisantheatre.si/index.php/the-agit-prop-theatre/.

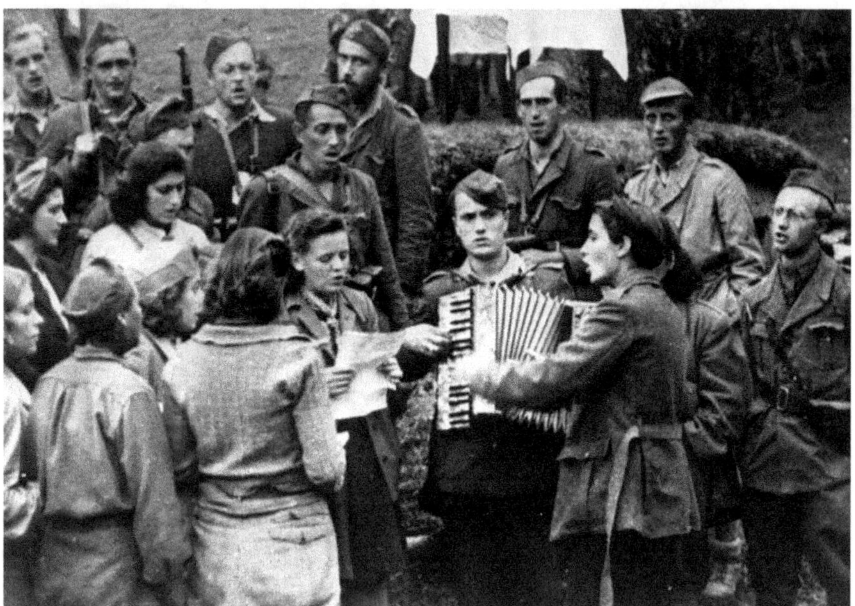

Figure 27: Performance by the cultural group of the XIV. Division, Kostja on the accordion. Jože Petek, summer 1943. Courtesy of MNZS.

Liberation, which was experimenting across liberated territories in Bosnia and Herzegovina, was very active from 1943.[156] I will argue that this was their anthem in that it drew strongly from the first experiences of the cultural production and dissemination of the oppressed, and articulated an ambitious expectation for Partisan art.

> *Anthem to Agitprop Theatre*
>
> We are all here Partisan–actors,
> Our home is nowhere, our stage everywhere.
> We are comrades by our fighters' side,
> Now we are here, sorrow somewhere else.
>
> Our words will not enlighten full-fed
> Conceited masters in the theatre boxes,
> Not in footlights but in deep forest,
> They touch the heart of a fighter hero.

---

156 See Milohnić (2016) and especially the figure of Vjekoslav Afrić and Žorže Škrigin who were the main motors of the experimental nature of the early theatre and performance of people's liberation.

Green forest is now our auditorium,
The floodlight – the moon shining from the sky
Nothing is more valid than Partisans' thanks
More than all the applause of the bourgeois world.

When the evening forest cloaks in darkness
And through it a secretive whisper runs,
Then through the night between the rocks
Echoes the free flight of our words!

And even if the distant voice disappears
Like shooting stars from the night sky,
Even then thousands sing within us

We are like the beat of one big heart.[157]

This poem touches on practically all the major topics that can be still seen as pivotal for social and aesthetic transformation in any struggle. Its programmatic nature – agitational theatre has an openly propagandistic character – does not exclude the author from profiling 'contingent' moments in the cultural process: everyone can be Partisan actor or artist (contingent agency); our home is nowhere – our stage *everywhere* (the contingent space of home and of performance); Now we are *here*, tomorrow *somewhere else* (the mobility of space); against the masters/the elite's

157 Mi vsi smo tu igralci – partizani,
naš dom nikjer, a oder naš povsod.
Borilcem smo tovariši ob strani,
sedaj smo tu, a jutri spet drugod.

Besede naše siti, domišljavi
Gospodi v lozah glave ne vedre.
V teatru svetlem ne, temveč v goščavi
junaku – borcu dvigajo srce.

Zelena hosta nam je zdaj dvorana,
reflektor – mesec ji sije z neba
in nič več nam je priznanje partizana
kot ves aplavz buržujskega sveta.

Kadar zvečer v temo se gozd odeva
in vanj zaveje tajnostni šepet,
takrat skoz noč med skalami odmeva
besede naše svobodni polet!

In dasi v dalji se izgublja glas
kot zvezd utrinek z nočnega neba,
a vendar tisoči pojo iz nas
smo kot utrip ogromnega srca! (In Paternu et al. 1998, 257).

audience – Partisan masses' applause (against a homogenous bourgeois audience, heterogeneity and the openness of the masses). This contingency that pins down and explores a further surplus over the war situation does not fall from the sky and would be impossible to conceive of without the liberation struggle. The liberation process made this radical contingency necessary.

More concretely, the anthem addresses the elementary modality of Partisan cultural work, which needs to be in constant flux, day and night, in city and village. At the same time, Partisan artists and cultural workers need to be inventive, they need to conceive new "floodlights" and use the "moonlight sky," or a small fire in the deep forest that can count on the additional play of shadows around the fire.[158] Furthermore, the anthem conveys a strong farewell to established institutions, abandoning the bourgeois canon and audience, while Partisan artists discover their stage being deterritorialised – anywhere. This does not mean that there was nothing before Partisan culture emerged and that there were no leaders in the Partisan movement. In the early stage, there were various more-or-less-established pre-war artists that joined the Partisans and contributed in a major way to their execution of ideas and of further experimentation by modest means. Nevertheless, these artists also had to 'unlearn' a large part of their previous cultural engagement and practice the maxim that "our stage is everywhere" in the liberated territories and in the illegal underground. Imagine small events in basements, or those theatre performances that took place in stables with minimal light and in whispers because the enemy was just a few hundred metres away (Milohnić 2016). This capacity and awareness of the modality and space of intervention relates to another key dimension: the specificity of Partisan cultural production and dissemination. Anyone who had the talent or desire to become a Partisan cultural worker or artist would be taken on board. Partisan artists then participated in creating and addressing their new audience: people from the villages and fellow Partisans and fighters. The author of the poem stresses that their recognition mattered more than the "applause of the bourgeois world." This was a proper coming together of the masses and Partisans, where various established artists, anonymous poets, amateur designers, actors and singers created the struggle's cultural means. And lastly and most importantly for the purpose of the counter-archive is the concluding highlight of the time of silencing and the "disappearing voice" of Partisan resistance. Despite the distance and gradual disappearance of cultural performance, song and theatre play, the echoes reach

---

158 There are many examples of how inventive cultural theatre workers were, from designing and creating puppets from various materials (for details on puppet theatre see Gerlović 1979) to making clothes for actors in Molière plays – even from Allied parachutes (Milohnić 2016).

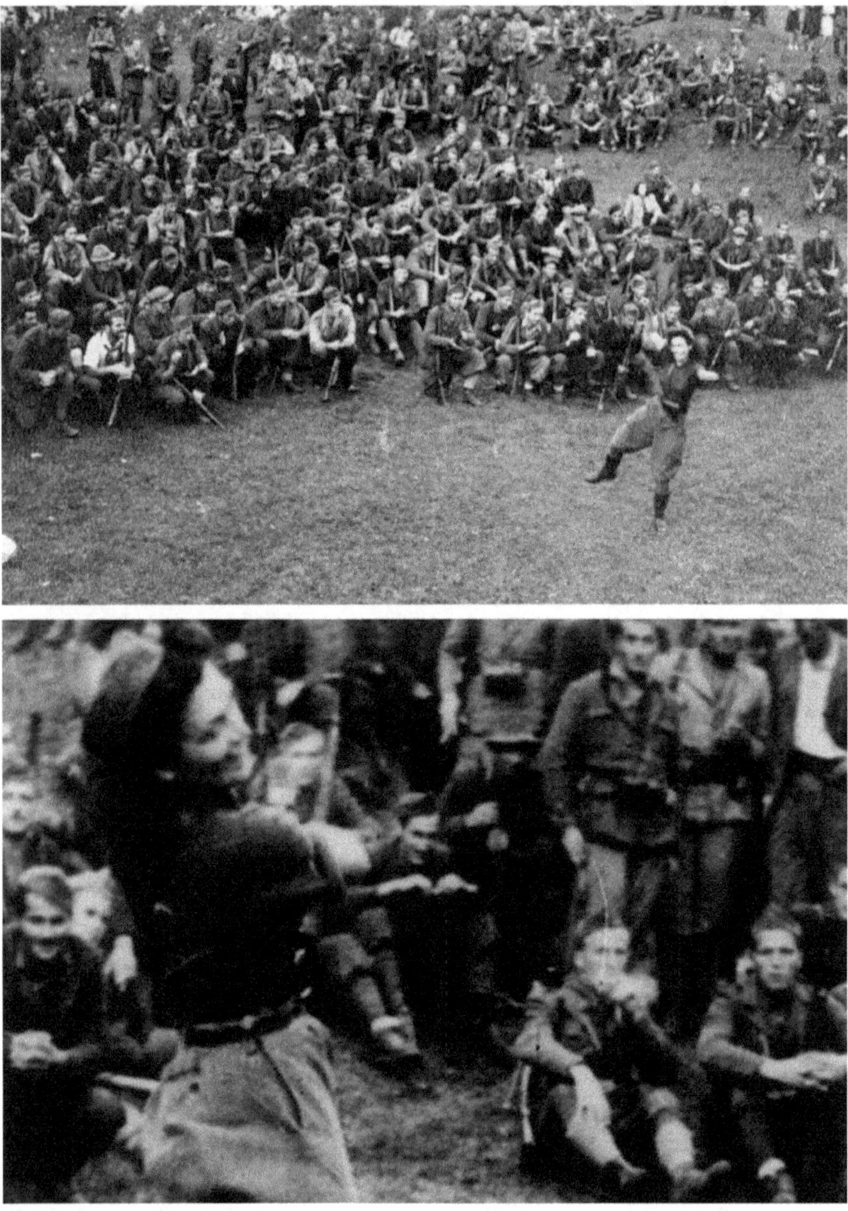

Figure 28a, b: Marta Paulin-Brina dances on the occasion of the oath and the foundation of the Rab Brigade, 23 September 1943, Mašun. Photo by Jože Petek. Courtesy of MNZS.

and extend to yet another multiplicity of voices, when the "thousands sing" and unite in the "beat" of the heart of resistance. Deleuze and Guattari's notion of the "monument to revolution" points precisely to such echoes and visions that bring together community-in-resistance, performing and living in the Partisan community.

The anthem to agit-theatre might not have been read by Marta Paulin-Brina -she was a great fan and a close friend of a partisan poet Karel Destovnik-Kajuh- yet I would claim that her Partisan performances are the most striking realisation, materialisation and re-mediation of the poem (especially anthem above) into dance. She was a modernist dancer before the war,[159] and entered the cultural group of Partisans. On one very symbolic occasion Marta Paulin-Brina was invited to perform. She struggled with the question of how to dance among the Partisans and especially before the Rab Partisan Brigade's inauguration,[160] which consisted of liberated survivors, among them dozens of Jews, who had survived the concentration camp on the Italian-occupied island of Rab (after Italy's capitulation). The event was fuelled by the symbolism of a homecoming and a struggle for freedom after the horrific experiences of a concentration camp. Marta Paulin-Brina's self-reflections on Partisan cultural techniques best explain her dance performance (see Figure 28a):

> I became a dancer, where nature became my stage. Instead of a wooden stage with boards I now dance everywhere. The feeling of balance becomes again a 'problem'; the musculature works differently, because one time the leg was searching for support on stones, another time on soft ground. This was the first thing that I observed. But then came more. This immense natural space gives you an opportunity and demands the expansion of movement. From a small move and gesture in the closed theatre one then creates a whole march in the open plane on a natural stage. This is also how dance moves could become big, clear and broad, that is, if I wanted to somehow command this huge space and establish myself in it. I also danced alone. Maybe my co-dancer in the hour of creation was most left on his own, away from all artists, because he had to realise my thoughts without any external help. Alone with his own mind and from his own body 'this something' had to be created. A conventional and unpersuasive ballet 'grace' would immediately wither away in nature, it would even become comical. In our case there was no so-called ballet in the broad sense of the word, but we could speak of a dance expression that was rooted in the liberated floors, with human participation in its historical creation of a nation or people. It was about

159 She attended the school of modern dance in Ljubljana run by Meta Vidmar who gained a licence from the internationally known school in Dresden (Wiggins). Brina was one of the brightest and the most talented dancers who established herself just as the war was starting (Milohnić 2018). For details on early modern and Partisan dance, especially on Kraigher, see Vevar (2017).
160 The Rab Brigade was formed after the capitulation of Italy and when internees of the major Rab concentration camp, among them many Jews, were released and a large majority of them formed the new brigade(s) (Romano 1980).

> participation in the liberation struggle of a people that knew no despair and that was aware of its strength and historical mission. Dance calls for struggle, and in this struggle, it is winning; it unties in joy; because of struggling and of constant efforts, because of power, because of the very historical act. In this dance circle we could all give each other a hand. Ours was a closed circle: in efforts and in suffering, in the midst of sighs and smiles, laughing – we were closely bound together. When I became a dancer, I found myself standing alone in front of the mass of fighters. I had this awareness of what I could do with my gift for dancing and my weak body, but how I could express that something, that which assembled us and brought us together? How would I be able to command this expanded disproportionate natural space? Suddenly, I felt an immense power in my legs, when I stood and pushed down hard on the ground of the earth. The hands felt the deep horizons of forests and were walking and climbing over the top of its trees. In my dance there was no imitation that could be related to formalistic moves. I rejected almost everything that I had learned in the years of my dance school training. I searched for dance expressions, original and fresh, which emerged from the human need to move. I found it in the game of balance, in balance with dynamic, rhythmical and voluminous dimensions, in tension and relaxation. Dance expression was a consequence of internal engagement. That I found this correct language of movement was only possible because of *people* and the *Partisan poem*, which was understood by everyone.[161]

Marta Paulin-Brina's self-reflection expresses one of the most profound wisdoms of Partisan dance and art that I would sum up in the following way: despite being highly skilful in modern dance techniques, she had to first 'unlearn' these techniques and relearn to dance under the new conditions in front of a new audience. Thus, she had to meet and experience all the unexpected varieties of landscape and at the same time carry a deep awareness of the mission. She was there for the people and because of the people, bearing in mind and body the task of liberation, while also trying to invent new artistic forms and practices. The performance was a 'surplus' from her past engagement as a dancer and a radical consequence of her 'internal engagement.'[162] Perhaps Paulin-Brina's performance could be best read as a lived anthem to Partisan dance.

---

161 Marta Paulin-Brina (1975, 25–26), my emphasis and translation. She was also inspired by Partisan poetry, most closely by the already mentioned Kajuh, who was her close friend in the XIV. Division and with whom they agitated and performed before the public at cultural meetings. She danced for half a year among Partisans only to lose her toes due to the harsh winter during the Partisan march in 1944.

162 Marta Paulin-Brina was not the only dancer among the Partisans. For instance, even during the war another woman named Živa Kraigher from the School of Modern Dance was performing a fixed choreography in Slovenia. She was active on the front, while she also worked on her dance secretly in the studio during the war. In her memoirs she writes that both the intensity of the Partisan experience and her reading of Matej Bor's poetry collection *Previharimo viharje* (1942) brought her to idea of thinking up and practicing for her own performance. Kraigher also admits that she did not want to perform her dance piece for a long time, as she felt it needed more

The last poem for the counter-archive represents one of the deepest poetic expressions of the whole Partisan struggle, and speaks from that impossible space of revolutionary temporality, between the past and future, thus evoking the complete intensification of the Partisan rupture. The poem was written by Pintarič-Švaba (1924–1942) and bears the title "Čemu pesmi?" (Why Poems?).[163] The original was lost during the war and the poem only survived as a German translation. Franc Pintarič-Švaba was certainly not a renowned poet – neither during nor after the war, but his personal tragic story deserves our attention. He was a fighter in the Štajerska Battalion and on 23 August 1942 he was poisoned by a local Nazi collaborator and died on the way to the Nazi encampment. No image remains of him, no real biography and no grave. All we have are his personal notes, which, as it turned out, were his poems. We do not know whether these poems were recited to the Partisan battalion or perhaps read silently during long nights with his fellow fighters, or even just by himself. There remains no memory, no testimony to this. Yet it is a historical fact that Pintarič's notes came into the hands of the Nazis, who with the help of the same collaborator who had poisoned him, translated them into German. They hoped to uncover important information on the morality of the movement and on the identity of Pintarič's fellow Partisans. Instead, as we will read, what they received were some of the most striking verses of Partisan poetry in memory. These poems remained in Nazi hands, and by a curious irony of history they survived in a Nazi archive, and only as a German translation. I should also add that the second family name of the author – Švaba [*Schwaba*] – is a Slovenian and also Serbo-Croatian derogatory term for a German. This only strengthens the profoundly tragic dimension of the fate of the poem and the irony that it would end up in Nazi hands. After the war, the Partisans confiscated part of the archive belonging to the Nazi occupation forces. These records were then moved to the archive of the new socialist republic where they remained practically invisible. In 1987, however, some 45 years later Boris Paternu et al. edited a large body of Partisan poems and also translated Pintarič's poems. Yet at the very moment the poem(s) finally appeared in Slovenian, ready to address the Partisan rupture once more, the bloody end of Yugoslavia

---

maturing. Thus, it was only first presented in 1953 and entitled "Resistance" (*Upor*). To think about conceiving one short performance of 5 minutes in a working process that lasted 10 years in the contexts of both during and after liberation would be something practically impossible in the current post-Fordist precarious and instantaneous conditions of artistic labour (Kunst 2015). I have to thank Bara Kolenc for this mention. For details, see Vevar's introduction to Kraigher (2017).

163 For a solid interpretation of this poem see Komelj (2008, 189, 342–343, 551). For more on Pintarič's other poems see Paternu et al. (1998, 294–297).

was readying itself and with it yet another denunciation of the Partisans by old local collaborators dressed in new clothes. This ironic moment reflects the failure of an historical mission: the real addressees of the poem are the future Partisan generations, but the historical context and absence of a critical-affirmative contextualisation had already disappeared. It seems that this historical coincidence corresponds to the specific paradoxical temporality inherent in the structure of the poem.

Why Poems?

We wrote poems in different times,
When we had nothing else to do.
But today,
When justice belongs to those in power,
When weapons do the talking,
Our poem is loud and clear:
'We want to live, to live freely in a free land.'

This poem of ours is our guidance,
It is our anthem.
Victims are falling for this poem
– innocent victims –
And they are falling by the thousands.

When this poem becomes a reality,
When freedom approaches in all its light and power,
Come forward, you poets and writers!
To the victims fallen for this poem –
(Write) poems of eternal glory and memory.[164]

Franc Pintarič-Švaba wrote this poem in the early summer of 1942, when the situation on the military front at home and abroad could still be viewed as one of defeat: Axis forces occupied the entirety of continental Europe and parts of Slovenian territory were annexed to the Third Reich at that time. The anthem,

---

164 Komelj had already refined the Slovenian translation, and I took the liberty of putting the text into poetic verse form:

V drugih časih smo pisali pesmi, ker nismo imeli drugega dela. Danes pa, ko je pravica na strani močnejšega, ko govori orožje, je naša pesem dovolj glasna in jasna: 'Živeti hočemo, živeti svobodno na svobodni zemlji.'

Ta naša pesem je naše vodilo, je naša himna. Za to pesem padajo žrtve – nedolžni – padajo tisoči.

Ko bo ta pesem postala resničnost, ko se bo svoboda približala v vsem svojem sijaju in moči, tedaj na plan, pesniki in pisatelji! Padlim žrtvam za to pesem – pesmi neminljive slave in spomina. (Komelj 2008, 551).

nevertheless, is directed against the tragic reality of this situation and attempts to elaborate the question written by the first Partisan poem, printed in December 1941 and directed at all Partisan artists (and poets). The famous poem *Veš poet svoj dolg?* ("Poet, Do You Know Your Duty?") by Oton Župančič was a call to take a (Partisan) side in the struggle. Similar political solicitations to poets (and artists) were very common in Partisan poetry. One key text in this vein was the call to arms written by Karel Destovnik Kajuh, which was also one of the earliest. His 'first' Partisan verses were written on the eve of the Nazi invasion of Yugoslavia when he called on poets to "sing today, like bayonets sing in the struggle. Poets need to spark the flame that is lit in people's hearts" (Kajuh in Paternu 1995, 207).

The higher duty of each individual and poet was then to go to battle using any and every means. I would argue that such calls to arms are most fully developed in Pintarič's poem, and are even the essence of the vocation of Partisan poetry. The very title of his poem "Why poems?" typically advocates that in times when weapons do the talking, words in turn should also become weapons. But what if one entertains the option of translating the poem's vocation in a slightly different manner? "Čému pesmi?" also means "Poems to What?" This title opens a different perspective by posing the following question: Who does the poem speak to and to what purpose is it addressed? This is no longer a simple call, not the mere duty of the poet to speak to others about the Partisan struggle; it rather addresses the Partisan struggle itself and offers one path to 'formalise' the rupture that took place during the war. This is an anthem that was written in and because of the Partisan struggle and it participates in the process of changing the existing state of affairs.

Such self-reflexivity offers a multi-layered view of temporality. As mentioned above, what is striking here is the temporal impossibility that is structurally inscribed in the poem and its vocation. The poem is first related to the past, *per negationem*, to earlier poems, poems that were written in a time of leisure and can no longer satisfy the demands of the 'vocation' of poetry. In the final paragraph, the poem refers to the poems of the future, poems, which will (only be able to?) commemorate the Partisan struggle. However, the gist of the anthem is concentrated on present impossibility, in the way Partisan poetry participates in the struggle to 'free' the land. This not only differentiates between the different vocations of poetry, but is also itself articulated from a paradoxical point in time; it evokes the perspective of the future, of that which does 'not yet exist' – or, in Pintarič's words, the perspective of the 'free land' to come. This is highly self-reflexive poetry that dramatises the tension between the past and future – both times of 'romanticism' (peace and glorious heroes) – but speaking from the position of the Partisan present. This is a poem that is a Partisan anthem engaged in the Partisan struggle, in its very interiority. A revolutionary situation necessitates a call to "overtake oneself towards the future" (Žižek 2008b, 460), which demands that one thinks and acts as if the future already existed, and thus effectuates the transformation before it takes place in reality. One dimension to this specific temporality therefore has to do with affirming something in the future, as if it has already come; but there is another side, and this side has to do with retroactively asserting that whatever has been asserted will be achieved. Žižek (2008) takes this conception of temporality from both Lacan and Badiou, who connect it to the *futur antérieur*. It is not enough for a revolutionary event to simply take place: in order for it to take hold it needs to be named, intensified on the one hand and retroactively acted upon in the future on the other hand.

Such a complex temporality is weaved into the very fabric of direct speech and communicates by way of prosopopoeia whereby the anthem gives voice to and impersonates the struggle itself: "We want to live, to live freely in a free land." This is one of the most precise formulations of the political maxim of Partisan struggle and it consists of three steps: firstly, against the regime of fascist death and murder, Partisans decide to live; secondly, life is affirmed not in its subjugated, controlled or obliterated form, but as free existence; and, finally, Partisans want to live freely in a free land. This seems an elementary formula but can also be universalised and seen in many other anticolonial experiences and subaltern subjectivities throughout the twentieth century. If struggle could speak or even be declaimed as a poem, it would impassion itself as a call to counter-interpellation, a poetic performative that goes against the apparatus of fascist occupation and the collaborationist tendency that either called for subjugation (and the obliteration of difference) or remained in the privacy of a pragmatic silence and empty expectation.

Pintarič's poem demands that future poetry replace the anthem when freedom comes. The future of poetry is now tasked with reciting and memorialising the glory of past struggle. Can it then be said that the Partisan anthem ultimately dissolves in nostalgia or in the socialist realist commemoration of the Partisan struggle? This invitation to future poets seems to dissolve the very vocation of poetry advocated within the foundation of Pintarič's poem. In other words, the future poems would be placed in the service of commemoration, whereby revolutionary weapons would be transformed into state weapons or ideological vehicles conveying the glorious aspects of past struggle. This would mean that new poetry would only reflect the memory agenda of the (new) state and would be relegated to the state archive. But then again, the relationship between future poems and a future political entity is not discussed in Pintarič's poem. Future poems can and should warn both against the forgetting of the past and explore Partisan struggle by other means. If we do not uphold this task, such experience will be lost for us despite being – or even by being – duly archived.

The anthem signals the immanent failure to commemorate what remains to be realised and hence what cannot be fully closed off. Is not the key characteristic of the anthem precisely its 'artistic' disappearance through its realisation as a political goal? Could we say that it will disappear the moment the land is freed? Within the Soviet avant-garde, new art was thought and realised through its very disappearance, but also through becoming an integral part of reality (a form of life) itself. Thus, if Pintarič's anthem was written solely for the purpose of liberation, it is clear that in the times that come after war and after the occupation ended, there is no need for it, for it is a fait accompli. This anthem remains a disturbing reminder even if freedom was formally obtained, be it in socialism or capitalism. The poem points to the never fully attainable character of universal emancipation and as such it traverses the specificity of any specific historical period. It is written for all the revolutions to come, which is why it is forever unfinished – the poem is a fait à accomplir. Without new struggles and the new poetry of such struggles, Pintarič's poem really disappears. If this section concludes with a peculiar temporal and poetic impossibility to commemorate the rupture, I will work on the peculiar and precarious (in)existence of Partisan film in the following section.

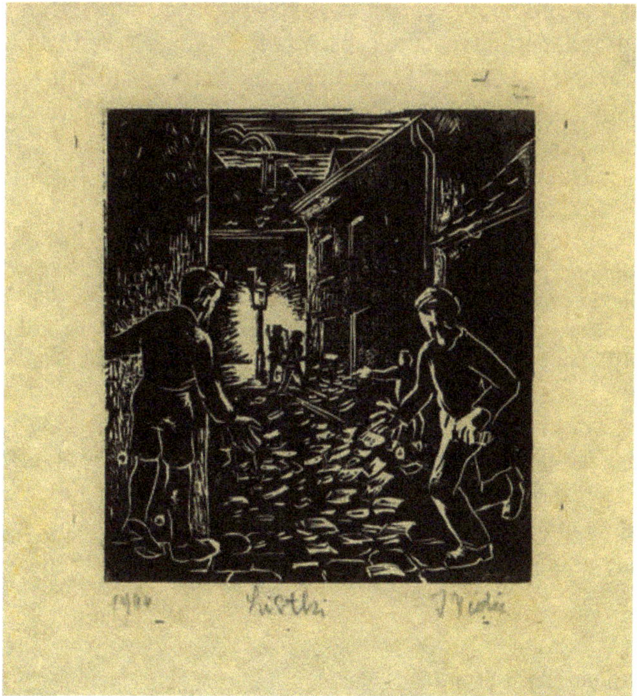

Figure 29: *Leaflets,* linocut by Janez Vidic. Courtesy of MNZS.

2.5 Between Partisan film documents and Partisan film "by other means"

Partisan film remains an under-researched field, and this is true for three main reasons. Firstly, Partisan troops did not have access to the necessary material means – i.e. cameras and any kind of film studio or laboratory. This was the result of a wartime context, and it was only after the liberation of Belgrade in October 1944 that this situation gradually improved. Yet to say that the Partisans did not have any material means would be incorrect: there were a few cameras circulating that the Partisans smuggled into the liberated zones from the pre-war period: some cameras and other materials were confiscated from the occupying forces. Still, it was exceptional for a typical Partisan unit to have a camera at their disposal. This activity was reserved for a very small number of individuals who were working for cultural units or propaganda sections as part of the liberation struggle.

Secondly, up until 1943, the use of cameras was politically restricted. The reasoning behind this restriction was designed to protect people: photographs or films could betray locations and serve to identify Partisans. This material could, and did, become a dangerous weapon in the hands of the occupiers and collaborationists. It served as a means of prosecuting Partisans' family members, taking them as hostages and/or deporting them to concentration camps. Nevertheless, despite the evident danger, the General Command of the Partisan struggle still had a need to document the conflict. The first decree for the Partisan archive was signed by the famous Jewish communist and Partisan Moše Piade, who on 20 October 1942 wrote that each Partisan unit should collect:

> a) one copy of each publication (a newspaper, booklet, leaflet, or any other cultural or other material) and also all future publications [...] b) one copy – of all photographs of our struggles and from behind the front, also the confiscated enemy's photographs [...] each photo needs to state who or what it represents, when and where it was taken, and from who this photo was taken [...] d) texts of Partisan poems and folk songs from the uprising.[165]

Piade's text is a first direct reference to an 'archive of the uprising,' which seeks to document not only the fight against fascism but the uprising itself (see point (d)). In reality, one can speak of more consistent photographic documenting of the struggle from 1943 onwards (within the propaganda units),[166] while Partisan film activity came to be consistently used only during the time after the liberation of Belgrade.

165 Quoted in Kurs (Miletić and Radovanović 2016, 106).

166 See Brenk (1966). For a recent publication on Partisan photography and archives see also the new and impressive book by Konjikušić (2019).

Dejan Kosanović (2003) argues that the first decree for the creation of a film division was passed on 5 December 1944, which was also the same period when the production and editing of the first Partisan newsreels appeared. There were other Partisan film documents that emerged before that, but many of those were lost and destroyed.

Thirdly, the precarious existence of Partisan film has to do also with one central assertion of film scholars, namely that Partisan films can be best described as "film documents" (Kosanović 2003), or as mere propagandistic newsreels, and as such possess no real intrinsic aesthetic value (Brenk 1979, 62). Most of the existing Partisan films are named as "Partisan film documents" (e.g. in the Archive of the Republic of Slovenia), and if we take a glance at these films, we gain the apparent impression that they are raw material.

2.5.1 Partisan film cases: Lost forever or found after the end?

Since the registry of Partisan films is rather poor and hard to find, this section first gathers some surviving fragments, including those documents scattered across various film archives in the former Yugoslavia. I will highlight a handful of cases from the first more spontaneous stage of Partisan film (1942–1944) and the second phase that belongs to institutionalising film activity after the liberation of Belgrade (1944–1945).

In 1942 and 1943, a Partisan by the name of Dušan Kveder-Tomaž shot the first important film footage, which was recorded on the Pohorje front in Slovenia on 8 mm film.[167] The Nazis destroyed all of the material in their offensive against Partisan forces in Gorenjska in 1943. During the same period, the first film footage was shot on the territory of Bosnia (Volk 1973). Kosanović asserts that the latter was more of an individual effort than a collective organisational one. He dates the first film footage to November 1942, more specifically to the first meeting of AVNOJ in Bihać, where Nikola Popović shot a film with a small 9.5 mm camera. He continued to film, but unfortunately everything has been lost.[168]

More lively cinematographic activity took place in Slovenia in the time from the capitulation of Italy up until October 1943, when the German offensive pushed Partisan forces back. Three Partisan filmmakers – Miloš Brelih, Čoro Škodlar and Božidar Jakac – documented the military and political events within the NOB: the Partisan assault on the major White Guard (Slovenian collaborationists) fortification in Turjak; the first meeting of the Slovenian Council of the Liberation Front in

167 Brenk (1975b, 119).

168 For a detailed view, see Kosanović (2003, 212–213).

Kočevje: the 9 October and later trials against the national traitors (collaborationists). These are also the oldest preserved Partisan film documents from the times of the NOB and are accessible in the Archive of Slovenia, found mostly in the post-war edited film "Partisan Documents" (Viršek 1965, 1972).[169]

Subsequent important film activity has been documented by Mihailo Švabić, who argues that an anonymous Partisan from the proletarian brigade systematically documented the liberated zone of Drvar and the meeting of the Communist Youth in April and May 1944.[170] Ana Peraica recently uncovered this anonymous Partisan, after discovering nine long-lost Partisan film tapes in her grandfather's sealed bunker.[171] Her grandfather, Antonio Peraica, worked for the Italian Cinecittà before 1943. After the capitulation of Italy, he joined the overseas brigade and the Partisans. Ana Perajica explains that he became the first Commissar for Film in the First Proletarian Brigade. Most of the film material consists of shots of Partisan marches and wounded Partisans, demolished cities and towns, but also some portrayals of everyday life in the liberated territories and the aforementioned meeting of the Youth Organisation.[172]

During 1944, Partisan filmmakers in Slovenia mostly used German confiscated 8mm cameras. The most exciting and innovative films were made by a talented photographer, Čoro Škodlar, who made his first full-length report on life during and between battles as part of the Partisan Ninth Division. Ambrožič remarked, "Škodlar filmed all units, on the march, in action, at work and occupied with different duties, also when resting."[173] He made photographic portraits of different Partisans and also of the Partisan hospital Franja. One of the most impressive pieces of footage comprises the Partisan attack on the fortification of the Home Guard at Črni Vrh above Idrija on 1 September 1944. Much of this material was sent to Moscow, and some speculate that it remains either in the archive of Samara in Russia or in the Krasnogorsk Archive.[174]

In the autumn of 1944, we enter the second stage that I name *institutionalised Partisan cinema*. On 7 October 1944, the Executive Council of the Liberation Front in Slovenia announced the formation of the Division for Film and Photography. France Brenk became the head of this section and immediately set to work on organisational activities. Continuous and more frequent air connections with the

---

169 Brenk (1975b, 119).

170 See Kosanović (2003).

171 Perajica published part of the restored documentary material with her own documentary *Take Care of the Film* (1945/2012, directed by Antonio/Ana Peraica).

172 From my personal correspondence with Ana Peraica.

173 Ambrožič, jr. (2008, 291).

174 From my personal correspondence with Polona Balantič.

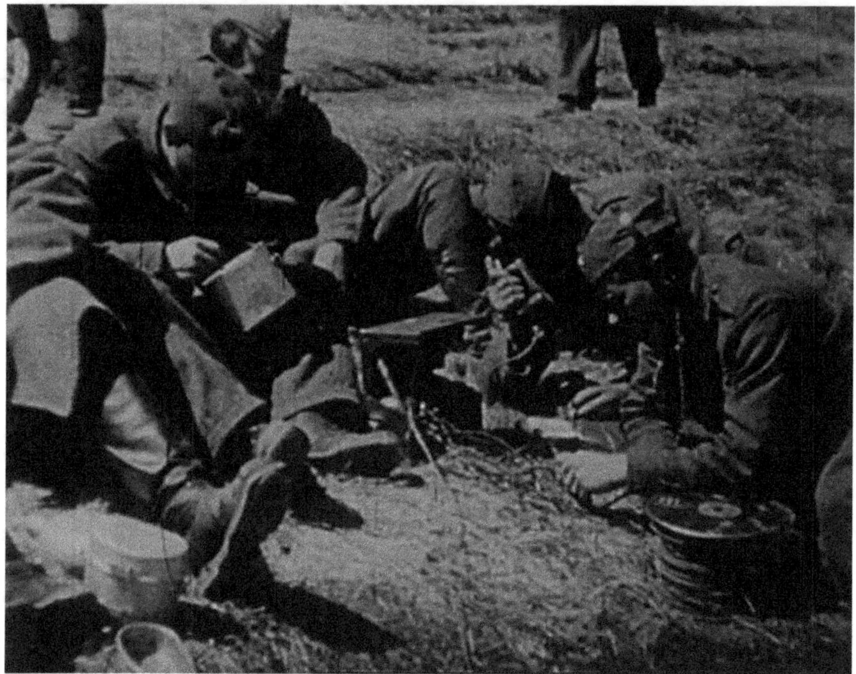

Figure 30: *Partisans During the Break.* Courtesy and source of the material: the Slovenian film archive at the Archive of the Republic of Slovenia, SI AS 1086, stills from the film *Partisan Documents 1941–1945*, Založba Borec, Ljubljana, directed by Stane Viršek.

Allied forces enabled the section to acquire more film material. Božidar Jakac, Čoro Škodlar and Stane Viršek filmed many events.[175] The figures 30–32 are taken from Stane Virsek's *Partisan Documents 1941–1945* and show a few impressive moments/actions of the partisans. Most of these films were developed only after the war, whereas in Črnomlje, in the liberated territory, a Partisan cinema operated from 1944 onwards.[176] The above-mentioned footage survived. It consisted of 1563 metres of 8mm film and in 1946 it was transformed in Zlin's laboratory (Czechoslovakia) into the normal 35mm format,[177] and is accessible in the Archive

175 As can be seen, the following titles suggest various events were filmed: *Transport of the Wounded, Srednja Vas, Allied Aid, Construction of the Bridge on Kolpa, The Coming of the Oversea Brigade to Bela Krajina, Manoeuvres of the First Slovenian Artillery Brigade in Suha Krajina, Transport of War Material and Wounded with Allied Aircrafts, Funeral of American Pilots, Evacuation of the Civilian Population* and *The Partisan March on Trieste, Sušak and Rijeka.* Some shots of the liberation of Trieste were made in colour. For further details, see Brenk (1975b), Duškovič (1988, 17), Nedič (1989) and Šimenc (1996, 57).

176 Golubovič (2009, 33).

177 The original documents were published in Brenk (1979, 53).

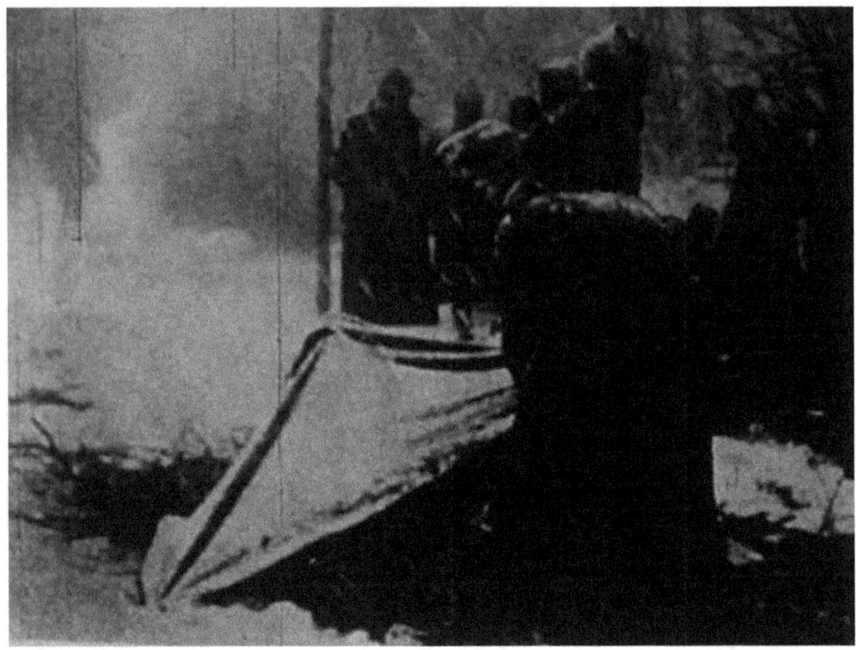

Figure 31: *Heavy Snow, Partisan Tents*. Courtesy and source of the material: the Slovenian film archive at the Archive of the Republic of Slovenia, SI AS 1086, stills from the film *Partisan Documents 1941–1945*, Založba Borec, Ljubljana, directed by Stane Viršek.

of the Republic of Slovenia. Later, Božidar Jakac gave the Archive of Slovenian Television his own personal collection of Partisan films that, in addition to *Partisan Documents* (400 m or 43 min, SLO 1972, directed by Stane Viršek) and *Partisan Documents 1941–1945* (1965), represent the oldest and also most valuable conserved material.[178]

After the liberation of Belgrade, the General Command issued a directive on 5 December 1944 for the formation of a Film Section in Serbia.[179] Radoš Novaković,[180] who had already worked tirelessly on film-related activities, was put in charge of the section. In January 1945, Vasiljević filmed the first Yugoslav newsreel that circulated in the liberated territories and was first screened in Belgrade. A very important assignment of the Film Section was given to Stevan Mišković,

178 Brenk (1975b, 120).

179 For a more detailed view, see Savković (1994).

180 He also filmed after the war and wrote some scripts for films on the Partisans, as did other Partisans such as Gustav Gavrin, Kosta Hlavaty, Nikola Popović, Žorž Skrgin, Franc Kosmač, France Štiglic etc.

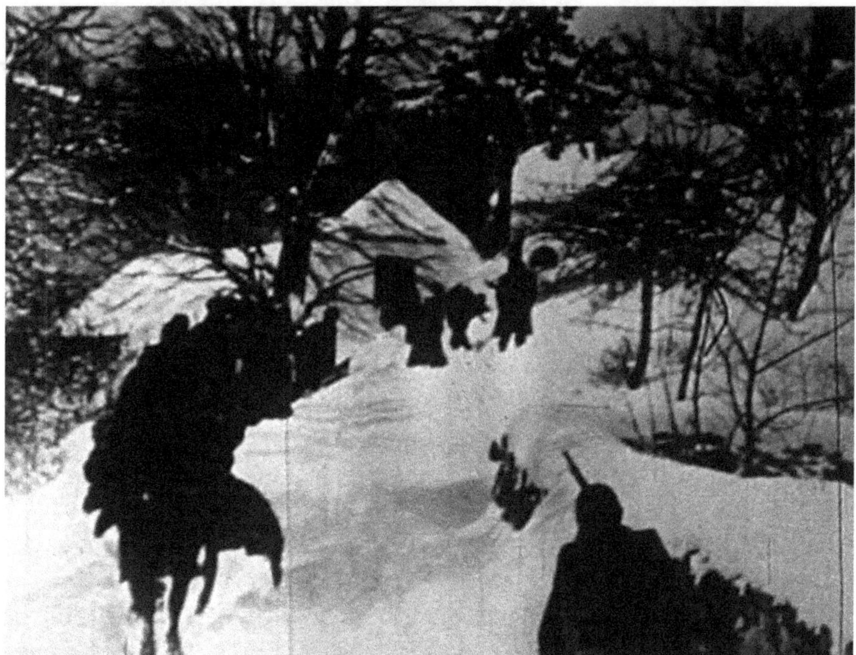

Figure 32: *Column in the Snow.* Courtesy and source of the material: the Slovenian film archive at the Archive of the Republic of Slovenia, SI AS 1086, stills from the film *Partisan Documents 1941–1945*, Založba Borec, Ljubljana, directed by Stane Viršek.

who had to document the fights in Bosnia. The Chetniks confiscated most of his material, while some of it was later developed incorrectly. The Film Section of Serbia imported hundreds of films from the United Kingdom and the Soviet Union and guaranteed their distribution and screenings. They had to completely reorganise and renovate the majority of cinemas or set up new improvised ones. Anton Smeh recorded a film documenting an Antifascist women's organisation in Sarajevo (number 6 newsreel), the arrival of the Sixth Partisan Division in Sarajevo and also the People's Council of Romanija [Romanija is a mountain in eastern Bosnia and Herzegovina] (number 8 newsreel). All these films are conserved in the archive of *Filmske Novosti* in Belgrade.

On Croatian territory, Kosta Hlavaty[181] and Oto Hervol made the only Partisan animated film on 16mm film that is accompanied by birdsong. Together with other cultural activists, they screened Partisan films in Croatian villages in the

181 In 1945, Hlavaty, in cooperation with Gustav Gavrin, shot the first documentary on the biggest concentration camp in Yugoslavia (*Jasenovac*).

region of Kordun (Škrabalo 1998, 134). Ana Peraica speaks of Karel Ravnić who, apart from being the commander of a Partisan unit, also used a camera to film. Unfortunately, this material was lost in nearby Korenica.

Ljubljana was the last city to be liberated after Trieste on the 9 May and two film crews covered her liberation. The first crew consisted of Stane Viršek, Franci Bar, Ivan Zalaznik and Janez Pogačnik who made the film *The Liberation of Ljubljana* (1945). The film crew of the production-company Emona shot the second and more famous documentary, in which Milan Kham organised a group of experienced cameramen comprised of Rudi Omota, Metod Badjura, Janko Balantič and Marjan Förster. They fixed the camera onto a car and filmed *Ljubljana Salutes the Liberators* (1945).[182] Some film material on the liberation of Trieste is still accessible in *Filmske Novosti* in Belgrade, while most of this footage can be found in the Archive of Slovenian Television in Ljubljana.[183]

From a strictly aesthetic point of view, one cannot speak of film proper, but of Partisan film documents. Yet then again, I would ask, what is essentially a Partisan film, and what does it mean to make film in such circumstances? In what way does one make a Partisan film? By what means? These questions prompted the interest in the Partisan counter-archive and were guided by Pavle Levi's definition of "cinema by other means" (2012) in order to 'unearth' different cases and intermediary forms of Partisan film. What Pavle Levi's book covered is, to a considerable extent, the history of avant-garde film experiments that show that proper 'cinematic effect' was only achieved through other artistic practices (i.e. through other means). Film was accomplished through theatre, design, photography and painting. According to Levi, the series of intermedial forms and experiments performed cuts and redefined what the field of cinema and film really consisted of (ibid., 25–46). If avant-garde artists experimented with early forms of media and produced intermedial works in the fervour of social and cultural change, then the WWII conditions of scarcity made Partisan artists experiment with the matter and means at their disposal. As will be shown below, the Partisans used minimalistic

182 Vrdlovec (2010, 162).

183 It is worth mentioning that some very important documentation material was produced by the Allied delegations and war-journalists during the diplomatic expeditions and cooperation with the Yugoslav Partisans. Perhaps the first film footage was made by the British film-maker Max Slade (*First Movies of General Tito*, UK 1944), and later his short film *Partisan Outpost* (UK 1944), Francis Burges' *The Nine Hundred* (documentary drama, UK 1944) and Jack Chamber's *Bridge* (UK 1946). The Soviet journalist Solomon Kogan probably made the documentary material *Liberation of Bihać* (UK 1945) and some other films in Bosnia. In 1945, the Soviet director and journalist Jelusin perhaps made the most important film for future research. It was simply entitled Yugoslavia (SU 1945) and combined confiscated German material with the Soviet and Partisan film archive.

means and other art forms, especially photography, poetry, literature and design to experiment with Partisan film. What follows are six case studies of Partisan film using other means.

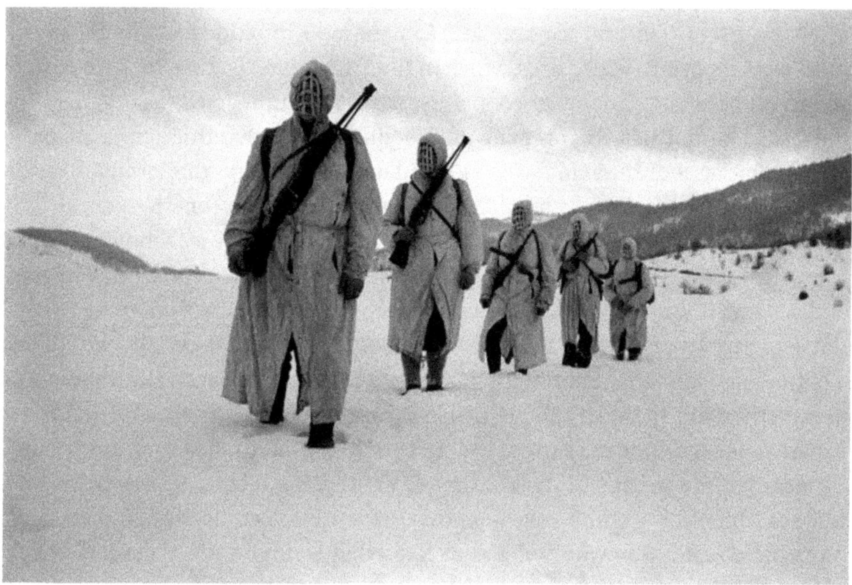

Figure 33: Partisan patrol of the Notranjska detachment, photo by Edi Šelhaus, winter 1944/1945, Babno Polje. Courtesy of MNZS.

2.5.2 Partisan sounds of resistance as the first film inscription

The very first Partisan film to use 'other means' dates to 12 December 1941. It was during this evening that the very last cultural performance of the Academic Choir France Marolt took place in the Italian-occupied Ljubljana, at the Union Hall. The choir succeeded in masking the anti-occupation event under the guise of cherishing Italian culture. The Italian commissar was present at the event and did not at all like what was happening. The very last song on the programme list was *Lipa zelenela je* (The linden tree is becoming green). This represented an important step in the Slovenian national awakening, as the last verses conclude with: "Sleep, sleep, oh linden tree, but you will not sleep forever, as green spring will bring new blossom blossoms. Again the birds, the happy birds will sing us our songs, whistle our songs." One of the members of the choir, the Partisan poet and lawyer Dr. Lev Svetek recollects:

> After we performed each song, there was major applause, but after the very last poem *Lipa* there was an enthusiastic hurricane of loud screams and applause [...] this was not a mere cultural event but a direct expression of political resistance [...] and at that moment I saw the Italian commissar accompanied by a civilian leaving the hall [...] The next day the Academic Choir was dissolved by the High Commissioner Grazioli."[184]

After this event, cultural workers and groups were forbidden, while those cultural workers sympathetic to or active in the Partisan resistance took an oath of silence, that is, they no longer cooperated in any cultural activities organised by the fascist authorities.[185] This song did not only echo down through testimonies but became part of the real Partisan counter-archive due to the formidable skill and courage of the film technician Rudi Omota.[186] At the time he was already a member of the Partisan Liberation Front and worked as a technician in the company Emona Film. As a technician with access to certain scarce film material, as the concert was to last only twenty minutes, he needed to find an additional three hundred metres of material. Firstly, in order to get enough tape, he created a cutting machine that cut the original 35mm film in two. Secondly, he was able to secretly plant the microphone inside the chandelier in the Union Hall a day earlier. Once the concert started, Omota closed himself in the room, from where he recorded the sounds of the resistance. Thirdly, the recording was made on a trace of film track – which was his proper invention (i.e. inscription on magnetophon tape). It is noteworthy that this musical inscription was recorded on split 17.5 mm film tape, which was a major step – unintentionally – for the technical discovery of inscribing sound directly on film: a discovery that developed globally only after WWII. Thus, the first Partisan moving image in Yugoslavia was equivalent to moving sound, i.e. a film recording of sound. Instead of the moving images (visual signifiers) Omota recorded and produced moving words (poetic signifiers). The entire reconstruction with the original recording of this event can be seen in Štader's documentary film on Rudi Omota.[187]

---

184 For a lengthier testimony of this event and a detailed overview of the cultural activities of the choir see http://www.apz-tt.si/en/o-zboru/zgodovina/1926-1941/.

185 The call for cultural silence in January 1942 by the Liberation Front meant that there should be no collaboration in cultural affairs. Ljubljana was one of the biggest resistance cities in occupied Europe, where a large majority population cooperated with the Liberation Front and had infiltrated the occupied apparatus. In February 1942, Italian forces erected barbwire with checkpoints and bunkers around the entire city, which remained until the end of the war (1171 days).

186 The song is now stored in digital form at the Archive of Radio Slovenia and is accessible online: https://ru-clip.net/video/JY-2Th14exI/apz-1941-lipa-zelenela-je.html.

187 Omota remained a pioneer in Yugoslav audio(ton) production, developing the magnetographic and other audio reproduction devices after WWII.

2.5.3 Partisan candid camera

Rudi Omota was a key actor in another important chapter of the Partisan film counter-archive. The event occurred on 10 April 1942 when the Liberation Front activist and member of the Communist Youth, Vilko Kopecki, raised a red flag at a Franciscan Church located in the very centre of Ljubljana. This was a night-time action, and the fascists tried to pull it down the next day. However, because of fears that the Partisans had mined the roof of the church, they were forced to perform some acrobatic feats and this gathered together a substantial number of Ljubljana's residents who observed the event with laughter. Rudi Omota and Milan Kham filmed this event secretly and lied to each other that they were shooting for purely documentary reasons. Even if they were both cooperating with the Liberation Front, the Front demanded such strict secrecy that at that point in time they still did not know that they were both members. When they developed this material, somebody from the Emona Film company denounced them to the Italian authorities. They were thus forced to destroy the very first film tape. Recently, the recording of this event has become available by means of cinematographic reconstruction.[188] Both of the initial 'films' were created with a great deal of technical skill and obviously undercover in occupied territory.[189] Most other Partisan films were filmed in the liberated territories.

2.5.4 Partisan film = photo exhibition + literary script

The material scarcity of film firmly marked out its limits, but even the absence of material and infrastructure was productively dealt with during the war. Among the Partisans, narrating past actions using film as a metaphor was quite a widespread practice. The reference to cinematic language was also utilised in many literary Partisan texts and stories.[190] To narrate and represent the intense and

188 Ljubič made a documentary about Kham, *Zadnja kino predstava* (2007; *Last Film Show*), where he reconstructed the first scene of the first Partisan film. The reconstruction of real Partisan events, places and people was a frequent technique used in films on the Partisans, see Brenk (1979, 65).

189 Milan Kham and Rudi Omota filmed several films under the command of the Nazis, such as *The Oath of the Slovenian Home Guard* (1944), *The Big National Anti-Communist Manifestation in Ljubljana* (29.6.1944), *Jelendol's Victims* (1944) and *Organisation TODT* (1944). The new government and judiciary of Yugoslavia used these materials after the war to identify and prosecute local collaborationists.

190 See Ambrožič jr. (2008, 291), for a typical literary rendering in cinematographic terms. See also the memories of the Partisan Kovačević (1959).

accelerated moments of action, the Partisan-eye transformed into the camera-eye and followed the movements. These film snippets were recreated through literary stories, but it seems as if these literary stories as well as the literary form itself were not sufficient in presenting the speed of events. I would like to include one example that expressed the desire for literary transformation in a cinematographic language and which has also become a kind of cursory film script. I will argue that this desire was not simply a desire to document the Partisan struggle more adequately, but a desire to make a film on liberation in the Partisan way.

It was a renowned writer and poet, the Christian socialist, Edvard Kocbek, who wrote the first script for Partisan film. I would claim that it is no coincidence that this happened during the high point of the Yugoslav Partisan struggle. Even though he never made a film – and he continued to use words (prose and poetry) – it is worth shedding more light on his historical-literary attempt. As mentioned in the previous chapter, in late November 1943 the delegates from the People's Liberation Councils were travelling from all the liberated and occupied territories to meet in the town of Jajce. The second meeting of the AVNOJ (Antifascist Council of the People's Liberation Struggle of Yugoslavia) declared the political autonomy of the new revolutionary Yugoslavia. Kocbek was one of the delegates and also spoke at the meeting of the AVNOJ. He began his speech with a description of a series of moving images – of how the seventeen delegates made it to AVNOJ's general assembly:

> one after another a soldier and a civilian left, an activist and then a Partisan, after the worker came the peasant, after the painter came the doctor, and after the poet came the priest. We went through numerous dangers, kilometre after kilometre, day and night, but united around a sole task for all the people of Slovenia. With us the whole people travelled, with their whole history and experiences, all their sacred goals, a people's genius. My eyes glanced over this delegation, when a characteristic glowing light appeared in front of us, a sacred figure just as in a poem by Blok. (1982, 231–232)

Kocbek does not name the figure, but the very last lines of Blok's famous poem *Twelve* refer to Jesus Christ.[191] Blok's famous poem is already asymmetrical in

191 "And so they keep a martial pace,
Behind them follows the hungry dog,
Ahead of them – with bloody banner,
Unseen within the blizzard's swirl,
Safe from any bullet's harm,
With gentle step, above the storm,
In the scattered, pearl-like snow,
Crowned with a wreath of roses white,
Ahead of them – goes Jesus Christ."

rhythm, highlighting the very dynamic of the October Revolution, while *Twelve* refers to the twelve Bolsheviks who can be seen as twelve apostles that follow the path, a departing red thread for the delegation: "All powers to the constituent assembly" (the Soviets). In the case of the Slovenian delegation, Kocbek was referring to the painstaking path of the struggle, but also to the delegation that had to cross so much enemy territory to arrive at the all-Partisan Yugoslav Soviet Council (AVNOJ).

Kocbek's most direct inspiration for a film, however, occurred just a few days earlier after he returned from a visit to the very first Partisan photographic exhibition in the Workers' Hall of Livno (see Figure 34a, b, c), where delegations from Slovenia, Croatia and cultural workers resided.[192]

On the way back to his accommodation, Kocbek met a local peasant who after the Ustasha terror action exclaimed: "The Partisans are our only hope, only they can make people live together and liberate them from the violence" (Kocbek 1982, 191). To this Kocbek added: "the old order is falling, and the rupture demands that we take a complete risk and make fundamental decisions [...]" (Kocbek 1982, 191). The impression from this exhibition[193] and his expectation of the political destiny of the Partisan struggle was left in heavy print in his diary.

> A huge number of people visited a very well conceptualised exhibition of photographs. I saw photographs that I would want to carry by my side for the rest of my life! How many precious moments will go to oblivion, if all this is lost before the end of the war! How many scenes will also go to oblivion in Slovenia! I saw the exhibition first in the group of people, but later I remained alone with these photos. I could not separate myself from this atmosphere [...] Suddenly I wanted to make a film with a friend. I would start shooting in this very space: with the camera directed to the centre of the room, showing parachutes from the Allied forces used as flags and ornaments, in between horrific and glorious photographs and docu-

---

The whole poem is accessible in Russian and English: https://kuscholarworks.ku.edu/bitstream/handle/1808/6598/BlokTwelve_RusEngTxt.pdf? sequence=1&isAllowed=y

192 The photo exhibition was accomplished thanks to the aforementioned decree by Piade, who encouraged such documentation (Miletić and Radovanović 2016, 106). This was not the first Partisan exhibition as earlier before during the Užice Republic in 1941 one exhibition was prepared for the celebration of the October Revolution, which travelled around to Požega, Gornji Milanovac, Arilje, Ivanjica, and Bajina Bašta. The Partisan exhibition was part of the first meeting of the Anti-Fascist Council for the National Liberation of Yugoslavia in Bihać. See also Dević (2018).

193 Another fascinating example of a Partisan exhibition took place in occupied Split in 1943, which "lasted for six months and encompassed around 80 artworks by eight local artists as members and sympathizers of NOB and the Communist Party: Nikola Ignjatović, Ivo Lozica, Ljubomir Nakić, Rudolf Sablić, Marin Studin, Vjekoslav Parać, Ivo Tijardović, and Antun Zuppa. From April until September 1943, the exhibition was continuously open to an audience that supported the anti-fascist movement, with an estimated 2,000 visitors." (Dević 2018, 68). The role of the exhibition was also practical since it was raising money for participating artists and fighters on the front.

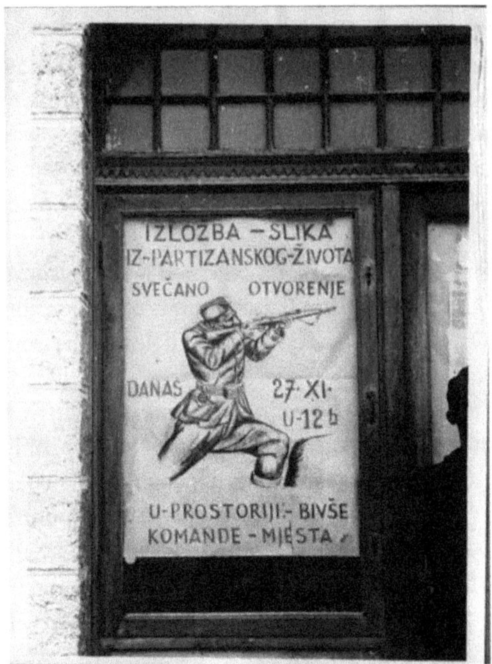

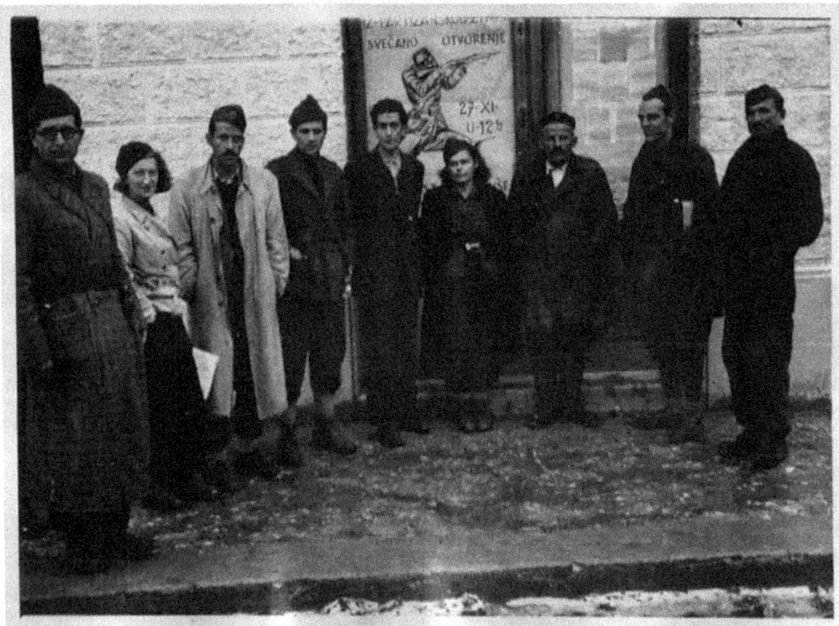

Figure 34a, b, c: Partisan photo exhibition in Livno, 27th November 1943; poster; group of artists; opening of exhibition. Courtesy of the Museum of the History of Yugoslavia (Belgrade).

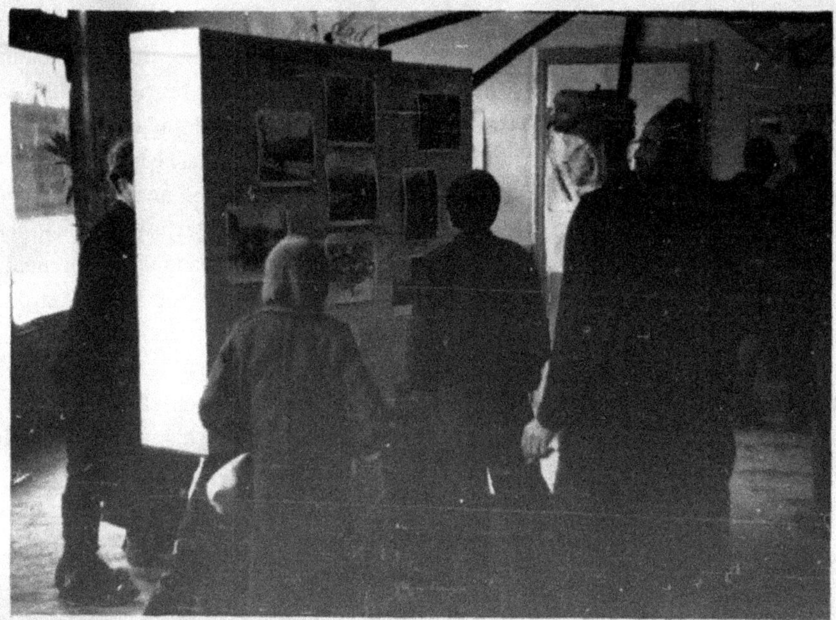

Figure 34a, b, c (continued)

> ments capturing the century old character. All this embraced by insecure and flashing lights, between mute visitors of these narrow spaces. These spaces surround the central hall, from where a mass of noises emerges incessantly. It is a real Babylon there: the youth has its choir practice, women have very important political meetings, theatre amateurs are preparing the play, whereas in the other corner the Partisans are playing pool on the green and torn table. Somewhere else, couples are holding each other, and many children are running around, as they enter the hall from the streets, because it has become dark outside. How many dark and light forces in one place! What kind of richness and feeling of being lost! Between these people there might be many enemy spies that will trigger tragic future events in Livno, this is how we might complicate the story in a tragic act in the so-called *My Film* [...]"[194]

Kocbek's script for his *Partisan Film* was triggered by Partisan travel and his visit to a photo exhibition that gathered images from different parts of Yugoslavia, from both the liberated and occupied territories. This film-related passage from his diary calls for a filmic form that has no problem with mixing a fictive and documentary dimension, of the past 'real' memory of Partisan life and the anticipation of events in the liberated area of Bosnia and Herzegovina. Kocbek also evokes details from social life that transforms the film into a thriller at the end.

194 Kocbek (1982, 515–516), my translation.

His premonition and anticipation of possible annihilation was confirmed only a few days later, when a large majority of the photographic – and some claim also film (Volk 1973) – material that inspired this script was burnt up in a Nazi bombing run on a plane that was departing on a diplomatic mission to Cairo. However, the real-existing fear of being annihilated by the fascists, and thus of also losing all of the Partisan archive that thought, imagined and documented the struggle, was not the main gist of Kocbek's demand for Partisan film. On the contrary, Kocbek did not want to simply conserve the past in some form of media that could somehow guarantee its afterlife. Rather, for Kocbek, it was his strong desire for a future film that made him move away from his favoured literary-poetic means of expression, to its expansion into another form. The time was ripe, even without possessing the material means to go beyond his own carefully kept diary and the scattered photo-material of the Livno exhibition (see also Figure 35). The name for this was the *First Partisan Film*.

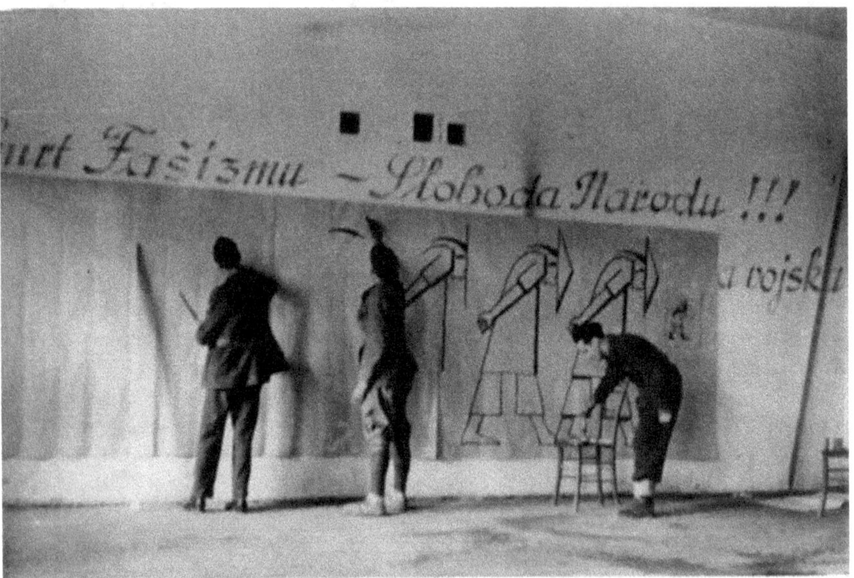

Figure 35: The entrance to the Partisan exhibition fresco-poster, which depicts Chinese peasants above them with the slogan "Freedom to People, Death to Fascism", unknown author. Courtesy of and source: znaci.net.

Just days after the exhibition and his writing the script, Edvard Kocbek became the first minister of culture in the newly formed revolutionary government of AVNOJ. As for its general orientation in matters of photography and film, AVNOJ

Yugoslavia remained predominantly, in relation to time and material used, documentarist.[195] However, even Kocbek's early fragments of the Partisan script show that he wanted to move beyond a documentarist or archivist conception. Kocbek's argument is in line with another Partisan artist, Božidar Jakac, who presented a lecture a few months later at the first congress of cultural workers of the Liberation Front in Semič, on 4 January 1944:

> When today, actually on a daily basis our eyes see a fleeting film of thousands of images and experiences all full of precious and valuable memories, everything is dependent on our experiencing and conceiving of all those moments; what kind of creation of these visible forms should be unfolded, what shall our ancestors see, how can a deeper image of our era be preserved in juxtaposition to daily reportage that is only an interpreter of events and cannot give us deeper and more permanent experiences?[196]

During the liberation struggle, this clarified an internal differentiation between documentation and a more fully developed photography and film of the people's liberation.[197] It does not mean that reportage and documentation are not important, but this new tendency articulated a need for film to liberate itself from an archivist role. Also of importance, as we saw above, the imposed borders between the media and arts, texts, photos, songs and poems and film were becoming porous. It is also true that some art forms – due to knowledge and material conditions – developed faster. Kocbek's initial reference to the Partisan photo exhibition, and its mobile variations, is not coincidental and puts forward the argument of the "cinematic effects" (Levi 2012) of other media. I will look at two such examples that might have further sparked the imagination for film.

2.5.5 Photo exhibitions with filmic effect

One of the most famous Partisan photo exhibitions in Slovenia took place on the liberated territory in the restaurant Lackner[198] in Črnomelj from 25 to 31 Decem-

---

195 See Volk (1973), who claims that the first film unit even operated just before the AVNOJ, but the film documentation was burned in an attack by a Nazi plane. Another film theorist and historian, Dejan Kosanović (2003), challenges the existence of these first films and concludes that it was instead part of the legend.
196 Quoted in Komelj (2008, 123–124).
197 France Brenk, who in October 1944 became head of the department for photography and film at the People's Liberation Council, promoted a more realistic plan for film production but that had to wait for more favourable material conditions for cinematography in post-liberation Yugoslavia (Brenk 1966, 51–60).
198 This was not just some ordinary restaurant but rather developed into a whole cultural complex that hosted exhibitions, ateliers and discussions, conferences and political meetings.

ber 1944. There were various Partisan cultural workers, artists – among them the above-mentioned Božidar Jakac – and journalists that prepared the exhibition and gathered photographs. The exhibition had its own poster (see Figures 36 and 37), flyers and even received material help from an English mission.

In terms of its reception, this exhibition was a big success: even if opened for a short time (one week) and in winter, it well exceeded expectations, since more than 1,000 visitors came to see the photos. The organisers did not want visitors to only watch the photos, but in the spirit of Soviet (film) exhibitions, they wanted

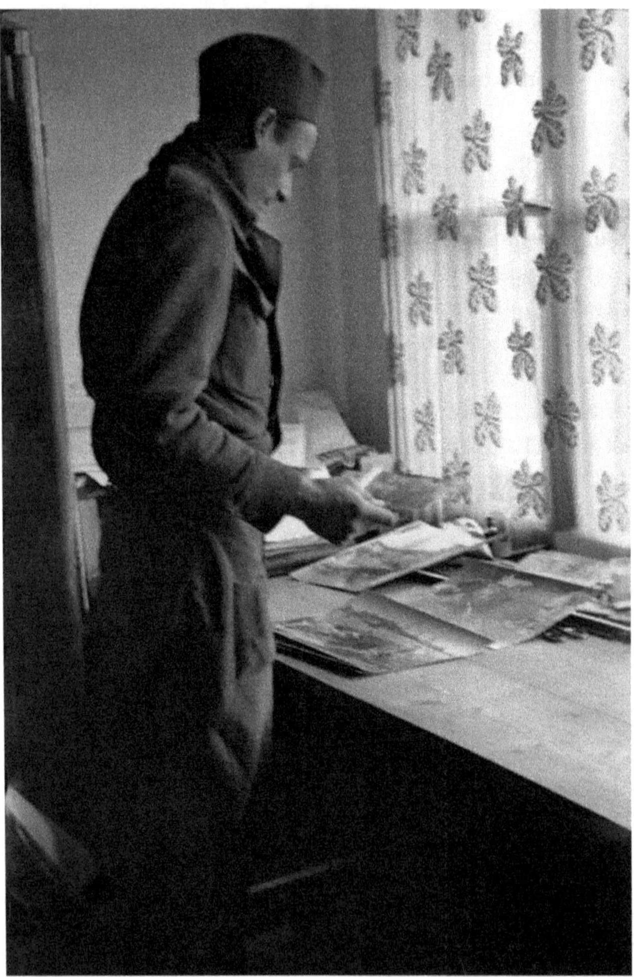

Figure 36: Workshop preparations for the photo exhibition in Hotel Lackner, photographed by Alfred Kos, December 1944, Črnomelj. Courtesy of MNZS.

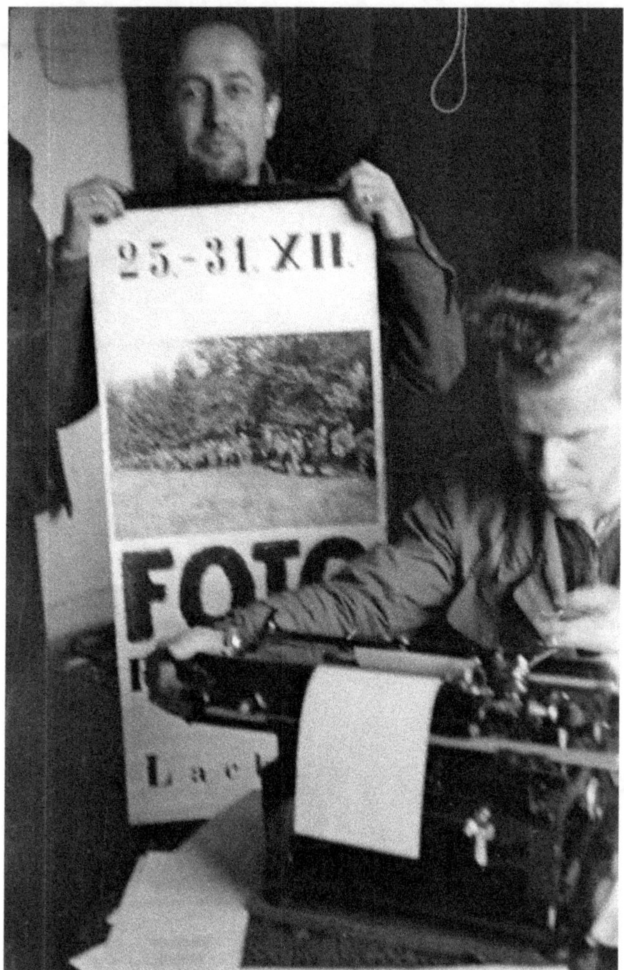

Figure 37: Workshop preparations for the photo exhibition in Hotel Lackner, photo by Alfred Kos, December 1944, Črnomelj. Courtesy of MNZS.

to engage visitors in educational purposes. The visitors were also invited to vote for the best Partisan photo (see Figure 38). The photo below won the first people’s photographic competition.

The exhibition’s constellation was rather simple. The graphic materials were provided by the English mission, while the wooden constructions were cloaked in textiles taken from the parachute of one American soldier. There were six wooden constructions (see Figure 39) that presented six different topics, into which the various photos were categorised: *Letošnja jesen* (This Autumn), *V Pohod* (Into

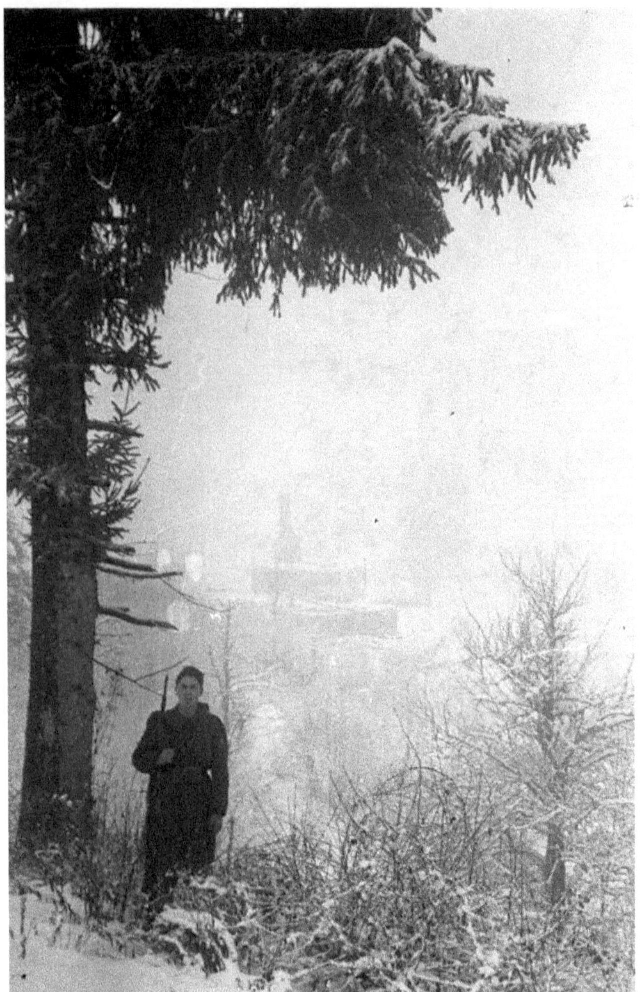

Figure 38: *Guarding Scout*, photo by Jože Bitenc, 13 December 1944, Kočevski Rog. Courtesy of MNZS.

the March), *Ruševine* (Ruins), *Ranjenci* (Wounded), *Grobovi Junakov* (Graves of Heroes), and *T* (T for Tito).

This categorisation bridged the divide between the effects of occupation (destruction, death, mutilation, ruination) and the first effects of Partisan resistance, including snippets from liberated territories and Partisan marches, as well as glimpses of future emancipation. The Partisan documentary photography often focused on destruction, misery and hunger, alongside more 'poetically' framed vignettes from Partisan life. Moving through this photo exhibition, one

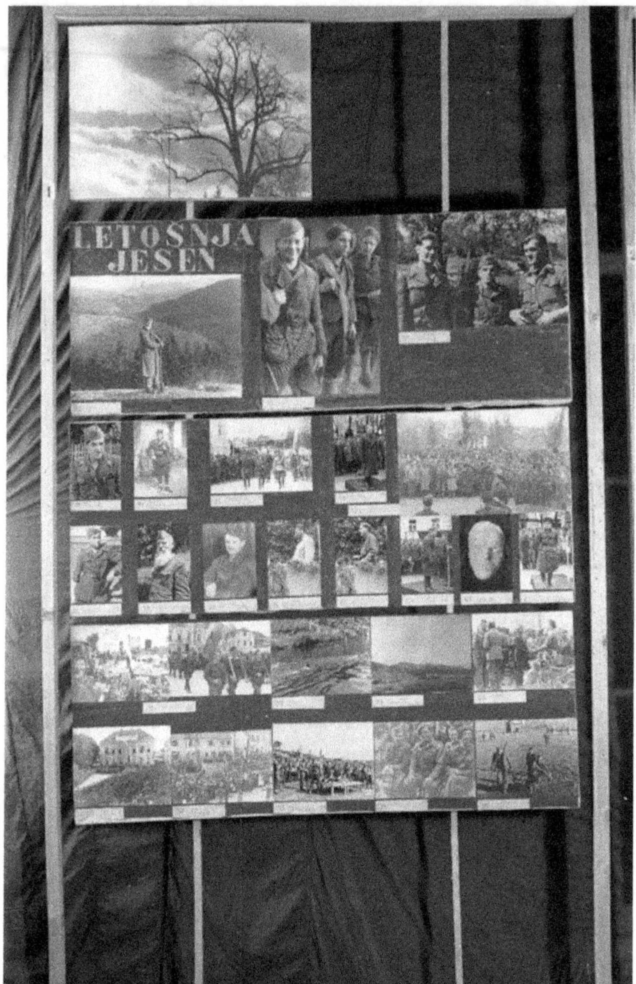

Figure 39: Photo Exhibition in Hotel Lackner, photo by by Jože Bitenc, 25–31 December 1944, Črnomelj. Courtesy of MNZS.

gained a sense of the organised people's/Partisans' gaze, as various photographers' edited photos formed a more coherent narrative and representation of the Partisan struggle. One can claim that this photo exhibition produced a filmic effect that offered a red thread of people's liberation, united by the dominant signifier – Tito's partisan leadership (see Figure 40).

The photo exhibition follows a certain Partisan convention – each cultural event was accompanied by the great leaders of antifascist alliances: Roosevelt, Churchill, Stalin – and from the Yugoslav context, Tito. One should note that

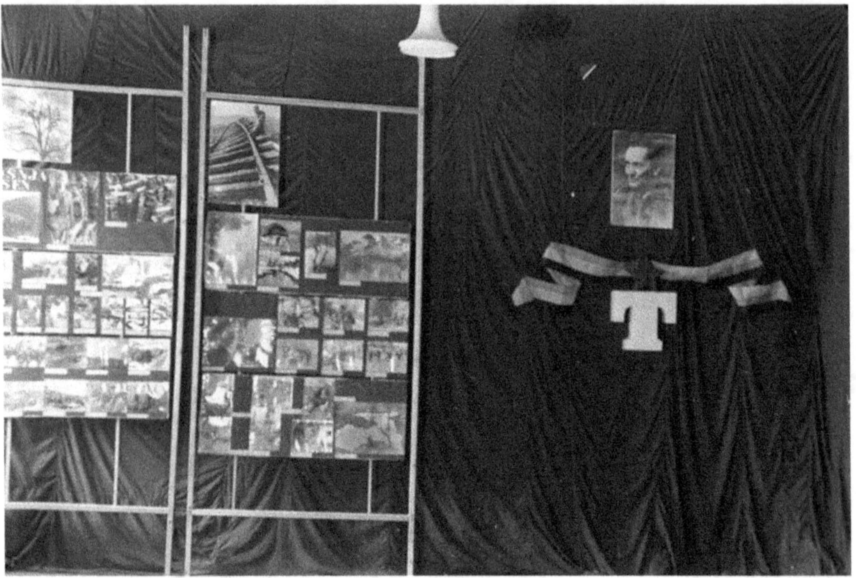

Figure 40: T (for Tito) at the photo-exhibition in hotel Lackner, by Jože Bitenc, 25–31 December 1944, Črnomelj. Courtesy of MNZS.

before WWII, Tito's name was taken as representative of an illegal and criminal organisation, the Communist Party. Anti-communism was part of the ruling ideology of the Kingdom of Yugoslavia – which made many people deeply suspicious. Furthermore, during the time of war, fascist propaganda and local collaborationist groups together with institutionalised churches spread words and images of that "leader of bandit gangs," the "Bolshevik and godless leader," who will confiscate all property. The resilience of the People's Liberation Struggle, as well as incessant cultural and political activities, made Tito's name synonymous with liberation. Instead of his painting or a photo, the somewhat terse end to the exhibition is presented by the letter T. This T ties together all the misery and enthusiasm for ending the war and defeating the enemy.

Such Partisan photo exhibitions are slightly better known within Partisan photographic history (Konjikušić 2019) and they were taking place across the liberated territories and their cultural spaces across Yugoslavia. I would like to highlight one additional format that remains under-researched, namely mobile and short-term photo exhibitions (see Figure 41). Such formats are precious since they demonstrate the deterritorialising nature of Partisan dissemination. Fabec and Vončina were the first to research such a format and explain that "mobile exhibitions consisted of 20 to 40 photographs mostly of the size 18 x 24 cm [...] and they were posted in visible spots in villages and squares in the cities" (2005, 115).

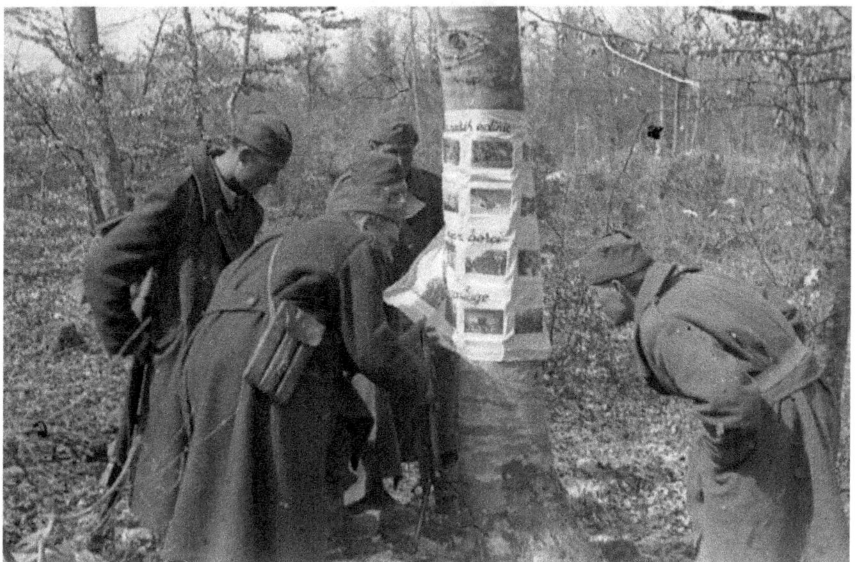

Figure 41: Fighters of 1. Battalion of the X. Brigade looking at the photos of a mobile exhibition installed on set on surrounding trees, photo by Milan Štok, 25 March 1945. Courtesy of MNZS.

These photos could be seen by local villagers, townsmen and Partisan troops, but also by enemies – they could be seen by anyone in that area. This gesture exposed precious material in a certain way and it also clearly demonstrated the presence not only of the Partisan resistance, but also of Partisan art.

Furthermore, if one speaks only on the level of circulation and the specific form of Partisan dissemination, one could say that the most appropriate cultural forms and formats of Partisan art were undoubtedly found in mobile photo exhibitions and mobile theatre groups that travelled around the liberated territory. The mobile theatre groups were especially successful in moving people and contributing to new Partisan performances and the dissemination of works and practices. If organisation and the editing of photographic material produced proper filmic effects in audiences, these mobile photo exhibitions pointed to invention – experimentation with the mobile format of the exhibition and photos thus went on the march with Partisans.

2.5.6 Partisan film = design + poetry

A widely accepted thesis in scholarship on Partisan art (Stepančić 2004) claims that Partisan graphic art was the most expressive and elaborate art form of the whole Partisan struggle. Its concrete materialisation stretches from drawings, caricatures, engravings (wood cuts), to bronze embossing and all kinds of imprints – found in Partisan publications, leaflets and posters. Indeed, the imagination and experimentation of Partisan artists and technicians were fully demonstrated in these new ways of printing, acquiring elementary material by scraping floors in houses and workshops (since linoleum and wood were often used). Since Partisan production and dissemination was conditioned by scarcity, this also nurtured an ethics of collective sharing and collective anonymous creation – mobility in use[199] – that was juxtaposed to the pre-war bourgeois regime of private property and invidual authorship. In terms of quantity we can speak of around 4,000 graphic works that were produced in Slovenia during WWII (Bassin et al., 1966). Graphic art was undoubtedly the most important visual medium (for one exemplary case by female partisan see Figure 42), while poetry with its 12,000 poems and songs was the most important narrative/poetic medium. Finally, it was the partisan theatre that was the most important interactive, performative and agitational cultural form of the Partisan struggle. These three art forms and their intermedial installations (see Figure 43) deeply permeated the liberatory imaginary. One of the major tropes presented a small partisan column moving in the snow, an elementary formation in the most extreme circumstances that pointed to the determination of the struggle.

This section will add one argument to the widely accepted thesis that graphic art spearheaded the visual imaginary of the struggle: I will argue that the graphic form expanded far beyond the limits of what was perceived as the graphic medium prior to WWII. Graphic art expanded and combined intensively with other art forms and formats, from verse (poetry and prose) to photography. We can follow a development of a hybrid intermedial form, which yet again operated using techniques that were cinematographic in orientation, which Levi named "cinema by other means" (2012). From the highpoint of its production, I will select two different design formats: firstly, I will present a few designs/linocuts from the portfolios and their exhibitions conceived as moving graphic-filmic images (especially the collective work of France Mihelič and Nikolaj Pirnat's *Naša Borba – Our Struggle*, 1944); and second, the unique example of the photo-graphic-poetic book *Zdravljica* by Prešeren (a would-be anthem of Slovenia, the work by Janez Vidic, 1944). Each of these graphic design forms or design portfolios – either standing alone or within Partisan exhibitions and an elaborated book format – invite us to reflect on intermediary forms. All these works became highly popular, massively read, watched, visited, discussed and sung during and after the liberation.

199 Partisans had to share and pass over any kind of publications they could get their hands on: *if you have already read it, pass it on.*

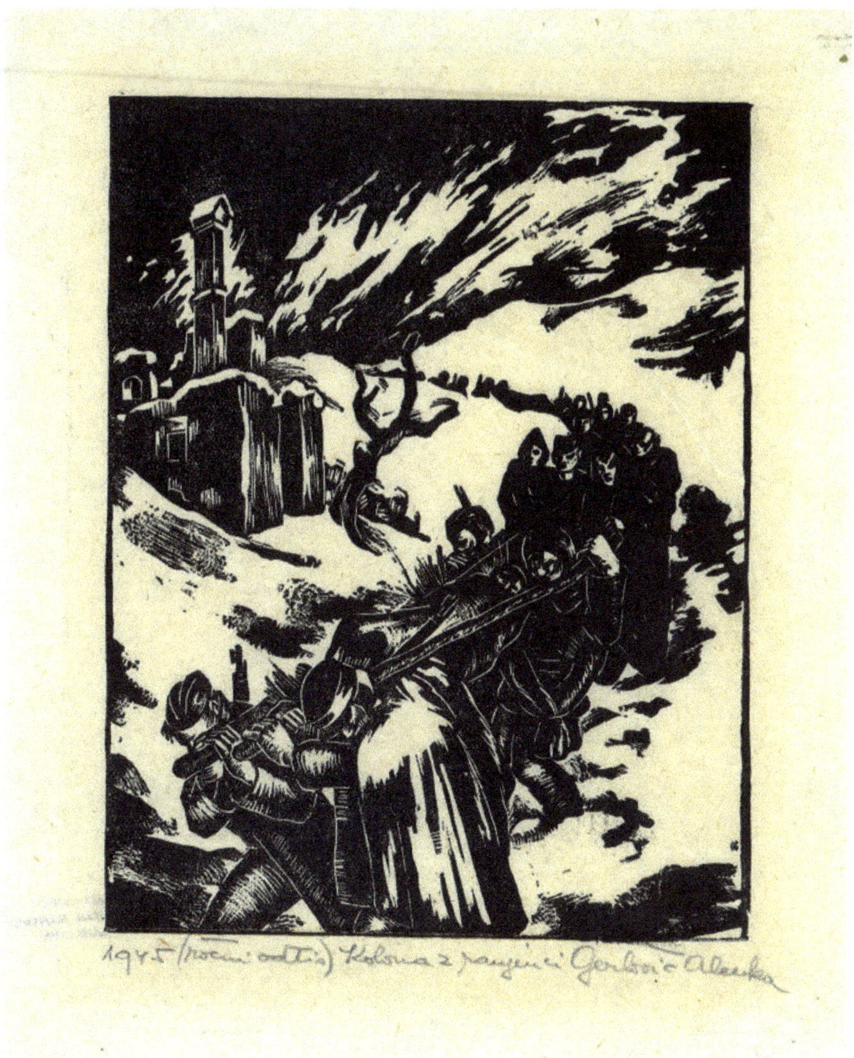

Figure 42: *Column with the Wounded*, linocut by Alenka Gerlovič, designed in 1945. Courtesy of MNZS.

The map *Our Struggle* was a joint work by two renowned and pre-war designers who both joined the Partisans early on: Nikolaj Pirnat and France Mihelič.[200]

---

200 This was, however, not the first graphic portfolio. The first one was produced in Slovenia in 1943 under the title *V Kristusovem Imenu* (In Christ's Name), made by a collective of sculptors, painters and architects who were primarily caricaturing the local fascist collaborators and the moral double standards that such a political position – collaborating with the occupier – imposed

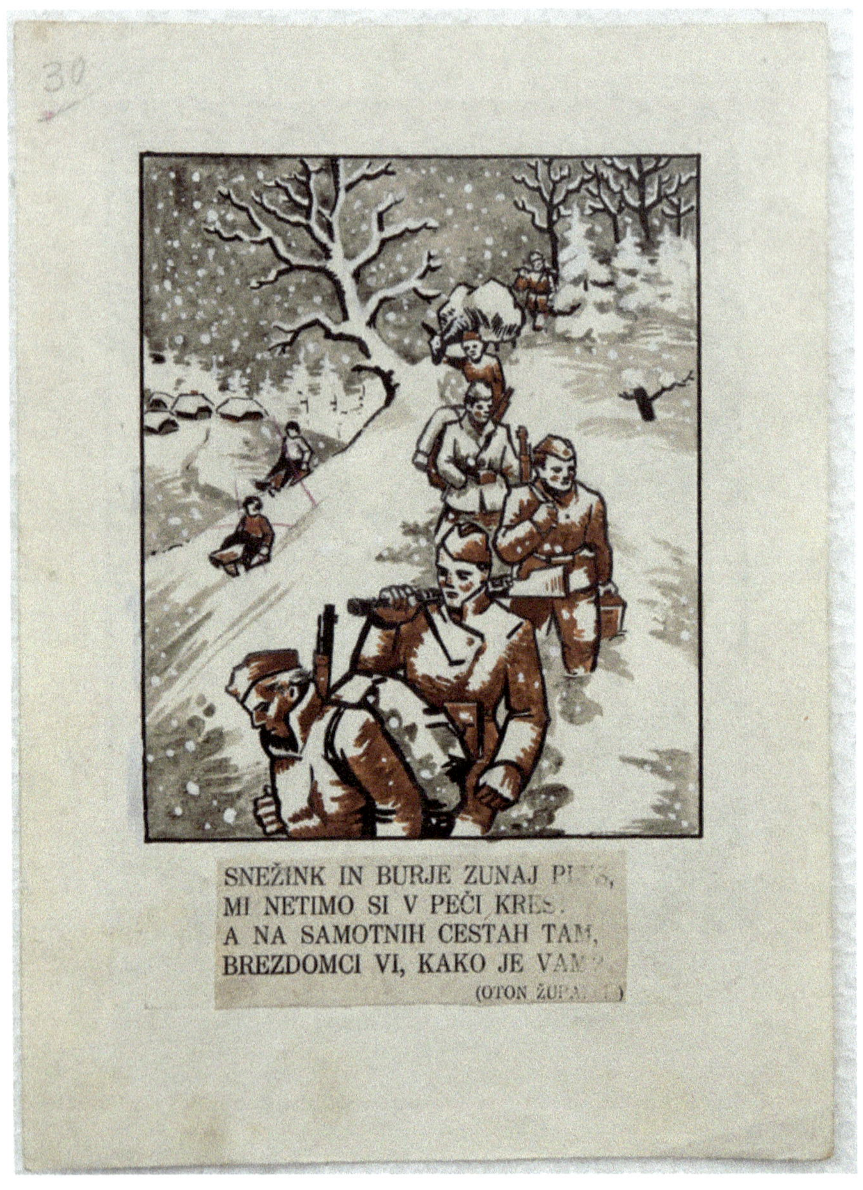

Figure 43: *Column in the Snow*. Pin-brush aquarel by Ivo Šubic. Illustration for children, which accompanies Oton Župančič's poem. Courtesy of MNZS.

The graphic map consists of twelve linoleum cuts – images of and to the People's Liberation Struggle. It was printed in early 1944 by the Partisan printshop Grafika Triglav and had a print run of 2,000 copies with an additional 150 luxury design copies. The latter were given as rewards to those who performed well in the battles, won competitions and also as gifts at diplomatic occasions with foreign representatives (for details see Visočnik 1969, 807–825). The print run of 150 special copies demonstrates that the leadership of the liberation struggle was aware of the significance and artistic quality of the Partisan portfolios, as something that would remain after the liberation. Such quality in production demanded extra effort and the use of very scarce material and became imprinted in the symbolic memory of resistance.

As the title of the map *Our Struggle* suggests, the twelve designs sought to portray and capture the essence of both the figure of the Partisan and the Partisan struggle in general. The map asks itself what moved the struggle and how the struggle itself moved? Each image includes a caption. The map was designed by two authors with a substantial difference in style: Nikolaj Pirnat practiced a more social realist style that was more agitational in its convictions (see Figure 45), while Mihelič's style could be seen as surrealistic (Figure 44; and in some cases he practiced expressionist/grotesque elements, for details see his another map, Figure 46 and 47). Some may see this graphic map as a politico-aesthetic compromise – in bringing together two such diverse artists – but I would suggest it was one of the best crystallisations of the controversy on the left over propaganda vs. autonomy.

The authors' formal differences are also reflected on through the subject of the struggle. Pirnat primarily orients himself towards single figures of Partisans, that is, one sees a Partisan in battle, either attacking or wounded. Mihelič is more focused on the general situation and the macabre atmosphere of the occupation: from the burnt villages to the Partisan detachment progressing slowly through the snow. Furthermore, and perhaps more 'controversially,' if some of the previous Partisan graphic designs had often portrayed fascists in a beast-like and grotesque way, then Mihelič used a similar style to portray the exhaustion and almost *übermenschliche* efforts of the Partisans in fighting the fascist beast, surviving and prevailing (cf. Dore Klemenčič 1944, see the above Figure 26). Despite the graphic map ending with an image of freedom, I would not like to single out any one image that united and represented the whole complexity of the struggle. Rather, the quality of the graphic map should be traced in its reconstruction of a

on patriots (Visočnik 1969). Elsewhere in Yugoslavia, in 1943 Marijan Detoni also prints his first graphic portfolio *Mapa U.* These graphic portfolios triggered many Partisan artists to think or work on/execute their own collective portfolios by the end of the war, immediately after the liberation.

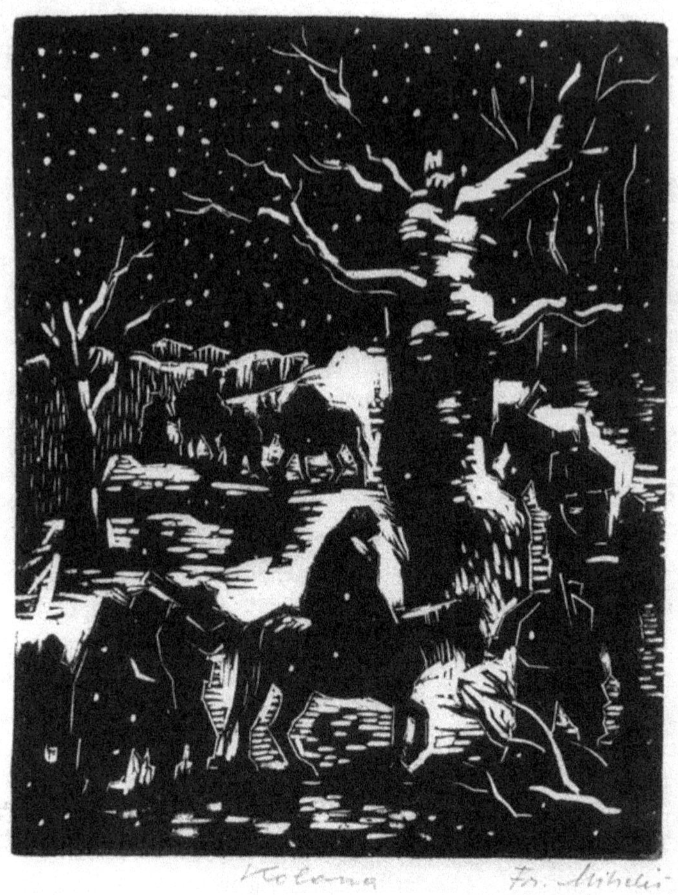

Figure 44: *Column in the Snow,* France Mihelič. From the graphic portfolio Our Struggle (1944). Courtesy of MNZS.

Partisan social tie – in the midst of destruction – between an individual Partisan figure and the collective cause of liberation. In other words, one can see a forceful dialectical movement between subjective engagement (heroism and hope) and the collective circumstances of war and struggle. The graphic map took the ambitious task of mapping and visualising the intensive experiences, structures of feelings and thoughts of the Partisan movement. Browsing through the graphic map back then and still today, offers the spectator a peculiar cinematic experience that crystallises the central figures and essence of the liberation movement.

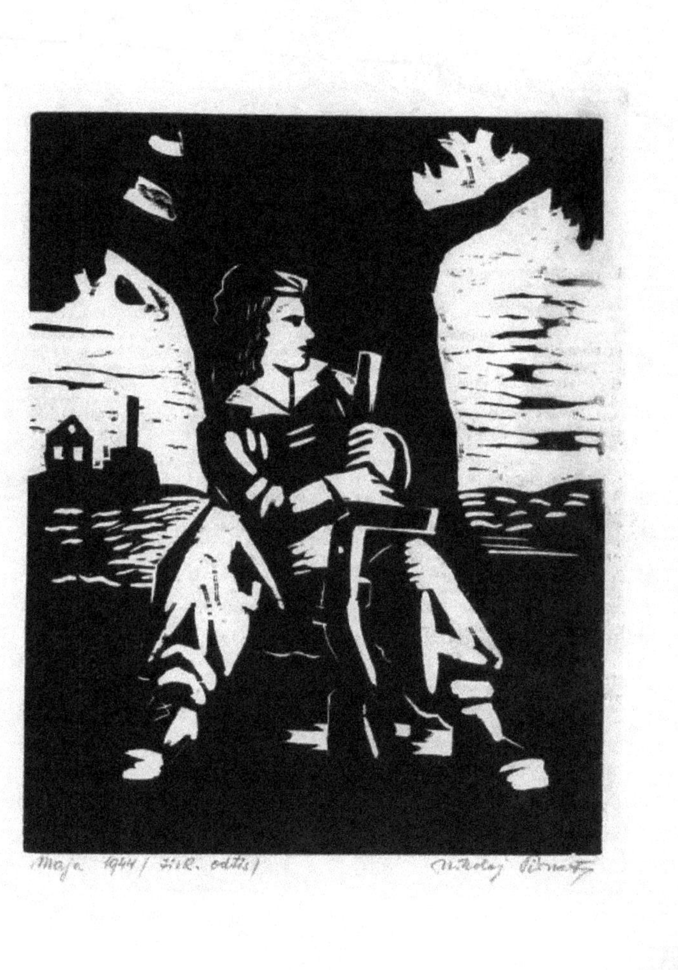

Figure 45: *Woman Partisan*, linocut by Nikolaj Pirnat. From the graphic portfolio Our Struggle (1944). Courtesy of MNZS.

I would claim that in a similar vein as the aforementioned photo exhibitions, these graphic maps were put on display at various Partisan exhibitions. The "Partisan" spectators could see the graphic portfolios (not only from Mihelič and Pirnat) and despite all the dynamics present in these photos, maps, images and documents, they had a fascinating effect on their audience. According to multiple testimonies, visiting the exhibition and looking at these Partisan artworks had an

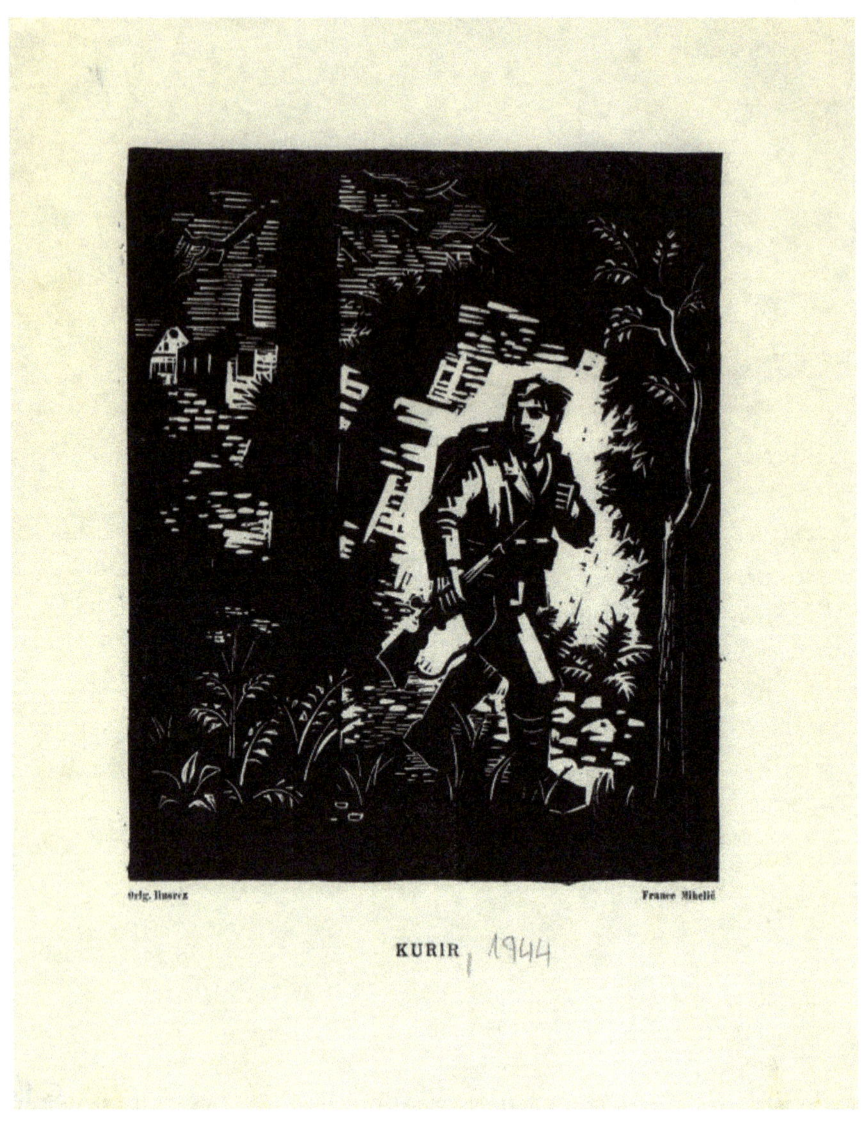

Figure 46: *Courier*, linocut by France Mihelič. Courtesy of MNZS.

almost freezing and evidently displacing effect. For many, it seemed to be one of the only ways of bringing back the whole of human dignity in these most brutal times. This structure of feeling (Williams 1961) is encapsulated in the lucid words from the diary of a Partisan who recounts a visit to one exhibition of a Partisan press in a small village:

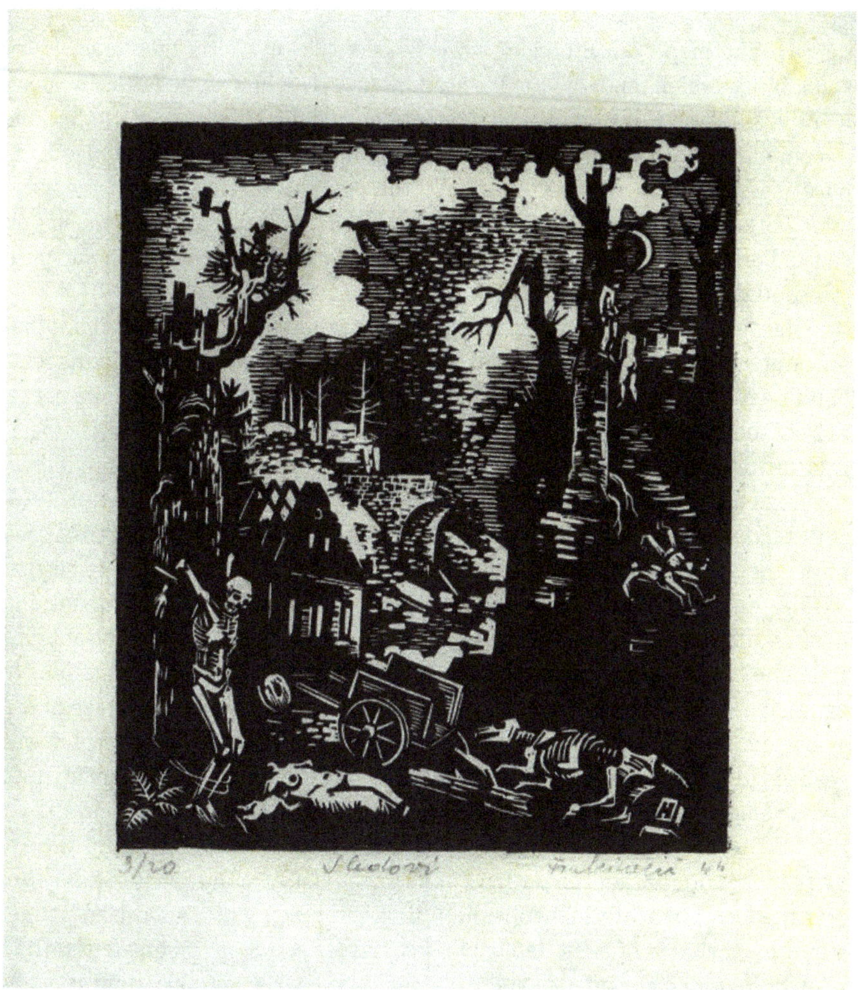

Figure 47: *Traces*, linocut by France Mihelič. From the graphic portfolio *Bloody Brotherhood*, 1945. Courtesy of MNZS.

> During Easter we had a chance to see a very well-designed exhibition on the liberated territory. Our propagandists and cultural workers had put different works on display, from the Allied print and Partisan literature to the work of artists fighting in the Partisan struggle. Our comrades did a splendid job in carefully preparing and working on the exhibition spaces, which made us forget that we were somewhere in the middle of the hills. (quoted in Visočnik 1969, 80)

Graphic portfolios within the exhibitions functioned as a film device in the literary sense: the portfolio became a series of moving graphic images on a spatial display. The map "Our Struggle" came to use Nikritin's term the "museum of static film," which rendered the Partisan intense dynamic of the Partisan movement visible and thus temporarily fixed its movement.[201] The portfolio became a mobile portfolio put on display numerous times, with extremely positive audience reactions, which triggered many other graphic designers and artists to start working on their portfolios.[202] Rather than for private use, such visual and sensual effects were produced through the encounter between the graphic portfolio and the exhibition.

The second important contribution to the counter-archive offered another encounter mixing graphic design, poetry and printed linoleum cuts (see Figure 48). This impressive book format was published in 1944 on the centenary of the publication of France Prešeren's *Zdravljica*. *Zdravljica* (Eng. a toast) was written in 1844 but censored and later on thoroughly edited due to its revolutionary spirit during the wave of Mazzini's "young Europe" (Paternu, 1995, 2009). *Zdravljica*, which is the current anthem of Slovenia, already possessed an iconic status relating to Slovenia's national awareness during the second part of the nineteenth century. And if the poem did not realise its dreams and desires during the dramatic failure of Vienna and the 1848 "Spring of Nations," then one hundred years later in 1944, the time was ripe not only for nations to emancipate themselves, but also for people and social revolution to take place. The poem can be literally read as a toast to freedom and liberation, which was realised in 1945, while other toasts to world peace and internationalism up until today remain within the utopian horizon, yet even more distant than in 1945.

The Partisan *Zdravljica* was printed in the Trilof printing house for the Regional Committee of the Liberation Front of Gorenjska.[203] The Partisan *Zdravljica* was the result of a fruitful cooperation between Janez Vidic, a Partisan painter who was in charge of eight linoleum cuts, and Marjan Šorli, an amateur technician who produced vignettes and designed a book. The edition's print run was 1500 copies, including a few copies woven into special albums. All 1500 copies were numbered and composed of extremely precious and costly material – what would be called a vintage-luxurious edition today. More than 160 kg of matter was used for the book, while vignettes were printed in red, gold and black and bound

201 For a detailed view of Nikritin see Tsantsanoglou (2013).

202 Another noteworthy graphic portfolio made by Dore Maj Klemenčič in July 1944 was titled *In the Name of Christ's Wounds*, and had a print run of 1000 copies. For the exhibition display, Partisan technicians sewed on silk from Allied parachutes (Klemenčič 1972).

203 The Gorenjska region was integrated directly into the III. Reich from early 1941. There was no press publishing in Slovene, but there was a small newspaper called *Karawanken Bote*, which mobilised Slovenian people to enter the fascist collaborationist army (Paternu 1995).

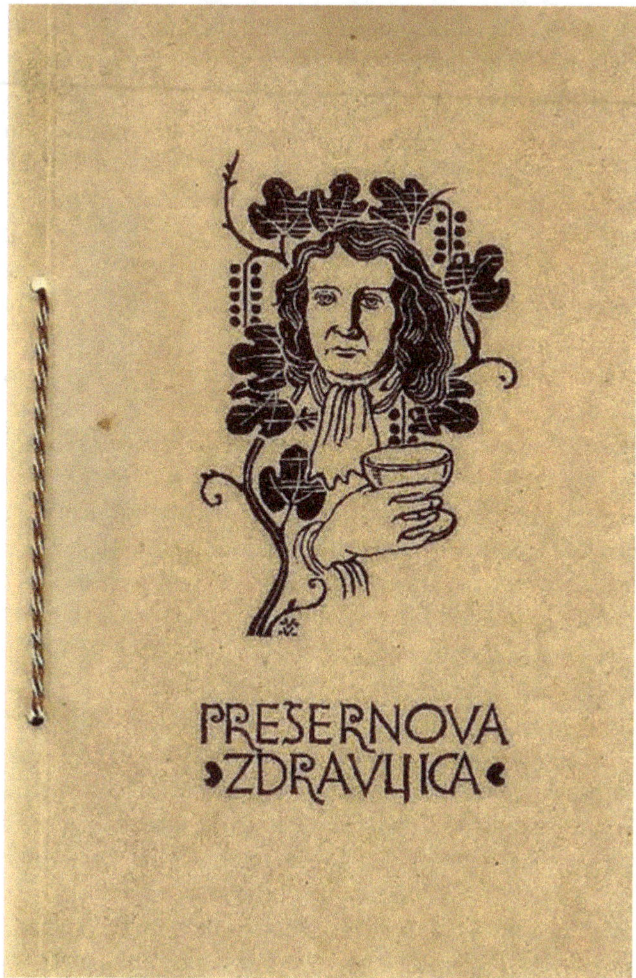

Figure 48: *Zdravljica/Toast*, designed by Janez Vidic and Marjan Šorli (1944). With permission of Luka Vidic.

with golden bronze into a neatly woven book accompanied by eight linoleum cuts. Instead of being rudimentary, propagandist and aesthetically weak, this edition in an almost baroque style was something deemed to be impossible, or even inacceptable in times of war. The location of the publication was also important: the cultural landscape of Gorenjska erased most of the traces of the Slovenian language and thus, to organise, design and make such a major vintage book was in itself a Partisan gesture. Immediately after its dissemination, *Zdravljica* became the most striking example of a WWII graphic poem and book; an example of a poem approached graphically and through film, with the aim of revitalising the liberationist legacy and mobilising new Partisans to fight for the new world, while at the same time singing a toast, a *zdravljica*.

Zdravljica has been analysed thoroughly by literary critics and historians in Slovenia.[204] Consequently, I will only refer to a few of the most vital analyses and moments. In a formal sense, Prešeren used a strategy called *carmen figuratum*, which means "word picture," a fine art poem that originated with the medieval monk Hrabanus Maurus. In the specific case of *Zdravljica*, translated as toast, the form is transparent and self-evident, since each stanza visually imitates a glass of wine (see Figure 49). In a certain way, the poem – its content and its visual form – directly identifies the message. Is perhaps this form present so that nobody misses Prešeren's political message, or can we speak of a specific doubling of readers' visual and poetic stimulation? Contrary to our basic perception that poems should be read, or listened to, here the visual perception is associated with wine tasting as a metaphor for poem tasting and freedom tasting. At the end the poem calls upon us to make a toast to the birth of a new nation and to the day when peace will reign among us all. Vladimir Nazor, one of the greatest Yugoslav poets (and a Partisan) parsed Prešeren's poetry and remarked in 1969: "This person invented the Slovenian nation" (quoted in Habjan 2016, 133). It was clear to Prešeren and to the Partisans that the liberation of the Slovenian nation and people would not be realised by a poem, but through the People's Liberation Struggle.

In the case of the Partisan *Zdravljica*, Janez Vidic and Marjan Šorli produced a powerful hybrid that further elaborated the *carmen figuratum*. Firstly, Šorli's vignettes strike readers as additional visual signifiers that place an emphasis on how to read the verses: today one could call them strong visual memes that exclaim instead of singing a chorus. The example of the image above portrays fists that refer directly to the stanza that speaks of "chains that bind us still and hold us fast (See Figure 50a, b)." In the official English translation, this part of the stanza can be read in the following way:

> May our dear realm in freedom grow.
> May fall the last
> Chains of the past
> Which bind us still and hold us fast!

In the translation, the "chains of the past [...] may fall" while in the original it is Slovenians who need to "crush the hands" of those who oppress the Slove-

204 For a detailed overview theorising Prešeren in Slovenian literary studies and sociology, see Jernej Habjan (2016).

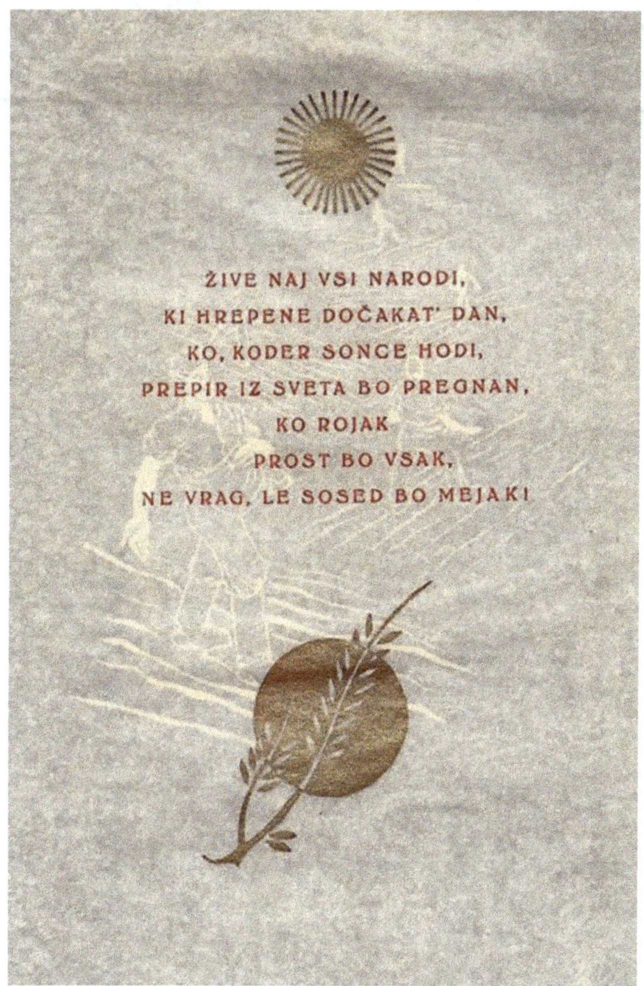

Figure 49: Representation of the stanza / *carmina figuratum* from Janez Vidic and Marjan Šorli's *Zdravljica*, 1944. With permission of Luka Vidic.

nian nation. In terms of visual analysis, of interest is not the mere doubling of poetic verse with a visual sign, but the presence of an empty space in between. Each reader, whether from 1844, 1944, or today can imagine the "invisible chains between the hands." This is why the poem and its vignette still touches us today, continuing to have an effect and affect, precisely because it does not name and portray the enemy (in mere nationalist terms), but rather tackles the problem 'structurally': what is it that chains us and subjugates us, and how are we to liberate ourselves from these chains? Secondly, Janez Vidic's linoleum cuts show

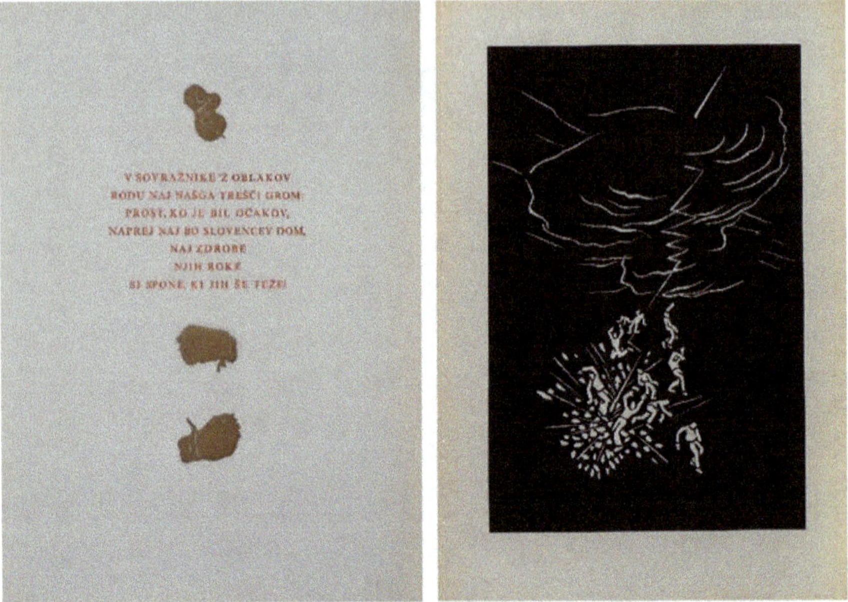

Figure 50a, b: Stanza and linocut on chains and strike of thunderbolt from Janez Vidic and Marjan Šorli's *Zdravljica*, 1944. With permission of Luka Vidic.

lightning that crashes in the midst of the enemies even if Prešeren's dictum says that thunder (and not lightning) will crash the enemy lines: "Let thunder out of heaven strike down and smite our wanton foe!" The small disparities between Vidic's linoleum cuts persist within the booklet, if on the one hand images relate and dramatise the poetic text, while on the other hand at least two out of eight images clearly move beyond the poem and represent the images of the Partisan struggle (see Figure 50a, b).

In each stanza, Prešeren skilfully zooms in and out of diverse social situations and calls different social groups to arms (Slovenians; women, who are actually machines who "induce fear in enemies; but especially young women and men"). The poem makes a toast to all the different subject positions in a very visual account, as given formally through the form of a cup (stanza), while in a cinematographic sense, these subject positions culminate in a final montage of "world history" in the penultimate stanza. The latter interpellates us – not as Slovenes, but rather as world citizens/revolutionaries – with a radical call and desire for collective work and struggle to reach a time when all nations can prosper and live in peace and freedom. Here the toast and subjective position is inscribed in the plural – in multiple nations and nationalities ("Long live all the nations [...]") – rather than in a singular form denoting a particular nation. Fraternity, sisterhood, the equality of all nations and freedom and liberation is underlined in both the original and the Partisan *Zdravljica* (see Figure 51). The ultimate goal of *Zdravljica* calls for the day when all splits and "strife will be banished from the world" (*"da koder sonce hodi, prepir iz sveta bo pregnan"*), or as the official translation says: "No war, no strife shall hold its sway."[205]

In the original and unpublished version of Prešeren's *Zdravljica*, the last trope in this stanza was completely changed. The ultimate goal of the freedom and equality of all nations is openly revolutionary, since all nations can live freely only when nobody is no longer subordinated, when there is "no enslaved head under the sun" (*"de koder sonce hodi, ne bod pod njim sužne glave"* – for this important distinction see Paternu, 1995).[206] Due to harsh censorship in the Habsburg Monarchy, Prešeren decided to change it and thus the message became more pacifist and was published in an extremely edited form.

Eric Wolf wrote an excellent study (1982/2010), which asserts that nations/people without history contributed to the formation of a new mode of production,[207] while this can be even further radicalised, arguing that the people without history can only become people with history by and through struggle. The people who do not struggle have no history, even less a future and will be silenced by the force of nature as Kosovel warned us before. *Zdravljica* is then not only a toast to one specific or chosen nation, but a toast to all those that struggle in the light of "ultimate struggle."[208] This is where the role of Partisan poetry joins hands with political declarations and action, where Partisan words organise the thoughts and "affect of enthusiasm" (zupančič 2005), which move Partisans and spectators onto the path to freedom.[209]

---

205 The English translation by Lavrin on the Slovenian government web page, and the other translations are mine: http://www.vlada.si/en/about_slovenia/political_system/national_insignia/france_preseren_zdravljica_a_toast/.

206 I owe this distinction between pacifist and revolutionary change due to censorship, to Rastko Močnik.

207 My research interests do not include assessing the transitional mode of production. One can say that a sort of 'Partisan economy' was organised, based on popular solidarity: a gift economy that was based on a belief in future liberation (Kirn 2019b). It is noteworthy that the Partisan struggle had its bonds and collected a "tax for national liberation" rather than confiscating material from the people – with the exception of collaborators/occupiers. For more details see Mikuž (1969).

208 Cf. Kelen and Pavković (2014).

209 One cannot impose a symmetry between fascist and Partisan affect. The extreme right and fascism mobilises fear and anger, and combines it with a viral hatred of others who do not belong to the chosen nation, race and/or religion. Fascists not only hate, but also bring to the fore an exclusivist love for one's presupposed eternal race, nation and/or religion. In contrast to this, Partisan affect is certainly not without anger, namely anger against domination and occupation,

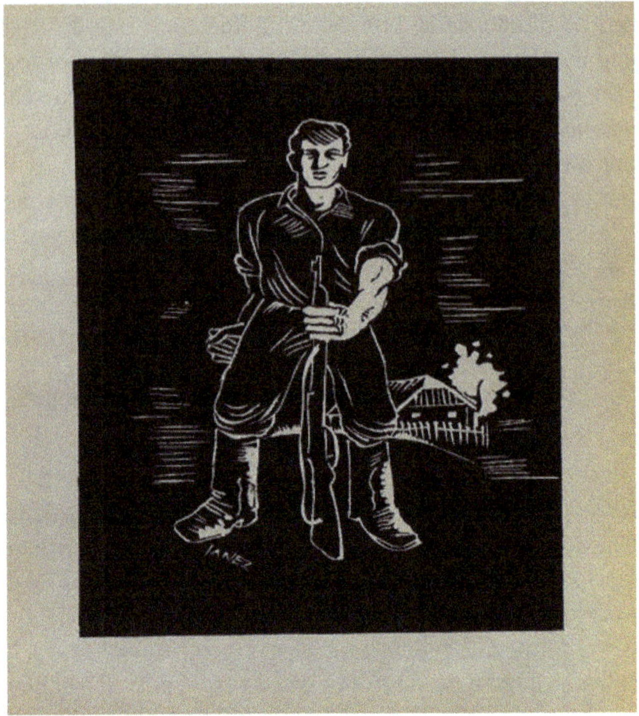

Figure 51: Figure of a Partisan fighter, linocut from Janez Vidic and Marjan Šorli's *Zdravljica*, 1944. With permission of Luka Vidic.

2.5.7 The liberation of Zagreb, the liberation of cameras

The liberation of different Yugoslav cities is fairly well documented in photos and also in certain films (I will come to this material in the next section), however, I wanted to include one story that was researched and re-montaged by Goran Sergej Pristaš in cooperation with Mila Pavićević. Pristaš retells the story of the liberation of Zagreb in May 1945 through a camera lens:

> The German and Ustasha forces are pulling out of Zagreb. Some film directors, mostly pioneers of Croatian film, are cooperating in the operation to save film equipment that occupation forces want to take with them. Part of the film equipment was hidden in the private store-

---

but it primarily operates on a level between enthusiasm and hope in building a new world based on equality. This gesture, however, has to reinvent love and humanity, which presupposes a comradely relationship towards others and to nature itself, and which does not exclude on the basis of national, racial, religious, and gendered 'natural' characteristics see also Malm (2018).

> houses, but large parts were impossible to hide. This is why the cameramen and film directors took cameras in their hands and were recording the retreat of the column from Zagreb. At the same time, they acted as if they would also be retreating and at some points soldiers even helped them accommodate the cameras. Branko Marjanović coordinated this action [...]; the retreating troops gradually forgot about the presence of film crews and the crews made it back to the city, so the film shooting continued. Some Partisans who came in, liberating the city, did not trust these crews and stopped filmmakers but they simply responded to them with the agreed Partisan password "Florian knows everything." But Florian did not really exist and this password was only agreed on between film crews – it enabled the film crews to somehow have a regular not so disturbed recording of the liberation. This is how the first film document *The Liberation of Zagreb* came into existence.[210] (Pristaš 2007)

There are two fascinating moments that deserve our attention in this case: firstly, and most obviously, the cameras and their film directors came to "Partisan" life by risking their lives on the very last day of occupation and liberation. They staged a never commissioned film in the interregnum, first acting as if they were leaving the city with the fascists. Moreover, they needed to work in a conspiratorial way even after the liberation. "Florian knows everything" – both an imaginary figure and revolutionary password – actually worked as a key filmic device that enabled them to continue shooting the liberation of Zagreb. Secondly, the film fragments that Goran Sergej Pristaš and Mila Pavićević brought back to life demonstrate the attitude of the people on the streets and in their windows. During the retreat of fascism, practically no one would say farewell to the Ustasha 'patriots': a few scared faces looked from the windows, while some people walked away. Once the camera had shot the liberation, the coast was clear and the whole city enthusiastically came onto the streets. The war had come to an end, but was not yet part of an organised communist gathering and ritual, instead consisting of spontaneous encounters between Partisans and people on the streets and squares.

The section on Partisan film showed that despite the extreme conditions of war, there existed both film documents and an array of artistic intermediary experiments that performed film by means of literary scripts, mobile photo exhibitions, design portfolios of major Partisan exhibitions, sound recordings and verses. Furthermore, the making of Partisan film by other means enhanced people's expectations, which led to a new awareness of the necessity of film during and immediately after WWII. This awareness ushered in the major task and role of Yugoslav film in the new socialist reality. In also looking to the analysis of Partisan photos and poems that evoke the gesture of an uprising and echo freedom,

---

210 A documentary film on the Zagreb liberation, which includes some of these film recordings, is accessible at: https://www.youtube.com/watch?v=WTzVqp4H_Zs.

I attempted to especially highlight their anonymous mass/collective production and dissemination. The counter-archive works through registers of Partisan texts and poems that were complemented and popularised by oral – singing – dimensions, or visual works that became moving images of struggle. The Partisan counter-archive therefore does not want to assign a medal conferring the highest aesthetic quality, nor mediate between those who see the peak in Partisan graphic art and others who see it in poetry, but rather points out the extremely creative combination of intermedial art forms and comradely cooperation between artists, cultural workers and amateurs who contributed to Partisan production and dissemination. The counter-archive covers the incessant development of Partisan rupture that built and enhanced social and cultural transformation. The selected records are not a closed selection, but a departing point for future research that holds a space that keeps (re)constructing solidarity between the oppressed, even if distant in time and space. What was to become one of the major tasks of socialist Yugoslavia was from the very start permeated by the Partisan struggle, and translated into political and cultural calls to commemorate, narrate and represent Partisan struggle. The extent to which they failed (the majority) and the extent to which they succeeded (the minority) will be the subject of the next chapter.

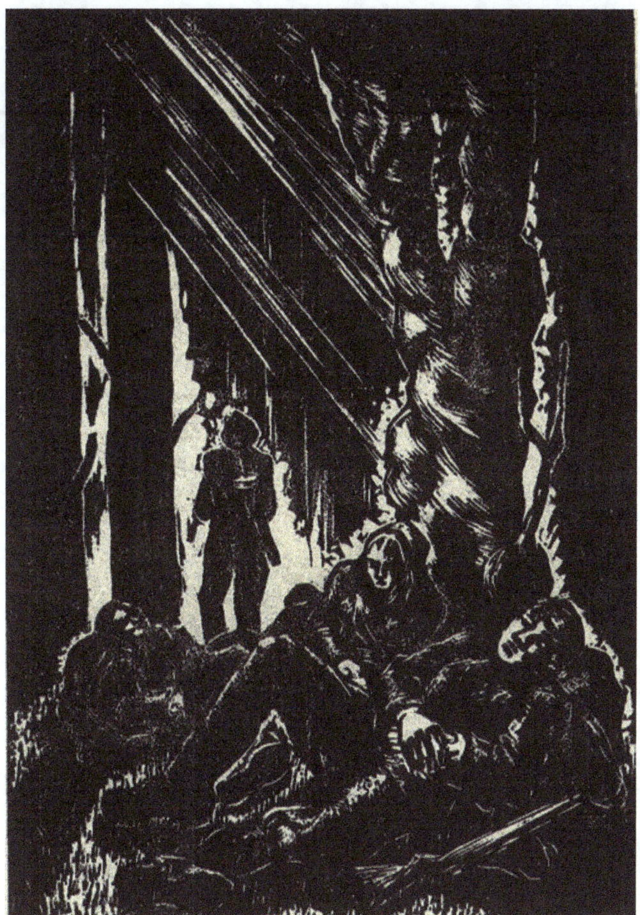

Figure 52: *Rest*, linocut by Alenka Gerlovič (1945). Courtesy of MNZS.

Chapter 3
Continuing the Partisan Rupture by Other Means: From Black Wave Films to Late Modernist Monuments to Revolution (1960s–70s)

> Memory from the heart of my native town,
> Neither thunder nor fire shall erase
> It shall live on also when the time overcomes
> And shatters brass and blasts the stone.
> Jure Franičević Pločar (1944)[211]

> Houses can be built again, railways tracks reconstructed,
> but a million and seven hundred thousand human lives
> will not be brought back to life. Each of these people had
> their own personal life, with hopes, troubles and joys [...]
> This was the high price we had to pay for our freedom.
> Josip Broz Tito, *Selected Military Writings* (1945)

3.1 Introduction: Partisan struggle as a dominant artistic genre

In the middle of May 1945, war ended in Yugoslavia and with it the end to the People's Liberation Struggle was almost complete. The period of heroic Partisan art came to an end and a space of vigorous aesthetic and political experimentation and engagement was not inscribed into this new historical mission: the building of the new Yugoslavia. Thus, calls rang out from the loudspeakers of the new political power: "There will be no rest, until we complete the reconstruction!" (*Nema odmora, dok traja obnova*!). The incessant political, cultural and economic struggle – the age of Yugoslav reconstruction that wanted to retain political autonomy from the West and East – brought with it deep reformist tendencies, revolutionary transformations and repressions. Clearly, the circumstances under which art was produced had changed from the wartime period.

211 „Spomen iz srca rodnoga mi grada
izbrisat neće gromovi ni plamen
živjet će i tad kad vrijeme svlada
i razmrvi broncu i raznese kamen."
This quote has been taken from Kolumbić (1982) and was often inscribed in the public spaces and partisan monuments in Dalmatia The translation is mine, edited by Darko Suvin.

https://doi.org/10.1515/9783110682069-004

Art was still conceived in a Partisan fashion: it needed to propagate and bear the torch for change, but now the tables had turned. The new Partisan art and many (former) Partisan artists openly participated in the institutionalisation of popular power: the *Federal People's Republic of Yugoslavia* and its cultural apparatus (1946). This is why some researchers asserted[212] that the People's Liberation Struggle (PLS) became *the* most dominant topic in artistic production – it became practically mythological – something that artists and artworks ought to celebrate and properly commemorate. Such a constellation might run against one of the major definitions of the counter-archive and its surplus and so it is fair to ask whether one can still speak of the Partisan counter-archive in this period? Did the counter-archive not become something completely different – "only" supporting the construction of the socialist state and glorifying the Partisan past? Or, might the Partisan counter-archive become embedded in the counter-hegemonic struggles within the new politics and culture of memory present within the dominant socialist archive? This chapter's hypothesis is to work further with Deleuze & Guattari's concept of a "monument to revolution" and select such cases that avoid a facile capturing by the state on the one hand, and those that produced an aesthetic rupture with the presupposed genre of Partisan art on the other hand.[213]

This hypothesis at first glance runs the risk of positing an over-simplified narrative on the Yugoslav socialist past imposed by an anti-totalitarian ideology[214] that categorises all socialist art along strict binary lines, either conceiving of socialist art as a reflection of state ideology or as a sort of dissident art (Jovanović 2012).[215] From this perspective, dissident art is anti-communist: something created by an individual genius locked within the iron cage and grey mediocrity of totalitarianism. Strictly speaking, this binary contradicts the anti-totalitarian enlarged historical perspective of the socialist past. For example, how can there even be dissident

---

212 Močnik (2005).

213 Močnik (2016) and Komelj (2016) revisit the famous polemical discussion on the birch tree, which asked to what extent Partisan artists had to follow political prerequisites during the PLS. The emblematic case was *how to paint a birch*? Representatives of a party line (socialist realism) claimed that the birch would have to carry traces of bursts of gunfire. However, the more autonomist – avant-gardist tendency won in discussions even during the war and rather posited something like Benjamin's "tendential art" that is radical in politics and in form.

214 Anything that refers to major political ruptures in Yugoslavia, be it the PLS, self-management or the non-aligned movement, has been deemed part of the ruling ideology of the socialist state. For details see Kirn (2019b).

215 The aestheticisation of socialist authority and ideology then brings all socialist countries into close proximity with the fascist authority. What this argument fails to recognise is how the Nazis fought vehemently against "entartete Kunst." And how they were so opposed to the avant-gardist and socialist realist currents.

art and artists if there was a totalitarian regime, which is defined by a high degree of violence, censorship and the complete absence of artistic autonomy?

Moreover, this binary coding of art collapses once we take a serious look at research on the cultural landscape of socialist Yugoslavia (see Jelača, Kolanović and Lugarić 2017; Hanaček 2019). It was the *League of Communists* that opened a path for the relative autonomy of culture and the promotion of academic modernism, as declared after 1952.[216] The results of the official cultural policy of (socialist) modernism were registered in both marginal and even mainstream cultural institutions, where support for critical, highly reflective and alternative cultural production took place.[217] Moreover, even if the League of Communists, with its cadre politics and ideological control, remained heavily involved in cultural production, the tensions between cultural autonomy and the state existed and intensified during the 1960s. I argue that this period can be seen as a realm where culture becomes the primary site (through 'overdetermination') of an open confrontation not only with the Partisan past but also with the socialist present. Artistic and social critique were practiced within the culture and in many ways foresaw the political and theoretical upheavals of 1968 (Kanzleiter 2011). Within the alleged opposition between pro-state and dissident artists, one thus discovers extremely rich and diverse artistic currents that contradict the anti-totalitarian standpoint and dichotomy. The history of art and culture in socialist Yugoslavia underwent a series of internal tensions, contradictions and developments (Praznik 2013). The counter-archival records do not qualify as 'dissident,' but as something that 'worked through' Partisan rupture, refracting echoes and visions for the new socialist present and communist future. These artworks were radical in form and content and expanded into "multi-directional memory" (Rothberg 2009) of WWII.

This chapter will work especially with works from the fields of (Partisan) film and monuments, that is, two major ideological investments by the socialist state. This is a litmus test for the rejection of anti-totalitarian ideology, which presupposes that the state had strict control over such ideologically invested fields. Evidently, film in Yugoslavia immediately became the most popular medium, and after initial economic stabilisation in the 1950s, Yugoslavia was familiar with both auteur films and high budget spectacles, such as epic Partisan films. The latter

216 Krleža's speech in 1952 entailed a win for relative cultural autonomy within national spheres (each republic had its own cultural infrastructure and sovereignty), while in terms of style, academic modernism and existentialism became the dominant forms (see also Močnik, unpublished essay).

217 For a general view on cultural and artistic production especially within the avant-garde scene in socialism see, Djurić and Šuvaković (2003) and Erjavec (2003).

dominated the public imaginary and the Partisan genre and often consisted of simple black-and-white portrayals of heroes (Partisans or victims) and villains (Nazis or local collaborationists). Along with other artistic forms of production that dealt with the Partisan struggle, such films produced intense ideological effects on their viewers. This resulted in the active and passive consumption of such cultural forms, rising Yugoslav patriotism, as well as a confrontation with the past and even indifference towards the Partisan past by the new generations (Bergholz 2007).[218] In this respect, Nebojša Jovanović contributed one important conceptual insight: instead of speaking of some homogenous genre of 'Partisan film' that mythologised Partisan struggle (Stanković 2005), we should rather speak of a "dominant genre platform" (Jovanović 2011). Expanding to the general field of new Partisan art, we could define the Partisan genre platform as a heterogeneous artistic formation comprised of different genres, styles, artistic formats, actions and performances – and even social criticisms – that were translated into the topic of war and liberation. The subject of the PLS proliferated in painting, design, prose-based literature, theatre and later in performance and, last but not least, in sculpture and architecture.

As a domain, film was seen by Tito and the communist leadership as an essential means of educating and reaching the masses. This is why building the infrastructure for film began immediately after the war and was decentralised, with each republic having at least one major film studio. But despite the socialist authority's large investment in the PLS and in film and sculptures/monuments in particular, there was an array of critical and engaged artworks that broke with the dominant canon and dissented from political control. This chapter argues that the most outstanding rupture within the dominant Partisan genre platform occurred in a few critical films and a large movement that created the "monuments to revolution." A selection of artworks emerged and changed the étatist narratives and ways in which one spoke about, observed, listened to and commemorated the PLS. The analysed artworks not only guarded the Partisan rupture, but even expanded it across new horizons. Spaces of culture and cultural works acquired an openly political nature – meaning that the then existing political problems of socialism were rethought and articulated within artistic matter.

218 Cf. the similar attitude described by researchers studying the relationship of local populations towards the monuments. These populations did not blindly follow official ideology, but rather the attitudes towards specific monuments speak of confrontation, enthusiasm, and also indifference. For details on general attitudes towards war memorials see Höpken (1999), whereas Velikonja (2017) conducted interesting research on graffiti in public spaces and monuments that relate to the question of the Partisans and Yugoslavia.

I have selected those artworks that openly dissented from the mythologising representation of the Partisan struggle, alongside those artworks that traced the Partisan 'surplus.' I will ask, especially with respect to Partisan monuments, if and how they formalised the idea of revolution, while for filmmakers, how did they film in a partisan way?[219] This chapter will analyse two films in detail: Želimir Žilnik's short *Ustanak u Jazku* (*Uprising in Jazak,* 1973) and Miodrag Popović's *Delije* (*The Tough Ones*, 1968). It will also analyse two monuments: Miodrag Živković's *Tjentište* (1971) and Dušan Džamonja *Kozara* (1972). In short, these artworks were – in form and content – opposed to major blockbuster Partisan spectacles, while they were still operating within the predominant cultural forms and media relating to memory: film and sculptures/monuments that 're-mediated' the legacy of the PLS. They fought a counter-hegemonic struggle on the protocols of how the people of Yugoslavia and beyond perceived, appropriated, but also negotiated and confronted images and narratives of the Partisan past.

3.2 Against state mythologisation: Partisan film between impossibility and collective memory-making

Daniel Goulding's seminal study on Yugoslav film (2002) concludes that the 1960s was the golden age of Yugoslav cinema, which coincided with relative economic and social stability on the one hand and a high degree of autonomy on the other hand. This material-ideological support for the arts, but also for alternative and amateur art was present especially in major urban centres across Yugoslavia.[220] Partisan films were *en vogue* throughout the whole history of socialist Yugoslavia – between 1945–1985 more than two-hundred films that dealt with Partisan topics were

---

219 One of the most recent exhibitions on Yugoslav architecture, modernism and utopia recently took place in MoMa, NYC (from July 2018 to January 2019) and includes an excellent catalogue with a few contributions focusing on Partisan monuments (Horvatinčić 2018).

220 "Technique to the People" was a slogan generated immediately after the war and supported by the special institution *Narodna tehnika* (Popular Engineering Society, 1946), which related to and continued the legacy of Partisan amateurism and the "do it yourself" attitude in a time of scarce resources. The major aim of this policy was, according to Janevska, to "organize, sponsor and promote different amateur activities. Even though they were under the 'political' control of the centre and were hierarchically organized, they were mostly left to their own devices as peripheral 'amateur reservations.'" (2012, 48). Amateur cinema received public assistance and young directors often worked with 8 mm and 16 mm film tape.

produced![221] However, it was during the period of the 1960s and 1970s that the magnitude and variety of both Partisan spectacles and critical independent films spoke of highly contested grounds concerning the narration and representation of the Partisan past. This would be of major importance since Yugoslav films entered the international stage, with circuits of consumption presenting the image of specificity of Yugoslavia. In broad terms, there were two types of Yugoslav Partisan films that reached international audiences: firstly, the independent auteur films received different awards and mentions at the film festivals (Cannes, Berlinale, Karlovy Vary etc.); secondly, more mainstream films, such as Štiglic's *Ninth Circle* (produced in 1960 at the Jasenovac concentration camp), or Veljko Bulajić's major blockbuster *Battle of Neretva* (1969), nominated for the best foreign film at the Oscars.

Before I move to analyse two film cases for the counter-archive, I need to juxtapose them with what became a mainstream genre of Partisan film. Some would call it the "red western" (cf. Štefančič), others, epic war films. Let me delve briefly into the most famous Partisan film, *The Battle of Neretva* (1969), produced by Veljko Bulajić. The film was the most expensive in the history of (post-)Yugoslav film. Estimates range from five to ten million dollars at that time. It took almost two years to produce, and it included sections of the Yugoslav People's Army, which left its manpower and infrastructure at the film crew's disposal. The casting was composed of such international stars as Orson Welles, Yul Brynner, Franco Nero, Sylvia Koscina and Sergei Bondarchuk, while Pablo Picasso designed the poster for the English version of the film, and the London Philharmonic Orchestra composed the music for English edition of the film.

The film plot focused on the turning point of the whole war for the PLS, the survival of the major body of the Partisan resistance under Tito who found themselves besieged by multiple fascist armies and collaborationist forces. This film has become a legendary Yugoslav epic. It presents the heroic overcoming of the siege and portrays the heroism and sacrifices of the Partisans, including their humanity to their wounded and typhoid-ridden comrades. All the events are dramatised through music and Partisan songs just as in any other Hollywood film. The film lasts for almost three hours and, seen in retrospect, it became a major monument in film and a dominant collective memory of the PLS's central battle. People may have forgotten much from the textbooks; some may remember fragments from personal testimonials, or film documentaries, but they do hold dear to specific passages of this film: the legendary singing of the wounded that

221 I will not enter into a discussion of the quantitative and qualitative poverty when comparing the golden age of the 1960s and 1970s with contemporary post-Yugoslav film production, which literally survives in comatose circumstances.

helps Partisan fighters push back against the Nazi annihilation, the resilience of Partisan fighters in the wake of being well-equipped and outnumbering the enemy, etc. The film also received major support from workers' collectives – it pursued a strong advertising campaign abroad and was an instant success with a huge rating. In Yugoslavia, more than 4.5 million spectators saw it in the first years of release, while outside Yugoslavia around 350 million people saw the film.[222] The mainstream epic Partisan films performed a double function: firstly, they became Yugoslavia's most celebrated film product (market); and secondly, internally they not only performed a filmic form of monument to the PLS that mythologised official memory, but the actors and topics also entered into Yugoslav popular culture and everyday life, strengthening the political legitimacy of the Partisan generation that still ruled the country.

That said, it is clear that any critical and independent filmmaker that wanted to make a film on the topic of the Partisans had a series of such Partisan films in his film-related conscious and unconscious imagination. During the period of the first severe economic crisis in Yugoslavia, it also became clear that the topic of the PLS had been instrumentalised by the socialist authorities in order to reposition and regain some ideological legitimacy. How was it then possible to remain an engaged and aesthetically innovative filmmaker, while avoiding the trap of repeating common tropes when speaking about the PLS? Furthermore, a large majority of critical filmmakers undoubtedly shared an open sympathy with the Partisan struggle, but the central challenge was to find a way of affirming the PLS without taking the authorities' declared position (from the League of Communists) and while differentiating such an affirmation from an established film genre? Despite the difficulties of such circumstances, a number of critical film directors took on the challenge and made some fascinating Partisan films that expressed their dissent either in terms of aesthetics or by choosing a more complex narrative structure. I would like to mention here a handful of such Partisan films that I categorise roughly into three groups. Firstly, there were the ethical–existential Partisan dramas that questioned the war itself and the difficult decisions that had to be made during the war, especially vis-à-vis fascist collaborationists and the civil war: Aleksandar Petrović's *Tri* (*Three*, 1965), Štiglic's *Balada o Trobenti in Oblaku* (*Ballad of the Trumpet and the Cloud*, 1961) Čap's *Trenutki Odločitve* (*Moment of*

222 Only one other Partisan action film, Hajrudin Krvavac's *Valter brani Sarajevo* (Valter Defends Sarajevo, 1972) surpassed expected spectatorship figures, becoming the most viewed film of all time with around a billion viewers. Valter is an action film and is based on a mixture of traits from Rambo (fearless, killing hundreds of Nazis) and James Bond (being undercover, charming and smart). The film earned eternal fame in China, which also explains the ratings. Valter now stars as a brand of beer in China, and a role model, while one film studio is considering filming a remake.

Decision, 1955); Bauer's *Ne okreči se sine* (*My Son Don't Turn Around*, 1956). Secondly, there were films that had a more neorealist influence devoid of any heroism in the life of the Partisan struggle: Veljko Bulajić's *Kozara* (1962), Mutapdžić's *Doktor Mladen* (1975), Živojin Pavlović's *Zaseda* (*Ambush*, 1969) and *Hajka* (1977). Finally, there were horror and surrealist films such as Puriša Djordjević's *Jutro* (*Morning*, 1967) and Miodrag Popović's *Delije* (1968); fourthly, there was a range of films that included a more complex depiction of the collaborationists, but also their authority from Lordan Žafranović's famous film, *Okupacija u 26 slika* (*Occupation in 26 Pictures*, 1977), to Miodrag Popović's *Čovek iz hrastove šume* (*The Man from the Oak Forest*, 1964), and also Vukotić's *Akcija stadion* (one of the first Holocaust films from Yugoslavia, 1977). All of these films and film genres had a variety of destinies. While some of the films became very popular, either being screened at the major Yugoslav film festival in Pula, or enjoying high-level distribution state-wide through the Yugoslav cinemas, others were screened mostly abroad, or on special occasions. What these critical Partisan films shared was an open challenge to the more epic war films that had become synonyms for the conventional mythological representations of the PLS. Put ironically, the holy trinity of Yugoslavia embodied by Tito, the Yugoslav People's Army and team sports received its film-music background in Partisan film blockbusters. The official ideology with its cinematographic regime of representation would not go unchallenged: an array of critical films offered a fresh engagement with the Partisan past.[223]

3.2.1 Žilnik's *Uprising in Jazak* (1973): How to make film in a Partisan way, or on the "banality of good"

Želimir Žilnik did not become famous for his films on Partisan struggle – in fact, over his very productive film career now spanning more than five decades, he made only one short film, *Uprising in Jazak* (1973), that presents an alternative form of remembrance by local villagers. He also made a more conventional documentary film, *One Woman One Century* (2011), that presents the story of one of the first female antifascist fighters from Istria in the 1930s and who was very engaged in the Partisan struggle during WWII. Despite this small number of Partisan films I would like to argue that Žilnik became a pioneer in Yugoslavia of making films in

223 They stood on politically very different foundations: from a more existentialist-humanist position (Petrović's anti-war message in *Three* points to the tragedy of the soldiers' deaths in the Kingdom of Yugoslavia, the Nazi occupation or Partisan forces) and revolutionary positions (Pavlović's *Zaseda*, which conveys revolutionary terror after the war), to a form of a people's approach to history from below (Žilnik's *Ustanak u Jazku*).

a Partisan way. He has continually challenged the ruling ideology in both socialist and capitalist contexts, while also paying special attention to the position of the oppressed and marginalised. This is not so surprising once we take into account his own trajectory that was marked by the most crass experience: he was born in the Crveni krst (Red Cross), an infamous concentration camp in Niš in 1942, and both of his parents were active communists and Partisans who were executed by (local) fascists during the war. His artistic career begins in the politically tumultuous years of socialist Yugoslavia, that is, in the latter half of the 1960s that were marked by the first severe economic, political and ideological crisis (Kirn 2019b). From his first films onwards, Žilnik worked on and developed a specific research and artistic method that later on received a name: docu-fiction.[224] This method not only preserves traces of fictive and documentary material without the complete blending of one into another, but also, Žilnik consciously worked with the team, either filming as the director on the stage, or presenting through his voice on the set, or interviewing the marginalised. The inclusion of the conditions of (film) production, the devices that signal the presence of film material and the film process to spectators and actors are heavily used in his films and testify to a deeply Brechtian influence on Žilnik's method (cf. Mazeriska 2013). Furthermore, the plot itself is based on a semi-prepared scenario, which demands both a degree of spontaneity in meeting and encountering the mostly amateur cast and a high level of focus on the part of the director, film crew and actors in responding to the situation of diegetic and real time and space. The trajectory of the plot and editing often gives the spectator the feeling that it could have developed in multiple ways. Žilnik's decision to decentralise the role of professional actors is also important. Amateurs might simply play their own roles, or respond to the questions, while at other times, Žilnik would insert them in roles they would feel more comfortable with, or would even push them to become actors.[225]

Žilnik's most famous and revolutionary works are his early short films *Unemployed* (1968), *Black Film* (1971), *Uprising in Jazak* (1973) and the feature film *Early Works* (1969), which all appeared in the late 1960s and early 1970s as

---

224 For a good overview of the political qualities and form present in Žilnik, see Mazierska (2013) and Prejdová (2000). Also see the whole essay section on the web page with an archive: http: //www.zilnikzelimir.net/essays.

225 Pavle Levi lucidly highlighted the political dimension present in this film method. Žilnik's film characters most often "represent border examples [...] between existing societies (within which they have no place) and possible, alternative, reorganized societies (within which – if these societies at some time were to be established – they would have clear and more stable identities). These characters are [...] the material for a process that Etiènne Balibar described as the constituting of 'the people,' which is initially non-existent because of the exclusion of those who are considered unworthy of citizenship." (2009, online).

part of the production house Neoplanta in Novi Sad. Neoplanta was directed by Svetozar Udovički, who produced and supported the works of Dušan Makavejev, Karpo Godina, Želimir Žilnik and many other experimental and political filmmakers who were not afraid to challenge the mainstream filmography or official ideology of Yugoslav socialism. If the late 1960s were the most productive historical moments for cultural and political activities, then the early 1970s saw a conservative backlash. Žilnik spoke of a certain turn to the re-Stalinisation of the League of Yugoslav Communists that led to the breakdown of leftist groups, students and workers' strikes on the one hand, and stronger ideological control over cultural production on the other hand. It was in 1971 that due to mounting political pressure over what was declared to be 'Black Wave Film,' an independent critical film scene took root. Late in 1971 Neoplanta's progressive director Udovički was substituted by Draško Redjep whose political line was in complete agreement with the suppression of cultural and political disobedience. One of the first steps under his direction was to compile a 'black list' and prevent or completely halt the distribution of past critical films. From 1972 onwards, the doors to Neoplanta and other major film studies were shut to political filmmakers across Yugoslavia.

Taking into account such a political climate and the predominance of Partisan film blockbusters in the early 1970s, the film *Uprising in Jazak* (1973) comes as a great surprise, and especially as something that radically disturbs the dominant way in which Partisan struggle is narrated, represented and finally remembered. Despite more recent anthologies, retrospectives, and analyses of Žilnik's work that evoke the importance of his films as documents of 'history from below,' this film is often overlooked and under-researched. It is noteworthy that this was the last film he made before leaving for West Germany. As mentioned, in the early 1970s Žilnik had to be inventive to continue making films, and together with some other filmmakers he had to return to cinema clubs, which were part of the self-management cultural infrastructure (Janevska 2012). It was in the Pančevo cinema club that Žilnik received a commission to film an advertisement for a hotel in Fruška Gora. In turn, Žilnik demanded that the club give him time and equipment to make a documentary film according to his own scenario in the village of Jazak.[226]

Uprising in Jazak is anything but a bombastic and epic representation of people in the village of Jazak in Vojvodina. The camera and crew arrive by car in Jazak, almost 30 years after the end of WWII. They start interviewing people,

226 For details on the production process, see the personal correspondence with Želimir Žilnik (2018).

including true witnesses and antifascists from the wartime period. A story of a local villager upon the arrival of the Nazis is accompanied by the visual passage of a shaky camera, the sound of moving tanks and shooting airplanes that attack and occupy the village. Žilnik makes the clear decision that he will not film and interview the national heroes, Partisan or communist leaders of yesterday or today, but the normal villagers, either supporters of the Partisans or those who eventually became Partisans. A large majority of these protagonists are neither politically 'articulate,' nor do they fit any heroic image of a Partisan fighter. What they do, however, is simply tell their stories in their own language. They speak of the arrival of the Nazis, then they show the camera the places where the torture took place and the techniques used – and where the executions took place. But they also speak about their ways of resisting, how they performed the Partisan oath, where and how women were hiding and feeding Partisans, but also where they were hiding guns and food and transporting them to Partisan fighters. In short, what makes Žilnik's inscription suitable for the Partisan counter-archive is his open countering of the mainstream film representation that postured Partisan fighters as heroic figures. The latter represented the major sacrifices of those in battle as the absolute good that cannot be questioned, while Žilnik makes a juxtaposition – I suggest – by inverting Hannah Arendt's term the "banality of evil," instead attributing what I call a specific "banality of good" to the local villagers. Since we often encounter the term "banality of evil" in reference to understanding the readiness of many ordinary people to collaborate and denounce Jews and political opponents to Nazi authorities, I would suggest the deployment in collective memory of something resembling a "banality of good." The latter is not to be understood as some sort of philanthropy on the part of those privileged enough to continue their 'normal living' in Nazi occupied Europe, nor does it refer to the noble gestures of rare individuals within the collaborationist apparatus (e.g. Schindler's list). Rather, I argue that this "banality of good" was a collective ethical choice made by the village community so as to perform an array of small gestures that contained a "weak messianic" power (Majewska 2019) that comes from 'ordinary' people. If the Partisan counter-archive during the war departed from the heroic gestures of Filipović and Radić before the execution that moved the masses (see chapter 2), then Žilnik's response to heroic gestures some 30 years later – in a very different political constellation – entailed the images and words of the resisting masses, of those from below that were allegedly not 'dignified' or 'educated' enough to remember, narrate and represent such a noble cause (see Figure 53a, b, c).

Žilnik's Partisan method can be praised to convey a more realistic and 'truthful' account of the Partisan past than the majority of Partisan films made at that time, while what I think is far more important is the way in which the film was made. The film's form consciously rejects any kind of aestheticisation and this

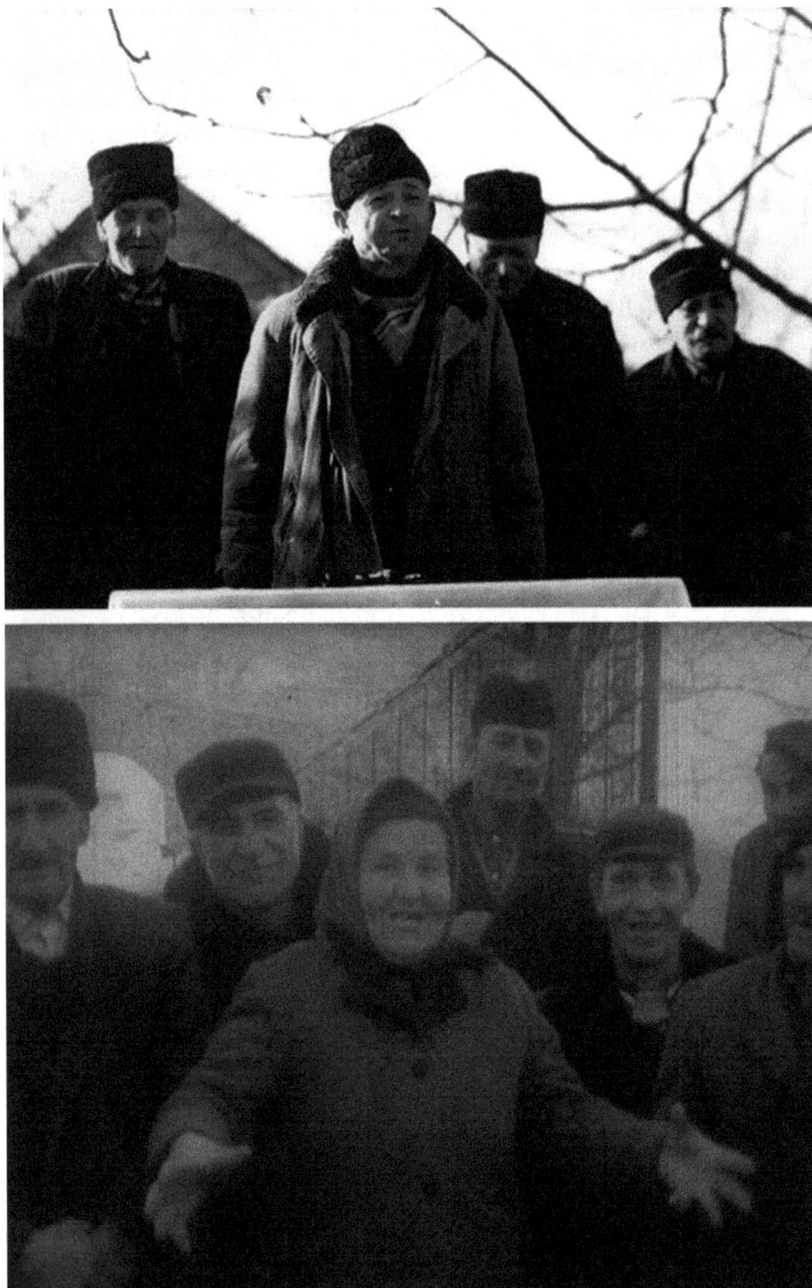

Figure 53: From the shooting of Žilnik's *Uprising in Jazak* (1972). Re-enactment of Partisan oath, reconstructing memory collectively, and cutting down the Nazi flag. With permission of Želimir Žilnik.

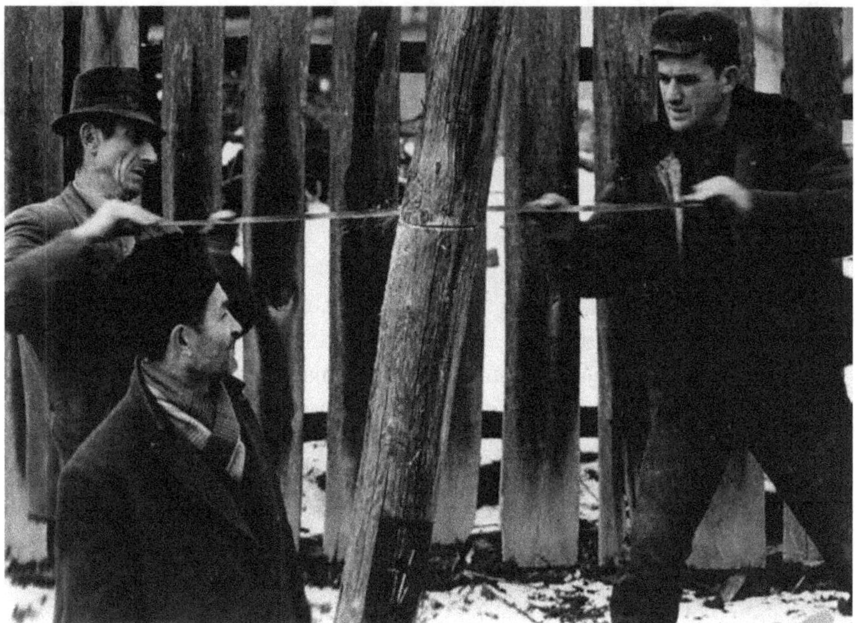

Figure 53 (continued)

is not only the consequence of a lack of material means for the film's shooting. Žilnik's use of the "raw image" (for details see Levi 2007) and the allegedly amateurish cutting that recurs in Žilnik's work, are not a sign of laziness on the part of the editorial team, nor of poor technical equipment, but rather express their conscious opposition to the aestheticisation of the Partisan struggle. The raw film material, raw peasant life, the raw circumstances of war and the struggle for liberation form a neorealist metonymic line of equivalence to Žilnik's arrival in and take on Jazak. Furthermore, Žilnik openly rejects the dominant mode of representing the war as a spectacular form that focused solely on and mythologised Partisan battles. This is a film that shows how the PLS and promise of a new world was conveyed to and materialised in the masses. The film explains why and how they struggled for the Partisan cause and not for the local collaborationists. Žilnik's perspective in this film is directed from the standpoint of the 'subjectivsation of masses' and could be seen as a reconstruction of testimonies from below, the film version of the "people's history of resistance" (Gluckstein 2012). These people are not only subjects worthy of political attention and media focus, but they became subjects that remember for us, for Yugoslav society and beyond. Žilnik also added an important layer in the format of a participatory survey, an addition in line with the Italian workerist tradition, which introduced collective participatory interviewing. This is masterfully inserted into the film dynamic, where the central events of village life and the resistance are narrated by the different voices of the participants. Their reconstruction is not simple and individualistic; during the filming these voices contradict each other and thus renegotiate the reconstruction of his/her-stories. This is how the Partisan surplus, the impossibility to remember the rupture – in the most truthful way – is traced by Žilnik. The constant movement of the plot is dynamised by the switches in camera movement and the changes in focus to different storytellers and multiple voices. This reconstruction takes the shape of a collective bottom-up process of a memorial narrative and imaginary of Partisan village resistance. There is not a single voice, nor retrospective Communist Party history of the PLS, but a mosaic of all those who participated in it. Due to the scarce material, spectators have to imagine – with the help of sound and different film devices – locations and objects that are missing on the set. For example, once Žilnik's film crew arrives in the village, the story brings us to 1941 and arrival of the Nazi planes and tanks in the village. The film crew's car is turned into a tank, and we see the images of the village and villagers from the moving car, which due to the conscious shaking of the camera and the editing of the sounds of moving tanks, imitate a tank passing through the village.

The collective Partisan reconstruction arrives at a clear political conclusion: the epic battles and the victory of the Partisan struggle would not have been possible without broad popular support, especially from those in the countryside who sacrificed their lives, preserved their dignity, harboured Partisans and practiced mutual aid. The countryside and popular support for the Partisans were the key infrastructures and the most vital means of reproduction for the entire PLS. Žilnik also undertakes a significant shift from the conventional portrayal of 'civilians' and farmers as passive victims of fascism to becoming protagonists of antifascism. As is clear in the film, not all of the local villagers waged battle with guns in their hands, however, all of them were actively involved in and supported the struggle throughout its duration. They become representatives of the 'banality of good,' of the existence of the struggle of those millions who supported and struggled on the side of great battles and cherished leaders. This film account offers a genuine memorial re-enactment of popular history through this raw but inventive aesthetical means. I claim that this is where the counter-archival Partisan gesture of the film lies: Žilnik repeats, through film, how people come to take sides – what matters for Žilnik, in both form and matter, is to make film in a Partisan way, and in this specific case to expand the echo and visions from those fighting from below, those masses who have been making history. Žilnik's film thus succeeds in putting those forgotten moments, traces and protagonists on display, protagonists who had been forgotten in the mainstream canon of socialist Partisan film history.

As mentioned at the beginning, Pančevo's cinema club made this film possible, yet there was a major obstacle to commencing the film's production. As was customary, the film was first sent to the commission that controlled film production in Vojvodina where it was rejected as unfit. From Žilnik's personal archive, *Uprising in Jazak* is designated as an "untruthful representation of the PLS [...] while Žilnik offends the revolution by engaging a group of bumps who allegedly represent Partisans."[227] In another very dramatic post-filmic unfolding of affairs, Žilnik, together with the most determined villagers-Partisans, entered the municipal office of the regional ministry of culture in Novi Sad. Having arrived without a formal invitation, they display their 1941 Partisan memorial, which confirms they fought for the PLS from the very start of the war. They rush into the office of the then minister Djordje Popović whom they force to tear up the decision to ban the film. After a formal apology – "banning the film seems to have been a mistake" – Popović granted their demand and gave his permission for the film's distribution. The film's distribution can be seen as yet another continuation of Partisan politics by other means – a means that resisted the regional bureaucracy and its attack on the engaged art/culture. This is how the Partisan memory of villagers, and Žilnik's methods of production and dissemination, come full circle. The first projection took place in the village cinema a few days later and Žilnik recollects that the cinema was completely full and the showing concluded with long standing ovations.[228] *Uprising in Jazak* was screened a few more times in the surrounding villages and in March 1973 at Belgrade's short film festival, where it received several positive reviews and was warmly received by the audience. In April the film went to the Oberhausen Film Festival and afterwards was withdrawn from distribution until 1984 when Žilnik finally received a copy of it.

3.2.2 Popović's *Tough Ones* (1968): A tough integration of the Partisan surplus

Another record for the Partisan counter-archive is a fictional film little discussed in film theory and history, both in Yugoslavia and internationally.[229] The most

227 From the personal correspondence with Žilnik (2018).

228 From the personal correspondence with Žilnik (2018).

229 Greg De Cuir, Jr's book has a chapter on *Tough Ones* (forthcoming). A few passages can be found in *Serbian Cutting* (Ilić, 2008) and Volk's authoritative but panoramic view (1973) and Daniel Goulding's account (2002). However, no major volume of a cinema journal or a monograph focuses on Popović's film work to my knowledge.

important reason for this lack of discussion is that the film and the filmmaker remained on the margins of film history, while also at the time of its appearance, *Tough Ones* was quickly removed from circulation. It was only in the late 1980s that the film would be made accessible, but at that time the topic of the Partisan struggle had become far less popular. The film director Miodrag Popović was in fact a recognised painter who was involved in artistic education during and after the People's Liberation Struggle. He briefly migrated to Paris in the early 1950s where he joined the art group *Informel*, while during the 1960s he started working on films, all of which strongly resonated with the public (Šašić 2012).[230]

Tough Ones was Popović's third film and was produced in the Belgrade Cinema Club with coproduction support from the major studio, Avala Film (see poster on the Fig. 54). This film went down in Yugoslav film history as the first film to explicitly address war trauma and post-traumatic stress disorder (PTSD).[231] The plot revolves around two brothers – Partisans – who fail to 'integrate' into post-war socialist society. They are traumatised subjects who cannot come to terms with the end of the war and the ruined landscape of early socialism. The conventional literary-autobiographical analysis (Šašić 2012) claims that this plot should be understood along the lines of Popović's own autobiography, who after his father was killed, joined the Partisans and relentlessly fought the Nazis until the end of the war. He also organised cultural activities but soon after the war Popović became disillusioned with the socialist revolution.[232]

Despite the autobiographical elements always present in artistic practice, I argue that Popović's film demands a psychoanalytic theoretical approach that attempts to trace the 'surplus' of the traumatic event and its negative dimensions, which propel two brothers onto this tragic trajectory. The opening sequence of

---

230 His first film *The Man from the Oak Forest* (1964) drew quite a lot of public attention at the main film festival in Pula. This was one of the very first films that offered a somewhat more complex and even mystical portrayal of the life of a Chetnik in a remote village in Serbia upon the arrival of the Nazis. Within the film, we encounter a local sage whose judgments on the situation of the coming civil war can be deemed existentialist, but not really openly supportive of the Partisan cause. After the first screening and initial silence, however, a standing ovation ensued – the film elicited a series of strong reactions, and as one can imagine, Party intellectuals heavily criticised the film.

231 The film deals with the psychological consequences of trauma and killing in the war, a topic that was not largely discussed nor addressed in Yugoslavia. Internationally, it was only with the war in Vietnam and with veterans returning home that such mental conditions became a topic of films and public culture, as well as of the pharmaceutical industry, army, hospitals, and psychological experts.

232 I need to thank Vedrana Madžar for these specific links between biographical, political and aesthetic trajectory of Popović.

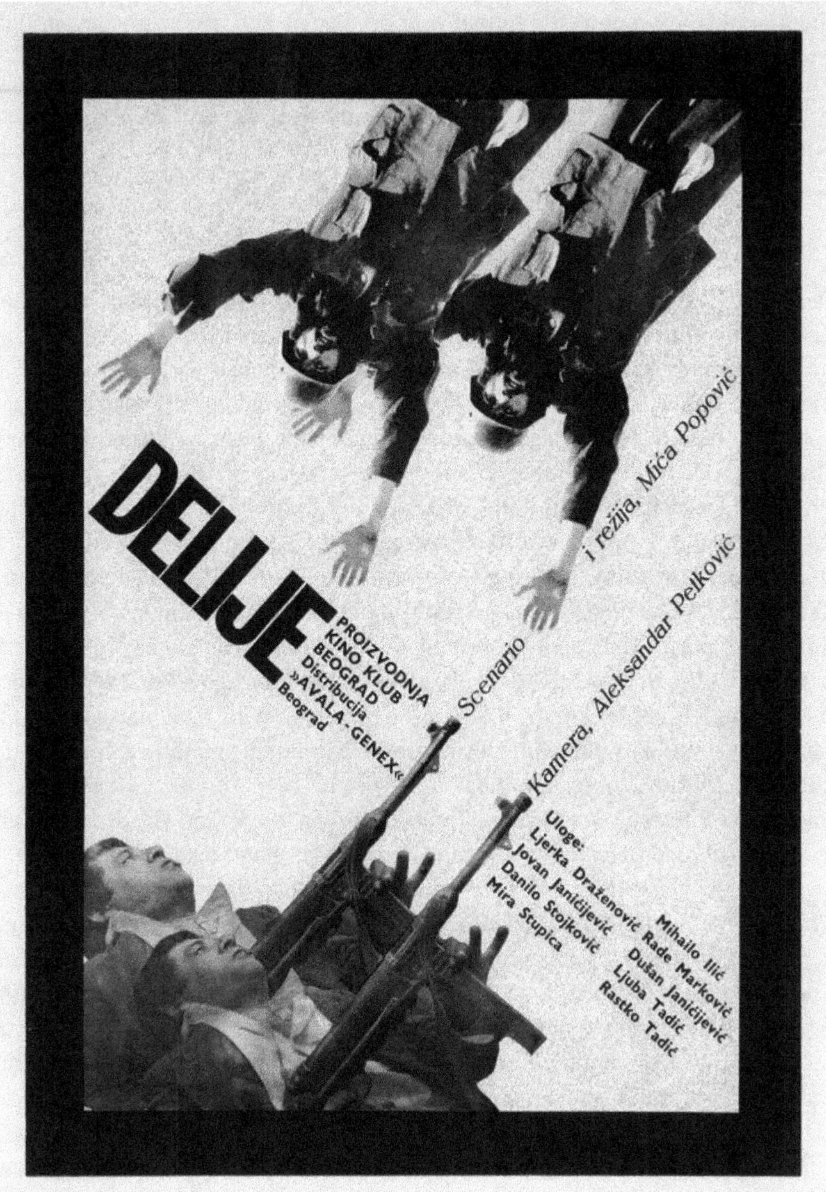

Figure 54: Poster of the film *Tough Ones* [Delije /1968/] by Miodrag Popović. Courtesy of Cinema Club Belgrade.

the film puts a symptomatic formal trait on display and a very unconventional 'credit giving' practice. The sequence is described very well by Greg De Cuir:

> Each of the principal characters is introduced with a 'mug shot' image and the sound of a cynically humorous off-screen voice that describes their personality traits. The sound of the voice is accompanied by the sounds of typewriter keys, and it becomes apparent that the voice is dictating text to be printed. Handled in this manner the credit sequence seems to be pronouncing a guilty sentence on the characters [...]. (forthcoming)

Delije is a film about two brothers named Gvozden and Isidor, who suffer feelings of guilt and trauma that span from WWII to the time of their childhoods and haunt their present inability to live 'normal' lives in the new socialist society. The primal traumatic scene that defines Gvozden's subjectivity is repeated through sporadic memory flashbacks illustrated by moments when a metal shade slams shut across the screen, and when one sees a "message on the shade that reads: 'three corner penalty'" (De Cuir forthcoming). Gvozden briefly relates to this "penalty" coming from his childhood football game and functions as a rem(a) inder of an unpleasant childhood event that is never fully explained. This return of the repressed and haunting and unexplained traumatic event is structured as a phantasy with the logic of *Nachträglichkeit* ['Afterwardsness'] as Freud lucidly explained (Freud (2000–2010)). Phantasy has a retroactive causality, which means that it is not important whether the phantasy really took place or not (the imaginary level), but that phantasy carries real traumatic-material effects for the subject concerned. Concretely, the phantasy of 'penalty' – with the effect of social and/or self-inflicted punishment – infects Gvozden and Isidor. The displacement to early childhood memories actually stands as an ideational representative, a *Vorstellungsrepräsentanz*, of representations of other traumatising war events. This is a perfect illustration in film of what Freud termed a "screen memory": something that works as a compromise formation between repressed elements and as a defence against them. The film itself does not show us war traumatic events; what we understand from Gvozden's phantasmatic return to childhood memory is a call for certain punishment. The latter is evidently illustrated by not only Gvozden's but also the damnation of both brothers and their incapacity to integrate into the new social order.[233]

The arrival of Yugoslavia's liberation returns the brothers to their home village, which is nothing but a ruin, both in their war memory and in reality. The 'Partisan' brothers cannot find work, they do not get married, and they persist

233 For some theoretical passages on how the logic of PTSD works, and on the status of the Real and the phantasmatic see Žižek (1989, 1997), and Verhaeghe (1998).

with a life in ruins in the village, which sustains their imaginary as if the Partisan struggle still continued. This imaginary frame intensifies once they encounter the new local madman, an ex-Nazi army soldier left behind by his fellow soldiers. His ordinary daily activity consists of throwing stones at anyone who comes too close. This is a transparent depiction of his suffering from war trauma. Their traumatic experiences encounter and set the stage for the renewed deadly struggle of World War II. The point of no return unfolds the moment the younger brother Isidor moves to action: he picks up his gun and kills the German (ex-)'soldier.' This death, however, does not become the tragic final step towards 'liberation' and peace time, but triggers Gvozden, the older brother, who explodes and turns against Isidor. We witness the final battle between the two brothers, which spectators might either associate with sheer irrationality and traumas from protracted fighting, or spectators might also relate it to the images of civil war[234] and the revolutionary excess of how the Communist Party moved against some of its own members and political opponents after the war.[235]

Killings, devastation, genocide and civil war within WWII followed by post-war killings – all these harsh and violent events were everyone's background on which Yugoslavia was reconstructed: everyone lost someone, while some lost whole families and homes. What I would suggest however is to not read this film as a mere representation of PTSD, and also not as an intensification of guilt by crimes the protagonists may have potentially committed and perhaps act out from fear of punishment or haunting memories from childhood (De Cuir, forthcoming). Rather, I would like to read the personal trajectory as an allegory for the dramatic dimensions of revolutionary process and failure to integrate the 'surplus' into the social order. What would be another name for this surplus-excess? It is not so much that after the liberation, when real freedom arrives, there is more freedom than in times of fascist occupation. Rather, in contrast and paradoxically, in times of war and during the liberation struggle there was an intensified feeling of fighting for freedom, of being free and so close to death. This was a trope I analysed in chapter 2 and which is reiterated in a handful of poems, songs and gestures from the Partisan counter-archive

---

234 There is a morbid scene with victims (in coffins) of revolutionary violence, which openly suggested that the Partisans and communists executed collaborators in the days after the war. The postwar killings was one of the more controversial topics, firstly presented in a few films in the 1950s and 1960s (for a good analysis of early Slovenian film on this topic see Stankovič 2005) and novels. I will return to this topic in chapter 4.

235 Internal purges saw a few trials after the war, but more systematic purges were conducted after the split with Stalin in 1948, where the infamous Goli otok, an island for re-education was created, and where mostly communists and former Partisans (deemed as Stalinists) would be sent. For details on this see Previšić (2013). This would be later thematised in the early film of Emir Kusturica: *Otac na službenom putu* (1985).

that moved beyond death. Rather than an abstract concept of freedom, or taken as a given in a liberated society, freedom within the PLS becomes one of the central political principles. Freedom was something worth dying for and even something that took over your personality and the Partisan collective.

Together with the constant movement, the uprooting, deterritorialising and liberating of new territories involved revolutionary changes for the once backward and conservative rural areas. Large masses of peasants and workers took the Partisan oath and became Partisans, that is, subjects-of-freedom that fully identified with the cause of liberation. As mentioned in chapter 1 and 2 in detail, within Yugoslavia, the quest for freedom was there not to reconcile, but to run through the deepest divisions (often reflecting class lines, yet often running within families) in a society that entered civil war. The objective conditions and subjective determination to break with such conditions brought an array of excesses with it. From excesses of violence to the excesses of revolution. The latter will interest me here, since they are based on a desire for freedom that suspends the normal border between life and death. The desire for freedom is another name for the Partisan excess/surplus. This is demonstrated by the high intensity of Partisan subjectivation and is materialised in the most fanatic fights of the proletarian brigades, but also in their complete investment in artistic activities and cultural education.

Returning to the film and the protagonists, Gvozden and Isidor, rather than suffering from their childhood memories and war sins, their memory is infected with the images, senses and sounds of freedom. There is something unbearable about freedom (a struggle) that demands our whole existential engagement (our life and all powers), while at the same time there was an absence of a centrally organised entity that would persistently sanction or tame the excess. I would thus not question whether Gvozden and Isidor were subjected to pre-war trauma (as with any unconscious subject, they are) or whether they committed some crimes: in short they were Partisan subjects who after the liberation struggle – during peace – continued their loyalty to liberation, the revolution and freedom. They fully embraced the Partisan surplus and did not let go. Taken out of the war context, the brothers become the tragic *Sancho Panza*, subjective remainders of revolution. Any revolutionary rupture, and Yugoslavia is no exception, leads to self-destructive and irrational actions that endanger either the lives of individuals, or the idea of revolution itself. The question of how to tame and protect the revolution in light of revolutionary excess has occupied political thought at least from the French revolution onwards. In a similar vein, in order to function somewhat 'normally,' the unconscious subject needs to protect him or herself from the traumatic Real. In the case of Gvozden and Isidor, this fails – the self-defensive mechanisms to control the revolutionary excess need to be imagined and developed for the future to come. For the fully loyal subject of freedom, the return to peace and normalcy – without a clearly defined enemy – might become more unbearable than war. After all the moments of collective enthusiasm and subjective engagement, was everything halted by peace? It would be naive to expect a socialist transition without any 'morbid' remainders and reminders of revolutionary surplus (Cf. Gramsci 1971, 275–276). Understood from this perspective, Gvozden and Isidor become symptoms of the end of Partisan struggle and the beginning of a new socialist society. Such a conclusion, then, does not only pose the evident question of PTSD and the failure of brothers to integrate into the new socialist order – it also poses the question of whether we can read their failure as the failure of the socialist state to continue the revolution?

3.3 Monuments to the People's Liberation Struggle: Revolution reloaded

Like the Partisan films, monuments to the PLS were a priority for the new socialist state. Between 1945 and 1990 several thousand monuments to the PLS were erected across all Yugoslavia. It is no secret that the production of Partisan monuments or monuments to revolution (the PLS) was formally influenced by the Alliance of Veterans' Associations of the People's Liberation War of Yugoslavia (SUBNOR), founded in 1947. As Sanja Horvatinčić argues, this became

> part of the official Yugoslav politics of memory in 1947 [...] related to the need to disseminate ideological propaganda as well as to legitimate the newly formed social and political order under the auspices of the Yugoslav Communist Party, which was the key and indispensable political factor in the liberation of the Yugoslav territory. (2014, 174)

However, the need to commemorate and produce monuments first came from below, from ordinary people wanting to mourn their victims or celebrate the victory over fascism. Many were built from the mid-1940s to early 1950s, thus in this first phase of memorialisation we encounter a combination of various popular and realist forms of sculpture. Interestingly, the large majority of monuments to the Partisan struggle in no way resemble the massive socialist realist monuments from the Soviet Union and Eastern Europe.[236] Nelida Silič-Nemec called them "people's architectonic monuments" (1982, 14), which had "vernacular" origins and forms. The spontaneous and omnipresent erection of these memorials across Yugoslav

236 For a good overview of the politics of memory in socialist Yugoslavia, see Karge (2010) and Horvatinčić (2014). The shift away from socialist realism was an outcome both of discussions on the left, as well as from party politics that stemmed from the split with Stalin in 1948.

space can be seen as an important part of ordinary people's mourning and a reflection and materialisation of popular memory not guided from above. A large majority of the monuments erected in the first ten years after the war were built in a broadly uncontrolled manner and were not directed by the Party apparatus. Often it was stonemasons who designed and built them, sometimes in cooperation with a local artist and other village volunteers. These self-initiated memorial practices resulted in a wide range of monuments: from simple plaques and small memorial rocks to sculptures of faces, and inscriptions listing the names of victims. They were mostly dedicated to local villagers and Partisans who had died in the struggle or were victims of fascist violence (one typical example see Figure 55).

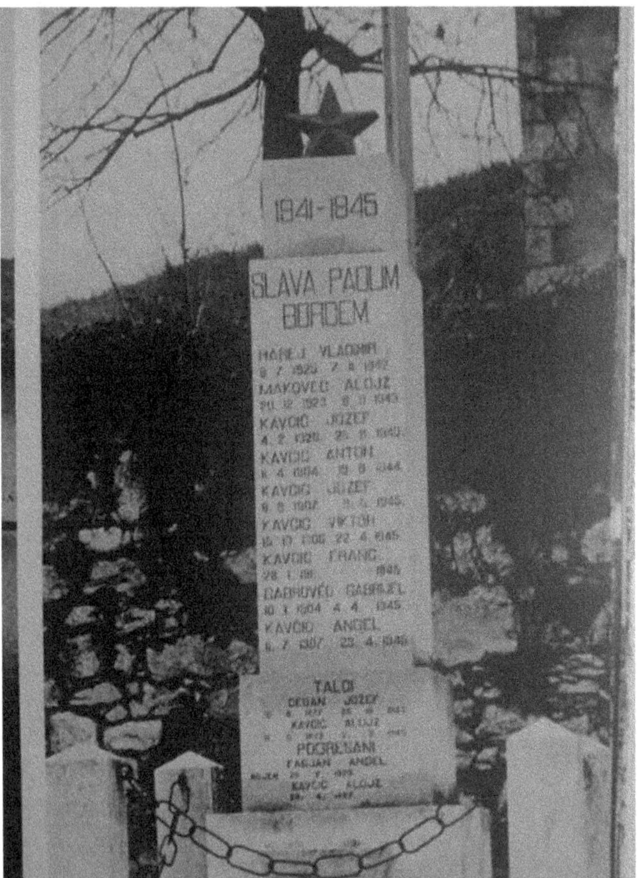

Figure 55: Memorial to the fallen of the PLS in Lipa (1952); photograph by Nelida Silič-Nemec, *Javni spomeniki na Primorskem, 1945–1978* (1982, 137); reproduced courtesy of Nelida Silič – Nemec.

After this more spontaneous and disorganised phase, the socialist authorities established the Commission for Ensuring and Developing Further the Traditions of the People's Liberation War and the Achievements of the Revolution (the commission hereinafter) for the building of monuments where experts, veterans and political representatives formally discussed questions of content, public competition for future monuments, as well as the conceptual formal question of what can be commemorated and under which formal conditions. Furthermore, larger monuments were organised by parts of the municipal and/or the republican political apparatus, which together with veteran organisations played an important role in providing the financial and material infrastructure for the monument-building (cf. Horvatinčić 2014, 2018; Karge 2010).

In the 1950s a more realist genre of monument emerged, taking the form of Partisan sculptures and large murals depicting historical battles, but also of larger pyramidal tombs to national heroes. This proliferation of realist monuments was largely coordinated by established organisations, especially the *Veterans Association of the People's Liberation Struggle* and the official *Commission*. These institutions pursued a more systematic memory politics besides financing larger projects in the cities and in the countryside. Their principal task was to initiate and publicly discuss new ideas for memorials, which would be suitable for the framing and formalising of such abstract notions as revolution, the People's Liberation Struggle, the figure of the Partisan, brotherhood and unity. In general, however, the commission failed to provide a clear answer as to how to represent these abstract notions, and did not prescribe a specific typology for the memorial sites. Instead, their work yielded a massive proliferation of memorials in the 'realist' mode, where pedagogical and historical inscriptions (content) were more important than aesthetic form. These realist monuments were not that much different from an emerging genre of memorial sites and monuments in the socialist East and the capitalist West, consisting of realistic (figurative) representations of victims and heroes, on the one hand, and more massive memorial plaques and tombs, on the other.

3.3.1 Monument to revolution, again

The term revolution is generally associated with the overthrow of government and violent upheaval that affects the whole of society. And since the violent side of revolution is often highlighted in the historical textbooks that cover the history of the twentieth century, revolution has been long associated with iconoclastic impulses. Once we overthrow the former elite, we also tear down the monuments representing former kings, or those institutions representing the old order (e.g. palaces and churches). Many artworks, from paintings to films, addressed the crumbling of the monuments and participated in the creation of the iconoclastic trope. Seen from such a perspective, whereby revolution is a violent and short event in the past, one can immediately ask: why would there be a need to commemorate something so iconoclastic? Why remember something violent, or merely the overthrowing of power? According to this logic, new monuments can only commemorate new leaders of revolution.

However, from the perspective described in this book, revolution is conceived of as a transformative process that continues the dismantling of oppression long after the overthrow of political power. Memory and monuments to/of revolution become paradoxical precisely at the moment when they are taken only as violence or as serving the new political elite (as monuments to new leaders). Rather, monuments to revolution commemorate something that does not want to seal political power forever, something inscribed in the utopian emancipatory horizon of the future. In other words, it can continue maintaining the revolutionary rupture and speaking, narrating and representing the oppressed. Critical history and memory then demand either a permanent or temporary space that addresses emancipatory transformation. This demand could be met by monuments understood as interventions in space that no longer presuppose the simple "passive spectator" (Rancière 2011). The monument to revolution "does not commemorate or celebrate something that happened but confides to the ear of the future the persistent sensations that embody the event: the constantly renewed suffering of men and women, their recreated protestations, their constantly resumed struggle" (Deleuze and Guattari 1994, 176).

The Yugoslav monuments to revolution were not the first to reflect and spatialise revolutionary temporality and monumentality in this form. One of the central predecessors to Yugoslav monument policy was undoubtedly Vladimir Tatlin, who in 1919 designed his *Monument to the Third International*. Tatlin's intervention, which was never realised, openly criticised the 'romantic' monuments – i.e. heads – that represented historical personalities from the French (e.g., Danton, Robespierre) and Russian revolutions (e.g. Lenin, Marx and Engels). Tatlin's work attempted to move beyond such representations, which only imitated reality and did not contribute anything new neither to monumental form and practice nor to (post-)revolutionary society (Buck-Morss 2002). The *Third International* (see Figure 56) was a 'monument' to a political organisation that still existed at that time and which was very much at the centre of a world history directed from below. This utopian monument was never (fully) realised, but this failure already points to the specific impossibility of directly translating the revolutionary idea into life. There can be no perfect monument or memory that truthfully represents and commemorates revolution. Notwithstanding the reservations and contradictions of such an idea for a monument,

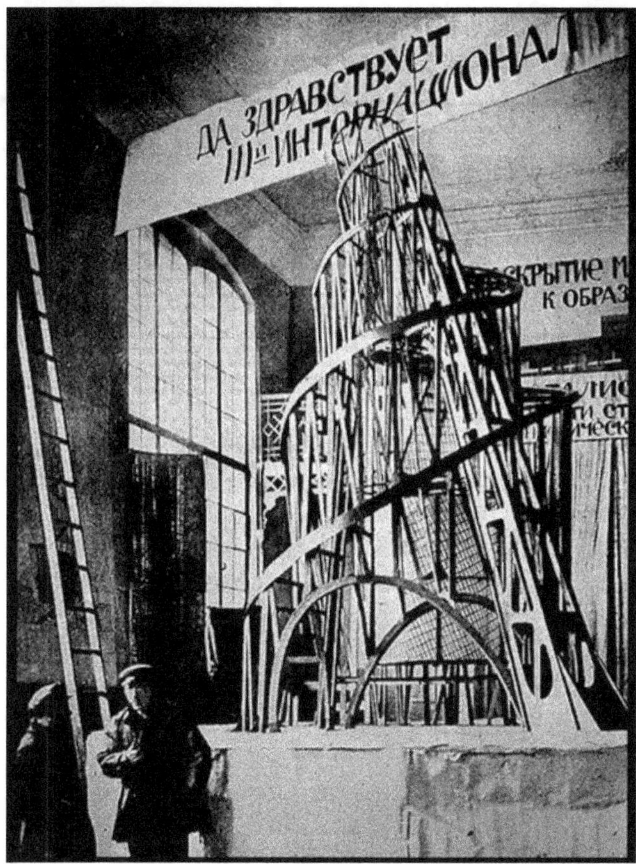

Figure 56: *Monument to the Third International*; Wladimir Tatlin (1919). Public domain.

Yugoslav architects and sculptors took some of these aspects seriously, and also succeeded in realising and elaborating them in practice.

The new Partisan monuments of the modernist movement were not content with any simple conceptual or spatial solutions – neither did they merely profess a specific pedagogical content, nor glorify the heroic individual figure of the Partisan. Rather, the new movement of sculptors that redefined and contributed to Yugoslav 'monuments to revolution' emerged in the 1960s and 1970s and paraphrased Marx's famous *11th Thesis on Feuerbach*: the point of new memorial form is not only to interpret the art history of the canon and to memorialise the past, but also to change it in light of the future communist society. One of the major contributions of the Yugoslav modernist monuments lies precisely in their investigation and materialisation of a revolutionary temporality and modality in the spaces they occupy. In other words, they embody a productive combination between discontinuity (with old traditions in form, oppressions in content) and continuity (speaking from the standpoint of the oppressed, referring to previous and future revolutionary subjects and forms), while also avoiding a purely educational-propagandist function.

The late and alternative socialist monumental modernism is not unified by a common typology, nor by a manifesto that brought sculptors and architects together. Rather than unity, there was a strong diversity and experimentation that marked their peculiar typologies: at times monumental and symbolic (representing fists, stars, hands, wings, flowers, rocks, etc.), while at other times bold and structurally daring, even otherworldly. The monument 'movement' was initiated by artists, architects and sculptors such as Vojin Bakić, Drago Tršar, Edvard Ravnikar, Bogdan Bogdanović, Dušan Džamonja, Miodrag Živković, Gradimir Medaković and others. Their works, together with discussions from above and from below, initiated an immanent process that managed to locate a series of aesthetic innovations in the field of monumental practice. Such 'aesthetic rupture' is a process that qualifies for a continuation of the political rupture of the PLS. Despite the continual destruction of the monuments to revolution during the 1990s as part of 'memorial cleansing,' or negligence by political authorities, which left them to the processes of natural decay, there are still quite a few of them that remain in good shape and they form a symbolic map of Partisan Yugoslavia (see Figure 57).[237]

Yugoslav monuments to revolution were erected on historic sites of Partisan struggle, in open landscapes outside villages and towns. As such, they do not occupy much more classic and visible public sites of representation, such as the avenues and squares of big cities, where they leave sovereign imprints on the daily life of citizens. These memorials are thus set in nature and often function as parks and leisure destinations with picnic facilities, restaurants and even hotels. In many of these memorial parks, one can visit museums or amphitheatres, which exist as open-air classrooms. Conceived in this way, memorial parks became hybrid complexes, merging leisure with education, architecture with sculpture, objects with the surrounding landscape. Monuments to revolution enter into dialogue with nature and due to their bold monumentality they intervene – one could even argue they overdetermine and de-nature nature itself. This is in line with an older model of socialist modernisation, which puts a frame around nature, while it simultaneously underlines the spatiality of the Partisan struggle. Importantly,

237 The fate and present state of some of these monuments will be briefly described in the following chapter.

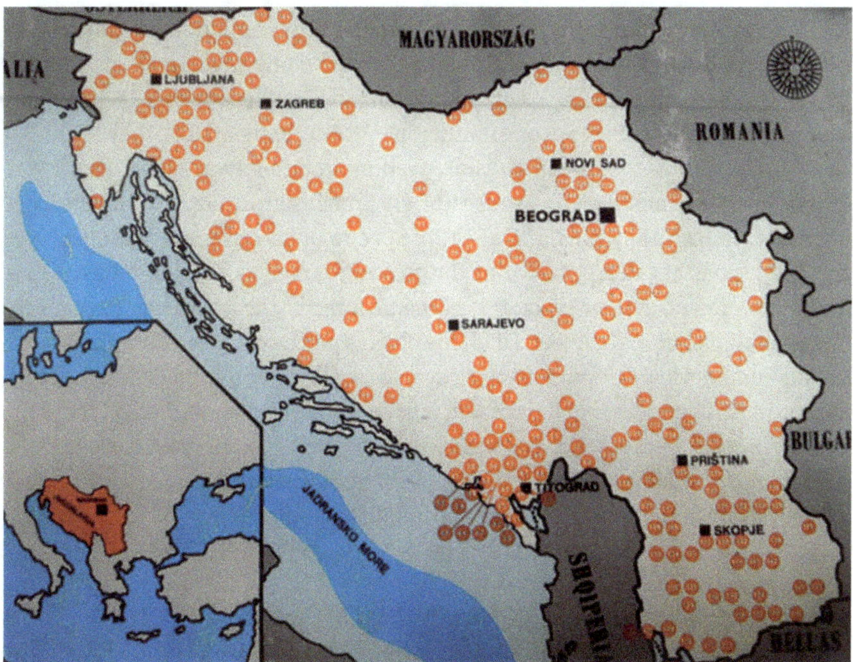

Figure 57: Map of Yugoslav monuments to revolution from the album *Spomeniki revolucije*, a popular album with stickers of monuments to revolution from the early 1980s, which included 190 of the most famous memorials. Public domain.

these monuments do not only mourn fallen Partisans and the victims of fascist violence, but celebrate the victory of the oppressed. To commemorate revolution means to incite, in audiences, cognition of the universal gestures of resistance, revolutionary emancipation and also transnationalism. It can be claimed that monuments to the revolution are late modernist, since they are aesthetically abstract and refer to the Soviet avant-garde legacy. However, due to their elaboration and proliferation we can speak of their own specific memorial modernist language that combined features that can be traced back to only a few other, mostly Soviet, monuments. In this respect, it is not an exaggeration to claim that the East developed a more complex and elaborate monument to revolution and victory over fascism than the West.[238]

238 Despite the purely aestheticising approach of Chaubin (2011), his photos captured a few impressive examples of late socialist modernist monuments in Soviet space that share the abstract, bold and otherworldly features of certain Yugoslav monuments. For a good overview and database of monuments to revolution see Niebyl (2018) and also his accompanying internet base.

Visitors who encounter Yugoslav monuments to revolution nowadays face diverse circumstances regarding the degree of their damage, abandonment, while in some cases solid conservation. What remains unquestionable is that these monuments will not leave anyone indifferent. As Burghardt argues, they are highly imaginative and can be seen as "ambassadors from far-away stars" (Burghardt 2009), or more concretely, witnesses of an unrealised future. Within the post-Yugoslav context, they turn into a sort of spectre of an unresolved and far more progressive past that keeps haunting the present of small nationalist communities. These monuments trigger memories of the historical drama and the wager of the Yugoslav transnational project. Of all the objects produced in socialist Yugoslavia, the monuments to revolution come closest to capturing and formalising the Partisan surplus. They succeeded in practicing a new 'politics of aesthetics' that criticised, or rather distantly departed from the existing canon of realist and popular memorials built after WWII. To illustrate some of the above points I will briefly turn to two case studies: the Kozara and Tjentište monuments.

3.3.2 The Kozara and Tjentište memorial sites: From resistant and asymmetrical circles to formal rupture

Kozara and Tjentište belong to the major memorial parks, conceived of as hybrid complexes, merging leisure with education, while they both reach the architectural peaks of the Yugoslav monumental 'movement.' In the case of *Kozara*, one finds that the museum and sculpture merge into one, while sculpture also becomes part of a greater amphitheatre. The amphitheatre works as an open-air classroom and discussion space, inviting people to congregate and enter into discussion with one another. Its natural setting triggers different public uses by visitors, from tourism and nature trips to organised school excursions featuring short lectures, presentations, dances and nowadays also nationalist-revisionist meetings.

These two memorial sites emerged in the changing political context of the late 1960s and early 1970s, when – for the first time since the end of the WWII – Yugoslavia entered into an economic and ideological crisis. It is noteworthy that the socialist authorities and Tito were first challenged by left-wing forces from the student movement and cultural initiatives to workers' strikes, which demanded more (genuine) communism. This was followed by the emergence of right-wing nationalism, especially the *Maspok* movement in Croatia (more commonly known as the Croatian Spring) and ethnic strife in the Kosovo region.[239] The ideological

239 For details see Dragović-Soso (2002), Kirn (2019b).

composition of the nationalist movements entailed anti-communist and traditionalist components, references to national culture and even the rehabilitation of local fascism. If the arrival of early 1970s saw the aesthetic peak of the modernist monument movement, its earlier discussions on the formalisation of revolution and Partisan struggle now became exposed to the rising tide of nationalism. The spectre of civil war (from WWII) was haunting the political sphere and in 1971 Tito himself underlined this in his speech: "Would you like to return to 1941? This would be a true disaster."[240] Hence, these monuments cannot be separated from their interventions in general discussions of that day: they were designed to counter (extreme) nationalism and strengthen transnational solidarity and revolution among the Yugoslav people and the nations that materialised through the Partisan struggle (cf. Neutelings 2010). This political inscription, which has so obviously faded away in and due to the post-Yugoslav situation, did not overshadow the aesthetic contribution of these monuments. The relationship between politics and aesthetics was forcefully tackled by Rancière, who claims that a strong "aesthetic rupture" (2009) has to do not only with the breaking of established aesthetic genre(s), but also with the launching of a democratic and open political process, be it on the side of the "emancipated spectator," or in terms of inclusion or disruption of what is, or ought to be represented. In this respect, the monuments I analyse below present precisely such an "aesthetic rupture": monuments that evidently form a break in terms of their abstract form from what I briefly showed to be the dominant monumental genre of Partisan monuments; however despite being abstract monuments (with museums and inscriptions), they openly address their historical references: if the monument to revolution in Kozara primarily deals with the scars of Partisan resistance and its defeat in the fascist siege, then Tjentište focuses on the major victory of the Partisan resistance.

The first example, the monument to revolution in Kozara, is located in northern Bosnia and Herzegovina on the highest point of the forested mountain range. Dušan Džamonja was – apart from Vojin Bakić – one of the most prolific sculptors of Yugoslavia and became internationally renowned for his sculptures during the 1950s and1960s. Džamonja experimented with bronze and iron, but also with wood, glass, concrete and polyester in his geometric 'plastic' sculptural interventions. Furthermore, from early on in his career he designed Partisan monuments (notably the monument to Stjepan Filipović in Valjevo, 1953) and also his first monument to revolution in Podgarić (see Figure 58).

In 1969 he won the all-Yugoslav competition for the monument to revolution in Mrakovica. Kozara memorial complex is the most ambitious and

240 In Rusinow (1977, 299).

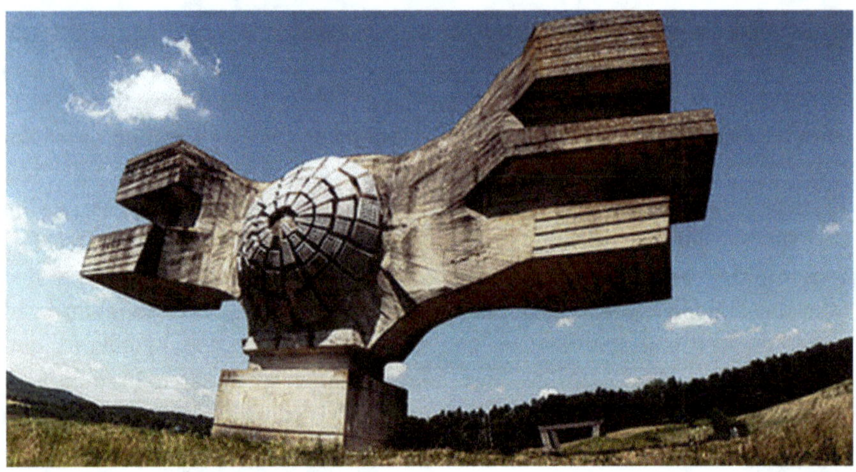

Figure 58: Monument to Revolution of the People of Moslavina, Dušan Džamonja and the architect Vladimir Veličković (1967), Podgarić (Croatia), courtesy of Marko Krojač.

comprehensive memorial site that he designed. The implementation was completed in 1972 (see Figure 59), 30 years after the siege and battle on Kozara. The memorial complex consists of two major parts; the first is approached by means of a plateau that leads through the forest to the central area of the monument. It generates an atmosphere for visitors by their walking through an area to see a monument gradually grow in front of their eyes. The monument is in the form of a cylinder consisting of twenty tall trapezoid pillars, made of concrete with conical gaps left between them. The visitors can enter the monument through these gaps, which are made exactly so as to allow human bodies to squeeze through them. The conical form of the gaps thus enables access to the monument, which makes it easier to get in than to get out; squeezing out of the monument is a physically unpleasant act. Inside the cylinder, visitors stand in a dark, chimney-like space from which they can only glimpse the outside via the vertical slits through which the light trickles in. The physical form thus produces an uneasy feeling of entrapment, which clearly refers to the horrific experiences that took place during WWII in the Kozara mountain range. Nazi troops surrounded the neighbouring forests with the help of Ustasha collaborators and closed in on Partisans and villagers. The military might of 40,000 fascists encircled 5,500 Partisan fighters and 80,000 civilians. From the siege some 1,600 Partisans and only a small portion of the civilian population (15,000) managed to escape. Thousands of young men were summarily executed, many children died in captivity (Barić 2016), while others were displaced in the Slavonia region, in concentration camps or sent as forced labour to Norway and Germany. The Partisans and people of Kozara paid a high

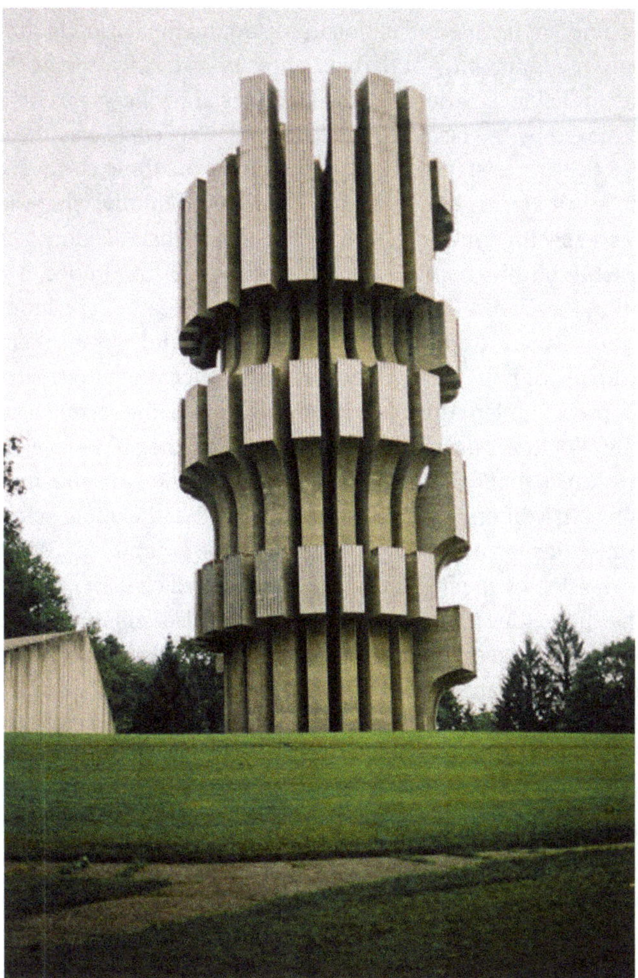

Figure 59: Monument to Revolution (Kozara); Dušan Džamonja (1972); photograph by Robert Burghardt, reproduced with permission.

price for their antifascist uprising and became an ethnically cleansed region haunted by the ghosts of resistance, of the displaced and executed Kozara people.

Apart from the imaginative constellation of amphitheatre, the strongest aesthetic feature of the monument to revolution (Kozara) is Džamonja's use of concentric circular forms, which can be traced to his previous experiments with sculptures. In this historical-cultural setting, with the Kozara region's legacy, these circular forms produced a triple echo. First of all, its circular form immediately recalls and highlights the idea of the *Kolo* (circle dance), a traditional dance that has been practiced by different people and nationalities around the Kozara mountains, people who were predominantly of Serbian ancestry. Secondly, the circle also refers to the claustrophobic experience of the Partisans and villagers as they were encircled and besieged by the fascist forces for weeks. This circle was there not only to break the Partisan resistance but also as a policy of ethnic cleansing and the erasure of the folk and inter-ethnic cultural legacy. And thirdly, what the monument hints at, as a specific synthesis, is that the circle as the *Kolo* does not only exemplify the general cohesive bond of a multinational peace time dance, but also its activation within Partisan resistance and antifascist solidarity. The latter moved the people within Kozara to dance with the Partisans and moved them beyond the ethnic principle of hate. Thus, there are three concentric circles: the lower representing the pre-war inter-ethnic folk legacy of the *Kolo*, the second representing the fascist siege of Kozara, and the third representing the above level of antifascist Partisan resistance that fought for the possibility of living together as a multinational community in a different world. The formal fact that the upper cylindric form remains open – directed at the sky rather than at the ground – does not only hint at the path travelled by the fraction of the Partisan and civilian population from the siege who succeeding in breaking through, but it also exemplifies the Partisan surplus in preventing these circles from being reduced to either the ethnic referent of one nation (the Serbian nation rising against fascism and the Croat Ustasha), or reduced to a fascist victory whose magnitude swallowed the Partisan forces or Serbian population. The encirclement and siege by the fascists can be broken only through the circle of solidarity and struggle. That struggle obviously builds on the folk and cultural legacy of that specific space, but it also transforms its allegedly 'authentic' legacy and propels it to the new future.

The second example I wish to analyse is the Tjentište Memorial Complex that historically also relates to the fascist siege of the major Partisan formation in central Bosnia and Herzegovina in 1943.[241] This fascist offensive has been described as the most tenuous moment for the whole Yugoslav Partisan movement in WWII. The core of the Yugoslav Partisan resistance and the General Command was trapped in the high mountains on the edge of Montenegro and Herzegovina and was carrying thousands of wounded fighters. Nazi, fascist and other collaborationist troops outnumbered the Partisans by almost ten to one; this was a 'live or die' situation for the Yugoslav Partisan movement that fought for its survival. Thousands of civilians and Partisans were killed in the forests close to the village

241 The battle is the fifth enemy offensive that gathered more than 120,000 fascist soldiers to fight around 15,000 Partisans (with thousands of wounded) and where almost 7,000 Partisans died. It is called *Sutjeska* and another blockbuster film made by Stipe Delić in 1972 paid homage to it. It is one of the rare Partisan films where Tito is the protagonist, played here by Richard Burton.

of Tjentište, but in the end, the Partisans, thanks to the courage of the military and surprise moves by the commander of the First Proletarian Brigade Popović and their persistence, were able to break through the siege. The breakthrough in itself also meant not only that the core Partisan detachments with the General Command survived, but also that soon after they became treated as the only real political and military force internationally supported by the Allies (see chapter 2).

Sutjeska was declared a national park after WWII and the memorial park began to be integrated in 1958, when the cemetery for 3301 Partisans received its first memorial form. The memorial space was extended in 1971 with the monument designed by Miodrag Živković, one of the most consistent sculptors who dealt with and produced an array of Partisan monuments across Yugoslavia. Furthermore, the final part of the memorial complex at Tjentište was built in 1975, when a memorial house was completed with fascinating murals painted by Krsto Hegedušić. He was a famous Yugoslav painter, who was helped on this occasion by a team of collaborators. The main part of the monumental complex is located near the village of Tjentište (see Figure 60a, b).

Živković's monument consists of two monumental concrete forms: rocks that mark the site of the breakthrough, and simultaneously form an artificial gorge. One approaches the monument by walking up a hundred stairs. The sculptural

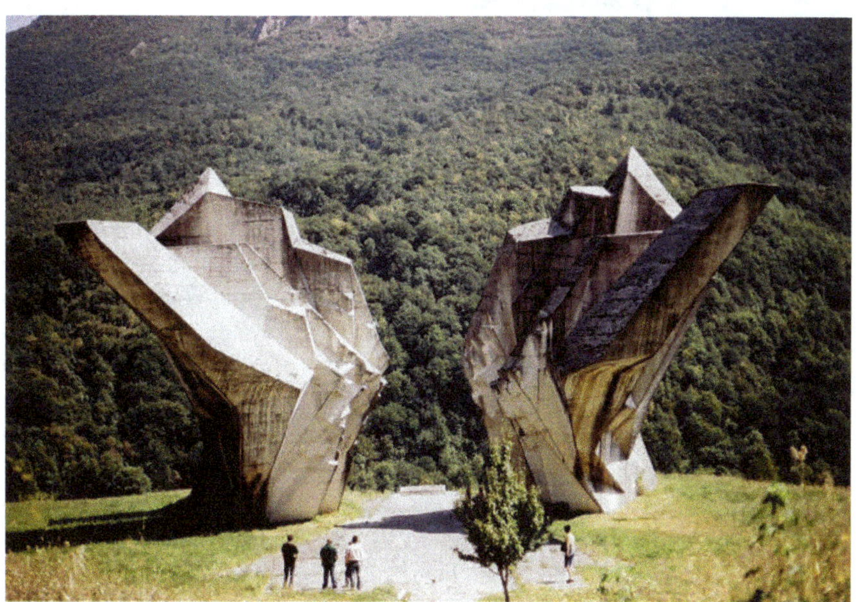

Figure 60a: Tjentište monument from afar; designed by Miodrag Živković (1971). Photo by Robert Burghardt, reproduced with permission.

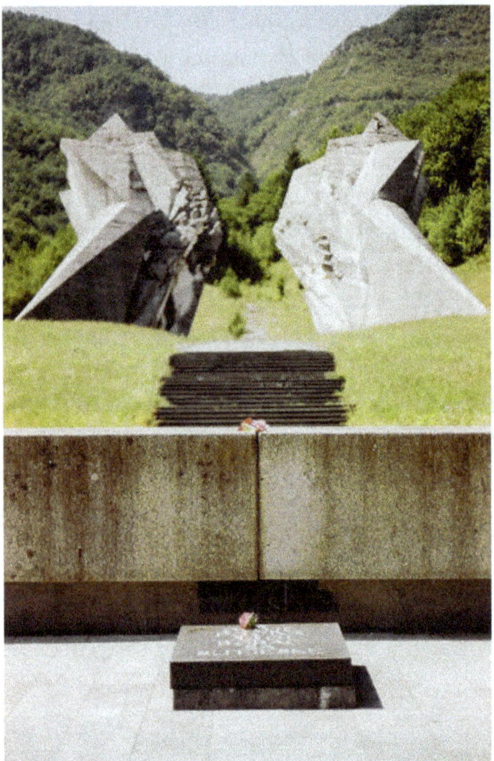

Figure 60b: Tjentište's amphitheatre; designed by Miodrag Živković (1971). Photo by Robert Burghardt, reproduced with permission.

form invites the visitor to experience marching through the mountains and being exposed on both sides. Its form also evokes the idea that even the hard rock of a siege can be broken. The configuration of the concrete forms constantly changes according to the point of view and movement of the visitor. When approached from below, the rocks seem massive and monolithic. Once the passage between the rocks is crossed, however, the form opens up and becomes more sophisticated, changing its initial quasi-symmetrical and monolithic appearance. Upon climbing further up the path and looking down to the monument, the rocks seem to turn into wings. And if from there one keeps walking along the path leading down to the small museum house, the rocks seem to dissolve into fingers. This is complexified by the subtle stylisation of distorted human heads (the Partisan dead) emerging from the rocks. Shifting perspectives on the object thus produce very subtle effects; the first impression of symmetry given by a frontal view of the rocks gives way to an impression of fundamental asymmetry once one has passed through the monument. The rocks are similar, without being exact copies of one another. Tjentište points to the asymmetrical nature of the struggle in which the Partisans managed to prevail over forces that were greatly superior in number and equipment. Finally, as an intervention in the natural space, in the natural park of Sutjeska, the Tjentište monument succeeded in overdetermining its picturesque natural surroundings, which is another typical modernist gesture. This meant that nature combined with a spatial monumental intervention looks even more magnificent, being a site of horrific executions and of the definite breakthrough of the Partisans (see Figure 61a, b).

The memorial house behind the monument houses thirteen large murals about the events, completed by Krsto Hegedušić and his associates. These still remain today – despite some of them being damaged (cf. Dimitrijević 2015). They are some of the most fascinating mural remainders dedicated to the PLS from the time of socialist Yugoslavia (see Figure 62 and 63a, b).

As mentioned at the beginning, the Kozara and the Tjentište monuments refer to similar historical events, i.e. operations relating to the fascists' offensives – besieging the Partisans and the subsequent Partisan breakthrough. If Kozara is seen as a defeat, Tjentište is seen as a victory. This might partially explain the very different solutions and aesthetic strategies employed in the sculptures. Kozara stresses the importance of the inner circle and of Partisan solidarity in order to break away from the fascist circle, while also transforming the authentic circle of the *Kolo*, while the Tjentište monument aesthetically portrays the breakthrough as a rupture with form and content. The rupture meant that the Partisan movement escaped annihilation and opened a path towards something new, as well as the possibility that monuments to revolution were later possible (in Yugoslavia). Ironically, the breakthrough did not follow an order by Tito and his military leadership, but was enabled by the courageous decision of Koča Popović, the commander of the First Proletarian Brigade. In his *War Diaries* he recollects the spirit in the following way:

> From an external point of view, the elements that are fighting have a heavy asymmetry: on the one side, there is sheer size (numbers), organisation, armament, garrisons, transport and guaranteed food provisions, while on the other side there is hunger, fatigue, naked feet, but also victory and a real indestructible force. (Popović, 1944/2008)

Can one not say that something of that experience of asymmetry and breakthrough was inscribed in the experience of the visitors who move around and through the monument? Once we move around the monument we can travel through the landscape: the monument and its forms become our binoculars that zoom in and out of nature. There are many aesthetic differences between the two monuments (and differences generally among the monuments to revolution). This should not

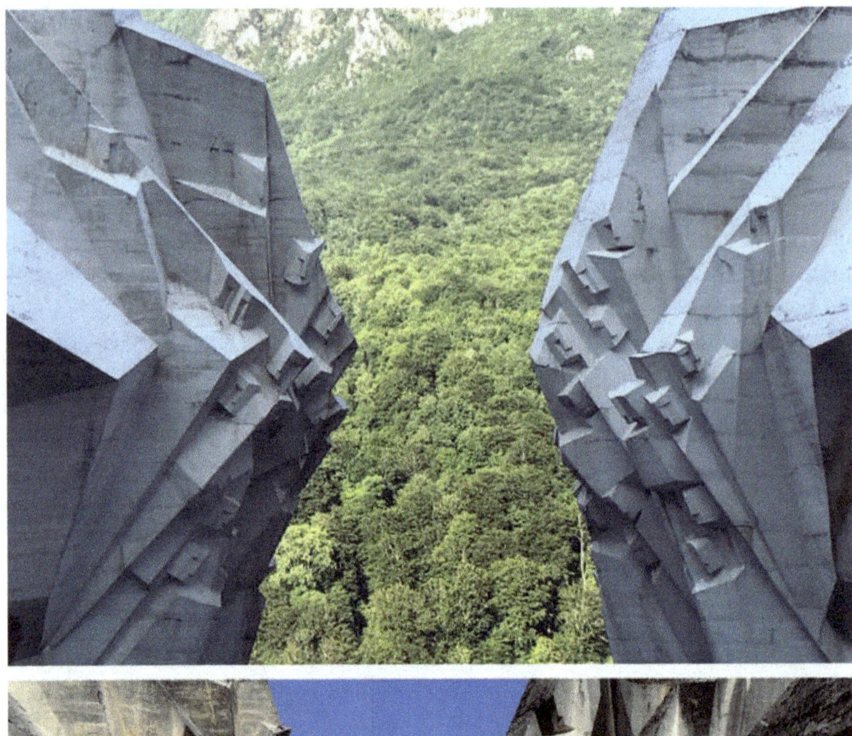

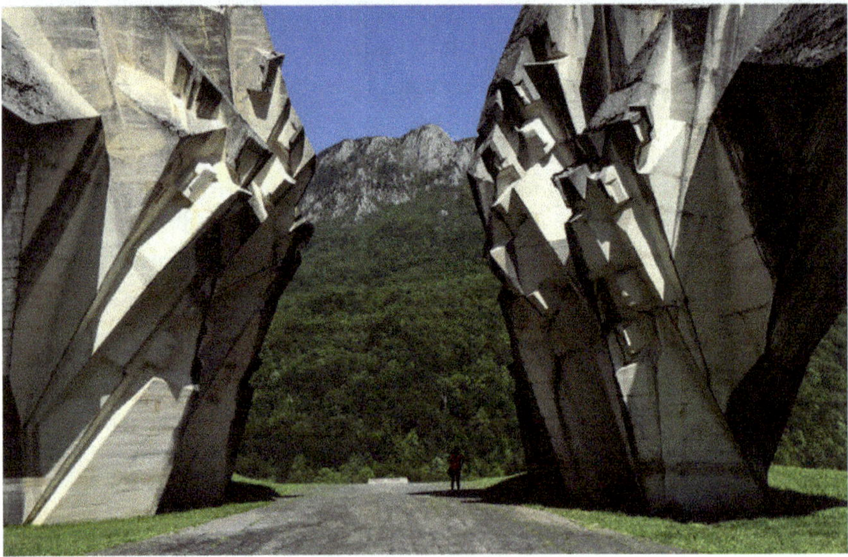

Figure 61a, b: Tjentište monument: details on the form and configurations of Partisans; Miodrag Živković (1971); photo by Michael Allen, reproduced with permission.

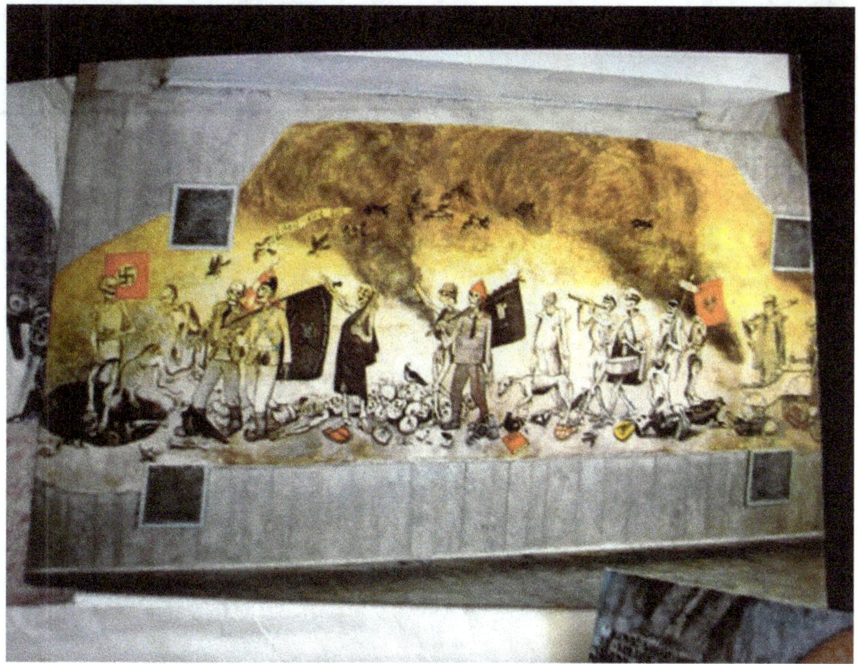

Figure 62: (Before) Photos of Hegedušić's mural during the time of socialist Yugoslavia. Public domain.

come as a surprise, it is rather precisely such a multiplicity of representations that testifies to the central lesson of the Partisan counter-archive: that Partisan rupture – however truthful and noble – cannot be narrated, represented or commemorated in one aesthetic style, or in one privileged format. Rather, all these different paths orient our gaze away from commemorating the past. These memorial forms encapsulate a promise of a different – better – future and instead of sticking with the past event as a fixed and closed set of premises, these monuments became involved in an expanded field of cultural and political struggles over the Partisan legacy. And they remain so today. These monuments have been inviting visitors to use long past events in order to reflect on the more recent past (the 1990s wars) and on a utopian future.

Thus, there is a central preoccupation with "time" – a temporality that I have already mentioned in the previous chapter's analysis of poems. A temporality of 'not-yet-existing,' or the *futur antérieur* is incited by their abstract and otherworldly form, connected to the real work of memory. Monuments to revolution do not remember instead of us (Young 1992), but are essentially meant for any future politics of emancipation. This is why for many nationalist agents and parties in

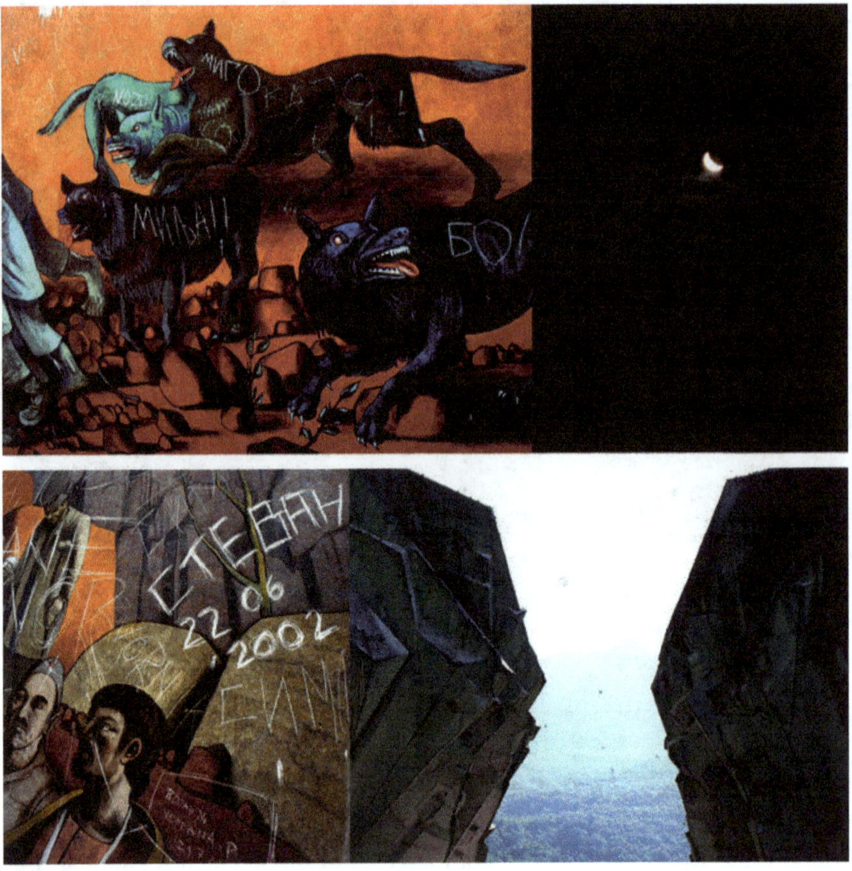

Figure 63a, b: (After) Photos of Hegedušić's mural interacting with the landscape after the war in BiH in 1990s. With permission of Goranka Matić.

the post-Yugoslav regions, these monuments remained as dark spots, as stains that disturb the eternal timescale of ethnic communities, which exclude anything related to the past and future revolution. If Partisan revolution could speak through a monument then it would want to exert its force on the present, and as such it needs to be retrieved and activated through cultural, memorial and political struggle. The major question posed by critical artists in Yugoslavia concerned how to formalise revolution and I would conclude that it received its most subtle and monumental answer in the sculptural/monumental 'movement.' These artists were far from being anti-communist dissidents, but expressed a commitment to continue the Partisan rupture through their own media and art practices. They took seriously the impossible task of narrating, representing and finding a form for the (Partisan) revolution, and therefore the memorial landscape became one of the most exciting and contested fields where multiple instances of the production and reception of Partisan memory were enacted and confronted. In the first few sections I sketched out how in the pre-existing memorial regime of visibility, i.e. realist monuments and popular architectonics, figurative monuments and elementary memorial language was pervasive. If the aesthetic gesture from the outside – due to its abstract language – may not immediately trigger political associations, it was precisely through the invention of new visual strategies and new experiences of monumentality that the reshaping, actualising and re-orienting of social attitudes and practices towards the Partisan past was achieved. These monuments are both powerful echoes and a vision of the revolutionary legacy. Their abstract vocabulary allowed for the appropriation of their meaning that could at once agree with official narratives, while also allowing room for disagreement with the official political line. By the mid-1980s this inventive movement, which is aligned with what I named the Partisan counter-archive, came to an abrupt halt. With the intensification of economic crisis and rising historical revisionism and nationalism, an era of anti-Partisan and nationalist monuments has begun. Emerging on new ethnically defined and in some places ethnically cleansed grounds, new 'revisionist monuments'[242] conformed closely with the new official ideologies. Furthermore, most of the revisionist monuments were much poorer aesthetically than their socialist predecessors. The process of undoing of the Partisan archive and counter-archive is the topic of my final chapter.

242 Together with Fokus Grupa (Croatia) we have been assembling an array of different monuments that we categorise under the adjective 'revisionist': nationalist, openly fascist, or those that focus on the 'totalitarian' crimes of socialism. See the web page: http://fokusgrupa.net/. The antifascist monuments – a backbone of postwar Europe – have come to assume a minor role from the 1990s onwards. There has been, with a few exceptions, very little investment in developing new antifascist or Partisan monuments, while the map and substance of revisionist monuments has been financially, institutionally and artistically explored.

Chapter 4
Undoing the Partisan Counter-Archive? From Nationalist(ic) Reconciliation to the Rehabilitation of Fascism

> Besides a small part of the intelligentsia, mostly of foreign blood, Croatian people rejected South-Slavism. These layers never felt as part of Slavdom, therefore they obviated, by their feelings, as something foreign and dangerous, Slavic and South Slavic propaganda conducted by Prague, Moscow and Belgrade. This fact provides us with further proof that Croats are not at all of Slavic, but of Gothic descent, a fact which had already been seriously discussed.
>
> Ante Pavelić, fascist collaborator and leader of the fascist puppet state, the NDH
> (*Kroatische Frage*, 1936)

> Ruins therefore often become the palimpsest of construction, use and decay. They give the past a palpable density, despite failing to represent any particular moment of the past. They convey various kinds of temporality, from slow partial decay to instantaneous catastrophic implosion. *Andreas Schönle,* from *Ruins of Modernity* (2010)

Chapter 2 followed the trajectory of the Partisan counter-archive during the heroic times of the Partisan struggle itself (1941–1945), while chapter 3 took a closer look at an ambivalent formation of memory politics and culture in the mature period of self-management socialism (1960s and 1970s). It pointed to a tense relationship between critical art and the socialist authorities in the field of Partisan memory. Chapter 4 wants to demonstrate how serious the project of historical revisionism and demonisation of anything connected with the Partisans in the socialist past became during the post-socialist condition. The process of dismantling the Partisan-socialist legacy took place on all levels of society. From a research perspective, one might be 'satisfied' with the level and number of new memorial artefacts in the post-socialist memorial landscape, which presents itself as a solid terrain of 'disputed memory.' The post-socialist memorial landscape has been a veritable site in which the Partisan rupture, antifascist and socialist legacy have been neutralised and eradicated, while constructions of nationalist myths and epics have received new monumental colours. Within the former East we can see historical revisionist monuments and memorial parks that stretch from seemingly more depoliticised and commercial forms of entertainment that put all

---

Note: Part of this chapter has developed from my current research that was published in Kirn (2019a).

https://doi.org/10.1515/9783110682069-005

totalitarian symbols and monuments on display (e.g. Budapest's Memento Park) to more consistent pedagogical and national museums of 'double occupation' that preach their national victimhood and anti-communist stance.[243]

Within the post-Yugoslav context, the post-socialist landscape is very vivid and the most brutal due to the civil wars of the 1990s. Just about anything connected with recent history can be called "dissonant heritage" (Tunbridge and Ashworth 1996), that is, it includes highly opposing interpretations of once commonly shared and recognised historical events – but arguably with very poor aesthetic expressions on all sides. In short, since the late 1980s the Partisan Liberation Struggle (PLS) is not seen as the only possible, reasonable or noble historic trajectory of nations and people from (ex-)Yugoslavia. It is now seen as one of the possible paths towards national independence (a liberal view), or a necessary step towards totalitarian dictatorship/Titoism (a right-wing view). Already in the mid-1980s various competing agents promoted diametrically opposed views on the recent past and challenged Yugoslav memorial politics. The most symptomatic case study for this memorial move was discussions over Bleiburg (fascist prisoners of war taken by British forces in southern Austria that were handed over to Partisans, some of whom were executed) and Jasenovac (the Ustasha concentration camp in WWII) that succeeded in 'ethnicising' the topic: the 'victims' were no longer organised around the historical struggle between fascism and antifascism, but according to their ethnic belonging. This soon became a battle over who killed more Serbs, Croats or Slovenians and with this came an array of historical falsifications that speculated on numbers, blowing up and minimising the numbers of fallen, while exculpating and de-contextualising the revolutionary and war events. For many political parties, Church representatives and WWII publics became one of the politically most acute dividing lines. Who was on the right side of history? Who was more patriotic, the Partisans or the fascist Home Guard? Who was the major victim and who were the real (or moral) victors and losers of WWII? Since the official commemorative policy of socialist Yugoslavia celebrated and commemorated the Partisan and People's Liberation Struggle, new nation-states saw this ideological-memorial complex as a central site for deconstruction, forgetting and destruction. New nation-states and their new model of governance required a new ideological legitimacy, which should be as distant from the communist, federalist, multinational past as possible. Historical revisionism participated in the creation of the ideological framework of one

243 See also Buden's analysis (2009) of the House of Terror Museum in Budapest and Radonić's detailed analysis (2009) of new national museums in the Baltic countries.

nation in one state.[244] This model was based on the principle of the ethnic cleansing of the territory divided up into its former sister nations. As the 1990s clearly demonstrate, this had disastrous effects that continue to be felt by the older and newer generations. The first targets of the new revisionism were symbols and representations as well as the narratives surrounding the Partisan and socialist memoryscape.

This brings us to three central commemorative political strategies of historical revisionism: firstly, the most radicalised format is destruction stemming from a more-or-less organised removal of monuments, which Žižić's documentary film rightly coined as *Damnatio Memoriae* (2001).[245] Secondly, the new commemorative policies launched a 'gentler' version of revisionism that entailed the transformation of the old Partisan monuments, whereby Christian crosses and the flags of the new states replaced every red star. Additionally, some of the monuments with the names of fallen Partisans were now updated with the names of fallen local fascists included, or those who had fallen in the homeland war of the 1990s.[246] Thirdly, new nationalist-reconciliationist-fascist monuments were erected that proliferated across the post-Yugoslav territories over the past three decades. Revisionist monuments were the major bearers of the 'anti-totalitarian' paradigm that demonised the old and advocated the new nationalist memory, be it celebratory and directed at important national personae and symbols, or openly rehabilitating local fascist collaborationism. Sometimes the new revisionist monuments were placed directly on sites where Partisan and socialist monuments had been removed. At times, new revisionist and fascist monuments were placed side by side with Partisan monuments in an alleged gesture of 'national reconciliation.' This strange co-existence has to do both with the severe extent of depoliticisation and also with the morbid symptoms of transition to new nationalistic communities. Then again, where it was felt appropriate, revisionist monuments sought out new places of commemoration and were erected through private and public initiatives. Most notably the

---

244 One critical analysis of how historical revisionism worked in the context of historical writing in Bosnia and Herzegovina was published by Arsenijević & Jovanović (2007). For a more general frame of rewriting Soviet history through totalitarianism, see Yurchak (2005).

245 Bogdan Žižić's documentary observed the magnitude of this process in the Croatian context, where during the 1990s around three thousand monuments disappeared. This occurred along with a policy that removed thousands of socialist-Partisan books from library bookshelves (Lešaja 2012). Lešaja analysed 19 years (1990–2009) of such cleansing of books deemed ideologically problematic in Croatia and estimated that around 14% of all library books have been removed either through their burning or other forms of destruction.

246 I wrote on this subject elsewhere in Kirn (2012c), see also Pavlaković (2018).

Church (which receives generous state tax breaks and subsidies), but also the local and state authorities cooperated and funded new public spaces and revisionist monuments. New annual commemorations were instituted, glorifying local collaborationism, whereby part of the political and Church elite countered the commemoration of Partisan memory with memories of local collaborationism. This group of monuments and commemorative practices entails a complex of ideological orientations but they also share a common break with the Partisan monuments analysed in the previous chapter.

This chapter presents an analysis of the most symptomatic cases of new revisionist monuments from my own context of Slovenia. I will present four cases that are most emblematic of commemorative revisionism: The first case will present a monument dedicated to the killing of fascist collaborators immediately after the end of the war (Kočevski Rog) and which was the start of an ongoing national reconciliation process. The second case can be seen as the peak of the 'national reconciliation' approach to memory that resulted in the *Monument to the Victims of All Wars*, a major site of commemoration in the very centre of Ljubljana. National reconciliation, I argue, opened the intellectual-memorial gates to the rehabilitation of (local) fascism. I support my analysis with a close reading of Spomenka Hribar's key texts, Slovenia's foremost authority on World War II memory. This leads me to the third case that commemorates a particular event during WWII (Grahovo) that symbolises the open rehabilitation of local fascism. The final example will show how 'anti-totalitarian' ideology returned to the heart of the European Union[247] in the form of a European Day of Remembrance for Victims of Totalitarian Regimes on August 23, the most important new commemorative event of its sort in the EU, which has been celebrated annually since 2009 on the anniversary of the signing of the Molotov-Ribbentrop Pact in 1939. In 2018, the European Commission announced plans to erect the very first anti-totalitarian monument in the central square of the EU district in Brussels. Ironically, this ideological equation between communism and fascism, which was defeated in the famous *Historikerstreit* during the late 1980s – Nolte's position included the relativisation of the horrific crimes of fascism – became the dominant form of memory politics in the former East and, it will be claimed, has now finally returned to the centre of Europe.

247 For a very thorough analysis of the criminalisation of communism within EU institutions, see Neumayer (2018).

4.1 The new "realm of memory": A commemoration to victims of totalitarian violence

Partisan commemorations were annually held events across all Yugoslavia and often occurred at the sites of the monuments to revolution and historic sites of great victories (and defeats) that occurred during the resistance. From textbooks to documentaries and public culture, a great majority of works took an openly positive attitude towards the antifascist Partisan struggle. The commemorations were seen as a central legacy of socialist Yugoslavia that was fiercely targeted by the new historical revisionism. The new revisionists did not only provide an array of historical falsifications and fake news but were diligent in imagining and designing new 'realms of memory' (Nora 1989). Primarily and from the start, these new realms of memory were related to the spaces of extra-legal killings that happened at the end – and immediately after the end – of World War II: Bleiburg and Kočevski Rog.

At the end of World War II, the Nazi army together with local fascist collaborators was pulling out of Yugoslavia. After many battles in mid-May 1945 they succeeded in crossing the border into southern Austria (Bleiburg), which was then held by British forces. Collaborationists themselves offered to fight in the potential anti-communist struggle that the West might have to start (Tomasevich 2001). However, British forces did not make any agreement with the profascist forces and were bound by the agreement antifascist Allied forces made in 1943, which became known as Operation Keehlhaus (Hornberger 1995, Epstein 1973). This meant that British forces returned 26,000 prisoners of war to the Yugoslav 3rd Army, the majority of whom consisted of Croatian Ustasha, followed by Slovenian Home Guards, while some of the fascist officers and leaders succeeded in securing a deal and fleeing abroad.[248] Especially in the new Croat revisionist historiography, this British decision is seen as a betrayal of the 'anti-communists,' while Bleiburg became the new realm of memory for pro-Ustasha advocates (Pavlaković and Brentin 2018). In addition to 26,000 POWs returning to Yugoslavia there were already some 40,000 fascist soldiers captured mostly on the territory of Slovenia at the end of the war. What happened to at least half of these POWs remains to this day a dark stain on the final stretch of the People's Liberation Struggle. Roughly half of them were sent to prisons, faced trial or were then or later amnestied, while another section of them were gathered together in the forests of Kočevski Rog. During May/June 1945 some 30,000 local fascists, Croatian Ustasha, Serbian and Montenegrin Chetniks, Slovenian Home Guards, and Nazis from Austria and

248 Čepič (2017, 426).

Germany were executed without trial by the secret service of the Communist Party and detachments of the 3rd Yugoslav Army (see Čepič, Guštin and Troha, 2017). The most recent historiographical study concluded that among those executed, 12,575 Slovenian prisoners of war were identified (Čepič, Guštin and Troha 2017, 436). Let me clearly state that these post-war killings were war crimes and also post-war crimes for which nobody was held accountable, and for which there is absolutely no political or moral justification despite the horrific crimes of the fascists during the four-year war in Yugoslavia. Under no circumstances, however, should condemnation of the post-war killings absolve the fascist collaborators of their war crimes and their betrayal of their nations and people.

The (re)discovery of the fascist 'victims' of the post-war killings occurred during the great crisis of the Yugoslav Federation, after the death of Tito in the 1980s. The first step in the new revisionism was to displace the commemoration of Ustasha crimes (and other fascist crimes) in the concentration camp of Jasenovac[249] and elsewhere onto the new realm of memory: Bleiburg. Bleiburg became the major profascist memorial site in Europe with an annual commemoration organised since the early 1990s by the Croatian Catholic Church and also officially registered as a Church event. This event has been attended by major pro-Ustasha civil groups and gathers around 20,000 people from across Europe who celebrate and network around this site of memory.[250]

The second realm of memory around which the post-Yugoslav extreme right has oriented itself and organises a pilgrimage, is located in Kočevski Rog, Slovenia. During the war these forests harboured the General Command of the Partisan Resistance in Slovenia, while from mid-May till July 1945 it became the major site of post-war killings conducted by the secret service of the Communist Party and a few Partisan detachments. Mass graves were dug deep in the forest and caves/old mines were used to bury the bodies. As mentioned before, the prisoners of war were profascist and consisted of Croatian Ustasha, Serbian and Montenegrin Chetniks, Slovenian Home Guards and other profascist soldiers who waged civil war and had committed many atrocities against the civilian population and Partisans during WWII.[251] It also has to be said that part of the leadership of the fascist

249 Jasenovac was a very brutal extermination camp, where hundreds of thousands of opponents to fascism were killed as well as Jews, Roma and other minorities.

250 It was in 2018 that the Austrian government forbid Ustasha and fascist symbols at Bleiburg. See a short television report by Austrian public television: https://www.youtube.com/watch?v=B_88PDnjyBw.

251 The highest casualties of WWII were Partisan antifascist fighters who were killed by occupation forces and local collaborationists. The second highest casualties were in the civilian population, who constituted almost one third of all killed. In this case, the large majority of these

collaboration was put on trial. This resulted in long stays of imprisonment and execution in many cases, while part of the fascist leadership succeeded by going into exile and fleeing from the camps held by British forces.[252]

The Croatian historian Jozo Tomasevich, in his authoritative book on war in Yugoslavia, described the Partisan treatment of the Ustasha (and the same goes for Serbian Chetniks, Slovenian Home Guards and others) in the following way:

> Considering the nature of the struggle among the various competing forces during the Second World War in Yugoslavia, the Ustaša atrocities against the Serbian population on the territory of the Independent State of Croatia and against all pro-Partisan Croats, the fact that the Ustaše adhered to the Nazis to the bitter end, and finally the fact that the Ustaša leadership wanted to put its troops at the disposal of the Western Allies for possible use against Yugoslav and other communists, no mercy on the part of the Yugoslav Partisans toward these troops could have been expected. (2001, 113–114)

In some historiographical accounts of those who survived the post-war killings, one can find descriptions of frenzied revenge and cruel reprisals for interwar atrocities (cf. Hayden 1994). This is true, but these acts were neither legitimate nor legal. Even if Partisans had lost whole families and their closest friends during the war in concentration camps, in battles or as civilians, such a frenzy should never have taken place. It is also clear that a degree of confusion was present among the highest-ranking officers, as suggested by a directive signed by Tito in May 1945 that demanded that prisoners of war were to be brought to prisons and put on trial. Some documents exist pertaining to the secret organisation Ozna, which point to parallel orders being given but without the signatures of the highest-level political leadership. In any case, one cannot relativise the graveness of the extrajudicial executions that should be viewed as a military and political crime in that the period of war had already come to an end. The conclusion of WWII and the civil war thus came to an end in the most brutal way.

Memories of the extrajudicial killings were kept under the rug in socialist Yugoslavia, even if there did exist some persons and works of art addressing this issue. Just after the war, the first to point out the killings was Kocbek, a former AVNOJ minister of culture who published an article that critically considered the post-war killings. He found such military acts unacceptable on moral, ethical and

---

deaths were also the responsibility of collaborationist-fascist forces, which used concentration camps as well as shooting civilian hostages (reprisals) and bombing and burning villages during offensives against the Partisan resistance. In Slovenia more than 100,000 people lost their lives during and immediately after WWII, which is more than 7.3% of the entire population. For details see Čepič, Guštin and Troha (2017, 423–434).

252 Some fled to Spain and the USA but most notably to Argentina, where they remained in very homogenous communities that retained an influence during the breakup of Yugoslavia.

political grounds. This was also one of the reasons for his isolation in socialist times.[253] This dark reminder of the end of the war resulted in traumatic experiences for those relatives who wanted to bury their dead or who wanted to know what happened. This silence was – at the end of socialism – used by the new revisionists in order to sharpen the conflicts and mobilise for the nationalistic cause(s).

The new revisionism has been focused on post-war killings and the effort to create commemorative realms in which a new national subjectivity could be performed and enacted. The Slovenian nation has to move beyond the Yugoslav context, which has been infected by such murderous crimes, and orient itself towards a new future. In the various ideological operations, fascist collaborators were humanised either by decontextualising their previous actions in WWII or humanising them as victims (Hribar 1987). Fascists became humanised victims manipulated by ideology, and Slovenians (i.e. the Home Guard) who were deserving of national mourning. Collaborators were consequently no longer understood as 'innocent victims' (the Catholic Church), but as 'true patriots', as advocated by the extreme right-wing and Church-supported NGO *Nova slovenska zaveza*. In this perspective the Home Guard became members of the only real Slovenian national army. The first array of monuments that I analyse employ a technique called silenced martyrdom, which is at times subtle and follows official requests from state representatives to rehabilitate the victims of post-war killings with a proper burial and the creation of new memorial sites.

The most important role in this process of rehabilitation has been played by the dominant churches across Yugoslavia – Catholic, Orthodox and Muslim, whose leadership found themselves in a very compromised position: they had either collaborated directly with the fascist occupation and assisted in the recruitment of volunteers for collaborationist forces, or remained silent during the time of national liberation. Such collaboration did not prevent a considerable number of lower-level clergy from entering or defecting to the Partisan cause during the war. With the fall of socialism and Yugoslavia, the churches not only regained their economic position as the largest landowner (through a denationalisation process), but also regained ideological strength through the repatriarchalisation

---

253 The writings of Edvard Kocbek, a Partisan and a Christian socialist, were heavily criticised after the war. He had to step down from all political and cultural posts and remained isolated for a long time. His interview that most openly criticised the post-war killings was published in 1975. His essays were appropriated in the mid-1980s by liberal and right-wing intellectuals to legitimate the quest of national reconciliation (Hribar 1987). I will come to this point in the following sections.

and retraditionalisation of societies.[254] In Slovenia, the Catholic Church became a major institution that both financed and venerated the erection of monuments that commemorated the killings of local fascists (the Home Guard). This is reflected both in the monuments' form as well as in the commemoration practices and discursive traits intrinsic to the new rituals (see for example Fig. 64 and Fig 65b, 66).[255]

Let me start with the most famous monumental complex to the post-war killings of the Home Guard located in Kočevski Rog, where already in 1990 the first reconciliatory gesture between a Slovenian bishop and a representative of the League of Communists took place and drew a huge crowd to commemorate the killings. The commemorations continued and it was in 1995 that the government of Slovenia decided to erect a memorial chapel beneath the hill. Since there were some problems with the tender, two chapels were erected in the end (Ferenc 2006).[256] The first monument was built by Metod Frlic to commemorate a 60-year anniversary, while the extreme right-wing NGO *Nova slovenska zaveza* contributed a wooden cross that was filled in with bronze. The first major monument, however, came in the form of a chapel in 1998. This memory site can be reached by driving deep into the forest area. Visitors enter forest paths before arriving at a central stage structured like a larger church chapel full of Christian signs and symbols.

The memorial bears the inscription: *Odpusti* (Forgive) and invokes one of the most important values of Christian morality (see Figure 65a). The massive layering of the crosses and figures of Christ's suffering in front of the chapel evokes the scattered bones of the fascist collaborators. It is certainly a less conventional form of burial site. It recalls that suffering is the highest and last will of Christ, which he bequeathed to his followers. This is now somehow conveyed in the suffering of true patriots, who were allegedly all proper Christians and Slovenians, and who seem to forget that they were also fascist collaborators! At the end of the day these true patriots were sacrificed on the altars of a totalitarian dictatorship in the

---

254 Cf. Buden 2009.

255 For a detailed overview of the discourse of the Home Guard, and of revisionism in Slovenia, see Luthar (2014, 2017).

256 Two major monumental sites have been erected in the 2000s and as Ferenc correctly argues, "Kren and Teharje presumably denote the sites of the most extensive executions of Slovenes. This standpoint was adopted by the media and a large part of the public. Yet neither the area beneath Kren nor the Teharje Memorial Park denotes the actual mass burial sites. While new monuments are being raised beneath Kren year after year, the Macesnova Gorica pit in Kočevski Rog, which seems to be the true largest burial site for victims of post-war executions, stands alone and is visited by no one" (Ferenc 2006, 153). This tragic twist evidently manifests something about the new revisionist discourse and its quest for 'new truth.'

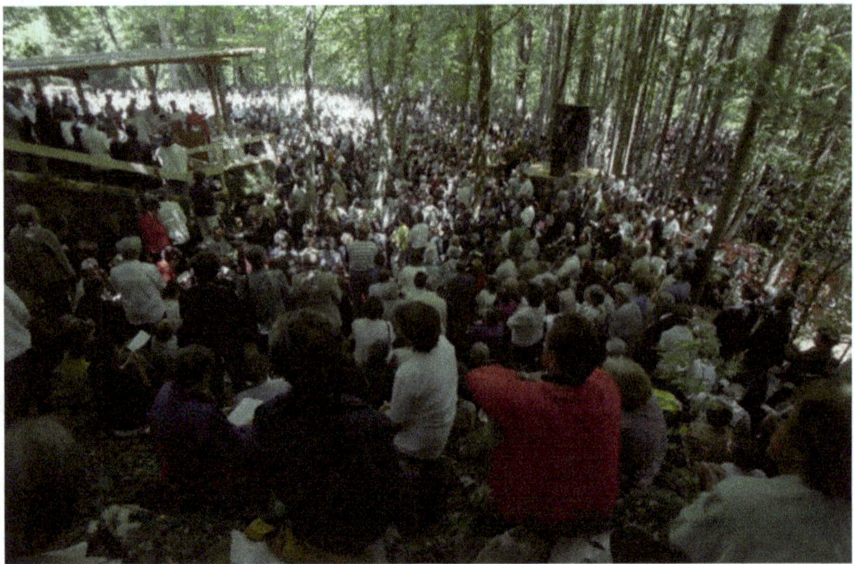

Figure 64: Early reconciliation, Catholic mass at/for the post-war killings at Kočevski Rog 2000, Teharje. With permission of Denis Sarkić.

making.[257] The whole memorial complex is surrounded by forest and its graveyard and chapel construction invites visitors to dwell in silence, with humble empathy and respect for the fallen victims (see Figure 65b). This act of mourning is only possible insofar as the fascist collaborators have been transformed into victims like water into wine; they are now recognised as subjects of injustice – extra-legal killings, or convicted by *ad hoc* war tribunals and summarily shot. The memorial park is shrouded in the dignified, calm, moral universe of Christianity with suffering and forgiveness being the most explicitly evoked feelings.

A little distance away from the first major memorial lies another chapel and monument that was completed on the initiative of the Slovenian Prime Minister Andrej Bajuk (who returned to Slovenia from Argentina in the 1990s) and the

---

257 This dictum is taken from the publications and arguments of *Nova slovenska zaveza*, an NGO that publishes notes, archival research, and delivers speeches on the yearly commemorations around these monuments. It is very active in finding locations and financing new monuments. As early as in 1990, the first reconciliatory commemoration dedicated to the post-war victims of communist violence was attended by 30,000 people. There, the former president of Slovenia and head of the Communist League of Slovenia, Milan Kučan and the now late bishop Alojzij Šuštar shook hands. The whole speech in Slovenian is accessible here: http: //www.bivsi-predsednik.si/up-rs/2002-2007/bp-mk.nsf/dokumenti/08.07.1990-90-92.

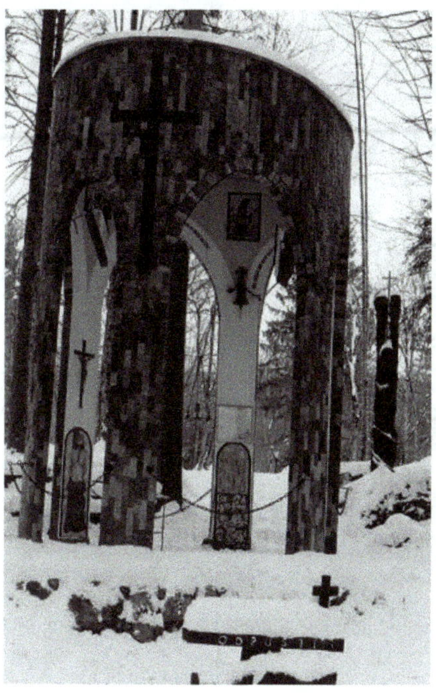

Figure 65a: Home Guard Memorial in Kočevski Rog in winter 1998. Photo by Manca Bajec, reproduced with permission.

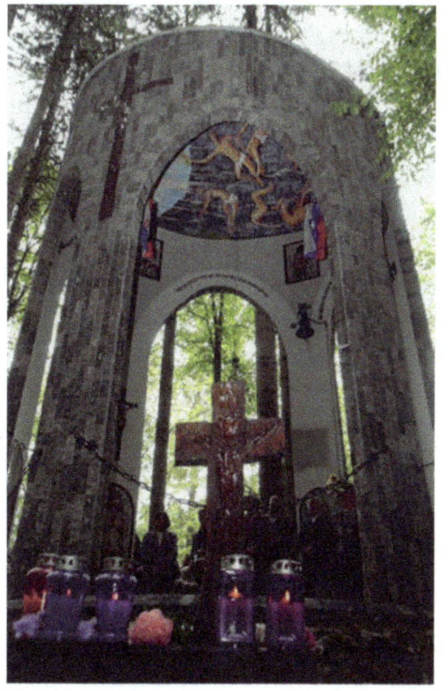

Figure 65b: Home Guard Memorial in Kočevski Rog at the time of the Catholic mass. Photo by Denis Sarkić, reproduced with permission.

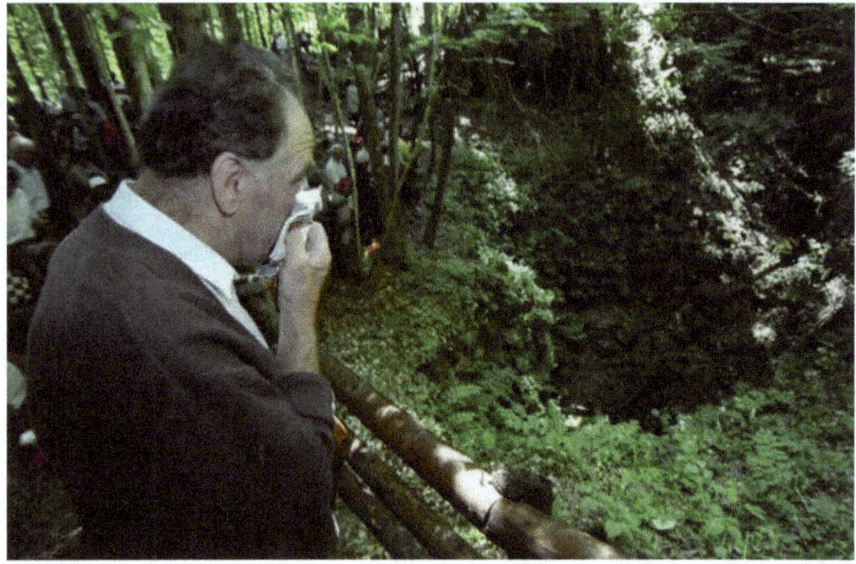

Figure 66: Image from a visit to the mass graves of the postwar killing / killed Home Guards at Kočevski Rog / Teharje, with permission of Denis Sarkić.

Association for Settling the Silenced Graves, conceived by Franc Perme. Within this memorial area a number of smaller tombs, plaques and crosses proliferated (also without permission) and one can follow different conservative inscriptions, such as: "Mother, Homeland, God" and "To the victims of revolutionary violence." The first slogan embodies the essence of a political ideology based on conservatism and the Catholic Church, while the second directly introduces a critique of a totalitarian regime in the face of seemingly innocent victims. The memorial strategy presents Home Guard members not as active protagonists, but as victims who should be recognised for their fight for the homeland and God and who, it seems, were entrapped into collaborating with the Nazis and killing their fellow compatriots only by mere coincidence.

Additionally, and more importantly, one locates two longer 'pedagogical' inscriptions that direct the interpretative line of the memorial site, the first of which was erected on 9 June 2002 by the extreme right-wing NGO *Nova slovenska zaveza* (see Figure 67).

It reads: "In this place lie four to five thousand soldiers of the Slovenian National Army, who were returned from Vetrinj by the English and were killed by communists in the first ten days of June 1945. Their names are not known. For which regiments and battalions they fought for three years for the freedom of the homeland is also unknown. They fell in this cave, where a thousand soldiers,

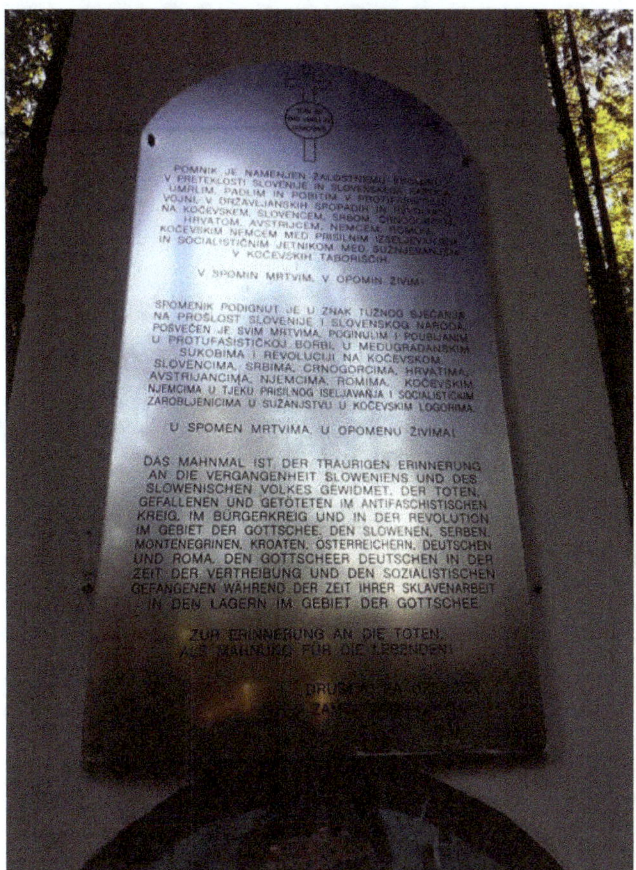

Figure 67: Memorial plaque on the monument by Nova Slovenska Zaveza, Teharje, public domain.

of the Serbian and Croatian Army, already lay. May God give them eternal peace and rest."

This inscription is factually misleading in the very title itself: the local fascists were no proper 'Slovenian National Army' as they were not only unrecognised by the Allies, but were also treated as fascist enemies. Moreover, even Italian fascists or German Nazi forces did not recognise them as the Slovenian Army. They were subordinates in the strict hierarchy of the SS military apparatus. Slovenian Home Guards swore oaths to Hitler and were mobilised in actions against the Partisans. Even the Yugoslav government-in-exile, which represented the former political ruling class, urged all anti-communist groups from September 1944 to join the Partisans, since the latter were recognised as the sole legitimate and legal political power. The inscription does not speak of Ustasha and Chetniks, but again normalises fascists by identifying them with the 'Croatian' and 'Serbian' Army respectively.

Once we zoom in on the chapel itself, visitors find ornaments, frescoes and a text that can be read in three languages: Slovenian, Serbo-Croatian and German. The inscription begins with a text supported by a cross, stating "We also died for the homeland (See Figure 68)."

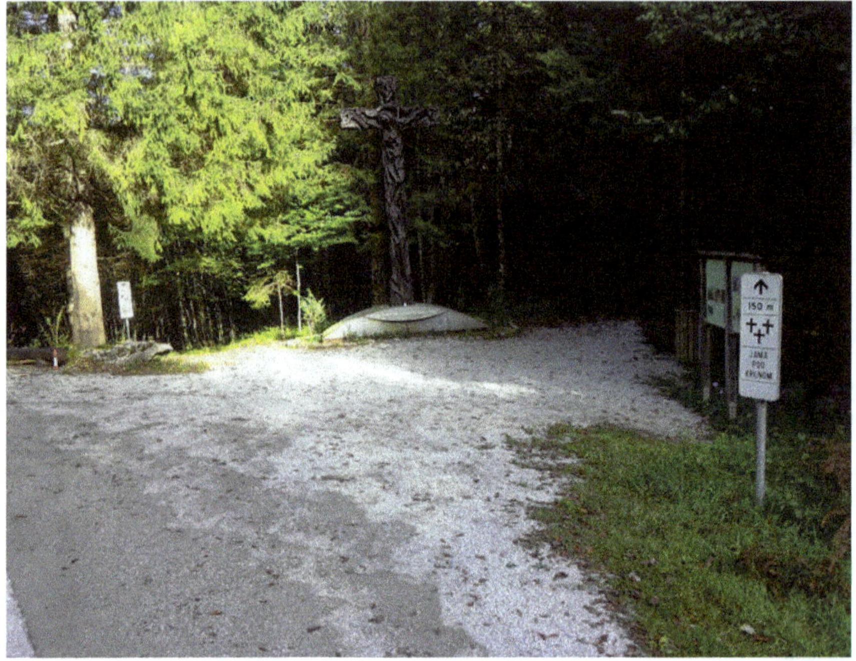

Figure 68: Entrance to the memorial complex for the postwar killing / killed Home Guards at Kočevski Rog, permission by Denis Sarkić.

> This memorial is designed as a sad memory of the Slovenian nation's past, those dead, fallen and killed in the antifascist war, in the civil war battles and revolution around Kočevje. Slovenians, Serbs, Montenegrins, Croatians, Austrians, Germans, Roma, Kočevje's Germans during the forced exile and socialist prisoners of the slave labour in Kočevje's camps. To the memory of the dead and a warning to those alive.

We should pay special attention to the peculiar wording once again. This monument commemorates those who have fallen in the 'antifascist war' and points out the real enemy of commemoration. The monument lumps together antifascists, Partisans and all those who carried out the social revolution. Moreover, it does not only refer to victims of the post-war killings, but also to those forced to labour as 'slaves' in the concentration camps. While in 1945 it was a widespread practice that prisoners of war assisted with the reconstruction of destroyed infrastructure, one could not say that there was some form of systematic slave labour or even something that would resemble extermination camps in the new Yugoslavia.[258] In juxtaposition to the antifascists-Partisans, the good side and new national heroes are not named as fascists, but as those who faithfully belong to the nation: as Slovenians, Austrians, Germans, and a few national minorities (Kočevje's Germans and Roma). The monument makes no mention of the fact that these members of ethnic groups were soldiers in fascist armies, thus clearly presenting the ideological viewpoint of the monument. Hence, the latter subtly includes fascist collaborators as moral victors who must be made part of the respective nation and as such, they succeed in normalising the extreme right military formations of WWII.

Since the post-war killings were little discussed in the time of Yugoslavia, with the demise of socialist Yugoslavia, simply turning the tables was an easy task. Now that the Partisans were labelled as 'communists,' they came to be treated as perpetrators who committed an injustice – the extra-legal killings. On this view, it is antifascists and communists who actually prevented the nation from healing. Apart from being counter-revolutionary and openly rehabilitating collaborationists, this monument also performs a definitive re-Christianization of the victims. What one registers in the repetitive memorial sites and commemorations is a biblical analogy with the martyrdom of Christ, as applied to the local fascists. I leave aside the very vulgar and blasphemous gesture that wishes to place local fascists directly on the cross. However, the narrative structure is indeed identical. On the side of the executioners one has totalitarian/communist violence, while the victims are the true patriots (fascists), who sacrificed their lives in the fight for the homeland and who had in that moment already attempted to prevent the unfolding of the communist catastrophe.[259] The new moral obligation to commemorate the resurrected was most directly alluded to in a striking speech in 2015 by the representative, Tone Rode, of the Christian newspaper *Družina*. At a

---

258 For a historical collective volume on Kočevje Germans and their exile after WWII, see Ferenc and Hösler (2011). After WWII, large parts of Europe were completely destroyed and ruined and a process of reconstruction began. In some places, this labour was conducted by the captured fascist soldiers, while in others they were re-integrated into normal life – when not assuming political responsibility and going on trial.

259 Nova slovenska zaveza on different occasions (see Stanovnik 1996, 2004) speaks of Jacobins and Communists sharing the dark legacy of the Enlightenment, which European civilisation needs to get rid of. Kočevski Rog is the material evidence of such a dark legacy.

commemoration that marked 70 years since the post-war killings, Rode argued that those who were killed are the "true martyrs of Christ" and embody an exceptional "spiritual force" that is "waiting to be really taken for our own [...] we live in the belief that only Christ's redemptive message can defeat the cancer in our wounded spirit."[260] In their poetic resentment and enthusiasm, historical revisionists present themselves as new apostles that capitalise on the repressed death of the fallen fascists, who will only be vindicated in the moment when a transitional society (e.g. Slovenia) not only acknowledges the injustice, but also dissociates itself for good from the remnants of the past and its "forces of totalitarian continuity" (continual demands for 'lustration'/purges). This ideological trope has been diffused by various media and material infrastructures in and across Slovenian space, such as the newspapers *Demokracija* and *Reporter*,[261] as well as public television documentaries and shows (most notably by a journalist Janez Možina and a historian Stane Granda), a major exhibition in 1998/1999 (*The Dark Side of the Month/Communism*), while on a more official political level, parties such as the (right-wing) Slovenian Democratic Party, led by Janez Janša, Nova Slovenija (NSi) and alongside them, the Catholic Church present themselves as the bearers of the new revisionist story.[262]

The revisionist monuments are not left alone for visitors to explore, but are integrated into annual commemorative pilgrimages, which are interwoven into the masses of bishops/priests and the speeches of right-wing politicians.[263] At least in the first years after independence and in the immediate proximity of civil wars in the 1990s, right-wing groups demanded commemoration – and did so

---

260 The whole speech online: https://www.casnik.si/tone-rode-govor-v-kocevskem-rogu/.

261 Let me take a few examples from *Demokracija*, where even their article titles point to ideologically driven 'reporting' that openly falsifies historical facts, which would be described today as 'fake news.' It did succeed in creating a continuous paranoia of communism among the supporters of and voters for the right-wing party that has been attempting to openly rehabilitate local fascist collaborators. In 2018 we could read the following titles: "Communism Still Dominates Slovenians with False Topics," "The Book Legacy *of Silence* Testimonies Disclose Communist Crimes That Did Not Even Spare Children," "The Commissar Woman Milja Used a Hammer to Nail Huge Nails into Brains through Skulls," "How the Creators of the Liberation Front (Partisans) Sent Innocent Children to Concentration Camps," "Ehrlich [a local collaborationist] Knew That Bolshevist Revolution Brings Evil, That Is Why He Was a Firm and Open Opponent of Communism," and so on. The whole discourse is centred on the trauma of the post-war killings and its repetitive nature in times of socialism, up until today when 'forces of continuity' (communism) still hold the strings and operate as 'uncles' from behind the scenes.

262 A similar constellation with a more radicalised degree of involvement in the rehabilitation of fascism is obvious across the entire former Yugoslav political landscape.

263 As mentioned above, the first commemoration in 1990 was attended by almost thirty thousand people, while the popularity of this commemoration later diminished.

successfully. They sought recognition for the injustices done to them in the post-war killings, which forced Partisan veterans and those advocating a complete understanding of the WWII struggle into a defensive position. Right-wing forces and even part of the left-liberal forces called for national unity and launched a process of 'national reconciliation.' 'National reconciliation' was a key dimension of Ciril Žebot's fascist national programme to break up Yugoslavia, while one could say it was to a large degree successfully integrated into the national programme of the new Slovenia. National reconciliation stems from a biologically based conception of the nation, which was reactivated during the 1980s and 'completed' in the wars of the 1990s.

4.2 National reconciliation: Ljubljana's *Monument to the Victims of All Wars* and its moral relativisation

Major speeches and texts by the new revisionists in the 1990s use two master signifiers: national reconciliation and denationalisation (the shift to private property). This was a highly paradoxical move. On the one hand, in order to become fully independent nations, states – gradually in some cases, faster in others – had to first expropriate working people from social ownership and collective wealth via denationalisation and privatisation (which produced a tiny class of local tycoons and war profiteers, see Kirn 2019b). On the other hand, the ideological voices of transition effused over national reconciliation and the healing of past-and-present wartime traumas, which would only be resolved in the fully realised future nation. Any serious discursive analysis must first ask a few very simple questions: Who was supposed to be being reconciled – and why? Were fascists now supposed to reconcile with Partisans? With their dead or with their current ancestors/promoters? Who was actually the intended subject of commemoration and why was there such a great ideological investment in this topic?

The key moment of reconciliation took place in July 1990, when Slovenia was still part of Yugoslavia, when the (now late) Catholic bishop Alojzij Šuštar shook hands with the head of the former Communist Party and first president of independent Slovenia, Milan Kučan. Kučan also gave a speech on the need for reconciliation between all Slovenians.[264] This was a declaration that marked the beginning of a long-term project involving very different agents: Church officials, intellectuals, civil initiatives, and politicians from all parties who all

---

264 The entire speech is accessible online: www.bivsi-predsednik.si/up-rs/2002-2007/bp-mk.nsf/dokumenti/08.07.1990-90-92.

insisted on settling scores related to World War II and the concomitant civil war that had divided Slovenia.[265] The agents of reconciliation agreed that the crimes of both sides must be fully acknowledged in order to move forward as a nation. However, the debate was asymmetrical, since the advocates of reconciliation also claimed that the time for a 'new truth' had arrived. It is noteworthy that in Yugoslavia the Partisan side enjoyed all of the attention and privileges of official commemoration, which meant that in the post-Yugoslav context, the time had come for the tables to be turned entirely. Old veterans from the Partisan struggle were deemed as nostalgics at best, and as glorifiers of totalitarian crimes at worst, while the advocates of national reconciliation claimed that the major historical wounds of civil war have to be 'healed' in order to move forward as a mature nation (Hribar 1987).

As a dominant banner of anti-communist dissidents, and later of all political parties, national reconciliation was realised in a very contradictory way. It is true that within ideological discourse and on the level of commemorative practice, this banner resulted in a new division between those who supported the Partisan cause and those who supported local collaborationists. But on a deeper level, reconciliation functioned as a form of state consolidation: the master signifier of reconciliation actually united the ruling class on its transitional path to Slovenian independence. National reconciliation became a dominant ideological platform that decorated the peaceful transition to a democratic and capitalist system and in a subtle way displayed a form of Slovenian nationalism. Reconciliation posited Slovenia as the morally superior 'nation,' and as it was already the most economically advanced 'nation' from the former Yugoslavia, it became the only one to undertake a 'decent' reckoning with its own bloody past. National reconciliation was introduced to renegotiate memories of the civil war during World War II, and I argue that it gradually opened a window for the rehabilitation of fascist collaboration.

Proponents of reconciliation established commissions for finding the rema ins of collaborationists and then organised gravesites and places of memory for them; it also publicly financed documentaries, books and exhibitions on the topic (see the introductory chapter). Retrospectively, one could argue that in the first decade after independence, Partisan and antifascist thought and practice were placed on a defensive footing and became increasingly marginalised across the post-Yugoslav landscape. Partisan and antifascist thought were pushed into a defensive position, as mentioned above, because they were deemed either nostalgic or totalitarian. Such thought was believed to no longer belong to common

265 For a good summary of Hribar's argument for national reconciliation, see Šumi (2015).

European memory and the future. Nationalist reconciliation openly rejected the transnational character of Yugoslavia and highlighted only the most violent revolutionary aspects of the Partisan past (the post-war killings).

The most elaborate account of dealing with the past came from the pen of the dissident intellectual Spomenka Hribar. She revealed her rediscovery of the post-war killings through Edvard Kocbek[266] in the essay "Guilt and Sin," published in 1986 and 1987 and which appeared in the most famous issue of *Nova Revija* that openly demanded Slovenian independence for the first time. Hribar's text on reconciliation built a humanist-Christian bridge between national, liberal, and Christian understandings of the nation and the citizen, and suggested a way of overcoming sins and guilt to heal the nation.[267] I will touch upon two major problems with Hribar's meditation: Firstly, as Irena Šumi cogently argues, Hribar's call for reconciliation is "morally vague," since it "disperse[s] the perpetrators and victims in a reciprocal way that would demand mutual apology and set the goal of reconciliation without unconditional recognition of guilt" (2015, 73). Secondly, Hribar decontextualises World War II and mentions neither (the fight against) Nazism nor the antisemitism that accompanied the anti-communism of the Slovenian Home Guard and the Catholic Church.

Another problematic moment in Hribar's embrace of reconciliation is its demand for a separation between individuals as 'human beings' and the 'ideology' they espouse:

> Reconciliation should be understood as agreement about our history. It would enable us to ultimately see both revolutionaries and counterrevolutionaries as unlucky 'sons from the same mother,' that is, from a perspective that recognizes them as people (of one epoch). This does not mean that we accept their ideology! Errors are human, but one need not accept and perpetuate them. But rejecting ideology does not also mean we must excommunicate its bearers; we need, then, to distinguish between the man AND his ideology. (1987, 102)

An elementary naiveté underlies this premise of pretending there is a way to separate individual citizens from ideology, and place them in some moral-liberal laboratory. It is itself symptomatic of the ideology at work in Hribar's text. She understands reconciliation primarily as a moral process that should be structured slowly

---

266 Edvard Kocbek was a major figure of Christian socialism and the first minister for culture in the Partisan revolutionary government founded in 1943. After the war he wrote a series of texts on (un)justified revolutionary violence during and after the war. The first officially published interview with such a condemnation was published in Italy in the journal Zaliv in 1975, and so Kocbek remained closely monitored until his death in 1981.

267 Her text was published in different issues of *Katedra* (1986), while some short sections appeared in her seminal article in *Nova Revija* (1987), which I refer to here.

around the 'heart' in vehement opposition to 'avant-garde hate' (Hribar 1987, 102). Reconciliation is an excavation of the 'soil, where *love* and *memory* grow' (Hribar 1987, 101) and can only happen 'between us as human beings' (Hribar 1987, 100). Most importantly, and here the evident ideological call is sounded, reconciliation should take place between us as human beings, but especially within the *national* context, that is, within the 'Slovenian nation.' It no longer has anything to do with European or Yugoslav history. The act of stripping the individual of all his or her ideological identifications while emphasising national belonging has been criticised by the historian Lev Centrih:

> [National reconciliation] has been understood as a call for the mutual recognition and respect of all sides engaged in the conflict, on the grounds that they all belong to the same motherland, to the same nation, even though they may perceive their devotion differently and are marked by errors and crimes. Nation and motherland have been perceived as pre-given qualities of every individual, that is, as essentially separate from one's affiliations to political, production or ideological practices. (2008, 70–71)

It would require too large a detour to analyse how Hribar's concept of ideology approaches it as a manipulative force instilled in an evil party.[268] However, it would be wrong to assert that Hribar proposes a conservative rehabilitation of fascism, as she spoke of the need to condemn fascist ideology and the crimes committed in its name. Furthermore, her intervention came during late socialism, when the silence surrounding the post-war killings was still strong, and so identifying her first target as 'avant-garde hate' was a direct attack on political bureaucrats.

However, the more problematic aspect of her argument is that to achieve the goal of national reconciliation, Hribar needs to beat the major enemy: the perpetuation of avant-garde hate (communism) that she says will prevent reconciliation between humans on Slovenian 'soil.' If her critique of the logic of the avant-garde and the infallibility of the party is to be taken seriously, we need to be very careful of one major ideological displacement in the text. Why is there no serious discussion of the principle of hate that started World War II? Hribar does not mention that the principles of ethnic hatred and 'national soil' actually instigated World War II. Nor does she note that local collaborationists openly adopted the fascist principle of ethnic and racial hate and stood with fascism until the very end of the war. Fascism existed in the Kingdom of Yugoslavia already before WWII, while

---

268 The theory of ideology is a complex topic with a long history of confrontations. Let me simply say that alongside the Heideggerian school of Spomenka and Tine Hribar, the Slovenian theoretical landscape of the 1980s served as a site for some of the most productive re-readings of Marx and Freud, e.g. those by Dolar (1982), Žižek (1989), and Močnik (1995).

fascist-collaborationist formations were vital to the military-political apparatus that terrorised and executed any political opponents (anti-communism), ethnic minorities (antisemitism) and all those who did not fit (Roma, LGBT) into the new order. Ethnic and political cleansing formed the *central political border* that Partisans and antifascists were not prepared to cross. This line divided the nation fundamentally and explains why the nation as a whole did not unite together against the occupation. This is what I named in chapter 2 the two *non-reconcilable* principles: on the one hand, there is the fascist principle of ethnic/racial hate under a collaborationist regime, and on the other, the Partisan inclusion of everyone who fought against fascism, worked for multinational solidarity and constructed a different, federative and multinational political entity. In a political sense, this translates into an ethical choice: either fascist occupation or a people's liberation struggle. The perversity of the moral universe of national reconciliation is that by accepting the premise, or the challenge, we perform a degree of moral relativisation and historical reduction relating to World War II. Conversely, we could give this call for national reconciliation a more generous reading and ask whether it meditates on a third option beyond these two, exclusive alternatives. On what moral and ideological grounds can citizens be forced to retroactively mourn all the victims of World War II, fascists and antifascists alike?

Despite its morally vague bearings, Hribar's text had at least one visionary effect. She called for a 'monument to national reconciliation' as early as the mid-1980s and largely defined the coordinates of the dominant memory politics in Slovenia:

> The obelisk should stand in the centre of Ljubljana [...] and scream to the sky about the tragedy of a small nation that, in the struggle for its own existence and incomprehensible human destiny, became simultaneously its own executioner and persecutor. This obelisk should read simply: 'Fallen for the Homeland.' Indeed, they *all* died for their homeland. Each dreamt of their own beloved homeland [...] All of us that are alive today are descendants of their yearning and suffering. If, as a nation, we cannot accept all this suffering as the suffering of our nation, then we cannot end the civil war that has decimated us. If we are not able to see a human being in the criminal, and if we feel no human pity for the criminal himself, then the sting of the war has not subsided and catharsis will not be reached.
>
> (Hribar 1986, 8, translation mine)

Her mnemonic call to arms interpellates us as current and future descendants of the Slovenian nation who must learn to see Partisans and fascists as belonging to the same 'homeland.' To live free and united, we must pity and forgive each other, even the criminals on both sides of the civil war. This moralisation and (de) criminalisation departs from the premise of cutting ties with ideology, while its final call for a new, revised memory identifies us (individuals) as subjects of the Slovenian nation organised around the central concept of 'national soil' alone.

The alleged exclusion of ideology, besides minorities and marginalised groups, is a cornerstone of (any) nationalist ideology and runs dangerously close to the ideology it allegedly also fights against: extreme nationalism.[269] After expressing moral condemnation of the totalitarianism of fascism (race) and communism (class), Hribar's text ends up with the inauguration of a new form of totalitarianism: that of the nation.

The second monument I wish to analyse materialised – as a realisation of Hribar's prayer – in the form of an obelisk two decades later, that is, after the European Parliament declared a proper acknowledgement of totalitarian crimes in terms of a commemorative day on 23 August for the whole of the EU. In 2009 the Slovenian parliament adopted a law on war cemeteries, which included plans for the *Monument to the Victims of All Wars* in Ljubljana, commissioned by the Ministry of Labour, Family, Social Affairs and Equal Opportunities. The monument's location was in the very heart of the country's capital, where it could embody the spirit of 'national reconciliation' and help to heal the Slovenian nation. The inclusively named *Monument to the Victims of All Wars* would stand just one hundred metres from the parliament building, on the edge of Zvezda (Star) Park, commemorating all the military conflicts, victims and fighters who died for the Slovenian cause in the twentieth century. The fact that the great majority of victims commemorated died during World War II speaks to the monument's dominant ethical requirement: the 'national reconciliation' of all Slovenians.

The Ministry of Labour, Family, Social Affairs and Equal Opportunities formed a commission that awarded first place to a group of architects: Rok Žnidaršič, Mojca Gabrič, Samo Mlakar, Žiga Ravnikar, Dino Mujić and Martin Kruh. The commission stated that the monument's particular symbolic strength lay in "its very neutral form that lacks unnecessary pathos [...] and does not carry any inappropriate monumentality in such place and time" (see Figure 69).[270]

The commission's conclusions can be reasonably challenged, both in relation to formal neutrality and the absence of monumentality. The topic, location, and, most notably, the act of erecting massive pillars in the middle of Zvezda Park are highly representative and monumental. I would even claim that Zvezda (Star) Park has now been overdetermined by this side square that I would name the 'Square of Reconciliation.' The chosen symbolism is not as neutral as the commission suggested. Another statement by the commission even contradicts this claim, stating that the monument represents:

---

269 See Spreizer and Šumi (2011).

270 The documentation is accessible online (www.zaps.si/index.php? m_id=natecaji_izvedeni&nat_id=119&elab_id=634#nagr).

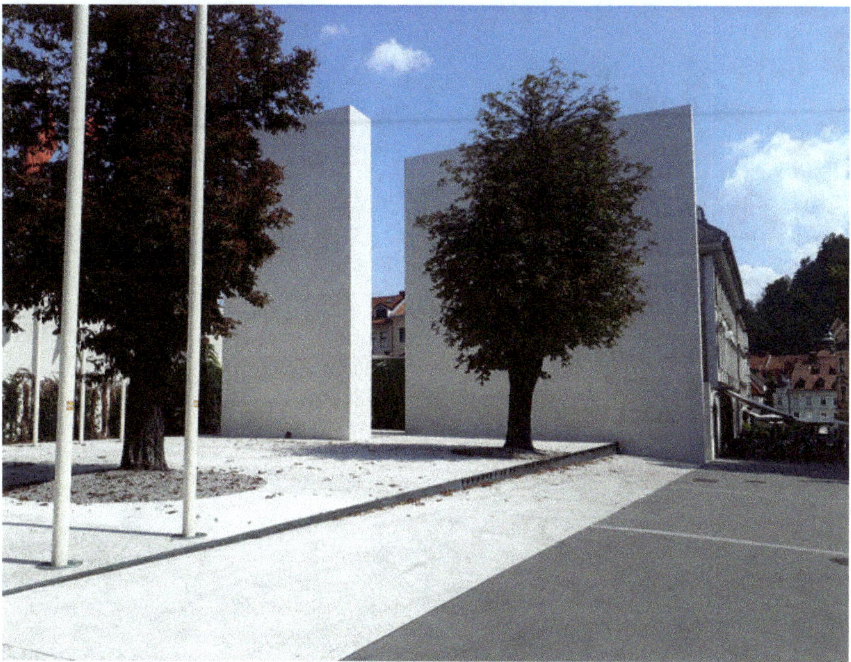

Figure 69: Monument to the Victims of all Wars, Ljubljana (Zvezda Square). Two concrete pillars. Photo by Gal Kirn.

> two pillars of nation connected at the base [...] this abstract form conveys both the metaphor of and allusion to the concept of unity in duality. The pillars are distanced from each other both along the length and depth, and this distance determines the central site of the monument, where wreaths (of flowers) can be placed.
>
> (Zbornica za arhitekturo, 2013, my translation)

This text and the monument's sheer monumentality do much to reveal the "political unconscious" (Jameson 1981) of nationalist reconciliation discourse. Surely the duality of form and the separate pillars of the unified nation refer precisely to the civil war during World War II. The form and symbolism express the divided nation, while the wounds of civil war are likewise evident in the monument (see Figure 70). Worse still, the reconciliation of the split nation is intended to be attained beneath the ground (this works as a kind of displacement of *Blut und Boden* to *Blut unter Boden*). This monument obviously materialises the proponents of reconciliation's call to work through memory so as to heal the Slovenian nation.[271]

271 www.zaps.si/index.php?m_id=natecaji_izvedeni&nat_id=119&elab_id=634#nagr.

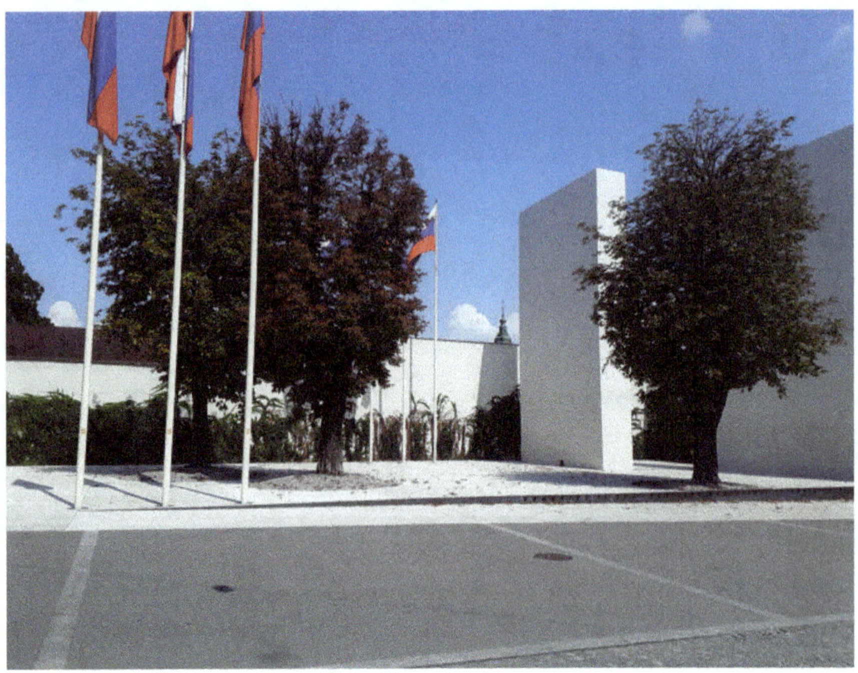

Figure 70: Side view from Zvezda Square of the Monument to the Victims of All Wars, Ljubljana. The platform inclines slowly; a quote by a Partisan poet appears in the bottom-right corner. Photo by Gal Kirn.

On the central square in which the monument lies, we can see two large rectangular slabs made from armoured concrete, consisting of white cement and stones from Slovenian rivers and quarries. A large inscription on the side, a quote by the renowned Slovenian poet Oton Župančič, reads as follows:

> Homeland is one that is given to all of us, and one life and one death.

The choice of quote selected by the ministry is neither coincidental nor uncontested. The poet's grandchildren objected to the choice and the decontextualisation of this quote. Evidently, this line is a perfect poetic embodiment of nationalist reconciliation: we live and die, regardless of our affiliation or the side we fought for, and we always return to the breast of the homeland and to the national soil. There are at least three scandalous facts that oppose such a nonchalant reading. Firstly, Oton Župančič was a Partisan poet whose poem "Do you know your debt, poet?" (1941) was the first printed Partisan poem in times of war. It called on artists in occupied Ljubljana to fight for the Partisans by any means possible. Secondly, the chosen verse was taken from the original (longer) poetic inscription that Župančič wrote for a Partisan memorial sarcophagus in 1949 (!). Thirdly, and even more problematically, a reading of the full poem gives us a sense of how reconciliatory decontextualisation and renationalisation of commemorated subjects occurs (see also Repe 2016):

> We are loyal to freedom, for the struggle we are chosen,
> what is life, what is death? The future is belief,
> whoever dies for it is elevated in life after falling into death.

This poem cannot be read as a rallying ballad for some eternal homeland that equally embraces all victims. For Župančič, it makes a whole world of a difference if and how we decide to fight. The centrality of the Partisan struggle entails a belief in a future (world) for which it is worth dying. The world of fascist occupation was structured around a cult of death and oriented towards the romantic past of an Aryan race unsullied by other ethnicities. It can be argued that quite a significant portion of Europe's population believed that such a world was worth fighting and dying for. But the Partisans dreamt of a profoundly different world: not only did Partisans and fascists embrace mutually exclusive principles during World War II, the Partisans fought against general oppression in the pre-war world. The causes for which the victims of "all the wars in the twentieth century" died are many, but the abuse and naturalisation of the fact that being born in the same nation can function as a point of unification for all the dead under the same monument is a troublesome ideological operation. With such moral relativisation and nationalisation of the Partisan and fascist past, the doors are opened for the rehabilitation of fascism.

4.3 From victims to heroes: The open rehabilitation of local fascism in Grahovo

Almost simultaneously, alongside the crowning of national reconciliation and the transformation of local fascists into victims of the post-war killings, extreme right-wing populists began to take steps to commission the first monument openly rehabilitating local fascism in Slovenia. This trend is also visible from 2013 onwards, while in other war-torn regions of the former Yugoslavia, it even existed from the early 1990s (Pavlaković 2018; Tepavčević 2017; Brentin and Pavlaković 2018). The new monuments and commemorative practices no longer simply commemorate the post-war killings, but now orient themselves towards the leaders of local collaborationism and their battles during WWII.

The third case study that I analyse here is a profascist monument located in Grahovo, a small town in Slovenia that already has a few World War II monuments:

three Partisan monuments and one honouring the poet France Balantič, who fought for the fascist Home Guard. To reiterate again, the Slovenian Home Guard was established by the SS just two months before the battle remembered in the new monument. The Home Guard was instrumental to the strategy of the SS: they waged a guerrilla war against the Partisans in Slovenia, massacred and tortured civilians and brought opponents and Jews to concentration camps. The new monument is dedicated to 32 fascist collaborators who died during World War II (22–23 November 1943) when the local unit of the Home Guard was besieged by a Partisan brigade at an important patrol post in the village. Despite demands to surrender, the Home Guard held their post until the morning of the 23 November, when the Partisans killed the large majority of the fascist unit.

The *Monument to Silenced Victims* was built on the initiative of the civil society group *Nova slovenska zaveza*, which has close ties with the Catholic Church and is also supported by the largest right-wing parties, the *Slovenska demokratska stranka* (SDS) and *Nova Slovenija* (NSi – the former Christian Democrats). In 2014 the initiators had to choose a day on which to erect the monument and instead of the obvious day of the battle, i.e. 23 November – also the day that most of the 32 collaborators died, the initiators choose 6 April instead. This was the day in 1941 when fascist forces invaded the Kingdom of Yugoslavia and the representatives of the old dominant political forces in Slovenia established the National Council (*Natlačen*), which openly collaborated with the fascist occupiers. This date was chosen strategically. Furthermore, the inscription openly framed their political message on the memorial plaque itself:

> On this site, in the year of our Lord 1943, a unit of the Home Guard of the Slovenian National Army was defeated by cannons and fire unleashed on them by communists, brothers in descent and strangers in thought. We await united in the earth, for the day when your proud lineage will break the lying chains of silence and our stolen honour may be restored; only the truth will revive your [descendants'] will for future growth. [my translation]

Without mention of World War II or of the fact that the Home Guards sided with the Nazis, the inscription reduces the context to the civil war and the 'bad guys' to the communists. At the same time, the Home Guard is transformed as representative of the Slovenian National Army. Again, the whole poetic interpellation is permeated with the biologisation of the divided nation ("brothers in descent") that must be cleansed of "strangers in thought" (ideological enemies, i.e. 'communists'). The open rehabilitation continues with the metaphor of resurrection and expresses hope that this fallen line will break the "chains of silence" and "restore" lost honour. The fascist trope of "blood and honour" on Slovenian soil is evidently inscribed in the monument itself. In contrast to the monuments to post-war killings, the central affect relating to the commemoration in Grahovo is resentment built on the defeat of local fascists. The *Monument to Silenced Victims* does not mourn the past but is future-oriented (the "will for future growth," see Figure 71).

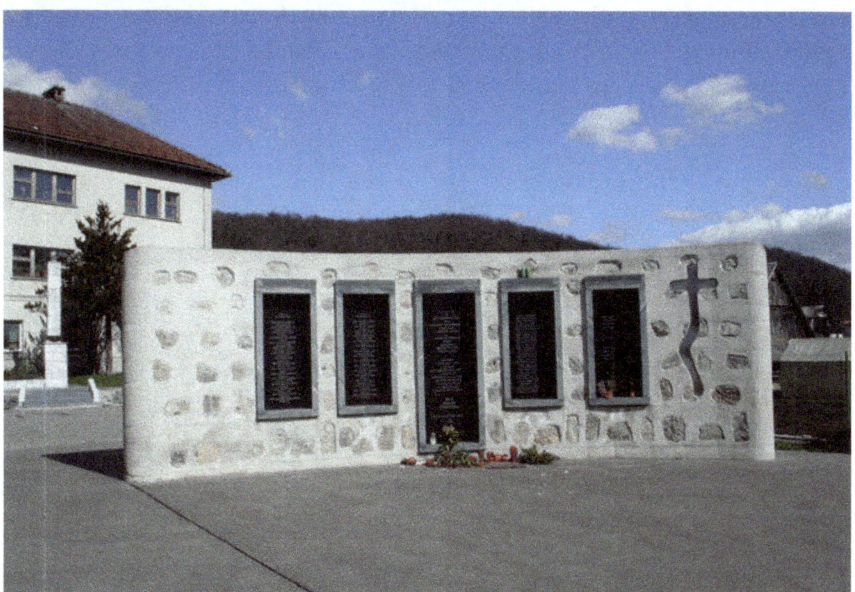

Figure 71: Monument to Silent Victims, Grahovo, Slovenia. Besides the memorial inscription, the monument wall refers to the house where fascist collaborators were killed, depicting a Catholic cross. To the left, a small Partisan monument is now all but invisible to visitors. Photo by/courtesy of Božidar Flajšman.

The local branch of the Association of Partisan Veterans (ZZB) issued a complaint to the Ministry of Culture, calling the monument a troublesome falsification because it "represents traitors to the homeland as the Slovenian Army." In addition, the position and sheer "size of the monument blocks the visibility of another monument, one dedicated to the victims of fascism."[272] The ministry rejected the complaint, arguing that the monument was located on private land. Consisting of a semi-circular wall 9 metres long and 3.1 metres high, the monument, it must be noted, is quite a substantial intervention in the town centre. It is shaped like the windows and doors of the besieged Home Guard post. On it are engraved the names of the 32 fallen fascists, along with the inscription quoted above. Close to

272 The report includes the major points of complaint: www.rtvslo.si/slovenija/v-grahovem-najprej-poklon-zrtvam-nacizma-nato-blagoslov-spomenika-domobrancem/333932.

the monument lies a table, also made of stone (a place for meditation and rest), and there are flag posts for displaying flags on commemorative flag days. The monument in Grahovo was designed by the architect Franc Popek (see Figure 72), the designer of many Home Guard memorial plaques, granite crosses and sites. Yet this monument marks a clear break from earlier forms of fascist commemoration: although Popek's early monuments commemorated the post-war killings, they were also very pious and symbolically Christian (see Kirn 2015a).

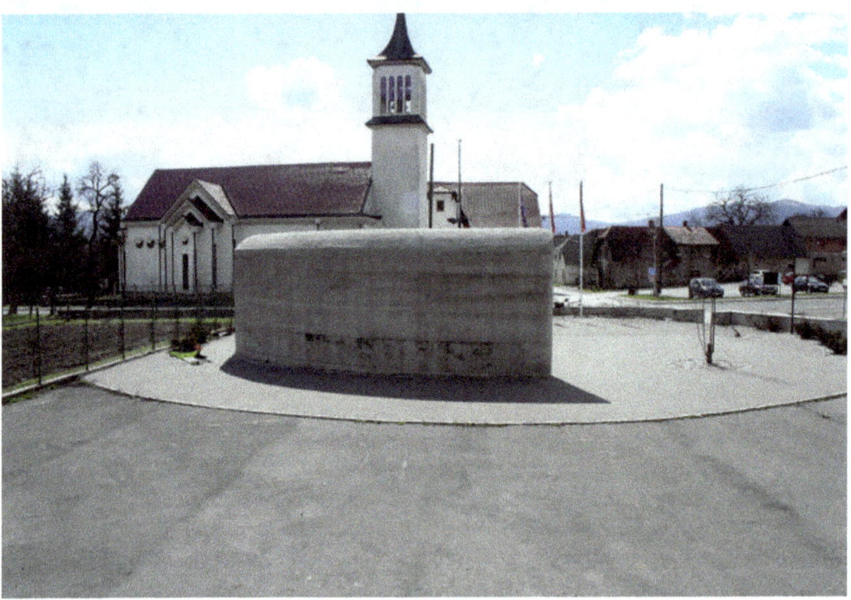

Figure 72: Rear view of the Grahovo monument that displays the centrality and magnitude of the monument, with the Catholic church in the background. Photo by/courtesy of Božidar Flajšman.

Last but not least, the ceremonial opening on 6 April 2014 was attended by the leadership of the right-wing spectrum in Slovenia. A representative of Nova slovenska zaveza and a local priest, Maks Ipavec, delivered the speeches, while Janez Janša, former prime minister and leader of the biggest right-wing party, wrote on Twitter that the visitors had come to exercise their "fundamental human right" to dignity, to grieve and to remember, and that they would not be "threatened by the advocates of this crime, their propaganda and lies" (6 April 2014). His claim that a wartime battle is part of a 'communist crime' is indicative of the recent radicalisation of the right wing, which is increasingly embracing the open rehabilitation of local fascism.

4.4 From antifascism to anti-totalitarianism: Brussels' new pan-European memorial

In the concluding section of this chapter, I want to show how the troublesome trend of historical revisionism and anti-totalitarianism returned to the heart of the European Union just two decades after ravaging the post-socialist landscape. At the time of writing, preparations are already under way for erecting the first *Pan-European Memorial for the Victims of Totalitarian Violence* in Brussels. The project was commissioned by the Platform of European Memory and Conscience, which brings together 55 private and public institutions across the European Union and has been long active in revisionist commemoration policies, research, networking and PR events that promote anti-totalitarian and nationalist perspectives. The Pan-European monument will be the crowning glory of the 23 August European Day of Remembrance for the Victims of Totalitarian Regimes commemorations. The memorial and the name of the event effectively equates fascism with communism, as does the selection of the date, the anniversary of the infamous Molotov-Ribbentrop Pact in 1939. This day of remembrance was designated in 2009 by the European Parliament and has subsequently been adopted by a large majority of national parliaments in the EU. Despite its stated aim of rejecting extremism and oppression, the commemorative day is an attempt to equate all victims and all regimes that go under the name 'totalitarian.'

Kirsten Ghodsee has warned that the moral equivalence present in this idea of totalitarianism can bring negative consequences for the political constellation and memory politics of the EU:

> If both sides of this spectrum are equally evil, then there will be no moral qualm in choosing the side more likely to serve Western political and economic interests, even if this means the institutionalization of a new nationalist xenophobia. If communism and fascism are moral equivalents, threats to the private property of the superrich or political acts that will destabilise global markets are the moral equivalents of the systematic murder of immigrants and internal others. The double genocide thesis and its production of the 'victims of communism' discourse not only aims to prevent a return of leftist politics. It can also be used to justify acceptance of neo-fascism. (2014, 137)

The commemorative aim of the Pan-European moment is to condemn the horrific purges and exterminations carried out by different political entities – Nazism, fascism and communism, which might contribute further to the blurring of the distinctions between such very different ideological, economic and political formations. If the Pan-European monument aims to represent the major mission and memory of Europe, then it fails to embrace "multidirectional memory" (Rothberg 2009), while also presenting no affirmative point that could mobilise common transnational identity. Are Europeans victims of totalitarian crimes? Are they also perpetrators of totalitarian violence? Are we only supposed to be protected by the common framework of the EU? This blending of differences cannot do justice as serious historical research: it is not as if all real-existing socialisms shared experiences of gulags or the imperialist tendencies of the later Stalinist period. Moreover, how do we explain the new EU focus on the 1939 pact while failing to address the historical context of Western military intervention after the October Revolution or, indeed, the fact that the first confrontation between the Soviet Union and Nazi Germany, and between international antifascists and Franco's fascists occurred during the Spanish Civil War, to which Western countries turned a blind eye?

When the fronts between antifascism and fascism were being drawn in Spain, most European governments were trying to prevent their citizens from going to Spain to fight for the republican antifascist side. Instead, (Western) European governments remained neutral and allowed fascism to take over Spain; also, in the aftermath of defeat, many brigadistas were incarcerated in concentration camps in France (e.g. at Gurs),[273] or had major problems returning back to their countries. Why, then, was the 23 August of 1939 chosen? Why not pick the official date of the Munich agreement, a year before, on 30 September 1938? This point was skilfully used by Putin's administration in order to point to the hypocritical stance of Europe, while legitimising Russia as the only real commemorative agent of antifascism – which is undoubtedly another tragic and ironic development of the cunning of memory. The date of 30 September 1938 can be seen as an open collaboration between Western Europe and Nazi Germany, which allowed Nazi Germany to annex major parts of Sudetenland/Czechoslovakia. Western European countries welcomed this 'historical' appeasement of Hitler with grand headlines about the evidently imperialistic attitude of central powers in Europe towards the eastern and southern countries on the one hand, and a tolerance of Nazi expansion in Eastern Europe on the other. Choosing the date of commemoration is thus not arbitrary, but testifies to the specific revision of history, in which it has already been made clear which political agents should be cast as the victors and who the enemies are, so that they can be projected onto European memory and its present Post-Cold War re-alignments. For these reasons, the date should have been addressed as a site of confrontation rather than alleged consensus. If acknowledging the horrors of Stalinism in Europe is an important

273 The multi-layered history of the Gurs concentration camp could serve as a specific portrayal of Western collaboration with fascism, where brigadistas were joined by socialists before Vichy, and then by the Jewish population: https://encyclopedia.ushmm.org/content/en/article/gurs.

thing to do, then why would we push for the moral equation of communism and fascism (Neumayer 2018), or also exclude another 'totalitarian' legacy of Europe: colonialism?

Nor can we ignore the historical fact that the bloodiest battles of World War II were waged between the Soviet Union and the Third Reich on the Eastern Front in 1942 and 1943, marking the major turning point of World War II. Remembering anti-totalitarianism on 23 August helps to erase this historical fact while it also contributes to the current downsizing of the role played by the Soviet Union and communist-Partisan forces in defeating fascism in World War II. In early 1943, with a few exceptions, continental Europe was a Nazi-fascist entity. Even before WWII, but especially during the war, Europe was not a space of freedom and democracy, but a site where fascist policies were jointly implemented by foreign occupiers and local collaborationists. This image of a united Europe should be also retained in public memory, while reducing the importance of communist parties and communist-inspired movements and groups in the fight against fascism is one major blind spot of the European Day of Remembrance for Victims of Totalitarian Regimes. It illustrates a major shift in post-1989 memorial focus: once decidedly antifascist, the memorialisation of post-war (old) Europe is redirecting attention from, for example, Holocaust memory,[274] to the crimes of communist regime(s).

Since the Pan-European monument has not yet been constructed at the time of writing, I can only analyse the public tender and the declaration of the winner(s) in April 2018. The monument will stand in central Brussels on Jean Rey Square in the European district and will serve as the central site of an annual commemoration every 23 August. This process was a major undertaking with an internationally renowned jury including the EU commissioner, Tibor Navracsics, the deputy mayor of Brussels, Geoffroy Coomans de Brachene and the architects Norman Foster and Julie Beckman. The competition announced that "no memorial yet has been created to the countless millions of victims of fascism, national socialism and communism in Europe."[275] There may be no such memorial in Brussels, but the Platform of European Memory and Conscience is certainly familiar with the proliferation of these types of memorials, monuments and museums in the former Eastern Bloc. Furthermore, the stated aim of the new memorial is to

---

274 Holocaust memory was not self-evident after World War II; rather, it emerged through a combined process of the continual efforts of historians, activists, and families of victims on the one hand, and decolonising movements on the other hand. The latter is a vital reference point for Rothberg's study on "multidirectional memory" (2009).

275 https://www.memoryandconscience.eu/wp-content/uploads/2017/04/Competition-announcement.pdf.

represent "the main reason for the existence of today's peaceful democratic European Union – the lessons learned from the totalitarian past and the determination to never allow history to repeat itself." Does the gradual lapse into extreme right-wing populism by many countries in Europe today not teach us instead that lessons have not been learned? The new memorial's main goal is to "visualise this humanitarian message" in the peaceful and democratic EU.

One of the main reasons that Europe could be reformed in the first place was the victory over fascism in World War II and the Marshall Plan afterwards. Oddly, the EU Commission call fails to provide a historical contextualisation or to mention any of the particular 'lessons learned.' It in no way differentiates experiences of Nazism from those of communism. It gives no other central reasons for the rise of fascism or how such ideas and organisations originated in the first place. Nothing is said of the global capitalist crisis or the intensified capitalist exploitation, which fuelled the colonial and imperialist projects that supported the logic of European political space from 1914 to 1945, therein triggering both world wars (Mandel 1986). There is no mention of the rampant nationalism and resentment after World War I or of Western interventions in Russia after the October Revolution, which led to the isolation of the Soviet Union after the end of the civil war. Even though major clashes occurred on the left (between social democrats and communists), Western liberal democracies' ongoing tolerance towards the emergence of fascism during the 1930s cannot be forgotten. In the stripped-down historical context of the call for a monument, these distinctions and lessons learned are blurred to enable a new form of commemoration, which stresses the European struggle against Nazism and communism. If the call clearly identifies Europe as a space where the struggle "for freedom and democracy" took place, the reader is left wondering which Europe that might be.

The memorial call and its execution are part of a top-down process that enjoys the high patronage of the European Commission. As such, a much more open, transparent and democratic process could reasonably be expected from an EU-led and organised project. For example, does this revisionist memory really reflect the heritage of the majority of Europeans, and the histories it leaves out? Red flags abound in both the call and the platform's previous and current projects, suggesting that conservative revisionism underlies the platform's commemorative policy. In fact, the call and the Pan-European monument are structured as self-fulfilling prophecies; they self-legitimise the perspective that Europe is a beacon of freedom and democracy while anticipating a future Europe that can move forward, free of guilt or remorse about the past, after having 'commemorated away' the 'foreign' occupations and catastrophes of Nazism and communism.

Unsurprisingly, the top three designs selected by the competition are aesthetically and politically mediocre. This is not entirely their fault, since they had to respond to the self-glorifying narrative of a Great Europe free of totalitarianism. Despite strong institutional backing and knowledge, the Platform of European Memory and Conscience seems to have ignored ongoing academic and artistic discussions on memory and monuments that in the last few decades have become increasingly critical of top-down projects that 'preach history' from a one-sided, self-legitimising perspective. The idea that one central monument in the centre of the new Europe can perform such an ambitious pedagogical task – teaching us the lessons to be learned and mistakes never to be repeated – is flawed and naive. How can a centralised monument commemorate and reflect upon theoretical and historical problematics if its organising principle is to equate all catastrophes and crimes – fascist, Nazi or communist – by blurring the definitions of 'totalitarian'? But even if we accept that the premises of such an ambitious call will always be problematic, we can still ask if the winning proposal for the Pan-European monument succeeded in giving future visitors a deeper understanding of totalitarian regimes.

The first place was awarded to Tszwai So, a member of the UK-based Spheron Architects (see Figure 73). The title of So's monument, *Echo in Time*, evokes the fantastic journey from the first book of Lindsey Fairleigh's *Echo Trilogy*, where time travel offers a route to Atlantis. If we conceive of the European Atlantis of the twentieth century as its communist and fascist catastrophes, then the new centre of power – Brussels – can finally learn, and commemorate, its lessons. Tszwai said that his design was heavily influenced by 40,000 letters he received from victims of totalitarian violence. His proposal consists of a very classical spatial solution common in 1990s monuments; it focuses on a floor plan on which the magnified letters of personal testimonies are engraved. This memorial solution will display the personal testimonies of numerous victims on the central square. Visitors walk on the content of the letters, which is written in many languages. At best, their multilingualism provides the most, if still limited, opportunity of evoking the shared experience of totalitarian crimes.

At the centre of the design is a woman in a red coat, perhaps recalling the iconic girl from Steven Spielberg's *Schindler's List*. Perhaps this image announces the girl's and Europe's maturity, now commemorating all twentieth century violence and horror through the same red coat? It is impossible to judge exactly where her gaze is pointed from the artist's rendering and the modest description on the website, but it points to somewhere below, towards a construction that suggests an opening.

The very commemorative process of walking and reading as you pass thro ugh the square resembles several Holocaust memorials in Berlin, such as the

Figure 73: Tswai So, winner of the public call for the Pan-European Memorial to the Victims of Totalitarian Crimes, to be erected in Brussels. From www.memoryandconscience.eu/2018/03/28/memorial-competition-winner/. Image removed at the copyright holder's request with apologies to readers of this book for the inconvenience.

monument to the violence of the Nazi regime at the Brandenburg Gate, or the book-burning monument in front of Humboldt University. In the Pan-European monument, the symbolic framework of the Holocaust is expanded to equate all types of violence. Extending this framework relativises the unique horror of the Holocaust. If we are to recognise and condemn the logic of terror, the purges and killings perpetrated by communist – especially Stalinist – regimes as well as the unique suffering connected to the memory of diverse groups and individuals, we must be careful to distinguish the differences between the logic that moti-vated this violence from Nazism and antisemitism specifically. These logics and regimes must be distinguished from each other not only when analysing the 'idea of communism' that is open towards a utopian and emancipatory horizon, and the liberal and European origins of Nazism (Landa 2015), but also when applying them to the scale and intensity of totalitarian violence, as well as to its targets. The industrially perfected extermination campaign of virtually the entire Jewish population of Europe in a matter of three years also targeted people with disabili-ties, Roma and Slavic people, communists and antifascists, to name a few.

We can compare the numbers of victims but cannot equate the ideological and political roots of the Nazi and different communist regimes. Asking who died under the brutal policies of the Soviet Union, especially in the Stalinist period, reveals a fundamental difference in its logic of terror. Rather than being driven by ethnic-racial hatred and the idea of a superior race, political violence in the Soviet period targeted a class enemy and was fuelled by the paranoia of Stalin and his entourage. It also extended to the cleansing of any dissenting voices within the party and Stalin's closest entourage. A closer look at the great purges and Stalinist trials shows that violence was directed at the innermost circles of the Communist Party, including dedicated members and long-term communists, Marxists and avant-garde artists, as well as towards workers and peasants, all of whom were deemed supporters of the Soviet state. Stalinism produced the most horrific mechanisms for consolidating political power and instilling fear in the masses across the Soviet space, but it did not designate a racial other or promote anti-Enlightenment ideology. By contrast, the victims of Nazi-fascist violence were profiled on racial, ethnic, and religious grounds on the one hand, and on political grounds on the other especially and first of all communists, anarchists and antifascists and eventually anyone aligned to liberal and democratic affiliations.[276]

The 'humanist' equation of all victims obfuscates an understanding of the historical events and logic that motivated the terror and extermination. The memory and history of violence and oppression is complex enough to demand a detailed analysis, not just a simple body count and personal testimonies. In addition, by not attempting a more truly all-encompassing representation, the Pan-European monument has missed another opportunity to commemorate the colonial legacy of the European project. The Pan-European monument could have invited visitors to make important historical connections with clear definitions and distinctions between socialism and communism on the one hand, and Nazism, Stalinism and fascism on the other hand. Alas, this type of memory would not be congruent with Europe's desired morally superior image as a place of freedom and democracy and would challenge the wisdom it has supposedly learned from its past.

***

The entire sequence present within the post-socialist memorial landscape can be generally observed as very negative for the Partisan – antifascist cause and

276 Žižek wrote an important contribution on thinking through the differences in terms of the anti-modern component to Nazism and the continuation of the Enlightenment on the side of communism (2001).

memory. The sections above analysed seismic shifts in post-Yugoslav and European memory resulting from the advances of historical revisionism. The latter was not only anti-communist, but also produced an array of revisionist monuments. In the landscape of Slovenian revisionist memory, I first analysed the arrival of the ruling ideology of national(ist) reconciliation, which attempted to reconcile fascists with antifascists by equating the crimes and ideologies of both camps (in the civil war during WWII). I pointed out how the displacement and decontextualisation from the wartime period of the post-war killings resulted in the reinterpretation of fallen and killed fascists as victims who also belonged to the same nation (Slovenia). The national reconciliation materialised in two different monuments, or rather, memorial complexes in Kočevski Rog and Ljubljana that both, in their own ways, contribute to Slovenian nationalism and healing the wounds of the nation. Nationalist reconciliation opened a path to a more extreme version, namely the commemorative practices and monuments that were installed after 2013 and which openly rehabilitated the local fascist collaboration (the Grahovo monument). In the final section, I analysed the Pan-European monument that crystallised the revisionist project of Europe, which instead of the antifascist and Partisan legacy orients itself towards an anti-totalitarian legacy. Memory within the new Europe is certainly not an innocent and self-evident activity, but an activity that should be treated with the utmost responsibility and care for historical detail and the current political situation. There is only one totalitarianism that nowadays endangers the free and democratic Europe – certainly not communism, but fascism. Thus, to entrust such a major project as a Pan-European monument to a politically biased grouping such as the aforementioned *Platform* reflects the sad state of affairs within the EU's dominant (memory) politics. These affairs have largely contributed to the emptying of antifascism in Europe today and to the undoing of Partisan (counter-)archive. Juxtaposed to this trend, I believe that it is politically and theoretically necessary to think, act, and strengthen both memory relating to fascist violence and antifascist and Partisan resistance: the Partisan counter-archive.

Conclusion: Retrieving the Counter-Archive Beyond Yugoslavia

> In conclusion
> I might be delusional,
> but its logical if you're reasonable everyone saying it's dark out there,
> but the glare of this has been staring us all in the face,
> we dropped the ball, took your eyes off the prize
> And the kids' veins are running ruthless, they're feeling their size
> clash: smoke and anger flaring up in the old empires' skies.
> Zena Edwards, *Revolving Anger* (2011)[277]

The central aim of this book has been to bring together various political moments and artworks that stemmed from and strongly related to the Yugoslav People's Liberation Struggle (PLS). I was interested in how far the specific encounter between revolutionary arts and politics was reflected, remediated and refracted within a series of artworks that I assembled under the title the Partisan counter-archive. The 'records' in this counter-archive have had prolonged reverberating and multiple effects that have continued to be felt up until today. This counter-archive is organised around a set of criteria that revolve around the Partisan 'surplus.' The surplus is another name for the revolutionary remainder that despite its singular past event has still been yielding effects and remains open to, or even opens the doors to, an emancipatory future. The records and documents of the counter-archive experimented with form and content, invented Partisan forms of production and dissemination and have continued the Partisan rupture by other means. These counter-archival works have also been able to contribute to alternative protocols of remembrance and inventive commemorative forms that have established a tense temporality, spatiality – and embodiment – of Partisan 'anti-memory.' The book unfolds according to the dynamic and changing constellation of Partisan art, politics and memory in three highly important periods for (post-) *Yugoslav* history: in the period of the People's Liberation Struggle (1941–1945), in the time of mature self-management (during the 1960s and in the early 1970s) and during the period of post-socialist revisionism undoing the Partisan (counter-) archive (from 1989 onwards). Why this enterprise – thinking about the Partisan counter-archive today – is not only theoretically but also politically urgent was made clear in the introductory chapter, where I paraphrased Marx in describing

277 I would like to thank Zena Edwards for the permission to use her quote as a motto for my conclusion.

https://doi.org/10.1515/9783110682069-006

the "primitive accumulation" of revisionist memory by the state and also in the concluding sections of chapter 4, which situate the Partisan legacy within the general landscape of European revisionism. Today, instead of transnationalism and an open society, the dominant ideology rather embraces an anti-totalitarian ideology that contributes to the evacuation of the antifascist and socialist past and a gradual, in other places fast, relativisation and rehabilitation of the fascist past. The Partisan counter-archive fights against the official national-ethnic conception of culture and the neoliberal policies that place a strong emphasis on nationalistic belonging and the individual pursuit of happiness. The counter-archive is a method and a call that participates in the mobilisation of emancipatory fragments of the past for a different future.

Chapter 1 gave a historico-political reading of WWII in Yugoslavia, of how the Partisan struggle created a new Partisan subjectivity, promoted emancipated figures of a new kind of man and woman, as well as of a collective-in-resistance. What took hold on the liberated territories during the war was a genuine political, social and cultural revolution that I named the Partisan rupture. In the first section of the chapter I focused on the intense encounter between Partisan politics and art that materialised – despite the impossible circumstances and scarce material – in an array of activities and artworks. Finally, the Partisan rupture yielded strong consequences in art: for an array of artists and artworks the immense novelty of the Partisan rupture came to the forefront of their consideration and commemorations. The second part of the chapter offered a definition of the Partisan "counter-archive," structured around a surplus with a set of criteria. Dealing with this surplus is an expression of the "tradition of the oppressed" and to a large degree I follow Deleuze & Guattari's conception of "anti-memory" and their call for a "monument to revolution" (1994, 176–177) that traces forms and modalities of revolution in its reflections, refractions, visions and echoes. The Partisan rupture was not simply one that armed new people in a military and ideological-political manner; it also became an activity and horizon of cultural empowerment and armament with a memory of future emancipation.

The selection of records, documents and images of the counter-archive follows three major criteria: firstly, the records resist being easily incorporated in official commemorations and national archives in the public sphere (by the state), since these artworks articulated that the surplus cannot be integrated into the existing state of affairs, but is rather projected towards the future. Records in the archive share a tense and contradictory relationship with memory and Partisan rupture.

Secondly, and connected to the first dimension, is the ability and form of the records that provided alternative protocols and forms with which to commemorate the Partisan rupture. In other words, their peculiar (revolutionary) temporality entails a tense relation between the not-yet-existing and unfinished project of revolutionary rupture on the one hand, and the already finite, present art form that attempts to formalise the rupture on the other.

Thirdly, records go beyond the then existing aesthetic-memorial canons and dominant expectations, which means they produced "aesthetic rupture" (Rancière). The Partisan counter-archive does not want to claim authenticity or neutrality, since the very modality of the Partisan surplus propels it beyond present and past state ideologies. This surplus dimension can be read as a revolutionary remainder and reminder that has to remain – through counter-archival practices – open to and not foreclosed by either the politics of the (former or current) state, nor by the aesthetic ideology of authenticity. The red thread of the subsequent chapters entailed taking seriously the continuation of Partisan rupture as a vital remainder that persisted, despite continual attempts to neutralise it or make it part of the history of the state. The Partisan counter-archive, either in its 'Partisan' production process and/or in its new forms of dissemination, points to the construction of a community-in-resistance. It might have been produced by anonymous Partisans, or appropriated from local popular, national and also international revolutionary traditions.

Irrespective of the political dangers that the achievements of past and future revolutions contain, which can always be reversed, there seems to be a certain element in Partisan counter-memory that further persists despite its 'failure' in different contexts. If authorities in the socialist Yugoslavia attempted to mythologise the Partisan past in order to ideologically cement and justify its own domination over working people, then current communities dominated by nationalism and neoliberalism completely disavow or demonise Partisan insurgency. Despite such forces, the Partisan surplus keeps resurfacing in alternative politics, theory and the arts as a legacy of the oppressed that does not want to be integrated into a state archive and that will not rest in 'peace' in the dustbin of history. The Partisan counter-archive resonates strongly with the concluding passages of John Akromfah's film *Handsworth Songs* (1986) that articulates a need for an archive of the oppressed after riots in the UK:

> These are for those to whom history has not been friendly, for those who have known the cruelties of political becoming, those who demand in the shadows of dying technologies, those who live with the sorrows of defiance, those who live among the abandoned aspirations which were the metropolis. Let them bear witness to the ideals which in time will be born in hope. In time, let them bear witness to the process by which the living transforms the dead into partners in struggle.[278]

278 I am indebted to work completed with Niloufar Tajeri for this counter-archival observation, with whom I have launched an archive on urban dissent (see https://www.pagesmagazine.net/en/articles/archive-of-suburban-dissent-1-introduction).

Akromfah speaks of the potentiality and the need for a process that can bear "witness" to the resurrection of the dead as "partners in struggle." How this alliance between the dead and alive is constructed and preserved is a major challenge of the struggle and memory of the oppressed. The case studies indicate that the surplus nature of the struggle and memory of Partisan revolution is something asymmetrical that cannot be integrated despite all – even 'positive' – attempts to narrate and represent it. This structural impossibility does not necessitate that we wait as bystanders of history and contribute to the silencing of the oppressed, rather, it forces us to invent new ways of retelling the legacy of the oppressed, in a constant critical dialogue with past and present, where the history of horrors and defeats is not separated from the history of victories of the oppressed.

Chapter 2 offers the richest matter of the Partisan counter-archive, which consists of a body of works now scattered and fragmented across the former Yugoslavia, yet produced during the Partisan struggle. The study tackles different Partisan art forms, especially poetry, film, graphic art and photography, each of which challenged the then existing fascist-collaborationist art institutions and pre-war bourgeois canons. Partisan artworks recorded in the counter-archive also armed the insurgency symbolically and commemoratively. I demonstrated that already during World War II there was a strong desire to commemorate the Partisan rupture. This acute awareness and sensibility that something exceptional was taking place sank into cultural activity and chosen artworks. My research retrieved poems written but never popularised (e.g. Pintarič's Partisan anthem *Why poems?*) as well as those that became popularised songs (e.g. the women's chorus Kombinatke's *Women anthem*). Furthermore, due to the scarcity of the material infrastructure of the PLS, Partisan artists were forced to invent intermedial formats: from the scrapped linoleum floor used to make linoleum cuts to the performance of film by other means. What kind of forms did the most emblematic Partisan figures take? From the photographs taken moments before execution (e.g. Stjepan Filipović, 1942 and Lepa Radić, 1943) to the joys of organising life and the new imaginary of liberated territories in forms such as major exhibitions (e.g. the Partisan exhibition in Livno, 1943) and major cultural meetings as in the theatre of the People's Liberation Struggle. Since existing studies on Partisan art have focused mainly on Partisan poetry and graphic art, my minor aim was to bring to light the peculiar (in)existence of Partisan film. As one of the media most limited by the impossible circumstances of war and absence of infrastructure, one may be surprised to encounter substantial film material: from real-existing film material (film documents that are preserved in different archives) and those films that were made by other means (e.g. Rudi Omota's registering of sound and song on film tape, 1941) to a film script from Edvard Kocbek's diary and graphic portfolios as moving images of the PLS (eg. Mihelič and Pirnat's *Our Struggle*, 1944).

I furthermore argue that precisely through this fragmentation, lack of means and scattered material, the deeper deterritorialising and universal nature of the Partisan insurrection itself emerged. Founded on the principle of the radical equality of all nations rather than the sovereignty of one nation, all those who fought against fascism assured that the Partisan counter-archive could never be fully controlled or centrally localised in a single mono-ethnic state. The insistence on the Partisan surplus that emerges through precarious fragments mimics the very precarious and painstaking path of building a new society and sustaining the struggle in future. This future classless and nationless society does not leave behind its counter-archive, but carries it forward in time, demanding the contemporaneity of all past struggles and realising them in new political forces. The return to the Partisan beginning should only ever be a new beginning oriented towards the future and should never be reduced to the function of commemorating the past.

Chapter 3 had a challenging task that bracketed off the nostalgic temptation of heroic times: how could one still speak of the Partisan counter-archive in the socialist Yugoslavia? What happened after the Partisans stopped their struggle and woke up from their dream for a future world? How is the task to commemorate the Partisan surplus to be met if we know that one of the major tasks assigned by the cultural bureaucracy after the war was to commemorate, narrate and represent the PLS? This central paradox of the Partisan counter-archive in Yugoslavia was traced to the inability of the Partisan surplus to be easily integrated into the state apparatus even if the representatives of the cultural apparatus demanded it. Yugoslav socialism – after the break with Stalin – did not follow a strict aesthetic model of socialist realism and from at least 1952 promoted academic modernism. However, there was still a major preoccupation with how to continue the revolution – the Partisan rupture – and move beyond party hierarchies and mythologisations of the PLS. I took most of the case study material from the period of mature self-management from the 1960s to the early 1970s. It is noteworthy that the mid-1960s was seen as a sign of a new era. The market reform in 1965 (Suvin 2014; Kirn 2019b) brought a series of negative consequences for the socialist model and inter-republican solidarity and for the first time after the war, the Yugoslav authorities witnessed an ideological crisis and political challenge. What took place in the late 1960s was a sort of new (Partisan) encounter between political revolt and agents (workers' strikes, student protests), theory (humanist Marxism – Praxis) and art movements (the neo-avant-garde, the new monumental sculpture movement, Black Wave films, etc.).[279] In response to

279 An interesting study on the connection between Praxis, the Black Wave and student movements was conducted by Stojaković (2011).

this encounter and criticisms, Tito and the party leadership launched a wave of repression in the early 1970s on the one hand, and a major campaign for new ideological legitimacy centred on the mythologisation of the Partisan beginning on the other hand. The dominant media – especially the major Partisan films of that time – became a major cultural complement to and justification of socialist authority. Furthermore, since the memory culture of the socialist Yugoslavia was centred so much on the topic of Partisan struggle, discussing and aestheticising it, it was extremely difficult to enter this dense commemorative forest. New critical artists had to depart from precisely such saturated circumstances, and fight both the dominant aesthetic-memorial genres and also the declared position occupied by Tito-as-Partisan leader and Tito-as-statesman (the Party). How can we move beyond those who are seen as direct inheritors of the Partisan revolution and the socialist project without succumbing to capitalist and nationalist temptation? Those tackling official Partisan memory answered by thinking about and finding new form of revolution, and also by re-enacting a collective memory built up by those from below. Žilnik's camera-eye *Ustanak u Jasku* (1973) brought the Partisan surplus once more to light by empowering those who were not worthy of being represented within the dominant blockbuster: simple peasants who were supporters of antifascism and who represented the major infrastructural veins of Partisan reproduction. Besides Žilnik, I selected Miodrag Popović's film *Delije*, which is a major filmic testament to the Partisan surplus, as illustrated by 'screen memory' and the subjective inability of dealing with traumatic and revolutionary excess, and consequently, its failure to integrate into the existing socialist state. Furthermore, the most advanced aesthetic answer and disruption of official memorial politics was materialised in a series of 'monuments to revolution' (eg. Džamonja and Živković). The monuments to revolution at Tjentište and Kozara both in their own way contributed to inventive spatialisations and incited a revolutionary temporality that oriented our imagination towards the future on the one hand, while also warning us of those who revise and destroy the emancipatory legacy of the Partisan past on the other hand. The critical artists of that time were not fervent anti-communist and nationalist dissidents, but part of a broader wave of critics who denounced real-existing self-management and called for a real communism that would continue the Partisan rupture. This is (from) where the new paths to commemorate the Partisan rupture broke with the dominant canon – be it realist or abstract modernist – and politicised those unheard and invisible in socialist society. The records in the Partisan counter-archive here opened a memorial space to individual and collective (re)thinking, facilitating multiple use and interpretations on the space of memory itself.

Chapter 4 works as a dramatic anti-climax that brings a sober moment to the Partisan dream and its socialist mythologisation, and offers a demonising form of memorialising the PLS. The late 1980s already entailed a clear exhaustion of Partisan rupture and the waning symbolic power of both the Yugoslav official commemorative policy on the PLS and the counter-archival and critical memory culture. This is a process that I called the undoing of the Partisan (counter-) archive and which places on display the whole power of revisionist history and memory in the dying stages of Yugoslavia and the transition to nationalistic communities within a capitalist system. Revisionism in ex-/post-/Yugoslavia was not only an exhibition in thought and academia, but also included an array of material effects that influenced how people read and saw events relating to World War II and the Partisan struggle. Revisionism firstly displaced the focus from memories of antifascism and of victims of fascist terror to memories of those fascist collaborationists killed at the end and immediately after the end of war. The dominant discourse in the early transitional phase – especially in Slovenia – was coined under the slogan of 'national reconciliation.' The reconciliation first of all aimed to place local fascist collaborationists and Partisans on an even footing, through moral relativisation: fascists also became 'victims' of wars and simply human beings who had been manipulated by ideologies (communist and fascist). This ethnic reinterpretation of Partisan struggle was designed as a therapeutic commemorative method that would heal the wounds of the (Slovenian) nation. In order to move to the future we need to forgive ideological exclusions and unite through the dead, based on a principle of ethnic belonging (Spomenka Hribar). Any kind of discussion of emancipation, Partisan resistance and antifascist solidarity was pre-emptively prevented: even those who kept the memory of the Partisan past alive – referred to as Yugonostalgics and who mostly consisted of Partisan veterans and left-leaning groupings – were pushed into a defensive position. Within this horizon, Partisan struggle became seen as a noble and important cause, yet also one vital for the constitution of Slovenian statehood. Thus, the revolutionary legacy and the Partisan surplus were almost completely wiped out from public space. The reconciliation process reached its peak with the inauguration of the *Monument to the Victims of All Wars* in the centre of Ljubljana in 2015. This became a central monument for diplomatic and top-level state commemorations. Furthermore, I claimed, and illustrated through examples of new revisionist monuments and critical analysis of the texts of a central authority on that issue (Spomenka Hribar) that nationalist reconciliation opened the gates to a *Blut und Boden* ideology that sailed towards the rehabilitation of fascism. If in other republics of ex-Yugoslavia, the transition in the 1990s resulted in ethnic/ civil wars that carried out ethnic cleansing and openly resurrected the fascist ghost of WWII, then in Slovenia the rehabilitation of local fascism took place with a temporal delay attached. It was in 2014 that Slovenia, more concretely the town of Grahovo, received the first monument that openly rehabilitated local fascists (the Home Guard) and their battle from 1943 that demonises the Partisan Bolsheviks. Apart from making local fascists new heroes (no longer victims) of true patriotism, the right-wing revisionist policies were able to transform former victors (Partisans) into criminals and creators of totalitarian regimes.

As regards memorial revisionism, the Slovenian and the post-Yugoslav contexts are not unique but share these features with all other countries expounding the European ideology of anti-totalitarianism. This ideology has been spearheaded by anti-communism and (local) nationalism, while the once explicit critique of fascism and nurturing of antifascism dropped in priority, or even completely disappeared from European new memory. If the former East presented a veritable ideological avant-garde of memorial revisionism – the iconoclasm of former monuments, Partisan or socialist and the building of new revisionist monuments – this process then found its its way to the core of the European Union, which in a certain sense revendicates the fascist historian Ernst Nolte. The European Union claimed the new commemorative date of 23 August (in 2009), which mourns all the victims of totalitarian regimes. Thus, anti-totalitarian ideology became the official ruling ideology of the EU, an ideology that blurs all sorts of social formations by making sweeping generalisations and propagating analytical weakness in thinking about the difference between violence, exterminations, purges and (counter-)revolution. Can we say that there can be any sort of equation between Hitler and Stalin, or Stalin and Gorbatschow or Dubček and Tito back with Hitler and Mussolini? The memorial peak of this process has materialised around the call – already completed, with a winner – of the competition for the *Pan-European Monument to the Victims of Totalitarian Crimes* in the heart of Brussels. In times when the neoliberal utopia and European project are in crisis, with the continuation of austerity politics and the withering away of the welfare state, this commemorative and revisionist turn that cherishes the civilisational achievements of Europe has been contributing to the emergence of extreme right-wing parties and profascist ideology in Europe.

That said, there has always been resistance towards established revisionism, be it due to progressive nostalgia, critical theory, or left democratic socialist groupings and antifascist organisations that have been pushing to link up contemporary antiracist and antifascist movements – movements that keep nurturing the memory of the antifascist past – and extending it in the fight of today. Also, within the post-Yugoslav context, at least from around 2008–2009, we can trace the emergence of an alternative and independent politico-cultural scene that affirmed the Yugoslav and Partisan past in a non-nostalgic fashion. This opened a space for the curating of different exhibitions and shows, for the staging of theatre performances, for women and other new Partisan choirs, as well as for the theoretical work of fellow scholars, the political work of groupings and left parties. The work of counter-archival memory that deals with the Partisan past claims that this past has never really closed. Rather, by affirming and retrieving Partisan fragments, we are already participating in a struggle for an emancipatory future.

The book *The Partisan Counter-Archive* concludes with two political lessons of the Yugoslav PLS: firstly, one can beat fascism only with a major popular front coalition, and secondly, this antifascist front needs to embody a transformational call that promises social emancipation and thus addresses the causes underpinning the rise of (neo-)fascism. The counter-archive has redefined both rupture and memory on rupture: the former (rupture) being not simple discontinuity or an overthrow of power, but something that yields strong consequences, while the latter (memory) should also not be taken as something fixed or at a standstill. The intense break and its continuation – by memorial/monumental/aesthetic means – encompasses different social fields and might trigger new discontinuities in the future to come. Thus, the relation between rupture and memory is neither linear nor mutually conditioning, but one of intense encounters, arrested developments, regressions, fast forwards and also contradictions between these two processes. This book has presented a modest contribution to the Partisan counter-archive, which might in a more collective fashion continue to systematise the artworks, voices, images and experiences of the oppressed that sustain the imaginary of radical discontinuity over space and time.

The geographical limits of this book and case studies relate to Yugoslav history, while the future aim is to enter into a dialogue with various geographic localities, encounters of politics, art and memories of the oppressed in the twentieth century and later. The Partisan counter-archive thus envisions future work from the very first Partisans in the aftermath of the October Revolution and Moroccan guerrilla units led by Abd el-Krim el-Khattabi to the international brigades and antifascists in the Spanish Civil War and the Partisans of WWII. The Partisan moment after WWII continued in the anticolonial struggles that stretch across different continents and with the urban guerrillas and in the militant feminist, antiracist and environmental movements – each of which have been fighting important struggles and had strong artistic and political effects. The Partisans of yesterday moved the world, shook it off from the established joints of hierarchy and domination, taking the side of a just world without oppression. The work of critical archival studies consists in articulating the counter-archival traces and effects. What immediately becomes apparent is that such things are no longer in the hands of a single author, or one book, but entail a collective effort expanding out to all of those groups and individuals that have already been collecting and interpreting the Partisan legacy and calling for a return to it. How such histories and memories of a past emancipated are to be remediated, retold, and resocialised to the present in the form of a new emancipatory politics is not only a theoretical task, but entails a political practice that remains to be awakened in our present and for our future. Even if distant in time and space, what the records in the Partisan counter-archive hold is a space that keeps (re)constructing solidarity between the oppressed.

Let me conclude this book with a final record for the Partisan counter-archive, which concerns the courageous political actions organised by antifascist women in June 1943 in the fascist occupied Ljubljana. Since Ljubljana was a major centre for resistance activities at the start of the war, from early 1942 the whole city came under the strictest military control. Italian fascist occupying forces organised mass raids, evictions, the executions of civilians as reprisals for Partisan actions, and mass internment into concentration camps, while it should also be noted that the whole city was encircled by barbed wire, fortresses and mine fields to prevent resistance. The Liberation Front and the core of activists and Partisans thus moved to liberated territories and forests, while the situation in the city became increasingly difficult for organised struggle. By June 1943 the prisons were not only overcrowded, with those detained tortured and killed, but there was also a shortage of information regarding the detainees and whether they had been sent to concentration camps. This forced antifascist women to organise one of the biggest – if not the biggest – women's demonstrations in the fascist occupied city during WWII: more than 10,000 women came to protest in a city that before the war had been home to around 60,000 people. Apart from those interned, killed or fighting in Partisans, this practically meant that all women from Ljubljana came to the protest. One can just imagine this crowd of young and old, these pale faces and weakened bodies, but also a strong and resilient female collective body that courageously faced the whole fascist machinery in front of the major court and administration. The fascist authorities were surprised that such a crowd had gathered in the first place, and might have realised the force of resilience and determination for liberation by that point. Standing without guns in front of the fascist enemy. In the war diary of the great Surrealist, Spanish Civil War combatant and commandeer of the First Proletarian Brigade, Koča Popović expressed such an unstoppable and indestructible will in the following fashion:

> The less we took breaks – the more solid and fresh we became,
> the worse we fed ourselves – the tougher we became,
> the worse we were armed – the more lethal we became
> without motorisation – we became faster.
> The costlier each of our deaths were, so our breathing gained a different, special value. As if all our miseries, efforts, difficulties condensed in a lethal spite, as if all this turned to our advantage.

Despite the women knowing that they were risking their lives in the face of evidently severe punishments, collective determination was stronger than fear. Being surprised by the turnout and afraid of its unfolding, the fascist police soon dispersed the protest, beat up some of the women and arrested a few dozen of them. The protest demanded the release of the internees and an improvement in their conditions, as well as the cessation of torture and the release of women. The action did not succeed in terms of its demands, however it inspired a continual imaginary of resistance that never gives up, despite all odds against it and despite horrific circumstances. There would be resistance even in the darkest hour of the century, and with resistance comes hope, creativity and a hunger for a new world. No photo of this event exists, but 10 years later a public competition for the commemoration of this protest was organised and I chose one painting that presentes the oppressed women protesting with their bare hands in the most dire circumstances of fascist occupation. (Fig. 74) by a Partisan designer and painter, Ive Šubic:

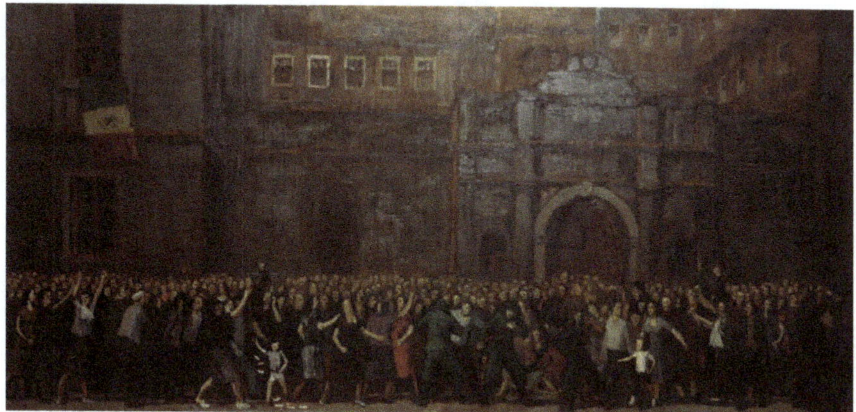

Figure 74: Women protest in front of the court in the fascist occupied Ljubljana, 24 June 1943, painting on oil by Ive Šubic (1953). Courtesy of MNZS.

Afterword
Concrete utopia lasts forever – Branko Miljković's *Yugoslavia*

Here is how she came to be on the day of her urgency
All that has no fire within burns out
What burns out becomes night
What does not burn gives birth to daylight
All that burns has to be set on fire
Whatever can be torn down and all that is not eternal has to be destroyed
Hope must be found in everything after all
Revolution, what remains is people
What passes is the past
The past that does not pass is the future and vigilance
Everything and everyone is an aspect of your hope
That is how she came to be on the day of her urgency
A shore to a Sea
A star over the Peninsula
Cape of Good Will
Bordered by infinity
Recommending love and reason to the fruit
In the factories people are canning sunlight
That manifests itself in the most diverse of ways
Equally in fruit and stone
Sweet the first time and scorching the next
Now she has all that is hers
The Sea in the south and clouds in the north
Cherries in the east and olive groves in the west
Constellations over the mountains, the most striking starry verses
In stone and in the water:
The cluster is a memory of their design
With its own future and her past
With its own path and its truth
Recommending love and reason to the fruit
A shore to a Sea
A star over the Peninsula
Cape of Good Will
Bordered by infinity
Foreign droughts would poison her springs
Strange deserts slander her sun and soil
Yet she is merciless towards what is real

Note: Branko Miljković's *"Jugoslavija"* is a poem taken from the edition Poezija „Smrću protiv smrti" (Poetry, With death against death, 1981) and translated by Borut Praper.

https://doi.org/10.1515/9783110682069-007

but also untrue, she does not give up the fight
The heart of her cities is the white sun of all people
She teaches the cities to be brothers to the Big City
That marries one end with the other
To each other and to the future
Explorers underground, in death, soldiers and miners
Explorers in the air, singers and icaruses
Explorers underwater, poets of the unconscious
Seek, find, rummage through all the treasures,
All the possibilities and all the names for your South
That recommends love and reason to the fruit.

List of Images

https://doi.org/10.1515/9783110682069-008

Bibliography

Academic Literature

Adorno, Theodor. "The Meaning of Working through the Past." *Critical Models: Interventions and Catchwords*. New York, Columbia University Press, 2005, pp. 89–103.

Adorno, Theodor. "Commitment." *Aesthetics and Politics*. London, Verso, 2007, pp. 177–195.

Agamben, Giorgio. *Homo Sacer*. Stanford, Stanford University Press, 1998.

Agamben, Giorgio. "Philosophical Archeology." *Law and Critique*, vol. 20, no. 3, 2009, pp. 211–231.

Akkerman, Mark. "The Business of Building Walls." *TNI*, 2019. https://www.tni.org/files/publication-downloads/business_of_building_walls_-_full_report.pdf. Accessed 12 December 2019.

Ali, Tariq. *The Extreme Centre: A Warning*. London, Verso, 2015.

Althusser, Louis. *Elements of Self-Criticism*. London, NLB, 1976.

Althusser, Louis, and Warren Montag. "On Marx and Freud." *Rethinking Marxism*, vol. 4, no. 1, 1991, pp. 17–30.

Althusser, Louis. *Philosophy of the Encounter. Later Writings, 1978–1987*. London, Verso, 2006.

Althusser, Louis. *On Ideology*. New York, Verso, 2008.

Andersen, Margaret, and Patricia Collins, editors. *Race, Class and Gender: An Anthology*. Belmont, Wadsworth Publishing, 1992.

Anderson, Benedict. *Imagined Communities*. London, Verso, 2010.

Ambrožič, Lado, jr. *Novljanovo stoletje* [Novljan's Century]. Ljubljana, Modrijan, 2008.

Apih, Milan, Rafael Ajlec, et al. *Vstanite, sužnji. Zbirka revolucionarnih pesmi narodov vsega sveta*. [Rise Up, Slaves. A Collection of Revolutionary Poems of People from the Whole World] Ljubljana, Založba Borec, 1976.

Arendt, Hannah. *The Origins of Totalitarianism*. New York, Harcourt Brace Jovanovich, 1966.

Arendt, Hannah. *Eichmann in Jerusalem: A Report on the Banality of Evil*. New York, Penguin Books, 1977.

Arsenijević, Damir, and Nebojša Jovanović. 'Protiv konsocijacijskih teza Mirjane Kasapović'. [Against the Sonsociationist Theses of Mirjana Kasapović]. *Agregat* 5, 11–12 (2007): pp. 22–27.

Ashworth, Gregory J., and John E. Tunbridge. *Dissonant Heritage, the Management of the Past as a Resource in Conflict*. New York, J. Wiley, 1996.

Badiou, Alain. *Conditions*. Paris, Seuil, 1992.

Badiou, Alain. *Metapolitics*. London, Verso, 2005.

Badiou, Alain, et al. *What is a People?* New York City, Columbia University Press, 2016.

Baldacci, Cristina. "The (Potential) Ongoing and Omnivorous Archive." *Fruit of the Forest*, vol. 4, 2013, pp. 30–36.

Balibar, Étienne, and Immanuel Wallerstein. *Race, Nation, Class: Ambiguous Identities*. London, Verso, 1991.

Balibar, Étienne. *We, the People of Europe? Reflections on Transnational Citizenship*. James Swenson, Princeton, translator. Princeton UP, 2004.

Balibar, Étienne. *The Philosophy of Marx*. Chris Turner, translator. London, Verso, 2007.

https://doi.org/10.1515/9783110682069-009

Balzac, Honore de. "The Wild Ass.'" *Skin*, vol. 1897, 12 Dec. 2019, https://archive.org/details/wildassskinother00balziala/page/n11.

Banac, Ivo. *The National Question in Yugoslavia*. London, Cornell University Press, 1984.

Barthes, Roland. *La chambre claire: Note sur la photographie*. Paris, Hill and Wang, 1980.

Barić, Nikica. "Kozara 1942. – sudbina zarobljenika, civila i djece". Casopis za drustvene i humanisticke studije, 22 (2), 2016: pp. 53–111.

Bassin, Aleksander, Vladimir Lakovič, and Vera Visočnik. *Revolucija in Umetnost*. [Revolution and Art]. Ljubljana, Knjižnica NOV in POS, Likovna zbirka, 1966.

Bassin, Aleksander, and Jože Kori. *Revolucija in Umetnost. Izbor slovenske partizanske grafike in risbe z motivi partizanskega zdravstva*. [Revolution and Art. A Selection of Partisan Graphic Art and Sketches with Motives from Partisan Healthcare]. Ljubljana, Knjižnica NOV in POS, Likovna zbirka, 1971.

Basu, Paul, and Ferdinand de Jong. "Utopian Archives, Decolonial Affordances Introduction to Special Issue." *Social Anthropology*, vol. 24, no. 1, 2016, pp. 5–19.

Baškovič, Ciril et al. *Študentsko gibanje 1968–1972*. [The Student Movement 1968–1972]. Ljubljana, Krt, 1982.

Benjamin, Walter. *Gesammelte Schriften*. In Schweppenhäuser, Hermann and Rolf Tiedemann, editors. Frankfurt a. M.: Suhrkamp. I. 3 (1974): pp. 1160–1161. Online translation by Sami Khatib, and Jacob-Bard Rosenberg: https://anthropologicalmaterialism.hypotheses.org/2082. Accessed 12 December 2019.

Benjamin, Walter. "Left-Wing Melancholy." In *Walter Benjamin, Selected Writings: 1931–1934*. Michael W. Jennings, Howard Eiland, and Gary Smith, editors. Cambridge, Massachusetts, Harvard University Press. II.2 (1999): pp. 423–427.

Benjamin, Walter. "The Author as Producer." In *Walter Benjamin, Selected Writings: 1931–1934*. Michael W. Jennings, Howard Eiland, and Gary Smith, editors. Cambridge, Massachusetts, Harvard UP. II.2 (1999): pp. 769–782.

Benjamin, Walter. "The Work of Art in the Age of Its Technological Reproducibility: Second Version." Edmund Jephcott, and Harry Zohn, translators. *Walter Benjamin, Selected Writings, Volume 3: 1935–1938*. Michael W. Jennings, and Howard Eiland, editors. Cambridge, Massachusetts, Harvard UP, 2002, pp. 101–133.

Benjamin, Walter. "On the Concept of History." *Selected Writings, Vol. 4: 1938–1940*. Michael W. Jennings, and Howard Eiland, editors. Cambridge, Massachusetts, Harvard UP, 2003, pp. 389–400.

Bergholz, Max. "Među rodoljubima, kupusom, svinjama i varvarima – spomenici i grobovi NOR 1947–1965" [Among the Patriots, Cabbage, Pigs, and Barbarians: Monuments and Graves to the Peoples' Liberation War, 1947–1965]. *Godišnjak za društvenu istoriju* 1–3, 2007, pp. 61–81.

Benjamin, Walter. *The Work of Art in the Age of its Technological Reproducibility*. London, The Belknap Press of Harvard University Press, London, 2008.

Bor, Matej. *Previharimo viharje*. [Overstorming the Storms]. Ljubljana, Cankarjeva založba, 1961.

Brenk, France. "Prispevek k zgodovini slovenskega in jugoslovanskega filma do 9.maja 1945." [Contribution to the History of Slovenian and Yugoslav film up until 9 May 1945]. *Dokumenti Slovenskega Gledališkega Muzeja*, vol. 6–7, no. 2, 1966, pp. 43–61.

Brenk, France. "Slovenski NOB film." [Slovenian Film in the People's Liberation Struggle] *Dokumenti Slovenskega Gledališkega Muzeja*, vol. 25, no. 11, 1975a, pp. 48–69.

Brenk, France. "Slovenski NOB film – nadaljevanje." [Slovenian Film in the People's Liberation Struggle – A Continuation] *Dokumenti Slovenskega Gledališkega Muzeja*, vol. 25, no. 11, 1975b, pp. 104–124.
Brenk, France. "O filmski in fotografski kulturi med narodnoosvobodilnim bojem." [On Film and Photographic Culture During the People's Liberation Struggle]. *Kultura, revolucija in današnji čas*, Franček Bohanc, editor. Ljubljana, Cankarjeva založba, 1979, pp. 61–67.
Brenk, France. "Slovenski film. Dokumenti in razmišljanja." [Slovenian Film. Documents and Reflections] *Kino*, vol. 17/18, 2012, pp. 79–95.
Brentin, Dario, Davor Pauković, and Vjeran Pavlaković. "The Controversial Commemoration: Transnational Approaches to Remembering Bleiburg." *Politička misao*, vol. 55, no. 2, 2018, pp. 7–32.
Brown, Wendy. "Resisting Left Melancholy." *Boundary*, vol. 26, no. 2, 1999, pp. 19–27.
Brown, Wendy. *Walled States, Waned Sovereignty*. Cambridge, Massachusetts, MIT Press, 2010.
Bilandžić, Dušan. *Zgodovina Socialistične federativne republike Jugoslavije: glavni procesi*. [History of the Socialist Federal Republic of Yugoslavia]. Mladinska knjiga, 1980.
Boatca, Manuela. "Coloniality of Citizenship and Occidentalist Epistemology." *Decolonial Theory and Practice in Southeast Europe*, 2019, pp. 55–77.
Bojić, Milosav, et al. *Prva Proletarska*. [First Proletarian] Ljubljana, Borec, 1966.
Bor, Matej. *Pesmi*. [Poems]. Slovenski knjižni zavod, 1946.
Buck-Morss, Susan. *Dreamworld and Catastrophe: The Passing of Mass Utopia in East and West*. Cambridge, Massachusetts, MIT Press, 2002.
Buck-Morss, Susan. *Hegel, Haiti and Universal History*. Pittsburgh, University of Pittsburgh Press, 2009. https://doi.org/10.2307/j.ctt7zwbgz.
Buck-Morss, Susan, and Jacir, Emily. *The Gift of the Past*. In: *dOCUMENTA (13)* Catalog 1/3: The Book of Books. Carolyn Christov-Bakargiev, and Bettina Funcke, editors. Ostfildern, Hantje Cantz, 2012.
Buden, Boris. "Još o komunistićkim krvolocima, ili zašto smo se ono rastali." [More on Communist Bloodsuckers, or Why We Broke Up]. *Prelom*, vol. 5, no. 3, 2003, pp. 51–58.
Buden, Boris. *Zone des Übergangs: Vom Ende des Postkommunismus*. [Zone of Transition: On the End of Postcommunism] Frankfurt, Suhrkamp, 2009.
Burchard, Marian, and Gal Kirn. "Beyond Neoliberalism? Social Analysis after 1989." *Beyond Neoliberalism*. Cham, Palgrave/ Springer, 2017, pp. 1–15.
Burghardt, Robert. "Partisan memorials in former Yugoslavia." *FZZ fanzine* 2009. fzz.cc/issue02PART.html. Last accessed 18 December 2019.
Butler, Judith. *Precarious Life: The Power of Mourning and Violence*. London, Verso, 2014.
Butler, Judith, et al. *Contingency, Hegemony, Universality: Contemporary Dialogues on the Left*. London, Verso, 2000.
Centrih, Lev. "O pomenu Komunistične partije Slovenije med drugo svetovno vojno in po njej." [On the Meaning/Role of the Communist Party of Slovenia During and After World War Ii]. *Oddogodenje zgodovine: Primer Jugoslavije*." *Borec*, vol. 60, 2008, pp. 61–80.
Centrih, Lev. *Marksistična Formacija*. [Marxist Formation]. Ljubljana, Založba /*cf, 2011.
Centrih, Lev. "The Socialist, Revolutionary and Antifascist Dimensions of the Liberation Front of the Slovenian Nation in Yugoslavia and Its Place in the History of Class Struggles," https://www.youtube.com/watch?v=aV9K8CP_6VU Ljubljana, Prvomajska šola, 2013.
Cesar, Emil. *Karel Destovnik Kajuh*. Ljubljana, Društvo piscev zgodovine NOB Slovenije, 1993.

Chakrabarty, Dipesh. "Death of History? Historical Consciousness and the Culture of Late Capitalism." *Public Culture* 41, 4.2 (1992): 47–65. https://doi.org/10.1215/08992363-4-2-47.

Chaubin, Frédéric. *CCCP Cosmic Communist Constructions*. Cologne, Taschen, 2011.

Clover, Joshua. *Riot. Strike. Riot*. London, Verso, 2015.

Čepič, Zdenko, Damijan Guštin, and Nevenka Troha. *Slovenija v vojni, 1941–1945*. [Slovenia in the War]. Ljubljana, Založba Modrijan, 2017.

Čolić, Milutin. "Umetnici, od volje' i vojnici revolucije." [Artists 'of Will' and Soldiers of Revolution]. In Života Marković, editor. *Užička Republika i Sječanja, I*, Belgrade, online: http://www.znaci.net/00001/59.htm. (12 December 2019). Titovo Užice: Narodni muzej, 1981, pp. 313–317.

Čolić, Milutin. *Jugoslovenski ratni film 1–2*, [Yugoslav War Film 1–2]. Belgrade/Titovo Užice, Institut za film/Vesti, 1984.

Čubelić, Tvrtko. *Ustanak i revolucija u riječi narodnog pjesnika*. [The Uprising and Revolution in the Words of the People's Poet] Belgrade, Znanje, 1983.

Daković, Nevena. "The Unfilmable Scenario and Neglected Theory: Yugoslav Avant-garde Film 1920–1990." *Impossible Histories*. Djurić, Dubravka and Miško Šuvaković, editors. Cambridge, CUP, 2003, pp. 446–489.

Daković, Nevena. *Balkan kao filmski žanr: Slika, tekst, nacija*. [Balkan As Filmic Genre: Image, Text, Nation] Belgrade, FDU, 2008.

Davis, Mike. *City of Quartz. Excavating the Future in Los Angeles*. London, Verso, 2006.

Davies, Norman. *Europe: A History*. London, Harper Perennial, 2006.

Dean, Jodi. *The Communist Horizon*. London, Verso, 2018.

Dean, Jodi. *Comrade*. London, Verso, 2019.

De Jong, Ferdinand. "At Work in the Archive: Introduction to Special Issue." *World Art*, vol. 6, no. 1, 2016, pp. 3–17.

De Cuire, Greg (forthcoming). *Yugoslav Black Wave*. Amsterdam, Amsterdam University Press. https://doi.org/10.1002/9781118294376.ch21.

Dedić, Jasminka, Jalušić Vlasta, and Jelka Zorn. *Izbrisani: Organizirana nedolžnost in politike izkljucěvanja*. [The Erased: Organised Innocence and the Politics of Exclusion] Ljubljana, Mirovni Inštitut, 2003.

Dedić, Nikola. "*Post-Yugoslav* Artistic Practices: Or, Art as ..." In *Post-Yugoslav Constellations*. Vlad Beronja, and Stijn Vervaet, editors. Berlin, De Gruyter, 2016, pp. 169–190.

Dedijer, Vladimir. *Tito Speaks*. London, Weidenfield & Nicolson, 1953.

Dedijer, Vladimir. *The Yugoslav Auschwitz and Vatican*. Buffalo, Prometheus Books, 1992.

Dedijer, Vladimir. *Novi prilozi za biografiju Josipa Broza Tita*. [New Notes on the Biography of Josip Broz Tito] Zagreb, Mladost Zagreb, 1980.

Deleuze, Gilles, and Félix Guattari. *What is Philosophy?* New York, Columbia University Press, 1994.

Deleuze, Gilles, and Félix Guattari. *A Thousand Plateaus*. New York, Continuum, 2003.

Denitch, Bette. "Dismembering Yugoslavia: Nationalist Ideologies and Symbolic Revival of Genocide." *American Ethnologist*, vol. 21, no. 2, 1994, pp. 367–390.

Derrida, Jacques. "Archive Fever: A Freudian Impression." *Diacritics*, vol. 2, no. 25, 2005, pp. 9–63.

Deutsch, Karl. *Nationalism and Social Communication*. Cambridge, Cambridge University Press, 1996.

Dević, Ana. "Hidden in Plain Sight: 'Illegal Artistic Exhibition.'" In *Exhibiting Matters*, Dubravka Sekulić, and Milica Tomić, editors. GAM 14, 2018, pp. 64–82.

Dimitrijević, Branislav (2015). “Đeneralov i ostali antifašizmi.” https://pescanik.net/djeneralov-i-ostali-antifasizmi/. Accessed 12 December 2019.

Djordjev, Bojan. *Not Red, but Blood*: https://bojandjordjev.wordpress.com/2014/nije-to-crvena-to-je-krv/. Accessed 12 December 2019.

Djurić, Dubravka, and Miško Šuvaković, editors. *Impossible Histories*. Cambridge MA, MIT Press, 2003.

Dragović-Sosso, Jasna. *Saviours of the Nation? Serbia's Intellectual Opposition and the Revival of Nationalism*. Montreal, McGill-Queen's University Press, 2002.

Dolar, Mladen. *Struktura fašističnega gospostva*. Ljubljana, Analecta, 1982.

Dugandžić, Andreja, and Tijana Okić. *Between Myth and Forgetting*. Belgrade, RLS, 2016.

Duškovič, Dejan. “Nekaj pripomb k naši obzorniški dokumentarni produkciji” [Some Comments on Newsreel Documentary Production]. In Zdenko Vrdlovec, editor. *40 udarcev: Slovenska filmska publicistika o slovenskem in jugoslovanskem filmu v obdobju 1949–1988*. Ljubljana, Slovenski gledališki in filmski muzej, 1988.

Dyker, Ivan, and David Vejvoda. *Yugoslavia and After*. London, Routledge, 1994.

Eng, David, and David Kazanjian, editors. *Loss: Politics of Mourning*. Oakland, California University Press, 2013.

Epstein, Julius. *Operation Keelhaul*. Old Greenwich, Devin-Adair, 1973.

Erjavec, Aleš, editor. *Postmodernism and the Post-socialist Condition: Politicized Art under Late Socialism*. Santa Barbara, University of California Press, 2003.

Erll, Astrid, and Ann Rigney, editors. *Mediation, Remediation, and the Dynamics of Cultural Memory*. Berlin, De Gruyter, 2009. https://doi.org/10.1515/9783110217384.

Fabec, Franc, and Dejan Vončina. *Slovenska odporniška fotografija*. [Slovenian Resistance Photography]. Ljubljana, Modrijan, 2005.

Ferenc, Mitja. “Poklon slovenskim žrtvam na napačnem kraju zločina.” [A Bow to Slovenian Victims at the Wrong Place of the Crime]. In *Mitsko in stereotipno v slovenskem pogledu na zgodovino*. Mitja Ferenc, and Branka Petkovšek, editors. Ljubljana, Zveza zgodovinskih društev Slovenije, 2006, pp. 153–164.

Ferenc, Mitja, and Joachim Hösler, editors. *Spurensuche in der Gottschee*. Potsdam, Deutsches Kulturforum östliches Europa, 2011.

Foster, Hal. “Archive Impulse.” *OCTOBER 110*, 2004, pp. 3–22.

Foucault, Michel. “Nietzsche, genealogy, history.” *Language, Counter-Memory, Practice: Selected Essays and Interviews*, Donald F. Bouchard, editor. Ithaca, Cornell University Press, 1977, pp. 139–165.

Foucault, Michel, and Jay Miskowiec. “Of Other Spaces.” *Diacritics*, vol. 16, no. 1, 1986, pp. 22–27.

Franke, Ansellm, Nida Ghouse, Paz Guevara and Antonia Majaca, editors. *Parapolitics*. Sternberg Press, Berlin, 2020.

Sigmund Freud, “Mourning and Melancholia.” *The Standard Edition of the Complete Psychological Works of Sigmund Freud, Volume XIV (1914–1916): On the History of the Psycho-Analytic Movement, Papers on Metapsychology and Other Works* (1964), pp. 237–258. https://doi.org/10.1097/00005053-192211000-00066.

Freud, Sigmund (2000–2010). *Complete Works*. Online: https://www.valas.fr/IMG/pdf/Freud_Complete_Works.pdf. Accessed 12 December 2019.

Freud, Sigmund. *Introductory Lectures on Psychoanalysis*. Eastbourne, Garnders books, 2014.

Fukuyama, Francis. *The End of History and the Last Man*. London, Penguin Books, 1992.

Gajić, Zoran, and Željko Popović, editors. *Kroz tranziciju*. [Through Transition] Novi Sad, Ako, 2011.

Gerlovič, Alenka. *Partizansko lutkovno gledališče.* [Partisan Puppet Theatre] Ljubljana, Borec, 1979.
Gerlovič, Alenka. “Moja partizanščina.” [My partisanship] *Borec* 39.2–3 (1987): pp. 109–143.
Glušič-Krisper, Helga, and Matjaž Kmecl. “Partizanska spominska proza” [Partisan Memory Prose]. *Slovenska književnost: 1945–1965. Prva knjiga: Lirika in proza.* Boris Paternu, Helga Glušič-Krisper, and Matjaž Kmecl, editors. Ljubljana, Slovenska matica, 1967, pp. 363–379.
Ghodsee, Kirsten. “Tale of ‘Two Totalitarianisms’: The Crisis of Capitalism and the Historical Memory of Communism.” *History of the Present: A Journal of Critical History*, 4.2., 2014, pp. 116–142. https://doi.org/10.5406/historypresent.4.2.0115.
Ghodsee, Kirsten. *The Left Side of History: World War II and the Unfulfilled Promise of Communism in Eastern Europe.* Durham, Duke University Press, 2015. https://doi.org/10.1215/9780822375821.
Gilić, Nikica. “Ne okreći se sine Branka Bauera: Stil i ideologija ratne (partizanske) melodrame.” [Style and Ideology of Partisan War Melodrama]. *Kino*, vol. 10, 2010, pp. 82–91.
Gluckstein, Donny. *A People’s History of the Second World War.* London, Pluto Press, 2012.
Goethe, Wolfgang. “Morphologie.” *Sämtliche Werke, Briefe, Tagebücher und Gespräche*, Abteilung I, Vol. 24, Dorothea Kuhn, editor. Frankfurt a. M., 1987.
Goethe, Wolfgang. *Metamorphosis of Plants.* Cambridge, MA, MIT Press, 2009 (Original work published 1798).
Goulding, Daniel. *Liberated Cinema: The Yugoslav Experience 1945–2001.* Bloomington, Indiana University Press, 2002.
Golubovič, Nataša. *Nastanek slovenske nacionalne kinematografije.* [The Emergence of Slovenian National Cinematography]. Koper, Fakulteta za humanistične študije, 2009.
Gramsci, Antonio. *Selections from the Prison Notebooks.* Quintin Hoare, and Geoffrey Nowell Smith, editors and translators. London, Lawrence & Wishart, 1971.
Gramsci, Antonio. *The Prison Notebooks.* London, ElecBooks, 1999.
Group of authors. “12 teza o projektu Jugoslavija.” [12 Theses on the Project of Yugoslavia]. 2012. *Novosti*: http://arhiva.portalnovosti.com/2012/03/12-teza-o-projektu-jugoslavija/. Accessed 12 December 2019.
Guevara, Che. “Guerrilla Warfare.” *Methods (San Diego, Calif.)*, vol. 1963, https://www.marxists.org/archive/guevara/1963/09/guerrilla-warfare.htm. Accessed 12 December 2019.
Habjan, Jernej, and Gal Kirn, editors. *Yugoslav Partisan Art.* Special edition of *Slavica Tergestina*, 16–17, 2016.
Hanaček, Ivana, Ana Kutleša, and Vesna Vuković (2017). “Problem umjetnosti kolektiva: Slučaj Udruženja umjetnika Zemlja.” [Problem of the Art Collective: The Case of the Association of Artists Zemlja]. *Lekcije o odbrani.* Miloš Miletić, and Mirjana Radovanović, editors. Belgrade, KURS, 2017, pp. 65–84.
Hanaček, Ivana. “Artists in Service of the Masses: The Untold Story of the Yugoslav Socialist Realist Project.” *Making Art History in Europe After 1945.* Noemi de Haro Garcia, Patricia Mayayo, and Jesus Carrillo, editors. London, Routledge, 2019.
Harvey, David. *Short History of Neoliberalism.* New York, Oxford University Press, 2005.
Hayden, Robert. “Recounting the Dead: The Redefinition of Wartime Massacres in Late – and Post-Communist Yugoslavia.” *Memory, History and Opposition under State Socialism.* Rubie Watson, editor. Santa Fe, School of American Research Press, 1994.

Heatherley, Owen. “Concrete Clickbait: Next Time You Share a Spomenik Photo, Think About What It Means.” Calvert Journal, 2016. http://www.calvertjournal.com/articles/show/7269/spomenik-yugoslav-monument-owen-hatherley. Accessed 12 December 2019.

Hercigonja, Nikola, and Djordje Karaklajić, editors. *Zbornik partizanskih narodnih napjeva.* [Collection of Partisan Popular Songs] Belgrade, Nolit, 1962.

Hercigonja, Nikola. “Muzička nastojanja u narodnooslobodilačkoj borbi.” [Musical Endeavours in the People's Liberation Struggle]. *Napisi o Muzici.* Belgrade, Umetnička akademija, 1972, pp. 187–194.

Hobsbawm, Eric, and Terence Ranger, editors. *The Invention of Tradition.* Cambridge, New York, New Rochelle, Cambridge University Press, 1983.

Hobsbawm, Eric. *Bandits.* New York, Delacorte Press, 1969.

Hobsbawm, Eric. *Nations and Nationalism since 1780: Programme, Myth, Reality.* Cambridge, Cambridge UP, 1992. https://doi.org/10.1017/CCOL0521439612.

Hobsbawm, Eric. *Age of Extremes.* London, Penguin, 1994.

Hofman, Ana. *Glasba, politika, afekt: Novo življenje partizanskih pesmi v Sloveniji.* [Music, Politics, Affect: The New Life of Partisan Songs in Slovenia] Ljubljana, ZRC SAZU, 2016.

Höpken, W. “War, Memory, and Education in a Fragmented Society: The Case of Yugoslavia.” *Eastern European Politics and Societies*, vol. 13, no. 1, 1999, pp. 190–227.

Hornberger, Jacob. *Repatriation. The Dark Side of World War II*, 1995. http://www.fff.org/freedom/0495a.asp. Accessed 12 December 2019.

Horvat, Srećko, and Igor Štiks, editors. *Welcome to the Desert of Post-Socialism: Radical Politics after Yugoslavia.* London, Verso, 2014.

Horvatinčić, Sanja. “Monuments Dedicated to Labor and the Labor Movement in Socialist Yugoslavia.” *Etnološka tribina: godišnjak Hrvatskog etnološkog društva*, vol. 44 no. 37, 2014, pp. 153–168.

Horvatinčić, Sanja. *Memorials from the Socialist Era in Croatia – Typology Model.* Dissertation thesis, Zadar University, 2017.

Horvatinčić, Sanja. “Memorial Sculpture and Architecture in Socialist Yugoslavia.” *Towards a Concrete Utopia.* New York, MoMa, 2018, pp. 104–112.

Hribar, Spomenka. “Narodna sprava.” [National Reconciliation]. *Katedra*, vol. 28, 1986, no. 1–3.

Hribar, Spomenka. “Logika sovraštva in sprava.” [Logic of hate and reconciliation]. *Nova Revija*, vol. 57, 1987, pp. 74–104.

Huberman-Didi, Georges, editor. *Soulevements.* Paris, Gallimard, 2016.

Huyssen, Andreas. *Present Pasts: Urban Palimpsests and the Politics of Memory.* Stanford, Stanford University Press, 2003.

Ilić, Mihailo. *Serbian Cutting.* Belgrade, Filmski centar Srbije, 2008.

Israeli, Raphael. *The Death Camps of Croatia: Visions and Revisions, 1941–1945.* New Jersey, Transaction Publishers, 2013.

Jagdhuhn Tepavčević, Nataša. “Walking Heritage. Performance as a Method of Transmitting a Confiscated Memory and Identity.” *Nostalgia on the Move.* Mirjana Slavković, and Marija Đorgović, editors. Belgrade, Muzej Jugoslavije, 2017, pp. 84–94.

Jakiša, Miranda. “Down to Earth Partisans: Fashioning of YU-Space in Partisan Films.” *Kino*, vol. 10, 2010, pp. 54–61.

Jameson, Frederic. *The Political Unconscious: Narrative as a Social Symbolic Act.* London, Methuen, 1981.

Jameson, Frederic. *Archaeologies of the Future.* London, Verso, 2005.

Jančar-Webster, Barbara. *Women and Revolution in Yugoslavia, 1941–1945.* Denver, Arden, 1990.

Janevski, Ana." We Cannot Promise to Do More Than Experiment! On Yugoslav Experimental Film and Cine Clubs in the 60s and 70s." *Surfing the Black: Black Wave Cinema and its Transgressive Moments.* Gal Kirn, Dubravka Sekulić, and Žiga Testen, editors. Maastricht, JvE Academy, 2012, pp. 46–77.

Javoršek, Jože. "Vstaja slovenskega naroda in poezija." [Uprising of Slovenian People and Poetry]. *Sodobnost*, vol. 29, no. 4, 1981, pp. 347–354.

Jezernik, Božidar. *Struggle for Survival: Italian Concentration Camps for Slovenes during the Second World War.* Ljubljana, Društvo za preučevanje zgodovine, literature in antropologije, 1999.

Jovanović, Nebojša. "Fadil Hadžić u optici totalitarne paradigme." [Fadil Hadžić through the Lens of the Totalitarian Paradigm]. *Hrvatski filmski ljetopis* 65/66 (2011): pp. 47–60.

Jovanović, Nebojša. "Futur Anterieur of Yugoslav Cinema, or Why Emir Kusturica's Legacy is Worth Fighting for." *Retracing Images: Visual Cultures after Yugoslavia*, Daniel Šuber, and Slobodan Karamanić, editors. Leiden, Brill, 2012, pp. 149–170.

Jovanović, Nebojša. *Gender and Sexuality in the Classical Yugoslav* Cinema, *1947–1962.* Budapest, CEU. Dissertation thesis, 2014.

Jelača, Dijana, Maša Kolanović, and Danijela Lugarić, editors. *The Cultural Life of Capitalism in Yugoslavia.* Cham, Palgrave Macmillan, 2017.

Kameda, Masumi. "Visual Framing of Red Martyrs: Soviet and Yugoslav Partisan Propaganda Compared." *Kultura*, vol. 138, no. 138, 2013, pp. 199–207.

Kanzleiter, Boris. *1968 in Jugoslawien: Studentenproteste und kulturelle Avantgarde zwischen 1960 und 1975.* [1968 in Yugoslavia: Student Protests and Cultural Avant-Garde between 1960 and 1975] Berlin, Gespräche und Dokumente, 2011.

Kampenaers, Jan. *Spomenik.* Amsterdam, Roma Publications, 2010.

Kapetanović, S. Odić, and S. Popović, editors. *Bihaćka republika I–II*, 1964. [Republic of Bihać]. http://www.znaci.net/00003/500.htm. Accessed 12 December 2019.

Kaplan, Robert. *Balkan Ghosts.* London, Picador, 2005.

Karamanić, Slobodan. "Kosovo after Yugoslavia." Special edition in English, *Prelom* 8.5, 2006, pp. 23–39.

Karamanić, Slobodan. "Balkan Socialist Confederation 1910–1948."
International Encyclopaedia of Revolution and Protest. Immanuel Ness, editor. NJ: Blackwell Publishing, 2009, pp. 337–339.

Kardelj, Edvard. *Spomini.* [Memories] Ljubljana, DZS, 1980.

Karge, Haike. *Steinerne Erinnerung Versteinerte Erinnerung? Kriegsgedenken in Jugoslawien (1947–1970).* Wiesbaden, Harrassowitz, 2010.

Keegen, John. The Second World War. New York City, Viking Press, 1989.

Kelen, Christopher. *Anthem Quality. National Songs: A Theoretical Survey.* Bristol, Intellect, 2014.

Kelen, Christopher, and Aleksandar Pavković. "'Zdravljica' – Toast to a Cosmopolitan Nation Anthem Quality in the Slovenian Context." *Nationalities Papers*, vol. 42, no. 5, 2014, pp. 828–847.

Kirn, Gal. "Spomin na partizane ali misel o partizanstvu?" [Memory of Partisans or Thought of the Partisans?]. Zdenka Badovinac, Bojana Piškur, editors. *Catalogue Museum on the Street*, Ljubljana, Muzej moderne umetnosti, 2009, pp. 104–112.
Kirn, Gal. *Conceptualisation of Politics and Reproduction in the Work of Louis Althusser: Case of Socialist Yugoslavia.* Dissertation. Nova Gorica: Univerza v Novi Gorici, 2012a.
Kirn, Gal. "New Yugoslav Cinema: A Humanist Cinema? Not Really." *Surfing the Black: Black Wave Cinema and its Transgressive Moments*, Gal Kirn, et al., editors. Maastricht, Jan van Eyck Academy, 2012b, pp. 10–46.
Kirn, Gal. "Transformation of Memorial Sites in the Post-Yugoslav Context." *Retracing Images: Visual Cultures after Yugoslavia*, Daniel Šuber, and Slobodan Karamanić, editors. Leiden, Brill, 2012c, pp. 252–281.
Kirn, Gal. "Multiple Temporalities of the Partisan Struggle: From Post-Yugoslav Nationalist Reconciliation Back to Partisan Poetry." In *Multistable Figures: On the Critical Potential of Ir/Reversible Aspect-Seeing*, Christoph F. E. Holzhey, editor. Vienna, Turia + Kant, 2014a, pp. 163–191.
Kirn, Gal. *Spominski park v Grahovem: Od ideologije narodne sprave do odprtega zagovora fašizma.* [Memorial park in Grahovo: From the Ideology of National Reconciliation to the Open Advocacy of Fascism] Borec, 2014b, pp. 164–168.
Kirn, Gal. *Partizanski prelomi in protislovja tržnega socializma v Jugoslaviji.* [Partisan Ruptures and the Contradictions of Market Socialism in Yugoslavia] Ljubljana, Sophia, 2015a.
Kirn, Gal. "On the Specific (In)existence of the Partisan Film in Yugoslavia's People's Liberation Struggle." *Partisans in Yugoslavia: Literature*, Film *and* Visual Culture. Bielefeld, Transcript, 2015b, pp. 197–226.
Kirn, Gal. "Towards the Partisan Counter-archive: Poetry, Sculpture and Film on/of the People's Liberation Struggle," *Yugoslav Partisan Art.* Jernej Habjan, and Gal Kirn. Editors. Special issue of *Slavica Tergestina*, vol. 16–17, 2016, pp. 100–126.
Kirn, Gal. "A Critique of Transition Studies on Post-Socialism, or How to Rethink and Reorient 1989?" In *Beyond Neoliberalism*, Marian Burchardt, and Gal Kirn. Editors. London, Palgrave/Springer, 2017a.
Kirn, Gal. "On Yugoslav Market Socialism Through Živojin Pavlović's 'When I Am Dead and Pale' (1967)." In *The Cultural Life of Capitalism in Yugoslavia*, Dijana Jelača, Maša Kolanović, and Danijela Lugarić, editors. London, Palgrave Macmillan, 2017b, pp. 139–158. https://doi.org/10.1007/978-3-319-47482-3_8.
Kirn, Gal. "Anti-Totalitarian Monuments in Ljubljana and Brussels." *European Memory in Populism.* Kaya Ayhan, and Chiara de Cesari, editors. London, Routledge, 2019a. https://doi.org/10.4324/9780429454813-3.
Kirn, Gal. *Partisan Ruptures: Self-Management, Market Reform and the Spectre of Socialist Yugoslavia.* London, Pluto Press, 2019b. https://doi.org/10.2307/j.ctvsrwbz8.
Klemenčič-Maj, Dore. *Izgubljeni zapiski.* [Lost Notes]. Ljubljana, Partizanska knjiga, 1972.
Klemenčič, Matjaž, and Mitja Žagar. *The Former Yugoslavia's Diverse Peoples.* Santa Barbara, ABC CLIO, 2004.
Klein, Naomi. *The Shock Doctrine.* London, Penguin Press, 2008.
Knežević, Vida. "Ilegalna grupa Život i levi umetnički front. Pitanje umetničkog organizovanja." [The Illegal Group Život and Left Art Front. The Question of Artists' Organising]. *Lekcije o odbrani.* Miloš Miletić, and Mirjana Radovanović, editors. Belgrade, KURS, 2017, pp. 85–128.

Kocbek, Edvard. *Tovarišija: dnevniški zapiski od 17. maja 1942 do 1. maja 1943* [The Comradeship: Diary Entries from 17 May 1942 to 1 May 1943]. Ljubljana, Državna založba Slovenije, 1949.

Kocbek, Edvard. *Listina. Dnevniški zapiski od 3. maja do 2. decembra 1943.* [Diary Entries from 17 May 1942 to 2 December 1943]. Ljubljana, Slovenska Matica, 1982.

Kolumbić, Mirjana, and Marinko Petrić. "Spomenici NOB-e i revolucije na otoku Hvaru." *Prilozi povijesti otoka Hvara*, Vol.VI No.1 (1982): pp. 7–72.

Komel, Mirt (2008). "The Yugoslav Wars As the Primordial Accumulation of Capital." In *Fast Capitalism*, issue 8.1. https://www.uta.edu/huma/agger/fastcapitalism/8_1/komel8_1.html. (12 December 2019).

Komelj, Miklavž. *Kako misliti partizansko umetnost?* Ljubljana, založba cf./*, 2008.

Komelj, Miklavž. *Ljubljana. Cities within a City*. Ljubljana, Likovne Besede, 2009.

Komelj, Miklavž. "The Function of the Signifier 'Totalitarianism' in the Constitution of the 'East art' Field." *Retracing Images: Visual Cultures after Yugoslavia*, Daniel Šuber, and Slobodan Karamanić, editors. Leiden, Brill, 2012, pp. 55–80.

Komelj, Miklavž. "The Partisan Art Revisited." *Yugoslav Partisan Art.* Jernej Habjan, and Gal Kirn. Editors. Special issue of Slavica Tergestina, vol. 16–17, 2016, pp. 86–99.

Komelj, Miklavž. "Od nadrealističke do partizanske revolucije." [From Surrealist to Partisan Revolution]. *Lekcije o odbrani.* Miloš Miletić, and Mirjana Radovanović, editors. Belgrade, KURS, 2017, pp. 45–65.

Komelj, Miklavž. Predgovor. In *Vsem naj bom neznan*. Ljubljana, Goga, 2019.

Kosanović, Dejan. *Kinematografija u Bosni i Hercegovini 1897–1945.* [Cinematography in Bosnia and Herzegovina 1897–1945] Sarajevo, Kino Savez Bosne i Hercegovine, 2003.

Konjikušić, Davor. *Red Light - Yugoslav Partisan Photography and Social Movement 1941–1945.* Belgrade, Rosa Luxembourg Foundation, 2019.

Kostja, Vojin. „Partizanska drzava." [Partisan State]. *Užička Republika i Sječanja, I*, Belgrade/Titovo Užice, Narodni muzej, 1981, pp. 214–227.

Kosi, Jernej. *Kako je nastal slovenski narod.* Ljubljana, Sophia, 2013.

Kosi, Jernej, and Lev Centrih. "Med slovenskim narodnim vprašanjem in slovensko nacionalno zgodovino – komentarji k *Slovenski novejši zgodovini*." [Between the Slovenian National Question and Slovenian National History - Comments on Slovenian Recent History]. *Zgodovina za vse: vse za zgodovine*, vol. 14, no.1, 2007, pp. 155–165.

Kovačević, Dušanka. *Women of Yugoslavia in the National Liberation War.* Belgrade, Conference for Social Activities of Yugoslav Women, 1977.

Kovačević, Veljko. *V okopih Španije. Spomini španskega borca* [In the Trenches of Spain. Memories of Spanish Interbrigadist Fighter]. Ljubljana, Založba Borec, 1959.

Kraševec, Igor. *Zapadnodolenjski odred.* [West Dolenjska Detachment] Ljubljana, Zbirka NOV in POS, 1985.

Krašovec, Primož. "O partizanski svobodi," lecture at WPU, 2007, Ljubljana. http://dpu.mirovni-institut.si/11letnik/krasovec.php. Accessed 12 December 2017.

Kristan, Ivan. "Kočevski zbor – rojstvo samostojne Slovenije." [Kočevje Assembly – Birth of Independent Slovenia]. *Teorija in praksa*, 10.7–8, 1973, pp. 600–609.

Križnar, Ivan. "Slovensko domobranstvo v boju proti NOB." [Slovenian Home Guards in the Struggle Against the People's Liberation Struggle]. *Osvoboditev Slovenije, 1945.* Ljubljana, Borec, 1977.

Krnić, Lovro. "U ime Tita, Partizana i Antifašizma Svetoga." [In the Name of Tito, Partisan and Holy Antifascism]. https://www.portalnovosti.com/u-ime-tita-partizana-i-antifasizma-svetoga. Accessed 12 December 2019.

Krleža, Miroslav. "Govor na kongresu književnika u Ljubljani." [Speech at the Literary Congress in Ljubljana]. *Republika*, 8.10–11, 1952, pp. 205–243.

Kuljić, Todor. *Umkämpfte Vergangenheiten. Die Kultur der Erinnerung im postjugoslawischen Raum*. Bonn, BpB, 2010.

Kunst, Bojana. *Artist at Work, Proximity of Art and Capitalism*. John Hunt Publishing, 2015.

Kuzmanić, Tonči. *Bitja s pol strešice*. Ljubljana, OSI-Slovenia/Mirovni Institut, 1999.

Labica, George. *L'expropriation originelle*. Paris, Les Nuits rouges, 2001.

Laclau, Ernesto. *On Populist Reason*. London, Verso, 2005.

Landa, Ishay. *The Apprentice's Sorcerer: Liberal Tradition and Fascism*. Leiden, Brill, 2009.

Landa, Ishay. *The Roots of European Fascism, 1789–1945*, Open University textbook, 2015.

Laplanche, Jean, and Jean-Bertrand Pontalis. *Vocabulaire de la psychanalyse*. Paris, PUF-Quadrige, 2004.

Laurelle, Francois. *General Theory of Victims*. Cambridge, Polity Press, 2015.

Lasić, Stanko. *Sukob na književnoj ljevici*. Belgrade, Liber, 1960.

Latas, Branko. *Dokumenti o saradnji četnika sa osovinom*. Belgrade, Institute, 1999.

Lebowitz, Michael. *The Contradictions of Real Socialism*. New York, Monthly Review Press, 2012.

Lenin, Ilyich. "On Slogans." *Lenin Collected Works*. Vol. 25, Moscow, Progress Publishers, 1975, (Original work published 1917) pp. 185–192.

Lešaja, Ante. *Knjigocid: Uništavanje knjiga u Hrvatskoj 1990-ih*. [The Destruction of Books in Croatia in the 1990s]. Zagreb, Srpsko narodno vijeće, 2012.

Lešnik, Doroteja, and Grega Tomc. *Rdeče in črno: Slovensko partizanstvo in domobranstvo*. [Red and Black: Slovenian Partisans and Home Guards] Ljubljana, ZIS, 1995.

Levi, Primo. *The Drowned and the Saved*. New York, Summit Books, 1988.

Levi, Pavle. *Disintegration in Frames: Aesthetics and Ideology in the Yugoslav and Post-Yugoslav Cinema*. Stanford, Stanford University Press, 2007.

Levi, Pavle. "Cine-Commune, or Filmmaking as Direct Socio-Political Intervention" (in Serbian), 2009. http://zilnikzelimir.net/sr/essay/kino-komuna-film-kao-prvostepena-drustveno-politicka-intervencija-1. Accessed 12 December 2019.

Levi, Pavle. *Cinema By Other Means*. Oxford, Oxford University Press, 2012.

Losurdo, Domenico. *War and Revolution: Rethinking the Twentieth Century*. London, Verso, 2015.

Lukacs, Georg. *History & Class Consciousness*. 1923. http://www.marxists.org/archive/lukacs/works/history/lukacs3.htm. Accessed 12 December 2019.

Lukić, Dragoje "Lepa Radic nije imala ni 18 godina." [Lepa Radic Was Not Even 18 Years Old]. 1968/2017. Retrieved online: http://www.yugopapir.com/2017/10/lepa-radic-43-nije-imala-ni-18-godina.html. Accessed 12 December 2019.

Luthar, Oto. "Preimenovanje in izključevanje kot sestavni del postkomunistične kultura spomina v Sloveniji." [Renaming and Exclusion As a Constitutive Part of Postcommunist Culture of Memory in Slovenia]. *Prispevki za novejšo zgodovino*, no. 2, 2014.

Luthar, Oto. "Memorial Landscape and Slovenian Post-Truth Historiography," conference paper, Zagreb, 2017.

MacKay, John. Interviewed by Francois Albera. "*Actualité de Dziga Vertov : l'avenir dure longtemps.*" *1895*, vol. 85, no.2, 2018, pp. 8–31.

Malm, Andreas. "In Wildness is the Liberation of the World: On Maroon Ecology and Partisan Nature." *Historical Materialism* 26 (3), 2018: pp. 3–37.

Magaš, Branka. *The Destruction of Yugoslavia*. London, Verso, 1993.

Mandel, Ernst. *The Meaning of the Second World War*. London, Verso, 1986.

Majewska, Ewa. "A Bitter Victory?" *Third Text*, 33:3, 2019: pp. 397–413.

Marx, Karl. *Theses on Feuerbach*. 1845. *Marx-Engels Archive*. www.marxists.org/archive/marx/works/1845/theses/index.htm. Accessed 12 December 2019.

Marx, Karl. *Trans. Ben Fowkes*. Vol. I. Capital. London, Penguin Books, 1990.

Mastnak, Tomaž. "Totalitarizem od spodaj." *Druzboslovne Razprave*, vol. 4, no. 5, 1987, pp. 91–98.

Mazierska, Ewa. "Eastern European Cinema: Old and New Approaches." *Studies in Eastern European Cinema*, vol. 1, no. 1, 2010, pp. 5–16.

Mazierska, Ewa. *European Cinema and Intertextuality: History, Memory and Politics*. Hampshire, Palgrave Macmillan, 2011. https://doi.org/10.1057/9780230319547.

Mazierska, Ewa. "Želimir Žilnik and Eastern European Independent Cinema." *Images*, vol. 13, no. 22, 2013, pp. 133–149.

Miletić, Miloš, and Mirjana Radovanović. *Lekcije o odbrani*. Belgrade: Rosa Luxembourg Foundation, 2016.

Miletić, Miloš, and Mirjana Radovanović. "Kulturna delatnost NOP-a: narodna/ revolucionarna." [Cultural Activity of the People's Liberation Struggle: Popular/Revolutionary]. Miloš Miletić, and Mirjana Radovanović, editors. *Lekcije o odbrani*. Belgrade, KURS, 2017, pp. 129–155.

Milohnić, Aldo. "O dveh sunkih veselega vetra partizanskega gledališča in o 'veliki uganki partizanske scene'." [On Two Pushes of the Happy Wind of Partisan Theatre and on the Great Enigma of the Partisan Stage]. *Dialogi*, vol. 51, no. 1–2, 2015, pp. 57–76.

Milohnić, Aldo. "Partizanski Molière kot simbolna gesta upora." [The Partisan Molière As a Symbolic Gesture of Resistance]. *Dialogi*, vol. 52, no. 1–2, 2016, pp. 34–56.

Milohnić, Aldo. "Marta Paulin-Brina. Ples, Misel, Spomin." *Dan, noč + človek = ritem: Antologija slovenske sodobnoplesne publicistike 1918–1960*. Ljubljana, Maska, 2018, pp. 73–80.

Mikuž, Metod. *Slovensko partizansko gospodarstvo*. [Partisan Economy] Ljubljana, Zavod Borec, 1969.

Mirzoeff, Nicholas. *The Right to Look*. Durham, Duke University Press, 2011. https://doi.org/10.1215/9780822393726.

Močnik, Rastko. *Extravagantia II: koliko fašizma?* [Extravagantia II: How Much Fascism?]. Ljubljana, Studia humanitatis, 1995.

Močnik, Rastko. "Partizanska simbolička politika." [Partisan Symbolic Politics]. *Zarez*, vol. 7, no. 161/162, 2005, pp. 12–14.

Močnik, Rastko. "Zgodovinopisje kot identitetna vednost: Trije slovenski zgodovinarji o razbitju jugoslovanske federacije." [Historiography As Identity Knowledge: Three Slovene Historians on the Destruction of Yugoslav Federation]. *Borec*, vol. 60, 2008, pp. 648–651.

Močnik, Rastko. "Will the East's Past Be the West's Future." Caroline Dacid, editor. *Les frontieres invisibles*, Oostkamp, Stichting Kunstboek, 2009.

Močnik, Rastko. "A Further Note on the Partisan Cultural Politics." Slavica Tergestina Unpublished essay / lecture in Belgrade FMS, 2018.

Monbiot, George. *Out of the Wreckage*. London, Verso, 2017.

Milinović, Daško, and Zoran Petakov, editors. *Partizanke. Žene u Narodnooslobodilačkoj borbi.* [Partisan Women. Women in the People's Liberation Struggle] Novi Sad, AKO, 2010.

Munitić, Ranko. *Živjet će ovaj narod, jugoslavenski film o revoluciji.* [This People Shall Live on, Yugoslav Film of Revolution] Zagreb, Publicitas, 1974.

Musabegović, Senadin. *Rat: Konstitucija totalitarnog tijela.* [War: Constitution of Totalitarian Body] Sarajevo, Svjetlost, 2008.

Nedič, Liljana. "Film v NOB" [Film in the People's Liberation Struggle]. *Enciklopedija Slovenije.* A. Dermastia, editor, vol. III, Ljubljana, 1989.

Nedeljkovic, Dusan. "Foreword" in *Antifašističke pesme* (3rd edition). Belgrade, Baraba, 2017.

Neumayer, Laure. *The Criminalisation of Communism in the European Political Space after the Cold War.* Milton Park, Routledge, 2018. https://doi.org/10.4324/9781351141765.

Nešović, Slobodan, and Neda Pagon, editors. *Prvo in drugo zasedanje AVNOJ.* [First and Second Meeting of AVNOJ]. Ljubljana, Komunist, 1973.

Neutelings, Willem Jan. *"Spomenik, The Monuments of Former Yugoslavia." Spomenik.* Jan Kampaeners, 2010.

Niebyl, Donald. *Spomenik Monument Database.* London, Fuel, 2018.

Nolte, Ernst. "Vergangenheit, die nicht vergehen will: eine Rede, die geschrieben, aber nicht mehr gehalten werden konnte." *Frankfurter Allgemeine Zeitung*, 6 June 1986.

Nora, Pierre. "Between Memory and History: *Les Lieux de Mémoire*." Marc Roudebush, translator. *Representations (Berkeley, Calif.)*, vol. 26, no. 1, 1989, pp. 7–24.

Opća enciklopedija JLZ IV, Zagreb, Jugoslavenski leksikografski zavod, 1978.

Ostojić, Stevo. *Rat, Revolucija, Ekran.* [War, Revolution, Screen] Belgrade, Spektar, 1977.

Paternu, Boris et al., editors. *Slovensko pesništvo upora 1941–1945. Prva knjiga.* Ljubljana, Mladinska knjiga and Partizanska knjiga, 1987.

Paternu, Boris et al., editors. *Partizanske.* Ljubljana, Mladinska knjiga and Partizanska knjiga, 1995.

Paternu, Boris et al., editors. *Slovensko pesništvo upora 1941–1945. Druga knjiga. Partizanske.* Novo mesto, Dolenjska založba, Znanstveni inštitut Filozofske Fakultete, 1998.

Paternu, Boris. "K virom Prešernovega 'frajgajstovstva'" (On the Sources of Prešeren's Free Thinking). *Slavistična revija* 57.2 (2009): pp. 301–10.

Paulin-Brina, Marta. "Plesna umetnost v partizanih" [Dance Art in the Partisans]. *Partizanska umetnost.* Filip Kalan et al., editors. Ljubljana, Zveza kulturno-prosvetnih organizacij Slovenije and Delavska enotnost, 1975, pp. 20–27.

Pavlaković, Vjeran. "Matija Gubec Goes to Spain: Symbols and Ideology in Croatia, 1936–1939." *Journal of Slavic Military Studies*, vol. 17, no. 4, 2004, pp. 727–755.

Pavlaković, Vjeran. *Yugoslav Volunteers in the Spanish Civil War*, Research Paper Series of Rosa Luxemburg Stiftung Southeast Europe No. 4, Belgrade, Rosa Luxemburg Stiftung, 2016.

Pavlaković, Vjeran. "Controversial Monuments." *Spomenici i politike sjećanja u BiH i Republici Hrvatskoj, kontroverze – Monuments and the Politics of Memory in Bosnia and Herzegovina and Croatia, Controversies.* Sarajevo, UDIK, 2018.

Pavičić, Jurica. "Igrani filmovi Fadila Hadžića" [The Fiction Films of Fadil Hadžić]. *Hrvatski filmski ljetopis* 34, 2004, pp. 3–38.

Pavlinec, Donovan. "The Partisan Print and Graphic Art." *Partizanski tisk / The Partisans in Print.* Breda Škrjanec, and Donovan Pavlinec, editors. Ljubljana, MGLC and Muzej novejše zgodovine Slovenije, 2004, pp. 60–94.

Petranović, Branko. *Istorija socialističke Jugoslavije I.* [History of Socialist Yugoslavia I] Belgrade, 1977.

Petranović, Branko. *Istorija Jugoslavije II: Narodnooslobodilacki Rat i Revolucija.* [History of Yugoslavia II: The People's Liberation War and Revolution] Belgrade, Nolit, 1988.
Petranović, Branko. *Balkanska federacija 1943–1948.* [Balkan Federation] Belgrade, Zaslon, 1991.
Petrović, Tanja. "The Past That Binds Us: Yugonostalgia As the Politics of Future." In *Transcending Fratricide: Political Mythologies, Reconciliations, and the Uncertain Future in the Former Yugoslavia.* Srdja Pavlović, and Marko Živković, editors. Baden-Baden, Nomos, 2013. https://doi.org/10.5771/9783845247601–129.
Pfaller, Robert. *Interpassivity.* Edinburgh, Edinburgh University Press, 2019.
Pirjevec, Jože, and Repe, Božo, editors. *Resistance, Suffering, Hope: The Slovene Partisan Movement 1941–1945.* Ljubljana, National Committee of Union of Societies of Combatants of the Slovene National Liberation Struggle; Trieste: Založništvo Tržaškega tiska, 2008.
Pirjevec, Jože. "The Strategy of the Occupiers." In *Resistance, Suffering, Hope: the Slovene Partisan Movement 1941–1945.* Joze Pirjevec, and Božo Repe, editors. Ljubljana, National Committee of Union of Societies of Combatants of the Slovene National Liberation Struggle; Trieste, Založništvo Tržaškega tiska, 2008, pp. 24–36.
Piškur, Bojana, and Soban Tamara. *This Is All Film: Experimental Film in Yugoslavia 1951–1991,* Museum of Modern Art, Ljubljana, 2010.
Popović, Koča. *Beleške uz Ratovanje.* [Notes During War/Struggle]. Belgrade, BIGZ, 2008. http://www.znaci.net/00001/29_6.htm. Accessed 12 December 2019.
Prashad, Vijay. *The Darker Nations.* New York, The New Press, 2007.
Prashad, Vijay. *The Red Star over the Third World.* New Delhi, LeftWord Books, 2019.
Praznik, Katja. *Intelektualno gospostvo: sodobna umetnost med vzhodom in zahodom.* Dissertation [Intellectual Domination: Contemporary Art Between East and West]. Ljubljana, Filozofska fakulteta, 2013.
Prejdová, Dominika. "Socially Engaged Cinema According to Želimir Žilnik," translated from Angažovaný film podle Želimira Žilnika." *DO III revue pro dokumentární film,* Andrea Slováková, editor. 2000, pp. 231–245. http://www.zilnikzelimir.net/essay/socially-engaged-cinema-according-zelimir-zilnik. Accessed 12 December 2019.
Previšić, Martin. "Broj kažnjenika na Golom otoku i drugim logorima za informbirovce u vrijeme sukoba sa SSSR-om (1948–1956.)". *Historijski zbornik,* 66, 1, (2013): pp. 173–193.
Pristaš, Goran Sergej. "Operacija, obnovljena izvedba, rekonstrukcija," lecture at various events (basis for film reconstruction and exhibition in 2015), 2007.
Pristaš, Goran Sergej. "Ne želim sodelovati pri vašem delu, če moram plesati." [I Don't Want to Participate in Your Work, If I Need to Dance]. *Dialogi,* vol. 51, no.1–2, 2015, pp. 107–118.
Pupovac, Ozren. "Projekt Jugoslavija: Dialektika revolucije." *Agregat,* vol. 4, no. 9/10, 2006, pp. 108–117. Project Yugoslavia: Dialectics of Revolution.
Pupovac, Ozren. *Post-Marxism and Post-Socialism.* Dissertation thesis at Open University, London, 2008.
Radanović, Milan. "Stjepan Filipović heroj radničke i antifašističke borbe," 2012. http://www.starosajmiste.info/blog/stjepan-filipovic-heroj-radnicke-i-antifasisticke-borbe-70-godina-od-smrti/. Accessed 12 December 2019.
Radanović, Milan. *Oslobodjenje. Beograd, 20. oktobar 1944.* [Liberation of Belgrade] Belgrade, RLS, 2014.

Radanović, Milan. “Kolaboracija je zločin“ [Collaboration Is a Crime], 2015. Online: https://lupiga.com/intervjui/intervju-milan-radanovic-kolaboracija-je-zlocin. Accessed 12 December 2019.

Radonić, Ljiljana. “Post-Communist Invocation of Europe: Memorial Museums’ Narratives and the Europeanization of Memory.” *National Identities*, vol. 19, no. 2, 2009, pp. 269–288.

Ramet, P. Sabrina. *Thinking about Yugoslavia. Scholarly Debates about Yugoslav Breakup and the Wars in Bosnia and Kosovo*. New York, Cambridge University Press, 2005. https://doi.org/10.1017/CBO9780511492136.

Ramet, P. *Sabrina. The Three Yugoslavias: State-building and Legitimation, 1918–2003*. Bloomington, Indiana University Press, 2006.

Rancière, Jacques. *La Nuit des Prolétaires: Archives du Rêve Ouvrier*. [Night of Proletarians. Archive of the Workers’ Dream] Paris, Fayard, 1981.

Rancière, Jacques. “Peuple ou multitudes?” *Multitudes online 9*, 2002.

Rancière, Jacques. *Politics of Aesthetics. The Distribution of the Sensible*. New York, Continuum, 2004.

Rancière, Jacques. “Aesthetic Separation, Aesthetic Community: Scenes from the Aesthetic Regime of Art.” In *Art and Research*, vol. 2, 2008.

Rancière, Jacques. *Emancipated Spectator*. London, Verso, 2009.

Rancière, Jacques. *Les Écarts du Cinéma*. Paris, La Fabrique, 2011.

Reč, Neime. “Za ‘ovu’ Jugoslaviju.” [For ‘this’ Yugoslavia], 2010. https://pescanik.net/za-ovu-jugoslaviju/. Accessed 12 December 2019.

Repe, Božo. “Partizanski tisk / Partisan Print.” *Partizanski tisk / The Partisans in Print*. Breda Škrjanec, and Donovan Pavlinec, editors. Trans. by Olga Vuković. Ljubljana, MGLC and Muzej novejše zgodovine Slovenije, 2004, pp. 42–60.

Rexhepi, Piro. “The Politics of Postcolonial Erasure in Sarajevo.” *Interventions*, vol. 20, no. 6, 2018, pp. 930–945.

Ristić, Marko. *Objava poezije*. [The Publication of Poetry]. Belgrade, Matica srpska, 1964.

Rodić, Milivoj. *NOB v narodnoj poeziji Kozarčana*. [The People’s Liberation Struggle in the Poetry of Kozara People] Belgrade, 1983, pp. 421–452.

Romano, Jaša. *Jevreji Jugoslavije 1941–1945, žrtve genocida i učesnici NOR*. [Jews of Yugoslavia 1941–1945, Victims of Genocide and Participants in the People’s Liberation Struggle]. Belgrade, Savez jevrejskih opština Jugoslavije, 1980.

Rothberg, Michael. *Multidirectional Memory*. Stanford, Stanford University Press, 2009.

Ricoeur, Paul. *Memory, History, Forgetting*. Chicago, University of Chicago Press, 2004. https://doi.org/10.7208/chicago/9780226713465.001.0001.

Rusinow, Dennison. *The Yugoslav Experiment 1948–1974*. London, Hurst, for the R. Institute for International Affairs, 1977.

Sabel, Charles, and David Stark. “Planning, Politics and Shop-Floor Power: Hidden forms of Bargaining in the Soviet Imposed State – Socialist Societies.” *Politics & Society*, vol. 11, no. 4, 1982, pp. 439–475.

Said, Edward. *Orientalism*. New York, Pantheon Books, 1978.

Salecl, Renata. *The Spoils of Freedom: Psychoanalysis and Feminism After the Fall of Socialism*. London, New York, Routledge, 1994.

Sindbæk Andersen, Tea, and Barbara Törnquist-Plewa, editors. *Disputed Memory: Emotions and Memory Politics in Central*, Eastern *and* South-Eastern Europe, Berlin, De Gruyter. 2016.

Samary, Cathérine. *Le marché contre l'autogestion: L'expérience yougoslave*. [Market Against Self-Management Yugoslav Experience] Paris, Publisud/Montreuil, 1988.

Savković, Miroslav. *Cinematography in Serbia during the Second World War 1941–1945*, Belgrade, Institut za pozorište, film, radio i televiziju. Fakulteta dramskih umetnosti u Beogradu, 1994. http://www.rastko.rs/filmtv/msavkovic-1941–1945.html#_Toc5526192. Accessed 15 October 2019.

Schmitt, Carl. *The Theory of the Partisan*. Michigan, Michigan State University Press, 2004.

Schönle, Andreas. *Architecture of Oblivion: Ruins and Historical Consciousness in Modern*. Illinois, Russia, Northern Illinois University Press, 2011.

Schöpflin, George. *Politics in Eastern* Europe *1945–1992*. Oxford and Cambridge, MA, Blackwell, 1993.

Schreel, Louis. "The Work of Art as Monument: Deleuze and the (After-) Life of Art." FOOTPRINT (2014): pp. 97–108.

Silič-Nemec, Nelida. *Javni spomeniki na Primorskem, 1945–1978*. [Public Monuments in Primorska]. Koper, Založba Lipa, 1982.

Smith, Terry. *What Is Contemporary Art?* University of Chicago Press, 2009. https://doi.org/10.7208/chicago/9780226131672.001.0001.

Smith, L, and Campbell G. "The Elephant in the Room: Heritage, Affect and Emotion." *A Companion to Heritage Studies*. William Logan, Mairead Nic Craith, and Ullrich Kockel, editors. Wiley Blackwell, 2015, pp. 443–460. https://doi.org/10.1002/9781118486634.ch30.

Spreizer, Alenka, and Irena Šumi. "That Which Soils the Nation's Body: Discriminatory Discourse of Slovenian Academics on the Romany, Foreigners and Women." *Anthropological Notebooks*, vol. 17, no. 3, 2011, pp. 101–121.

Stanković, Peter. *Rdeči trakovi. Reprezentacija v slovenskem partizanskem filmu*. [Red tapes. Representation in Slovenian Partisan Film]. Ljubljana, Založba FDV, 2005.

Stanković, Peter. "Je mogoče o jugoslovanskem partizanskem filmu govorit kot o žanru?" [Is It Possible to Speak of Yugoslav Partisan Film As a Genre?] *Kino*, vol. 10, 2010, pp. 22–54.

Stanovnik, Justin (1996): "Komunistična revolucija." [Communist Revolution]. *Revija Zaveza 21, 1996*. Online: http://www.zaveza.si/zaveza-st-21-komunisticna-revolucija-justin-stanovnik/. Accessed12 December 2019.

Stanovnik, Justin. "Aktualni politični komentar Nove slovenske zaveza." [Actual Political Comment of Nova slovenska zaveza]. *Revija Zaveza 59*, 2004. http://www.zaveza.si/zaveza-st-59-aktualni-politicni-komentar-nove-slovenske-zaveze-justin-stanovnik/. Accessed 12 December 2019.

Stepančič, Lilijana. "O razstavah partizanskega tiska / On Partisan Art Exhibitions." *Partizanski tisk / The Partisans in Print*. Breda Škrjanec, and Donovan Pavlinec, editors, trans. Olga Vuković. Ljubljana, MGLC and Muzej novejše zgodovine Slovenije, 2004, pp. 10–20.

Stojaković, Krunoslav. *"Praxis als kognitiver Rahmen der Kultur." Praxis, kritika i humanistički socijalizam*. [Praxis As a Cognitive Frame of Culture] Belgrade, RLS, 2011, pp. 50–55.

Stojaković, Gordana. *AFŽ Vojvodine 1942–1953*. [The Women's Antifascist Organisation in Vojvodina]. Novi Sad, 2007.

Stojanović, Branimir. "Politika Partizana." *Prelom*, vol. 5, no. 3, 2003, pp. 48–51. Politics of Partisan.

Streeck, Wolfgang. *How will capitalism end?* London, Verso, 2016.

Subotić, Jelena. *Yellow Star, Red Star. Holocaust Remembrance after Communism*. Cornell University Press, 2019. https://doi.org/10.7591/9781501742415.
Suvin, Darko. *A Life in Letters*, Washon Island, Paradoxa, 2011.
Suvin, Darko. *Samo jednom se ljubi: Radiografija SFR Jugoslavije*. [One Falls in Love Only Once: A Radiography of the Socialist Federal Republic of Yugoslavia] Belgrade, Rosa Luxemburg Stiftung, 2014.
Šašić, Branko. *Znameniti Šapčani i Podrinci II*. [Famous People from Šabac and Podrinje II]. Šabac, Čivija print Šabac, 2012.
Šelhaus, Edi. *Fotoreporter Edi Šelhaus ponovno v Škednju*. Ljubljana, Borec, 1982.
Šimenc, Stanko. *Panorama slovenskega filma*. [Panorama of Slovenian Film] Ljubljana, DZS, 1996.
Škrabalo, Ivo. *101 godina filma u Hrvatskoj 1896–1997: Pregled povijesti hrvatske* kinematografije. [101 Years of Film in Croatia]. Zagreb, Nakladni zavod Globus, 1998.
Štefančič, Marcel. "Bo ta film pomagal dobito vojno? NOB po h'woodsko." [Will This Film Help Win the War? Partisan Struggle in Hollywood Style.] *Kino*, vol. 10, 2010, pp. 126–158.
Štrajnar, Milena, and Tanja Velagić, editors. *Ilegalčki: Vojna Ljubljana 1941–1945*. [Illegal Partisan Children in War Ljubljana] Ljubljana, Društvo ZAK, 2004.
Šumi, Irena. "Slovenski antisemitizem, živ pokopan v ideologiji slovenske narodne sprave." [Slovenian Anti-Semitism Drowned in the Ideology of National Reconciliation] *ČKZ*, 260, 2015, pp. 69–84.
Taylor, Diana. *The Archive and the Repertoire*. Durham, Duke University Press, 2003. https://doi.org/10.1215/9780822385318.
Tempo-Vukmanović, Svetozar. *Revolucija koja teče I–IV. Memoari*. [Revolution in Flux I–IV. Memoars] Zagreb, Globus, 1982.
Timofeeva, Oxana. *The History of Animals*. New York, Bloomsbury, 2018.
Tito, Josip Broz. *Selected Military Works*. Belgrade, Vojnoizdavčki Zavod, 1966.
Todorova, Maria. *Imagining the Balkans*. Oxford, Oxford University Press, 2009.
Tomashevich, Jozo. *War and Revolution in Yugoslavia, 1941–1945: Occupation and Collaboration*. San Francisco, Stanford University Press, 2001.
Tomšič, Samo. *The Capitalist Unconscious*. London, Verso, 2015.
Traverso, Enzo. *Left-Wing Melancholia: Marxism, History, and Memory*. New York City, Columbia University Press, 2017a.
Traverso, Enzo. "Totalitarianism between History and Theory." *History and Theory Journal*, Special Issue: Theorizing Histories of Violence, 2017b, pp. 97–118.
Tsantsanoglou, Maria. "The Soviet Icarus: From the Dream of Free Flight to the Nightmare of Free Fall." *Utopian Reality*. Christina Lodder, Maria Kokkori, and Maria Mileeva, editors. Leiden: Brill, 2013, pp. 43–56. https://doi.org/10.1163/9789004263222_005.
Vaingurt, Julia. *Wonderlands of the Avant-Garde: Technology and the Arts in Russia of the 1920s*. Noyes St. Evanston, Northwestern University Press, 2013.
Velikonja, Mitja. *Titostalgia: A Study of Nostalgia for Josip Broz*. Olga Vuković, translator. Ljubljana, Peace Institute, 2009.
Velikonja, Mitja. "*Yugoslavia After Yugoslavia*: Graffiti About Yugoslavia in the Post-Yugoslav Urban Landscape." *The Cultural Life of Capitalism in Yugoslavia* Diana Jelača, Maša Kolanović, and Danijela Lugarić, editors. Palgrave Macmillan, 2017, pp. 323–343. https://doi.org/10.1007/978-3-319-47482-3_18.
Verhaeghe, Paul. "Trauma and Hysteria Within Freud and Lacan." *THE LETTER*, vol. 14, 1998, pp. 87–106.

Veselinović, Ana, et al. *Izgubljeno u tranziciji*. [Lost in Transition] Belgrade, RLS, 2011.
Vevar, Rok (2017). "Predgovor" (Foreword). *Ko se zgodi ples. Zapisi, dokumenti spomini*. [When Dance Happens. Notes, Documents and Memories]. Kraigher, Živa, Ljubljana, Maska, 2017.
Visković, Velimir. *Sukob na ljevici: Krležina uloga u sukobu na ljevici* [Controversy on the Left: Krleža's Role in the Controversy]. Belgrade, Narodna knjiga-Alfa, 2011.
Visočnik, Vera. *Revolucija in umetnost: risbe iz zaporov in taborišč*. [Revolution and Art: Drawings from Jails and Concentration Camps]. Ljubljana, Knjižnica NOV in POS, Likovna zbirka, 1969.
Vittorelli, Natascha. "With or Without Gun: Staging Female Partisans in Socialist Yugoslavia." *Partisans in Yugoslavia: Literature*, Film *and* Visual Culture. Miranda Jakiša, and Nikica Gilić, editors. Bielefeld, Transcript Verlag, 2015, pp. 117–136. https://doi.org/10.14361/9783839425220-006.
Vogman, Elena. *Sinnliches Denken: Eisensteins exzentrische Methode*. Berlin, Diaphanes, 2018.
Volk, Petar. *Hronika jugoslovenskog filma 1896–1945*. [Chronicle of Yugoslav Film 1896–1945] Belgrade, Svedočenje, 1973.
Vrdlovec, Zdenko. *Zgodovina slovenskega filma*. [A History of Slovenian Film]. Radovljica, Didakta, 2010.
Vrečko, Janez. "Srečko Kosovel in evropska avantgarda." [Srecko Kosovel and the European Avant-Garde]. *Primerjalna Književnost*, 28. Special issue on Kosovel's poetics. Ljubljana, 2011, pp. 45–57.
Wachtel, Andrew Baruch. *Making a Nation, Breaking a Nation: Literature and Cultural Politics in Yugoslavia*. Stanford, Stanford University Press, 1998.
Williams, Raymond. *The Long Revolution*. Harmondsworth, Chatto, and Windus, 1961. https://doi.org/10.7312/will93760.
Williams, Raymond. *Resources of Hope*. London, Verso, 1989.
Woodward, Susan. *Balkan Tragedy*. Washington, The Brookings Institution, 1995a.
Woodward, Susan. *Socialist Unemployment: The Political Economy of Yugoslavia 1945–1990*. Princeton, Princeton University Press, 1995b.
Woodward, Susan. "The Political Economy of Ethno-Nationalism." In *Socialist Register*, 2003, pp. 73–92.
Wolf, Eric. *Europe and the People without History*. Santa Barbara, California University Press, 2010.
Young, James. "Counter-Monument: Memory Against Itself in Germany Today." *Critical Inquiry*, vol. 18, no. 2, 1992, pp. 267–296.
Yurchak, Alexei. *Everything Was Forever, Until It Was No More: The Last Soviet Generation*. Princeton UP, 2005.
Zgonik, Nadja. "Od partizanskega mitinga do akcije." [From Partisan Meeting to Action] *Dialogi*, vol. 51, no. 1–2, 2015, pp. 77–88.
Žilnik, Želimir and Kirn, Gal. Personal corresondence (email archive), 2018.
Zupančič, Alenka. "Enthusiasm, Anxiety and the Event." *Parallax*, vol. 11, no. 4, 2005, pp. 31–45.
Živković, Andreja. "From the Market … to the Market: The Debt Economy After Yugoslavia." *Welcome to the Desert of Post-Socialism*. Srečko Horvat, and Igor Štiks, editors. London, Verso, 2015, pp. 54–78.
Žižek, Slavoj. *The Sublime Object of Ideology*. New York, Verso, 1989.

Žižek, Slavoj. "Multiculturalism, or, the Cultural Logic of Multinational Capitalism." *New Left Review*, vol. I/225 1997, pp. 28–51.
Žižek, Slavoj. "Carl Schmitt in the Age of Post-Politics." *The Challenge of Carl Schmitt*, Chantal Mouffe, editor. London, Verso, 1999, pp. 18–37.
Žižek, Slavoj. *Did Somebody Say Totalitarianism? Five Interventions in the (Mis)Use of a Notation*. London, Verso, 2001.
Žižek, Slavoj. *Violence*. New York City, Macmillan, 2008a.
Žižek, Slavoj. *In Defense of Lost Causes*. London, Verso, 2008b.
Žižek, Slavoj. *Living in the End Times*. London, Verso, 2011.

Filmography

Recent post-Yugoslav and Yugoslav film (partisan, critical, documentary focus)

Bajer, Josefina, Daniela Mehler and Aleksandra Vedernjak (2010, GER). *Hej Sloveni! YU-Nostalgia as phenomenon of everyday life.*
Bauer, Bruno (1956, YUG). *Ne okreči se sine* (My son don't turn around).
Bulajić, Veljko (1962, YUG). *Kozara.*
Bulajić, Veljko(1969, YUG). *Bitka na Neretvi* (Battle on Neretva).
Čap, František (1955, YUG) *Trenutki Odločitve* (Moment of decision).
Delić, Stipe (1972, YUG). *Sutjeska.*
Djordjević, Puriša (1967, YUG). *Jutro (Morning).*
Dragojević, (2011, SER). *Parada* (Parade).
Golubović, Srdjan (2013, SER). *Krugovi* (Circles).
Hribernik, Jasna (2012, SLO). *Franja.*
Jugoslavija u Ratu (1991, SER), Yugoslavia in war documentary series online: http://www.youtube.com/watch?v=tmwdK2IULlk&feature=BFa&list=FLPODexyrsVoQ9aUs6tizXww (15 October 2018).
Krvavac, Hajrudin (1972, YUG). *Valter brani Sarajevo* (Valter defends Sarajevo).
Kusturica, Emir (1985, YUG). *Otac na službenom putu* (Father on business trip).
Kusturica, Emir (1995, SER). *Underground.*
Ljubič, Milan (1965, YUG). *Vojna Poezija (War poetry).*
Ljubič, Milan (2007, SLO). *Zadnja kino predstava* (Last film show).
Mutapdžić, Midhat (1975, YUG). *Doktor Mladen.*
Neonazimessen in Österreich – Kroatische Hitlergrüße in Kärnten (2017). Report vom 23.05.2017 [ORF2, AUS], report on Bleiburg. Online: https://www.youtube.com/watch?v=B_88PDnjyBw
Pavlović, Živojin *When I am dead and pale* (1967, YUG).
Pavlović, Živojin (1969, YUG). *Zaseda (Ambush).*
Pavlović, Živojin (1977, YUG). Hajka (Hunt).
Petrović, Aleksandar (1965). *Tri (Three).*
Popivoda, Marta (2013, Serbia / France / Germany). *Yugoslavia, how ideology moved our collective body* (film essay, 62 min).
Popivoda, Marta (forthcoming, Serbia / France / Germany). *Landscapes of Resistance.*
Popović, Miodrag (1964, YUG). *Čovjek iz šume* (Man from Oak Forest).

Popović, Miodrag (1968). *Delije* (The Tough Ones).
Oslobodjenje Zagreba, 1985, YUG (Liberation of Zagreb). Online: https://www.youtube.com/watch?v=WTzVqp4H_Zs.
Štader, Dražen (2004, SLLO). *Rudi Omota – Hidden Chapter of Slovenian Cinematography.*
Štiglic, France (1961). *Balada o Trobenti in Oblaku* (Balada about trumpet and cloud).
Štiglic, Franc (1960, YUG). *Deveti Krog* (Ninth Circle).
Turajlić, Mila (2010, SER). *Cinema Kommunisto* (documentary film).
Vukotić, Dušan (1977, YUG). *Akcija stadion* (Action Stadium).
Weindner Krese, Jakob (2014, SLO). *To, česar burja ni odnesla* (What was not taken away by burja, documentary film).
Žafranović, Lordan (1977, YUG). *Okupacija u 26 slika* (Occupation in 26 pictures).
Žilnik, Želimir (1968, YUG). *Nezaposleni* (The Unemployed), 13 min.
Žilnik, Želimir (1969, YUG). *Early Works.*
Žilnik, Želimir (1971, YUG). *Black Film*, 14 min.
Žilnik, Želimir (1973, YUG). *Ustanak u Jasku* (Uprising in Jasak), 18 min.
Žilnik, Želimir (2011, SER). *Jedna žena jedan vek* (One Woman one century).
Online archive of Želimir Žilnik: http://www.zilnikzelimir.net/.
Žižić, Bodgan (2001, CRO). *Damnatio Memoriae* (Damnation of Memory, Documentary film).

Mentioned partisan films and material from WWII

Bar, France, Viršek, Stane et al. (1945, YUG). *Liberation of Ljubljana.*
Badjura, Metod et al. (1945, YUG). *Ljubljana salutes the Liberators.*
Burges, Francis (1944, UK). *The Nine Hundred.*
Elusin (1945 USSR). *Yugoslavia* (documentary).
Hlavaty, Kosta and Gavrin Gustav. (1945/6, YUG). *Jasenovac.*
Jakac, Božidar (1972, YUG). *Partisan Documents.*
Kham, Milan and Omota, Rudi (1944, SLO). *Jelendol's Victims.*
Kogan, Solomon (1945, USSR). *Liberation of Bihać.*
Omota, Rudi (1944, SLO). *Organisation TODT.*
Omota, Rudi (1944, SLO). *The Big National Anticommunist Manifestation.*
Omota, Rudi (1944, SLO). *The Oath of Slovenian Home Guards.*
Omota, Rudi (1941, SLO). Recording of the song "Lipa zelenela je" on 12.12. 1941, archival recording accessible: https://ru-clip.net/video/JY-2Th14exI/apz-1941-lipa-zelenela-je.html.
Perajica, Antonio and Ana (1945/2012, YUG/CRO). *Take Care Of The Film.*
Slade, Max (1944, UK). *First Movies of General Tito.*
Slade, Max. (1944, UK). *Partisan Outpost.*
Viršek, Stane (1965: YUG). *Partisan Documents 1941–1945.*
Viršek, Stane (1972: YUG). *Partisan Documents.*

Online material relating to revisionist monuments / memory

Article on reconciliation process in totalitarian paradigm in Croatia: "Dan sjecanja na zrtve totalitarnih i autoritarnih rezima" http://www.index.hr/vijesti/clanak/dan-sjecanja-na-zrtve-totalitarnih-iautoritarnih-rezima-i-hrvatska-je-cesto-u-tomesudjelovala/567891.aspx. (12 December 2019)

Article on reconciliation in Montenegro in the wake of preparation for the monument to Wehrmacht soldiers from WWII: http://www.dwworld.de/dw/article/0,,15331844,00.html?maca=ser-Blic+Online-2569-xml-mrss29 . (December 2019).

Budapest's Memory Park: http://www.szoborpark.hu/index.php?Content=Szoborpark&Lang=en. (12 December 2019).

Center of national reconciliation's (research center financed by the government of Slovenia) public statement "In Slovenia we can speak of regression of reconciliation process" (22 August 2011). http://www.rtvslo.si/slovenija/v-sloveniji-lahko-govorimo-o-regresijispravnega-procesa/264551. (12 December 2019)

Exhibition and publication on totalitarian history (Slovenia): http://www.muzej-nz.si/eng/eng_razstavni_katalogi_03.html. (12 December 2019).

Macedonian memorial project Skopje 2014 – PR video: http://www.youtube.com/watch?v=iybmt-iLysU. (12 December 2019).

Report on new collaborationist monument from Grahovo (6 April 2014) http://www.rtvslo.si/slovenija/v-grahovem-najprej-poklon-zrtvam-nacizma-nato-blagoslov-spomenika-domobrancem/333932. (12 December 2019).

Report on Monument to Victims of all Wars (Ljubljana, Ministry of Labour): https://www.zaps.si/index.php?m_id=natecaji_izvedeni&nat_id=119&elab_id=634#nagr. (12 December 2019).

Online accessible documentation and a report of commission of the Monument to victims of all wars (Ljubljana): http://91.185.212.27/~majafaro/foto/spomenik_a_-_porocilo.pdf. (12 December 2019).

Repe, Božo. "Manipulation with partisan poet," 2016. https://www.mladina.si/175915/m-anipul-acije-s-p-artiz-anskim-pesnikom/. (12 December 2019).

Commemoration speeches

Kučan, Milan. "Spravna slovesnost v Kočevskem rogu," speech of president of Slovenia at Kočevski Rog, 8. julij 1990: http://www.bivsi-predsednik.si/up-rs/2002–2007/bp-mk.nsf/dokumenti/08.07.1990–90–92. (12 December 2019).

Rode, Tone "Speech on 70th anniversary of postwar killings in Kočevski Rog." Družina, 2015. https://www.casnik.si/tone-rode-govor-v-kocevskem-rogu/. (12 December 2019).

Report on the speech of the Bishop of Celje (Slovenia), Anton Stres at the memorial in Teharje (5 October 2008): http://www.rtvslo.si/modload.php?&c_mod=rnews⊕sections&func=read&c_menu=1&c_id=184117&tokens=stress. (12 December 2019).

EU totalitarian revisionist process

European declaration and day of memory: http://en.wikipedia.org/wiki/European_Day_of_Remembrance_for_Victims_of_Stalinism_and_Nazism. (12 December 2019).

European Parliament. "Resolution of 2 April 2009 on European Conscience and Totalitarianism.": http://www.europarl.europa.eu/sides/getDoc.do?pubRef=-//EP//TEXT+TA+P6-TA-2009–0213+0+DOC+XML+V0//EN. (12 December 2019).

Platform for European memory and conscience: https://www.memoryandconscience.eu/ (12 December 2019).

Ronald Reagan, 1985 (5 May): "Remarks at a Joint German-American Military Ceremony at Bitburg Air Base in the Federal Republic of Germany." http://www.vlib.us/amdocs/texts/reagan051985.html (30 September 2019).

Online links to the revisionist articles of the right-wing journal Demokracija (in Slovene)

"Ehrlich knew that bolshevist revolution brings evil that is why he was firm and open opponent of communism" (18 September 2018). http://www.demokracija.si/fokus/helena-jaklitsch-ehrlich-je-vedel-da-boljsevisticna-revolucija-prinasa-zlo-zato-je-bil-neomajen-nasprotnik-komunizma.html. (12 December 2019).

"How the creators of Liberation Front (partisans) were sending innocent children into concentration camps" (27 April 2018). Online: http://www.demokracija.si/slovenija/kako-so-tvorci-of-nagnali-nedolzne-otroke-v-koncentracijska-taborisca.html. (12 December 2019).

"Book *Legacy of Silence* testimonies that discloses communist crimes that did not spare even kids" (17 June 2018): http://www.demokracija.si/slovenija/v-knjigi-dediscina-molka-pricevalci-razkrivajo-grozljive-komunisticne-zlocine-ki-niso-prizanesli-niti-otrokom.html. (12 December 2019).

"Communism still subjugates Slovenians with false topics" (21.8. 2018): http://www.demokracija.si/slovenija/zgodovinar-dr-granda-komunizem-se-vedno-zasuznjuje-slovence-z-laznivimi-temami-ki-nimajo-nobene-zveze-z-resnico-ter-izrablja-clovesko-stisko-za-poglabljanje-razdora-med-slovenci.html. (12 December 2019).

Online sites related to the mentioned concentration camps, casualties of WWII, and collaborationist groups

The table of casualties across regions/nations in WWII: http://en.wikipedia.org/wiki/World_War_II_casualties. (12 December 2019).

Concentration camp on Rab (largest island held camp managed by Italian occupationist forces): http://en.wikipedia.org/wiki/Rab_concentration_camp (12 December 2019).

Concentration camp Jasenovac (managed by collaborationist regime Independent State of Croatia, NDH): http://www.jasenovac.org/. (12 December 2019).

Concentration camp Gurs in France: https://encyclopedia.ushmm.org/content/en/article/gurs; http://www.gonarsmemorial.eu/. (12 December 2019).

Foundation of Slovene Home Guard under SS command, 23 September 1943, journal *Slovenec*, online: http://www.dlib.si/details/URN:NBN:SI:DOC-9Z762QHI. (12 December 2019).

Oath of Slovenian fascist Home Guards "Führerju za rojstni dan" (For birthday of Führer). https://dlib.si/stream/URN:NBN:SI:DOC-BUM9HW2A/f5eb01d4-a28c-48d9-a1b3–9ee62ac31ee1/PDF *Slovenec*, 21 April 1944. (12 December 2019).

On the German organization that helps funding and organizing SS veterans: https://en.wikipedia.org/wiki/HIAG. (12 December 2019).

Online accessible avant-garde and partisan poems/songs

Antifašističke pesme (3rd edition). Belgrade, Baraba, 2017.

Blok, Aleksandr. "Twelve." 1918. https://kuscholarworks.ku.edu/bitstream/handle/1808/6598/BlokTwelve_RusEngTxt.pdf?sequence=1&isAllowed=y (12 December 2019).

Kosovel, Srečko. "Tragedija na oceanu" [Tragedy on ocean], 1925. https://sl.wikisource.org/wiki/Tragedija_na_oceanu. (12 December 2019).

Levstik, Vida. (1944)."Ženska himna." [Women anthem] *Pesmi za mladenke* (Poems for young women) variation of *Women Anthem* from Kombinatke: http://kombinatke.si/Pesmipdf/zenska_himna.pdf.

Mayakovsky, Vladimir. "Brooklyn Bridge." 1925. (https://macaulay.cuny.edu/eportfolios/smonte10/files/2010/08/Mayakovsky.pdf). (12 December 2019).

Mayakovsky, Vladimir "At the top of my voice." 1930. https://www.marxists.org/subject/art/literature/mayakovsky/1930/at-top-my-voice.htm). (12 December 2019).

Miljković, Branko. Poezija „Smrću protiv smrti" (Poetry, With death against death). Belgrade, Novo pokolenje, 1981.

Racin, Kosta. "Balade to Unknown Soldier," 1943. https://slikepartizana.wordpress.com/2017/04/20/balada-o-nepoznatom-vojniku-kosta-racin/ (12 December 2019).

Prešeren, France. *Zdravljica* (Toast), 1844. Accessible in English with an official translation by J.Lavrin: http://www.vlada.si/en/about_slovenia/political_system/national_insignia/france_preseren_zdravljica_a_toast/ (12 December 2019).

Webpage of Kombinatke women choir (SLO) contains impressive number of songs that relate to the international resistance legacy, some of them also translated into English: http://kombinatke.si/. (12 December 2019).

Sources from the Archive of Republic Slovenia (Ljubljana) and Archive of Museum of Contemporary History (Ljubljana)

Bor, Matej (1944). *Pesmi*. (Poems). Issued by propaganda section of Regional committee of Liberation Front for Gorenjska. Ljubljana, Plenum kulturnih delavcev OF and Cankarjeva založba, 1979.

Kajuh, Karel Destovnik. *Pesmi* (Poems). Issued by cultural unit of XIV.partisan division in November (6, brochure 266), 1943.

Klemenčič-Maj, Dore. *V imenu Kristusovih ran* ... (In the name of Christ's wounds; portfolio with 10 linoleum cuts), issued by Propaganda section of IX. corpus of people's liberation army (14, brochure 504), 1944.

Kranjc, Cene. *Slovenske partizanske tiskarne v borbi za svobodo.* [Slovenian partisan printing shops in the struggle for freedom] Issued by Propaganda committee of the People's Liberation Army, 1944.
Mihelič, France and Nikolaj Pirnat. *Naša Borba* (Our Struggle, portfolio). In Archive of Museum of Contemporary History, Ljubljana, 1944 (see list of figures).
Naša žena. Glasilo (Slovenske) protifašistične ženske zveze [Our woman. Journal of Slovenian antifascist women organisation], MNZS: Ljubljana. 24. 06 1943.
Pesmi (1943). [Poetry]. Issued by Okrožna tehnika KPS (Technique Section of Communist Party of Slovenia). Ljubljana (20, brochure 759), 1943.
Prešernova Zdravljica 1844–1944, issued by Regional Committee of Liberation Front for Gorenjska (23, brochure 862–864 designed by Janez Vidic and Marjan Šorli), 1944.
Propaganda Section of Executive Committee of Liberation Front, nr. 1.
Župančič, Oton. "Pojte za menoj!" [Sing after me]. *Slovenski poročevalec*, Ljubljana, 6. september 1941.
Žena u Borbi (1943). [Woman in struggle] *Journal of Women Antifascist Front of Croatia*, 1.

Online sources for the counter-archive

Archive of resistance: http://www.resistance-archive.org/. (12 December 2019).
Archive of Women Antifascist Organisation: www.afzarhiv.org. (12 December 2019).
Archive mostly on black liberation: http://www.coloursofresistance.org/.
Archive of decolonising practices. (12 December 2019).
http://www.internationaleonline.org/research/decolonising_practices/. (12 December 2019).
Archive of urban dissent: https://www.pagesmagazine.net/en/articles/archive-of-suburban-dissent-1-introduction. (12 December 2019).
Archive of interference: https://interferencearchive.org/. (12 December 2019).
Brabrat (2017). "Stjepan Filipović: everlasting symbol of anti-fascism" (2017). https://libcom.org/history/stjepan-filipovic-everlasting-symbol-anti-facism. (12 December 2019).
Description of different battles and related material to partisan warfare in Yugoslavia: http://www.vojska.net/eng/world-war-2/yugoslavia/.
Edwards, Zena (2018). "On the expanded concept of hunger and riots." Lecture at IfA/Acud, Berlin. https://youtu.be/3wdNMbsuGkA. (12 December 2019).
Exhibition in HKW "Parapolitics: Cultural Freedom and the Cold War" https://www.hkw.de/en/programm/projekte/2017/parapolitics/parapolitics_start.php. (12 December 2019).
Exhibition and online resources from Huberman's *Uprising* (Paris, 2017): http://soulevements.jeudepaume.org/cartographie/. (12 December 2019).
Exhibition Partisan Print (not press) (Stepančić) at International Centre of Graphic Art. Ljubljana, 2004. http://www.mglc-lj.si/eng/index-razstave.htm. (12 December 2019).
Exhibition and call for Bakić's monument Petrova Gora in Zarez (by Vesna Vuković). : http://www.zarez.hr/clanci/jucer-sutra. (12 December 2019).
Exhibition curated by WHW "Janje moje malo", 2016. http://www.whw.hr/galerija-nova/izlozba-janje-moje-malo-cetvrta-peta-epizoda.html. (12 December 2019).
Internet database on partisan theater activities with some interviews (in Slovenian and English): www.partisantheater.si. (12 December 2019).

Internet database on late modernist monuments on WWII (Donald Niebly): http://www.spomenikdatabase.org/. (12 December 2019).
Manucci, Lando. "Division Garibaldi in Monte Negro." http://www.montenegrina.net/pages/pages1/istorija/cg_u_2_svj_ratu/divizija_garibaldi_u_crnoj_gori_lando_manuci.html. (12 December 2019).
Online portal www.znaci.net contains photo material, archival material, copies of the books related to WWII, memoirs and analysis, from occupiers and partisans. (12 December 2019).
Online portal of Academic Choir France Marolt and description of their last event of resistance in 1941: http://www.apz-tt.si/en/o-zboru/zgodovina/1926–1941/. (12 December 2019).
Pristaš, Goran Sergej and Mila Pavićević, "Liberation of Zagreb, notes for a reconstruction" at the Urban Festival http://urbanfestival.blok.hr/13/en/liberation-of-zagreb/. (12 December 2019).
Public discussion „Primitive accumulation in the post-socialist transition" at WPU (2013): http://www.delavske-studije.si/primitive-accumulation-in-the-post-socialist-transition-and-the-eu-accession-period/. (12 December 2019).
Various letters, texts and artworks can be found in the webpage curated by Ivana Momčilović: http://edicijajugoslavija.org/index.html. (12 December 2019).
Webpage https://uzicanstveno.rs/ contains some historical photos and description of Užice republic. (12 December 2019).
Women antifascist histories and guided tour in Zagreb by Barbara Blasin and Ana Lovreković. https://www.portalnovosti.com/ana-lovrekovic-i-barbara-blasin-zene-su-medju-prvima-ustale-protiv-fasizma. (12 December 2019).
Young partisan woman that encapsulates the dedication and importance of women in the resistance. https://www.youtube.com/watch?v=MQICfRlIs1s. (12 December 2019).

Index

https://doi.org/10.1515/9783110682069-010

www.ingramcontent.com/pod-product-compliance
Lightning Source LLC
LaVergne TN
LVHW010853110826
845149LV00005B/1396

* 9 7 8 3 1 1 0 9 9 4 9 5 7 *